W9-BHL-490

INTERNATIONAL LIBRARY OF
AFRO-AMERICAN LIFE AND HISTORY

1. Crispus Attucks

2. Ira Aldridge

3. Henry Ossian Flipper

4. Aleksander Pushkin

5. Harriet Tubman

6. Willie Mays

7. Thurgood Marshall

INTERNATIONAL LIBRARY OF

AFRO-AMERICAN
LIFE
AND HISTORY

HISTORICAL
AFRO-AMERICAN
BIOGRAPHIES

BY

WILHELMENA S. ROBINSON

THE PUBLISHERS AGENCY, INC.
CORNWELLS HEIGHTS, PENNSYLVANIA
under the auspices of
THE ASSOCIATION FOR THE STUDY OF AFRO-AMERICAN LIFE AND HISTORY

To

ANTOINE LARUE ROBINSON, II

who, it is hoped,

will one day be included

in the realm of this volume

Preface

THE Association for the Study of Afro-American Life and History joins with Pubco Corporation in presenting this new series of volumes which treat in detail the cultural and historical backgrounds of black Americans. This Association, a pioneer in the area of Afro-American History, was founded on September 9, 1915, by Dr. Carter G. Woodson, who remained its director of research and publications until his death in 1950.

In 1916 Dr. Woodson began publishing the quarterly *Journal of Negro History*. In 1926 Negro History Week was launched, and since that time it has been held annually in February, encompassing the birth dates of Abraham Lincoln and Frederick Douglass. The *Negro History Bulletin* was first published in 1937 to serve both schools and families by making available to them little-known facts about black life and history.

During its sixty-one years of existence, the Association for the Study of Afro-American Life and History has supported many publications dealing with the contributions of Afro-Americans to the growth and development of this country. Its activities have contributed to the increasing interest in the dissemination of factual studies which are placing the Afro-American in true perspective in the mainstream of American history.

We gratefully acknowledge the contributions of previous scholars, which have aided us in the preparation of this *International Library of Afro-American Life and History*.

Our grateful acknowledgment is also expressed to Charles W. Lockyer, president of Pubco Corporation, whose challenging approach has made possible this library.

Though each of the volumes in this set can stand as an autonomous unit, and although each author has brought his own interpretation to the area with which he is dealing, together these books form a comprehensive picture of the Afro-American experience in America. The three history volumes give a factual record of a people who were brought from Africa in chains and who today are struggling to cast off the last vestiges of these bonds. The anthologies covering music, art, the theatre and literature provide a detailed account of the black American's contributions to these fields—including those contributions which are largely forgotten today. Achievement in the sports world is covered in another volume. The volume on the Afro-American in medicine is a history of the black American's struggle for equality as a medical practitioner and as a patient. The selected black leaders in the biography book represent the contributions and achievements of many times their number. The documentary history sums up the above-mentioned material in the words of men and women who were themselves a part of black history.

CHARLES H. WESLEY

Washington, D.C.

Table of Contents

Introduction

THIS volume of the *International Library of Afro-American Life and History* is designed to present biographical sketches of Afro-Americans in the mainstream of history around the world. Close to four hundred personalities are included. These individuals are not presented as "great" or "famous" but rather as representative of the socio-economic aspects of the life of the Afro-American in his struggle for the attainment of freedom and equality. This theme is pursued in the organization of the volume into three parts: "The Fourteenth through the Eighteenth Centuries," "The Nineteenth Century" and "The Twentieth Century." In each of these divisions, the lives of individual Afro-Americans are presented to give evidence of their ingenuity in making adjustments to their environment, or to show the development of their abilities and talents in their contributions to the mainstream of world culture and in their role in the struggle of justice and the dignity of man.

Dividing the work into centuries automatically created problems of overlapping. Some of the lives of individuals naturally extended from the closing period of one century into the opening decades of the next. This problem was handled by placing each person in the century to which he made a greater contribution according to the basic theme of this volume.

Unfortunately, some of the exact birth dates could not be ascertained. The historical period in which the individual made his mark was used in determining where to place the biographical sketch. For instance, many of the Afro-Americans who participated in the American Revolution made their contribution in the eighteenth century and were automatically placed in that period. In each of the three parts, the biographies appear in alphabetical order; captions are included in the titles to indicate each individual's area of contribution. No attempt was made at presentation by areas, such as music, art, sports or scholarship, as many individuals could be included in several different categories of this type.

The introductory statement to each part expresses the continuing thesis of the inalienable right of man to liberty, equality and the pursuit of happiness, whether in America, Europe or Africa. The winds of change of the mid-twentieth century, along with the events accompanying a gradual swing from Social Darwinist-type theories of the inferiority of the Afro-American to the rapid attainment of recognition and equality—or independence, as in the case of the African states— inspired the production of this work on the Afro-American. While the coverage is broader than that of any other volume of this type produced so far, it was not designed to be all-inclusive. These sketches are primarily examples of typical individuals—some, very ordinary persons—whose lives are representative of or similar to the lives of other people who are found in the mainstream of history. There are numerous individuals of the present century who merit inclusion in the volume but were omitted because space was limited and also because information on contemporary figures is easily available through the current news media. Athletic stars, entertainers and civil rights workers of today receive extensive coverage in the major journals, newspapers and television networks. Instead of attempting to present all of the widely known individuals, the author concentrated more on introducing the reader to those lesser-known individuals who pioneered in many areas to open the way for those of the present day.

These biographical sketches were collected from many widely scattered sources to bring to the reading public a one-volume general reference on the lives of Afro-Americans who have contributed, extensively or in a pioneering effort, to the stream of world culture from the thirteenth century to the present. The bibliography appearing at the end of the volume represents the sources from which the material was collected. It will also guide the reader to additional information on the subject of the text.

Historical Afro-American Biographies was conceived by Dr. Charles Harris Wesley, author, and editor of this series. While writing on the general history of the Afro-American, he saw the need for an accompanying volume of biographical sketches giving more details on individual personalities who were casually referred to in the broader historical treatment. The organization and thesis of the volume were left entirely to the writer, who was inspired and encouraged by the editor in each phase of the research and writing.

The close collaboration of Mrs. Patricia Romero, who collected materials and the pictures as well as supervised the work of compiling the volume at the office in Washington, D.C., made it possible for the work to be completed on schedule. Credit for the design and layout goes to Allan Kullen of Pubco Corporation.

Acknowledgment is due the members of the library staff of Central State University for making their collections available to the writer even during the vacation period. Credit must be accorded to the author's students in two history courses at Central State University, who entered into the project with enthusiasm and rendered invaluable service in the collection of biographical material.

WILHELMENA S. ROBINSON

Wilberforce, Ohio

PART I

The Fourteenth through the Eighteenth Centuries

Introduction

THE rise of modern Europe in the fifteenth and sixteenth centuries marked the end of an isolated European culture. The forces let loose by the Renaissance and the commercial revolution of this period brought about the opening of commercial contacts with the people of Africa and other lands. News of the great empires of African people below the Sahara had now reached European circles. The African rulers of the fourteenth, fifteenth and sixteenth centuries were in contact with the Arabs of the Near East, as they had been converted to the Islamic faith. Accounts of their wealthy caravans across the desert to Mecca for the holy pilgrimage were known to the Europeans. Knowledge of these thriving, well-organized empires stimulated the Portuguese maritime interest to explore the coastal waters around Africa during the fifteenth century.

Once the Europeans established contact with the Negroes of Africa, an interchange of trade and commerce followed. The African Moslem rulers exchanged human beings for the trinkets of European traders, as slavery was an accepted institution of the Arabs who had converted them to the Islamic religion. Thus, a thin trickle of African migration reached Europe. The stimulus of the philosophy of the Renaissance, added to the revitalization of the economic life of Europe as a whole, contributed to the opening of new avenues to the acquisition of wealth and power. Traffic in human beings was one of the new sources of wealth which the Europeans tapped toward the end of the fifteenth century. Thus Negroes were on hand to participate in the discovery, exploration and settlement of the New World.

The possession of Negro slaves was a novelty in Europe, and in many cases traders gave them to their monarchs, or to noblemen across the continent of Europe, as far away as Poland and Russia. The records show that the offspring of many of these Africans became substantial contributors to the cultural development of Europe.

Dutch traders put an end to the Portuguese monopoly of commerce with African rulers. And as Europeans emigrated to the Americas, they brought with them the Negroes from Africa. The purchase of the Africans by the British settlers was carried out on the principle that they were bonded servants similar to the white indentured servants from England. When the Africans had completed sufficient work to defray the cost of their purchase, they were set free and were permitted to own land or to develop their own enterprises to earn a living.

3

This practice of the English settlers was but one example of the prevailing philosophical thought of eighteenth-century colonial life. These early American settlers believed in the ideals which had been expounded by the scholars of the Enlightenment: that all men are created equal and are entitled to the inalienable rights of life, liberty and the pursuit of happiness. The disappointment of the English colonists when the mother country denied them the inherent rights of the "Glorious Revolution of 1688" smoldered in their minds until the latter half of the eighteenth century, when the floodgates of the American Revolution were opened.

This revolutionary philosophy had spread to the Negroes of the colonies; and they responded to its appeal by joining the patriots in the struggle for the attainment of these ideals. Crispus Attucks gave his life for American freedom. Other Negroes joined the Continental Army to help achieve the idealistic goals that had been set down in the Declaration of Independence, thinking that its philosophy would be applied to them in their state of bondage after the war.

This section contains biographical sketches of Negroes who lived during the period of the fourteenth through the eighteenth centuries. A few were rulers of the great empires of Africa; some took part in the discovery and exploration of America; and others contributed to the struggle for man's inalienable right to freedom. In the last category, some overlap into the nineteenth century; their role was to continue the struggle because of the failure to achieve in the eighteenth century the basic rights of man.

These truly are the Brave,
these men who cast aside
old memories, to walk the blood-stained pave
of Sacrifice . . .
. . . to suffer and to die
for Freedom—when their own is yet denied!

Roscoe Jamison

Abderrahman Es-Sadi

Sudanese Historian

Abderrahman Es-Sadi (1596–1660), Sudanese writer of the 17th century, gave to the world a descriptive picture of the civilization then flourishing in this section of West Africa. It is in his book *The Tarikh Es-Soudan* that the history of Timbuktu comes to life. Even though he was a Moslem and denounced the customs of the natives who resisted Islam, his glowing accounts of trade, the university centers, and the rulers constitute a useful history of the people.

As a secretary and a notary in the service of a traveling official, he took advantage of every opportunity to collect the documents and facts needed to write his account of the history of Timbuktu. The information it imparts concerning the basic culture of the area coincides with that of his contemporaries as well as with that of more recent scholars.

Es-Sadi was born in the Sudan and grew up in the tradition of the Islamic faith. As a devout believer in the teachings of Mohammed, he interpreted the history of the West African civilizations through the bias of his Islamic heritage. He tended to attribute the great achievements of the people to their acceptance of the Islamic faith. Thus he was highly critical of the traditional native customs of the masses.

Allen, Richard

Church Founder and Bishop

Richard Allen (1760–1831), the organizer and first bishop of the African Methodist Episcopal Church, was born a slave in Philadelphia in 1760. While a young lad, he was sold to a farmer near Dover, Delaware. He soon was converted to Christianity and began to preach. Allen impressed his master with his persuasiveness and zeal to such an extent that he was allowed to conduct services in the farmer's home; and in 1777, he converted his master and was allowed to purchase his freedom.

In 1784, a conference of the Methodist Church was held in Baltimore, Maryland. Allen apparently was present and became acquainted with the evangelist Richard Watcoat, who permitted Allen to travel with him on the Baltimore circuit. Later, Francis Asbury, the first bishop of the Methodist Church in the United States, gave Allen frequent preaching assignments.

After the Revolutionary War, Negroes were discouraged from worshipping with white congregations. One Sunday in 1787, Allen and other blacks were asked to go to the gallery of St. George's Methodist Church in Philadelphia. However, Richard Allen did not lose faith in Christianity; instead, he set about organizing a new denomination. He

RICHARD ALLEN

established his first church, Bethel, in Philadelphia just a few years after the exodus from St. George's. In 1816, sixteen independent Negro Methodist congregations from the different states of the Union formed the African Methodist Episcopal Church. Allen became its first bishop. The church expanded under his leadership, and by 1826, there were two bishops, a total membership of 7,927 and financial assets of $1,151.

The economic and social conditions of the free Negroes of the North, in 1787, had led Allen, together with several of his friends, to found the Free African Society. When the yellow fever epidemic hit Philadelphia in 1793, Allen and Absalom Jones, at the urging of Dr. Benjamin Rush, advised the members of the society to nurse the sick regardless of race or color. During the War of 1812, Richard Allen and Absalom Jones ex-

pressed their patriotism by recruiting more than two thousand Negroes to help defend Philadelphia. It was a normal reaction for Allen, in 1817, to denounce the American Colonization Society, which was organized for the purpose of returning the free Negroes in America to a colony in Africa. He vehemently denounced the society before an audience of three thousand Philadelphians in Bethel Church. In 1830, Allen started the first national movement for resettling free Negroes in Canada.

Amo, Anton Wilhelm

German Philosopher

Anton Wilhelm Amo, 18th-century professor of philosophy at the University of Wittenberg, Germany, was born in Axim on the Gold Coast of Africa, in what is now the independent nation of Guinea. He was captured as a child to be sold into slavery. Fortunately, his purchaser was the Duke Anton-Ulrich von Braunschweig of Amsterdam, Holland, and Amo was placed in the Duke's home as a companion for his son. The Duke's wife reared him with her son. He was an apt pupil; therefore, the Duke undertook an experiment designed to prove to a friend that the Negro's mind was intellectually equal to that of any other person.

Amo was enrolled in Halle University, Saxony, where he mastered Hebrew, Greek, Latin, French, Dutch and German in addition to studying astronomy, literature and philosophy. He earned his degree of Doctor of Philosophy with his dissertation *De Jure Maurorum*. He continued his studies at the University of Wittenberg, where his genius was acknowledged by the Council of the University. He contributed to the development of the German school of philosophy during the 18th century. In 1734, he was appointed to the Chair of Philosophy of Wittenberg. The Prussian Government recognized his superior contribution to scholastic achievement by awarding him the title of Councillor of the State. His inaugural address upon assuming his Chair of Philosophy was a discourse on the apathy of man.

Unfortunately, Duke von Braunschweig died just as Amo reached the height of his success. He was deeply attached to the Duke, and in his grief, decided to return to Africa, where he spent the remainder of his life in seclusion and meditation.

In 1753, the famous explorer Henry Gallaudet found him living the life of a recluse. In the 19th century, the scholar Abbé Grégoire produced a book entitled *Literature of Negroes,* in which he included the life and contributions of Anton Wilhelm Amo.

Armistead, James

American Spy

James Armistead collected valuable information concerning the British forces at Portsmouth, Virginia, for the French Major General Marquis de Lafayette during the American Revolution. In 1781, Washington ordered Lafayette, with a selected force of twelve hundred troops from New England and New Jersey, to Virginia to block the advance of the British forces under General Cornwallis. When Lafayette arrived in the area of Williamsburg, he badly needed information concerning the strength and movements of the enemy. One of his most valuable agents who carried out these dangerous intelligence missions was James Armistead, a slave of New Kent County, Virginia.

Armistead hovered around the British camps, collecting information and passing it on to other spies for delivery to the French general. The general later said of his agent, "His intelligence from the enemy's camp were industriously collected and . . . faithfully delivered." Armistead was emancipated by an act of the Virginia legislature in 1786.

The bill states that Armistead "kept open a channel of the most useful information to the army of the state."

After the war, Armistead returned to New Kent County, where in 1816 he purchased a farm of 40 acres of land. In 1819, Virginia granted him a pension of $40 per year as well as an award of $100. He took the name of James Lafayette, after the famous Frenchman, who returned to America on his well-known tour in 1824. It was a highlight in the life of James Lafayette when, in October 1824, he had the honor of greeting his former commander in Richmond.

Askia Mohammed Ture
(Askia the Great)

Ruler of Songhay (West Africa)

Mohammed Ture (?–1538), African reform ruler of Songhay, had distinguished himself as a general under his predecessor, Sunni Ali Ber. Internal strife followed the death of Sunni Ali in 1492, and within a year Mohammed Ture had secured the throne, taking the name Askia. He won the loyalty of his administrative officials, placed the army on a professional basis and installed his brother Omar as the chief lieutenant. He avoided recruiting farmers and artisans by using slaves and captives. A loyal Moslem, he conferred special favors upon the mosques and centers of learning and encouraged scholars to come to the empire.

Although his pilgrimage to Mecca was less spectacular than that of Mansa Musa, Mohammed Ture accomplished much for his subjects through his study of government, principles of taxation, commerce, banking and religious toleration. When he returned to Songhay, he established intellectual centers at Gao, Walata, Timbuktu and Djenne, to which he invited scholars. The University of Sankore in Timbuktu was the outstanding medieval institution in West Africa. As

ASKIA MOHAMMED TURE

Attucks, Crispus

Martyr for Freedom

Crispus Attucks (*c.* 1723–1770), one of the first men to die for American freedom, was a fugitive slave who had escaped from his master and had worked for twenty years as a merchant seaman. When Samuel Adams, prominent leader of the struggle against British domination of the American colonies, called upon the dock workers and seamen in the port of Boston to demonstrate against the British troops guarding the customs commissioners, Crispus Attucks responded to the plea. Aroused by Adams' exhortations, a group of 40 to 50 patriots, armed with clubs, sticks and snowballs, approached the British soldiers. Attucks was apparently in the front line of the aroused citizens, urging them on. Suddenly there was a terse order—"Fire!" The British troops responded with a barrage of rifle fire.

a religious reformer, Askia practiced tolerance toward Jews and Christians. Banking, credit and commerce were supported by new laws, and a lucrative system of trade was carried on with the Arab traders of the North and East. He also had canals built to irrigate the desert sections of his farmlands.

At the University of Sankore, literature, science, law, medicine and geography were taught, and scientific experiments were encouraged. While Askia was carrying out his extensive reform program, Omar was busily engaged in extending the boundaries of the empire.

Near the end of his life, Askia became blind; and in 1529 he was dethroned by his son Mussa. Disorder followed, and the empire suffered from strife and insurrections for a period of twenty years.

CRISPUS ATTUCKS

Crispus Attucks was the first to fall in the celebrated "Boston Massacre" of 1770. Four other Americans died that fatal night from the action. Samuel Adams used the incident to incite the colonists to further rebellion. Although only five people were killed, Adams termed it a "massacre" of innocent citizens by the tyrannical mother country. Paul Revere published a poem and a drawing of this famous incident in the *Boston Gazette* on March 12, 1770. Writers who omit Crispus Attucks' name from the accounts of the American Revolution might as well dismiss the "Boston Massacre" as an irrelevant incident in the struggle for independence.

Banneker, Benjamin

Engineer and Scientist

Benjamin Banneker (1731–1806) was born near Ellicott's Mill (now Ellicott City), Maryland. His formal education was limited to attending a Quaker school near Joppa, Maryland. While still a youth, he made a wooden clock which ran accurately for the rest of his life. From 1791 until 1802, Banneker published a yearly almanac. He was the first of his race to publish scientific and astronomical materials in the United States. He published also a treatise on bees and computed the cycle of the seventeen-year locust.

Banneker led a most unusual life—he studied the stars at night and slept during the day. When he was not sleeping, he worked on mathematical computations. He was noted also for the many followers he acquired. Men from distant places journeyed to his farm. He showed them around dressed in a suit of dark cloth, carrying a cane, and wearing a large beaver hat. In later life, Banneker sold the farm in order to devote all of his time and energies to his scientific work.

Benjamin Banneker, born a free man, was aware of the manifold evils of slavery and wrote a now-famous letter to Thomas Jefferson, challenging the latter's liberalism:

I apprehend you will embrace every opportunity to eradicate that train of absurd and false ideas and opinions which so generally prevail with respect to us [Negroes]; and that your sentiments are concurrent with mine which are: that one universal Father hath given being to us all; that He not only made us all of one flesh, but that He hath also without partiality afforded us all with these same faculties and that, however diversified in situation or color, we are all the same family and stand in the same relation to Him.

Banneker contributed also to the field of engineering. He was a member of the surveying team which laid out the city plan for the nation's capital.

In accordance with his antislavery philosophy, Banneker was an advocate of pacifism. In his almanac he published an article which stated that if there was to be a Secretary of War there should also be a Secretary of Peace.

BENJAMIN BANNEKER

Burr, Seymour

American Soldier

Seymour Burr, a slave in Connecticut caught in the web of circumstances, heeded the British promise of freedom if he would serve the mother country. He was captured in an attempt to join the British. After explaining to his master that he wanted to be free, he was promised his freedom if he would join the army of the patriots. Seymour then enlisted in the Seventh Massachusetts Regiment and participated in the Battle of Bunker Hill.

His desire for liberty urged him on through many trials during the war. During the siege of Fort Catskill, he endured the extremely cold weather and the shortage of food. He suffered, along with the thousands of other patriots in the Continental Army, to attain his freedom after the war. His master, brother of the controversial political figure Aaron Burr, honored his promise to Seymour in 1783. As a free man, Seymour assumed his master's last name, Burr, and settled in Canton, Massachusetts, where he reared his family.

Captein, Jacques Elisa Jean

Dutch Philosopher

Jacques Captein, 18th-century philosopher, painter and poet, was educated by his Dutch master, M. Manger, as an experiment to determine whether Africans were intellectually equipped for the successful study of literature, science, philosophy and art. He was captured at the age of seven on the Andreas River by a slave trader, who gave him to a friend. The young slave's master began instructing him in the rudiments of the Dutch language during the trip to Holland. The boy learned rapidly and soon after his arrival in Europe was converted to Christianity. According to the European concept of Chris-

JACQUES ELISA JEAN CAPTEIN

tianity, the training of an African as a missionary to convert other Africans would enable the Church to fulfill its manifest destiny.

One day the master discovered the boy sketching a picture of Moses when he was supposed to be studying. He had already painted several large Biblical scenes. It was decided then that he should have further training at The Hague. There he was taught painting as well as Greek, Hebrew, Latin and Chaldean. He was sent to the University of Leiden for four years to study theology. On completing his training, he was sent to Elmina, Africa, to fulfill his duties as a Christian missionary. By the time he returned to Holland, the slave trade was a profitable enterprise; and, as Europeans were bent upon justifying their acts by rationalizing the principles of Christianity, they called upon Captein to endorse slavery. The fact that he had not been subjected to the hardships of slavery, but rather had benefited from his benevolent master's protection, indulgence and instruction, may explain why he wrote a dissertation in defense of slavery in 1742. He attempted to demonstrate that slavery was not contrary to the principles of Christianity. Though his argument is not convincing, the work is, nevertheless, brilliant in its literary form and significant as a political document.

Before embarking upon this aspect of his career, Captein had published collections of sermons and poems in Amsterdam, thereby proving that an African was capable of mastering all of the thought processes of the European.

Charlton, Samuel

American Soldier

Samuel Charlton (1760–1843), soldier in the Battle of Monmouth, in New Jersey, was placed in the Continental Army by his master at the age of 16 or 17. He was born in New Jersey, and following the war he resumed his servitude. However, his master liberated his slaves on his death and provided for Charlton a lifetime pension. Upon his liberation Charlton, with his wife, moved to New York City, where he died in 1843.

Samuel Charlton, like many other Negroes, served in the Revolutionary War as a substitute for his master. He fought in the Battles of Brandywine, Germantown, and Monmouth. Of the fifteen thousand Americans engaged at the Battle of Monmouth, it is estimated that seven hundred were Negroes. Washington's army had come out of Valley Forge eager for combat. The men had suffered starvation, cold and every form of distress. They were inspired and encouraged when they encountered the British evacuating Philadelphia and engaged them in battle at Monmouth Courthouse on June 28, 1778. While the battle was a victory for neither side, it was the last major engagement in the North.

The "Black Patriots" of the American Revolution endured suffering and hardships along with their companion white patriots for love of country and were willing to pay the price of liberty.

Christophe, Henri

King of Haiti

Henri Christophe (1767–1820), or King Henri Christophe of Haiti, had his first lessons in war during the American Revolution and returned to Haiti to become a confidant and successor of Toussaint L'Ouverture. Henri Christophe served as a sergeant in the legion of mulattoes and free Negroes commanded by the Viscount de Fontanges at the siege of Savannah, Georgia, in 1779. In what was called the most brilliant feat of the day, this Negro detachment contained the British attack and permitted their comrades to carry out an orderly withdrawal. Christophe was wounded at Savannah, but he returned to Haiti with new concepts of freedom and independence.

During the Haitian Revolution, Christophe joined the forces of L'Ouverture and rose rapidly to the rank of general. When the first stages of the revolt were over, he was made governor of Cap Français and the surrounding region. After L'Ouverture was captured by Leclerc and taken to France, and Dessalines had himself made governor of Haiti for life, Christophe was next in line to assume leadership of the Negroes of the island. Dessalines' tyranny proved to be worse than that of the French. He was assassinated in 1806, and Henri Christophe became the new ruler of Haiti.

So much dissension developed on the island over the leadership of Pétion, who was the elected president of the Republic of Haiti, that Christophe was convinced that he should create a monarchy. The republic was a government of mulattoes and was under the rule of a mulatto. The monarchy was to be a dominion of the pure blacks, sustained by a hereditary nobility, who would support the throne and maintain order among the subjects.

Christophe was not an educated man, but he employed several educated mulattoes as secretaries to read to him several hours a day. Thus his knowledge of history was extensive and accurate. Frederick the Great of Prussia was his idol, and he borrowed the name of his palace Sans Souci from Potsdam.

King Henri's rule was resented by many because of his increasing pressure for production and his ruthless system of punishment for those who did not work to make Haiti the "Pearl of the Antilles." He suffered a stroke in 1820, and many of his subjects rejoiced that he was disabled. On October 8, 1820, he was carried to his citadel, where he shot himself. His son, Prince Victoire, was assassinated, thus ending the royal line.

Cromwell, Oliver

American Soldier

Oliver Cromwell (1753–1853), a patriot of the Revolutionary War who valiantly served his country, stayed with Washington's dwindling forces and was selected to participate in the Battle of Trenton. He was one of the soldiers who accompanied Washington when he crossed the Delaware River on Christmas night in 1776. The expeditionary force surprised the British troops who were celebrating the Yuletide season, confident that the American patriots were too inept to make an attack. Cromwell saw action at the Battles of Trenton and Princeton in 1776–77, Brandywine in 1777, Monmouth in 1778, and Yorktown in 1781. He lived to the age of one hundred and delighted in telling his friends and admirers that he had witnessed

the surrender of the British General Cornwallis at Yorktown, as well as the last of the casualties of the Revolution.

Cromwell was born in Columbus, Burlington County, New Jersey, and is believed to have been born free. He enlisted in the Second New Jersey Regiment under the command of Colonel Israel Shreeve and was one of the longterm soldiers of the war, as he served six years and nine months, which was longer than many of the white patriots. He received a Federal government pension of $96 a year in recognition of his honorable military service. After his discharge from the army, he settled on a farm in New Jersey and reared a family of six children.

Cuffee, Paul

Colonizer

Paul Cuffee (1759–1817), Negro shipowner and colonizer, was born near New Bedford, Massachusetts. As a free Negro whose father had been a slave, Cuffee became greatly concerned over the status of the Negro in his native state and throughout America to the extent that he became one of the first to advocate African colonization as a solution to the incipient racial problem. In 1811, he traveled to Sierra Leone, a British colony on the West Coast of Africa, where he founded the Friendly Society of Sierra Leone, for the emigration of free Negroes from America. In 1815, he spent $4,000 of his own funds to transport 38 Negroes to Sierra Leone. He had planned more expeditions to Africa, but his health failed and he died in 1817.

A successful shipbuilder and shipowner, he accumulated an estate worth more than $20,000. In 1797, at the price of $3,500, he purchased for himself and his Indian wife, Alice Pequit, a farm on which he built a school for free Negro children. He and his brother, John Cuffee, entered a suit, as tax-

PAUL CUFFEE

payers, against the state of Massachusetts for the right to vote; but they were unsuccessful in winning the case. Several years later, legislation was adopted to correct this unjust practice. The Negro entrepreneur campaigned regularly against discriminatory practices faced by the free Negroes in America. His association with whites was unquestioned, and he was received by the Quakers as a member of the Westport Society of Friends.

de Pareja, Juan

Spanish Painter

Juan de Pareja (*c.* 1606–1670), famous pupil of the Spanish painter Velázquez, was born in Seville, Spain. He was purchased on the slave market in Seville in 1623. As a slave in the household of Velázquez, his duties were to grind the colors, clean the brushes, and keep his master's studio clean and orderly. Juan was not allowed to study with his master because it was illegal for a slave to paint; but he was thrilled at the touch of brushes and responded to the canvas as if drawn by magic. He would rush through his other duties in order to get to the studio while it was empty of pupils and the master was absent, so that he could paint.

In 1649, Juan accompanied Velázquez to Rome, where he was exposed to the great Italian painters. When de Pareja was in his forties, his passion for painting could no longer be resisted, and he started a painting which he carefully kept out of his master's sight. After they returned to Spain in 1651, King Philip IV became a frequent visitor to Velázquez' studio. During one of his visits, he noticed a canvas turned toward the wall and insisted that he be allowed to view it. In fear of losing his life, de Pareja obeyed the King's order. Velázquez did not recognize this work of art, and Juan confessed that it was his own painting.

JUAN DE PAREJA

Instead of punishing the slave for such a liberty, King Philip ordered Velázquez to grant Juan his freedom as a reward for his great talent. The master granted him his freedom and accepted him as a pupil. De Pareja developed into one of the chief followers of the Velázquez school of painting and an outstanding religious and portrait painter. He was already widely known as the subject of one of Velázquez' masterpieces, a beautiful portrait of the African slave, which had been exhibited in Rome.

Juan de Pareja's works, in some instances, became nearly indistinguishable from those of his teacher; but he was more than a learned and skillful disciple of Velázquez. His works give evidence of a genius of his own and show much of the style of the best schools of Genoa and Venice; they also reflect the influence of the Flemish Masters.

The following known works bear his signature: "The Portrait of the Architect Ratis"; "The Presentation of Christ in the Temple"; "Baptism of Christ," which is now in the Santa Trinidad gallery in Toledo; "The Calling of St. Matthew," which is now in the Prado Gallery in Madrid; and "St. John the Evangelist, Orontius and the Madonna," which now hangs in the Chapel of the Recollects in Madrid.

De Pareja remained in the Velázquez household after the death of the master and until his own death in 1670.

Derham, James

Physician

James Derham (1762–?), pioneer in medicine, was born a slave in Philadelphia before the American War of Independence. He was sold to Dr. John Kearsley, Jr., who taught him to read and write and used him as an apprentice in prescribing medicines for patients. He was purchased by Dr. George West, a surgeon in the Sixteenth British Regi-

ment during the Revolutionary War. He developed more skills under Dr. West, particularly in the treatment of wounded soldiers.

When the British troops withdrew from American soil after the Treaty of Paris, in 1783, Derham was sold to Dr. Robert Dove of New Orleans. Continuing to serve as an apprentice, or slave assistant, to men in medical practice, Derham learned as much about medicine as was possible in the America of his day and time.

Dr. Dove allowed Derham to purchase his freedom on liberal terms and helped him establish his own medical practice. Derham had acquired an excellent education from his former masters, who were cultivated men, and with his extensive knowledge of the art of healing, he soon developed a lucrative practice in New Orleans. Working among the multi-lingual population of the area, he soon became fluent in French and Spanish. As a physician he became deeply interested in the relationship of disease to climate and became well versed in the use of drugs for the diseases of the Mississippi delta region.

Du Sable, Jean Baptiste Pointe

Pioneer Settler

Jean Baptiste Du Sable (1745–1818), adventurer, trader and one of the first settlers of Chicago, was born in Saint Marc, Haiti. Some historians think that he was the son of a successful Frenchman from Marseilles, France. His mother was a former Negro slave. Du Sable was sent to France for his education and was described by contemporaries as "a handsome, well-educated Negro." He came to New Orleans in 1765 with a friend and former schoolmate, Jacques Clemorgan of Martinique. They came to America as representatives of the expanding company of Du Sable and Son, but soon after their arrival the French territory of Louisiana was taken over by the Spanish government.

Desiring to escape Spanish rule, the two friends left New Orleans for St. Louis, another thriving settlement of French fur traders on the upper Mississippi River. For two years they carried on a bustling trade with the Indians. The adventurous comrades moved farther north into Indian territory and settled with the Peoria and Potawatomy tribes. While living with the Indians and participating in fur trapping expeditions, Du Sable traveled along trails which led to the present sites of Chicago and Detroit and parts of Canada. Finally, in 1772, he decided to build a fur trading post on the Chicago River near Lake Michigan. The single cabin built by Du Sable developed into a growing trading center. In referring to his settlement at Chicago, Du Sable later remarked that "the first white man to come to Chicago was a Negro." When the jurisdiction of the United States extended into the area, Du Sable sold his holdings and moved to Missouri, where he died in 1818.

de Saint-Georges, Le Chevalier
French Musician and Soldier

Le Chevalier de Saint-Georges (1745–1799), celebrated Negro artist of Paris and soldier of the French Revolution, was born at Basse-Terre, Guadeloupe, December 25, 1745. His father, Jean Nicholas de Boulogne, was councillor for the King of France and served as comptroller of the treasury. Although his mother was a Negro slave, his father claimed the boy and brought him back to France with him. He was well educated and was taught the arts of fencing, horsemanship, marksmanship and dancing. He possessed a talent for music and studied under Jean Marie Leclair and under Gassec, the director of the Concert des Amateurs.

The indulgent father provided his son an inheritance of eight thousand pounds per year, which enabled him to pursue his studies

LE CHEVALIER DE SAINT-GEORGES

and to live lavishly in Paris. In the aristocratic circles of France, he was acclaimed as the most skilled in the art of fencing. As a musician, he performed as a violinist and introduced two of his original concertos for violin with orchestral accompaniment in 1772–1773. He became noted as a composer of string quartets and eventually succeeded his former teacher, Gassec, as director of the Concert des Amateurs. He also became assistant director of the orchestra of the opera in Paris.

The versatile artist wrote and produced three dramatic operas: *Ernestine, a Comedy in Three Acts; La Chasse;* and *The Anonymous Lover.* His other musical publications are *La Fille-Garçon* and *Le Marchand de Marrons.*

Military power was another of Saint-Georges' triumphs: in 1791, during the French Revolution, he was made a captain of the National Guard. However, not pleased with the latter, he switched sides and joined the revolutionists. He succeeded in recruiting an entire regiment of Negroes. He advanced rapidly, becoming chief of brigade and the legion commander. In the turbulent and chaotic years of the Revolution, he was accused of misusing funds and was tried and sent to prison for a year. Many outstanding citizens came to his defense with declarations attesting to his bravery and honesty; he was finally released and returned to his former command. Disheartened and disillusioned over the failure of the Republican dream, the artist-soldier retired to private life and died in obscurity on June 12, 1799.

Dessalines, Jean Jacques

Emperor of Haiti

Jean Jacques Dessalines (c. 1748–1806) was made Emperor of Haiti, with the title Jacques I, on October 8, 1804. The second in command to Toussaint L'Ouverture during the Haitian Revolution against French rule, he was made governor of a province by L'Ouverture. Napoleon was determined to regain control of the former possession and, in 1802, dispatched General Leclerc to Haiti to suppress the uprising. Through trickery and violence, Leclerc reestablished French rule temporarily. He ordered the return of plantations to their former French owners and the reinstitution of slavery for all blacks. This decree further incited the former slaves. To reduce resistance, Leclerc resorted to bribery of the revolutionary leaders. L'Ouverture was sent to France, and an attempt was made to assassinate Dessalines. News of the attempt led to a new revolt. The blacks and the mulattoes joined forces and drove the French into the sea. Saint Domingue (Santo Domingo) was declared a republic, with the name Haiti.

The movement's hero, Dessalines, was named governor general for life. He was empowered to establish laws, to declare war, to make peace and to appoint his successor. After consolidating his power, Dessalines be-

JEAN JACQUES DESSALINES

came notorious for his tyranny. He especially antagonized the mulattoes, who resented domination by the blacks. On April 28, 1806, he issued a proclamation that all the French residents on the island were to be put to death. The massacres that followed shocked his subjects, and when he turned his vengeance on the mulattoes, they formed a secret conspiracy against the black monarch. On October 17, he was ambushed and shot to death by mulattoes at Port Rouge.

Diaz, Henrique

Liberator of Brazil

Henrique Diaz (?–1661), famous Negro general, was born a slave in Recife, Brazil. According to Portuguese custom, if a slave was industrious he was awarded opportunities for advancement. The young Henrique was an alert child who learned to read and became interested in the history of his country. Seeing the grievous plight of his country under the rule of the Dutch, who had seized the bulk of the Portuguese colonies around the world, the young man decided to become a soldier so that he could fight the Dutch masters.

The weakness of the Portuguese Army in Brazil and its failure to defy the Dutch aroused Henrique's determination to liberate the entire land. In 1633, he called upon a group of his friends to join with him in offering their services to the governor by enlisting in the army. The bravery of the young soldier soon became a legend as he went into battle resolved never to retreat. He displayed such valor that he was promoted rapidly until he became a general. He combined skill and cunning with his daring exploits against the Dutch and outwitted and confused the Dutch generals until they were forced to capitulate.

In the battle of Porto Calvo in 1645, Diaz was hit by a bullet in his left hand. Despairing over the time it took the wound to heal,

HENRIQUE DIAZ

he had the hand cut off. He received the "Cross of Christ" decoration from Philip IV for his bravery in this battle but vowed never to wear his "Cross of Christ" until the Dutch were driven out of Brazil.

The brave soldier who helped liberate Brazil from the Dutch died in 1661. It was not long afterward that the Portuguese changed their policy toward Negro slavery. Instead of the liberal, humane treatment of the first half of the seventeenth century, they made the lot of the slave intolerable. They forgot that a Negro slave had been instrumental in saving the country for them.

Dumas, Thomas Alexandre

French General

Thomas Alexandre Davy de la Pailleterie (1762–1806) took the name of his mother, Louise Cessette Dumas, thus beginning the "dynasty" of the famous trio of Dumas in modern French history. His mother was a Negro woman of Santo Domingo; and his father, a marquis, was the descendant of an ancient Norman family. The Marquis left the court life of Versailles in 1760 and settled in Jérémie, where he became one of the richest colonists on the island. When he decided to return to France, he took his son Thomas with him. The boy was sent to Bordeaux to study, but at the age of 16 he enlisted in the Queen's Dragoons, under the name of Dumas.

When the French Revolution broke out in 1789, he enlisted in the Corps of Saint-Georges to fight for the principles of "liberty, equality, and fraternity." By 1792, he had so distinguished himself for his bravery and endurance that he was advanced in rank to general. He was made a commander of the army of the Pyrenees in 1793 and campaigned with Napoleon Bonaparte in Italy, in the Tyrol and in Egypt. He won the nickname "the Horatius Cocles of the Tyrol" in an amazing feat while in command of the cavalry. He was a soldier, sincerely devoted to the Revolution, but he detested the cruelties committed in the name of the republic. When he realized Napoleon's intentions of creating an empire instead of maintaining the republican government, he did not attempt to hide his dissatisfaction and requested permission to return home from the Egyptian campaign. On his return to France, he was captured by the Bourbon government of Naples, where he was imprisoned for two years. By the time he was released from prison, Bonaparte had control of France, but he never forgave his General Dumas for speaking out against his ambitions of creating a French empire.

Dumas was forced to retire with a small pension, and he died in poverty in 1806. He left behind a widow, a daughter and his son, Alexandre, who later became one of the literary geniuses of France. Dumas is still revered by the French for the services he rendered during the Revolution. This gratitude is expressed in the monuments erected to him, his son and his grandson on the Place Malesherbes in Paris.

Estevanico (Little Stephen)

Explorer

Estevanico (*c.* 1500–1539), discoverer of New Mexico and Arizona (the Seven Cities of the Zuñi Indians), was born in Morocco around the year 1500. He sailed from Spain in 1527 with an expedition of 506 persons to explore the interior of the New World. After landing on the coast of Florida, their number diminished to 240 within three months; and by the end of the year only 4 of them remained. For eight years, these four explorers, including Estevanico, lived among the Indians, serving as "medicine men." Three of the group eventually returned to Spain, but Estevanico settled in Mexico, where he learned the customs and languages of the Indians. Because of this knowledge, he was selected in 1539 by Fray Marcos to serve as a guide for the expedition in search of the legendary Seven Cities of Cibola.

He was instructed to proceed in advance of the exploring party and to send back crosses varying in size according to what he had found. On the fourth day, he sent back a cross as tall as a man, and the messenger informed Fray Marcos of the seven large cities with houses of stone and lime. Instead of waiting at a safe distance from the Indian cities until the exploring party caught up with him, Estevanico pushed on into the Indian territory alone, and was captured and subsequently murdered when he tried to escape. Hearing of the death of Estevanico, Fray Marcos fled from the area without finding the famous Seven Cities.

THOMAS ALEXANDRE DUMAS

Flora, William

American Soldier

William Flora (?–1820), one of the valiant heroes of '75, was on guard at Great Bridge south of Norfolk with other sentinels of Colonel William Woodford's Second Virginia Regiment on December 9, 1775, when the British stormed the bridge with two hundred troops. Although only a volunteer sentinel, Flora continued to fire at the onrushing British regulars after his comrades had withdrawn to their redoubt. The staunch defense of the bridge by the patriots threw the British forces into confusion, making it possible for the American troops to engage the British in guerrilla warfare. The British were forced to evacuate Norfolk and to withdraw to their ships lying in the harbor.

Flora was a free-born Negro of Portsmouth, Virginia, one of the one thousand free Negroes of military age in the colony at the outbreak of the Revolution. Even though the royal governor had promised emancipation to all slaves who would join the British Army to repel the rebellious patriots, most of the Negroes expressed their loyalty to the American struggle for independence and freedom.

In the opening conflict of the War of 1812, William Flora again rose to the defense of his country. When fighting occurred near Norfolk, Flora took up the old musket that he had used at Great Bridge and enlisted as a marine on a gunboat.

As a veteran of the Revolution, Flora was awarded the usual land bounty of one hundred acres and distinguished himself between the two wars as a successful property owner and businessman. He acquired and operated a livery stable in Portsmouth. For over thirty years, he enjoyed the patronage of the leading citizens of his community. He left a large estate to his son and grandson, including many horses and carriages that were used in his livery business.

Forten, James

Abolitionist and Inventor

James Forten (1766-1842), a free Negro of Philadelphia, was a capitalist-equalitarian-abolitionist who fought to win respect for the Negro's fitness to share in the common heritage of America. He received a few years of education in the Quaker-conducted school of Anthony Benezet, but at the age of ten he had to go to work. At fourteen, he entered the Navy in the service of his country during the War for Independence. From his experience in the Navy, he developed a device for the handling of sails and became a highly respected businessman as the owner of a sail loft employing both Negro and white workers. He became the wealthiest Negro in Philadelphia and used his fortune for a wide range of causes, such as women's rights, temperance, peace and the equalitarian rights of the Negro. He became the most important Negro in the abolitionist movement of his day. Feeling that his record as an American entitled him to full recognition as a man and a citizen, he fought the policy of deportation advocated by the American Colonization Society. In 1817, he spearheaded a meeting at the A.M.E. Church in Philadelphia to denounce the designs of the colonizationists.

He was one of the organizers of the Convention of Free Negroes in 1830, which gave its attention to the plight of the free Negro and struck against the deportation idea. Forten and the members of the National Convention of Free Colored People were responsible for consolidating Northern Negro opinion against emigration on the basis that they were entitled to first-class citizenship as they were of old American stock.

As an abolitionist, Forten is reputed to be responsible for the conversion of William

Lloyd Garrison and Theodore Dwight Weld to the belief in racial equality. He believed that the welfare of all Negroes in America depended upon the emancipation of their brethren in slavery. A man of wealth and the descendant of several generations of free men, Forten stands out as the first militant champion of civil rights for the Negro.

Gomez, Sebastian

Spanish Painter

Sebastian Gomez (1646–1682), famous artist of 17th-century Spain, is remembered for his paintings executed in Seville, two of his most beautiful being "Our Lady with the Child Jesus in Her Arms" and "Saint Anne." Today, many of his paintings are owned by private individuals in Spain and throughout Europe. He excelled in the production of harmony of color, executed with a freedom of touch and a profound knowledge of shade and light. This famous painter was the son of a Negro slave who had been brought to Spain in the early period of the slave trade. As a slave of the famous painter Murillo, the boy's duties were to clean his master's brushes and studio.

In this capacity, the young Sebastian carefully watched his master mix the colors and instruct his pupils. Then, one day while cleaning the studio, he attempted to paint. When Murillo found one of his paintings and questioned all of the pupils as to who had painted the picture, Sebastian kept silent. This happened again, and he was questioned by the master, but he denied any knowledge of the work. Finally, Murillo caught him painting one day, and he could deny it no longer. Begging forgiveness of his master, the young boy was shocked when Murillo praised his work and announced that he would become his pupil. The master not only recognized the artistic talent of the boy but considered him a genius.

SEBASTIAN GOMEZ

Gomez was released from slavery; and Murillo adopted him as a son, sponsored his marriage and worked with him as a painter to perfect his style. He wanted the famous Sebastian Gomez to go down in the cultural history of Spain as the mulatto son of Murillo.

Hall, Prince

Fraternal Leader

Prince Hall (1735–1807), founder of the oldest Negro fraternal organization in America, was born in Barbados, British West Indies, in 1735, the son of an English father and a free Negro mother. He was first trained to become a skilled leather worker but after a few years of training gave up that apprenticeship and migrated to Boston, Massachusetts, where he became a leader in the Negro community of the city.

During the Revolutionary War, Prince Hall and 14 other free men of color were inducted into the Masonic Lodge by a group of British soldiers stationed in Boston. When the British Army evacuated the area the following year, Hall organized the first Masonic Lodge for Negroes in America. He obtained a charter from England in 1787 for the African Lodge Number 459. He was elected master of the organization and set up African lodges in Philadelphia and Rhode Island in 1797. The name African Grand Lodge was changed to the Prince Hall Grand Lodge after the organizer's death in 1807.

The founder of Negro Freemasonry was a champion of Negro rights. A self-educated man and a clergyman, he recognized the value of education and, in 1787, campaigned for the establishment of schools for Negro children in Boston. He was a property owner of the city, which entitled him to vote and participate in the affairs of the state. He petitioned the Massachusetts legislature to support the cause of emancipation and especially the protection of free Negroes from kidnapping and being sold into slavery.

As a patriotic citizen of Massachusetts, he had asked the Committee of Safety for the Colonies to allow him to join the Continental Army, which was organized by the Second Continental Congress with George Washington as the commander-in-chief. His petition was approved, and he served in the Continental Army during the Revolution.

Hammon, Jupiter

Poet

Jupiter Hammon (c. 1720–c. 1800) was born a slave in New York in the colonial period. He was given an education of sorts by his master, Mr. Lloyd, and turned to writing poetry as an intellectual and emotional outlet, since slavery prevented most other forms of expression.

The Lloyds were fond of Hammon and, since the type of verse that he wrote was not critical of slavery, they helped him place his works before the public. Most of his works were concerned with salvation and, therefore, closely identified with religion. This was typical of the period in which he lived and indicates that he had close ties to a formal religion.

The first work published by Hammon was the poem "An Evening Thought: Salvation by Christ, with Penitential Cries," written in 1760. Following its publication, he continued writing sporadically until 1787. He was a contemporary and admirer of Phillis Wheatley and dedicated 21 stanzas of poetry to her in 1778.

Hammon was unpopular among many of his race, however, because of his acceptance of the role in which life had placed him. His last work was the essay entitled *An Address to the Negroes of the State of New York,* and in this message Hammon admonished other slaves to be humble in their roles until such time as the race earned its freedom.

Hannibal, Abram

Russian Officer

Abram Hannibal (1697–1782), great-grandfather of Russia's greatest poet, Pushkin, was captured in Africa and was sold as a slave on the Constantinople market to a Russian nobleman. At the age of eight, he was given to Tsar Peter the Great, who grew fond of him and saw to it that he was educated and baptized in the Russian Orthodox Church. When he completed his schooling, he went with Tsar Peter to Paris, where he studied military engineering.

Hannibal remained in France for seven years. He became a favorite of the Duc d'Orleans and was permitted to join the French army. The Duc d'Orleans tried to persuade him to remain in France, but Hannibal chose to return to his adopted land of Russia so that he might serve the Tsar

ABRAM HANNIBAL

as an engineer lieutenant. In the meantime, his family in Africa had discovered that he was in the service of the Tsar, and his brother traveled to Russia and requested Peter to allow Hannibal to return to his family. Hannibal, however, elected to remain in Russia.

As long as Tsar Peter lived, Hannibal enjoyed his favor and sponsorship; but after the death of Peter his good fortune waned. Queen Catherine and Peter II exiled him to Siberia. The punishment was harsh and unendurable. He attempted to escape but was recaptured and returned. In 1741, he was saved by Elizabeth of Russia, who pardoned him and reinstated him to high rank in the army.

He was given many responsibilities and duties to carry out in the name of his new ruler. In the boundary-line dispute between Sweden and Russia, Hannibal was commissioned to represent Russia in settling the issue. As an engineer, he was appointed a

member of the staff to inspect Russia's army fortifications and the construction of the Logoda Canal. Shortly before he died, Hannibal was appointed commandant of the city of Reval (now Tallinn).

Haynes, Lemuel

Minister and Minuteman

Lemuel Haynes (1753–1833), Congregationalist minister of New England, was born of a white mother and a Negro father at West Hartford, Connecticut, in 1753. He was deserted by his mother and grew up in the home of Deacon David Rose of Granville, Massachusetts. Lemuel attended the district school and was instructed in the Christian religion. It was the custom to read a noted minister's sermon on the evening before the Sabbath, and Deacon Rose, who was practically blind, had assigned the task of reading to the young Lemuel. One day Lemuel read to the family a sermon which seemed a little unusual, and the deacon insisted on knowing the author. Lemuel had to confess that it was his sermon. The family was so impressed with the quality and profoundness of the sermon that they all agreed he was destined for the ministry.

His training for the ministry was interrupted by the Revolutionary War. He joined the revolutionists, first as a minuteman in 1774, then as a regular soldier after the Battle of Lexington. When he returned home from the Continental Army, he began the serious study of theology. He studied Latin and Greek under Daniel Farrand of Canaan, Connecticut, and William Bradford of Wintonbury.

He was licensed to preach in the Congregational Church in 1780 and was ordained soon afterward. He became the pastor of the Congregational Church of Middle Granville and served for five years. His next church was in Torrington, Connecticut, where he

LEMUEL HAYNES

was one of the first black ministers of a white congregation. Some of the members of the church were displeased over having a "nigger minister"; but the disgruntled were soon converted to acceptance of Reverend Haynes. At West Rutland, Vermont, he became noted for his revivals and was called upon to conduct services in the other churches of the area. Both the Connecticut and Vermont Missionary Societies called upon him to conduct revivals in the backwoods of their states. Haynes was active in the "Great Awakening" of the church and the revival of Christianity.

He participated in the exciting controversy with Hosea Ballon over religious practices. In the debate, he silenced Ballon with his famous sermon, "Ye Shall Not Surely Die."

During the War of 1812, he spoke out against the anti-Federalists who were threatening to secede from the Union at the Hartford Convention in 1814. Because of his ridicule of the states' righters of New England, many of his church members turned against him. He thought it best to resign and accept a church in Manchester, Vermont. From Manchester, he moved to Granville, New York, where he was pastor at the Congregational Church until his death in 1833.

Hector, Edward

American Soldier

Edward Hector (?–1834), a private in Captain Hercules Courtney's company of the Third Pennsylvania Artillery, displayed an example of patriotism at the Battle of Brandywine Creek in 1777 that merits recording. Hector had answered his country's call in the opening crisis of the Revolution by enlisting in the army on March 10, 1777. He saw action that summer, when the British launched their invasion of Pennsylvania with the objective of taking Philadelphia, where the Continental Congress was in session. Washington's heroic effort to halt the British at Brandywine Creek was in vain, but the bravery of his men, especially Edward Hector, deserves attention.

Hector had charge of an ammunition wagon attached to Colonel Proctor's regiment. An order was issued by the officers for the wagons to be abandoned to the enemy when Washington's army was forced to retreat. Hector refused to sacrifice his horses to the enemy; and in the confusion of the retreat, he took up and used the muskets which had been left on the field by the fleeing soldiers and retired safely, with his wagons, in the face of the victorious British.

After the war, attempts were made to procure a pension for the hero of Brandywine, but the request was not honored until 1833, the year before his death. The legislature of Pennsylvania granted him $40 for his services in the Revolutionary War.

Jones, Absalom

Minister

Absalom Jones, rector of the first separate Protestant Episcopal congregation for Negroes, was born a slave in Sussex, Delaware. As a child servant in his master's house, he learned to save the pennies given to him by visitors. He was encouraged to use his pennies to purchase a speller and a Bible in the endeavor to learn to read. When his master took him to Philadelphia to work as a handyman in his store, one of the clerks taught him to write. He received permission to attend night school, where he rounded out his formal education.

The thrifty young slave purchased his wife's freedom and later his own. As free Negroes, they continued to work for their former owner and in time purchased a home and other income property. As a respected member of the community, he worshipped in St. George's Methodist Church and participated in the establishment of the pioneer Free African Society along with Richard Allen and other prominent freemen of Philadelphia.

In 1787, when trouble developed over the seating of blacks in St. George's Church, Absalom Jones was pulled from his knees during prayer by an usher, with the command that he was to retire to the balcony of the church. He and Richard Allen led the Negro exodus from the mother church. With the members of the Free African Society, they endeavored to organize independent Negro churches. The two friends parted when Jones preferred to follow the Anglican tradition while Allen created the African Methodist Episcopal Church.

During the yellow fever epidemic in 1793, the two leaders helped set up relief measures for the citizens of Philadelphia. They continued to cooperate during the War of 1812 and raised a company of militia for service in the army. While Allen became the first bishop of the A.M.E. Church, Jones organized many Negro parishes in the African Protestant Episcopal Church.

ABSALOM JONES

Latino, Juan

Spanish Scholar

Juan Latino (de Sesa), 1516–1597, scholar and university professor of Spain, was captured on the Barbary Coast at the age of twelve and sold into slavery in Seville, Spain. He was purchased by the family of the famous Spanish soldier-hero, Fernando Gonzalo de Cordoba. The young slave Juan was assigned to the family heir, the third Duke de Sesa. Juan attended the young master, who was eight years younger than he, carrying his books to and from the lecture room. Peeping in the books, the older boy became

JUAN LATINO

curious and asked what the mysterious symbols meant to one so young. The Duke explained the secret to his slave, and with the family's approval Juan was permitted to study with his master.

Granada had become the chief center of learning in Spain, and Archbishop Pedro Guerrero was liberal enough to accept the admission of the slave into the classes with his master. Here he mastered the Latin language and amazed the teacher with some poems written in Latin. For his excellence in mastering the language, he became known as Juan Latino instead of Juan de Sesa. The best of his poetical works, "Austriad" and "Translatione," attracted a great deal of attention.

He also mastered Greek and taught both languages, earning his degree in 1546 from the University of Granada. He was noted for his quick wit, musical ability and his charm. He was awarded the Master of Arts

degree in 1556 "without prejudice of Color" and was highly honored in 1565, when he opened the academic year of the university with a Latin oration.

The life of this Spanish scholar was revived in 1935 by the presentation of Encisco's dramatic version of Latino's career. The play centers around his love for Doña Ana, a Spanish noblewoman whom he married.

Lew, Barzillai

American Soldier

Barzillai Lew (1743–?) was the son of a free Negro, Primus Lew, who had migrated from Haiti to Massachusetts. Barzillai was born in Groton, Massachusetts, and was a cooper by trade. This giant of a man responded to the lure of adventure on the trails across the New England mountains in pursuit of the French and Indians in the 1760's and was ready to use his skills in the struggle for independence in the 1770's.

As a veteran of the French and Indian War, having served for nine months in a Massachusetts company commanded by Thomas Farrington, Lew brought to the amateur volunteers of the Continental Army a record as a seasoned and experienced soldier. He enlisted on May 6, 1775, in the 27th Massachusetts Regiment and participated in the Battle of Bunker Hill and the siege of Boston as a soldier and a fifer. Lew remained in the army for the remainder of the Revolution. His military career included dangerous and daring assignments of anti-British guerrilla warfare activities in New England.

Lislet-Geoffroy, Jean-Baptiste

French Scientist

Jean-Baptiste Lislet-Geoffroy (1755–1836) was a botanist, natural philosopher, zoologist and astronomer. His contributions were made in the name of France, yet he never visited France. He was born on the Ile de France, or Mauritius, an island situated in the Indian Ocean about five hundred miles east of Madagascar. His father was a Frenchman; his mother was the granddaughter of Touca Miama, an African King of Galam. She was enslaved and carried to the Ile de France in 1730. The Frenchman, Geoffroy, freed her, and she bore him a son in 1755. The father adopted the child and christened him Jean-Baptiste Lislet-Geoffroy.

Jean-Baptiste was placed in the engineering corps at the age of 15, where he studied mathematics and astronomy under a former admiral. He became an expert draftsman and designer. His interest in scientific pursuits led him to study geology, geography, biology, zoology and natural phenomena. He developed maps of the Ile de France and gave minute descriptions of the highest mountains of the island. As a consequence of this contribution, in 1791 he was made guardian of maps and plans.

He was elected a member of the famed French Academy of Sciences. In the archives of the academy may be found many of his manuscripts containing his meteorological observations and his hydrographical journals. In a report of a voyage that he made to the Bay of St. Luce, he gives detailed descriptions of the manners and customs of the people. In a recommendation to France, he suggested they develop the island's resources as exchangeable commodities to promote an advantageous and lucrative commerce, rather than leave the natives in a constant state of war in order to supply slaves to the white traders.

When the British took over the island in 1794, he had already risen to the rank of captain of the engineers under the French army. Therefore, the British designated him chief of the engineer commission.

Mansa Musa

Ruler of Mali

Mansa Musa, 14th-century descendant of the first Emperor Sundiata of Mali, was one of the outstanding rulers of this West African empire. Mali stretched from the mouth of the Senegal River on the Atlantic Ocean to the right bank of the Niger River. To the north, the territory extended into the Sahara Desert, where it included valuable salt deposits and copper mines.

The wealth and splendor of the Mali Kingdom was revealed in 1324, when Mansa Musa made his famous pilgrimage to Mecca in accordance with the Islamic custom. He took with him a caravan of 60,000 persons and 80 camels, each carrying about 300 pounds of gold dust. He impressed the people of the Middle East greatly with the wealth and magnificence of his West African kingdom.

He rebuilt the city of Timbuktu and fostered learning by building mosques and schools in many of the towns. Learned scholars from the University of Fez were invited to teach in the schools. His large army consisted of some 100,000 men, with approximately 10,000 cavalrymen. This military might, and his political administration, held the vast empire together.

Matthews, Saul

American Spy

Saul Matthews, soldier and spy for the Virginia Army of the American Revolution, was born a slave in Virginia but earned his freedom for "many very essential services rendered to the Commonwealth during the late war." When many of the Negro slaves of Virginia were following the British forces in hopes of gaining their freedom, Saul Matthews took up his musket and offered his services to the Virginians. In 1781, when

Cornwallis occupied a position that gave him control of Portsmouth, Virginia, there was urgent need for information concerning his troops, their positions, strength and movements on the James River. Lafayette and Baron von Steuben issued an order to the commander of the four counties of the area, Colonel Josiah Parker, to obtain the desired information. Colonel Parker dispatched the trusted Negro enlistee, Saul Matthews, to penetrate the British lines for the purpose of gathering the desired information.

Matthews accomplished his mission successfully and was responsible for leading a raiding party against the British on the very night of his return to his lines. They captured many British prisoners and so harassed Cornwallis' forces that he was eventually forced to shift his troops to another position.

Colonel Parker praised Matthews' services as a soldier and a spy, stating publicly that he deserved the acclaim of his country. In 1792, the Virginia legislature granted him his freedom from slavery.

Pétion, Alexandre Sabès

Haitian Leader

Alexandre Pétion (1770–1818), mulatto leader of the Haitian Revolution and president of the Republic of Haiti, was educated in one of the best military schools of France and had served in the French Army in Europe. In the three-sided struggle for control of the French island of Haiti, the French General Leclerc, through intrigue and bribery, pitted the mulattoes against the blacks, with the intent of crushing the revolt for independence. In 1803, Dessalines, the strongest of the insurrectionist generals, defeated the French at Cap Français and was elected governor of Haiti for life. He placed his four most prominent leaders in command of the four departments of the island. Christophe, the black general, and Pétion, the

ALEXANDRE SABÈS PÉTION

mulatto, were entrusted with two of the divisions. The despotic rule of Dessalines resulted in his assassination in 1806, and this led to rivalry between Christophe and Pétion for control of the island.

Pétion, as natural leader of the mulattoes, dreamed of an ideal republic controlled by his people. Through the support of the mulattoes, he was made chairman of the committee to draft the constitution and was elected president. Christophe immediately waged war on the republic, but it ended in a stalemate. Pétion was proclaimed president of the south and west, forming the Republic of Haiti. The government of the republic was more liberal and democratic than the monarchical state in the north. Pétion carried out land redistributions as rewards to the veterans of the revolution and put into practice his ideas of self-sustaining agriculture.

In 1816, Pétion aided Bolívar in his liberation of northern South America. He offered the liberators refuge in his republic and provided equipment to the insurgents. By so doing, he became one of the instruments in the freeing of Venezuela, Colombia, Ecuador, Peru and Bolivia. He was elected president of the republic for life in 1815 but lived only three years afterward.

Poor, Salem

American Soldier

Salem Poor, distinguished soldier in the Battle of Charlestown during the Revolutionary War, was a member of a regiment made up largely of white men. He earned the praise of his officers while in battle for his gallantry and courage. A petition dated December 5, 1775, was presented on his behalf to the General Court of Massachusetts by fourteen Massachusetts officers. It stated that "a Negro man called Salem Poor of Col. Frye's regiment, Capt. Ames' company in the late battle at Charlestown, behaved like an experienced officer, as well as an excellent soldier. . . . We would only beg leave to say, in the person of this said Negro centers a brave and gallant soldier. The reward due to so great and distinguished a character, we submit to the Congress."

Salem Poor also served his country at Valley Forge and White Plains. He fought for the principles of life, liberty and the pursuit of happiness even though he had undergone the degradation of being a slave.

Prosser, Gabriel

Insurrectionist

Gabriel Prosser (1777–1800), a slave insurrectionist, was born in Virginia in 1777 and was hanged in 1800 for his plot to march on the city of Richmond, seize the arsenal, strike down the whites and liberate the slaves. His plan was frustrated by a fearful storm on the night of August 30, 1800, plus the fact that two slaves informed their master. The magnitude of the plot forced Governor James Monroe to declare martial law to defend the city. Prosser's band of recruits was organized on a military basis. Three columns were to attack Richmond: the right wing was to seize the arsenal, the center wing was to encircle the town, while the left wing was to seize the powder house. Had the plan succeeded, Prosser was to seize other cities and the entire state of Virginia.

Prosser won followers by impressing them with testimony from the Bible, claiming he was their chosen leader. He was described as "a fellow of courage and intellect above his rank in life." He was assisted by his brother Martin; his wife, Nanny; and another unusually capable leader, Jack Bowler. Each Sunday, Gabriel visited the city of Richmond noting the various locations of arms and ammunition as well as the layout of the town. His followers made crude weapons—swords and bayonets, and about five hundred bullets—in the spring of 1800. On Saturday, August 30, Tom and Pharaoh, slaves of Mosby Sheppard, informed him of the plot. He, in turn, reported it to Governor Monroe, who acted with speed and secrecy, calling in over six hundred men to give notice of the plot to every state militia commander.

Gabriel attempted to escape when his plot was foiled by a storm and the informers, but he was captured in Norfolk on September 25. He was convicted and sentenced to hang on October 7. He was personally interviewed by Governor Monroe in the hope that he would talk. Gabriel and 15 of his associates were hanged on the same day. At least 35 Negroes were hanged for participating in the plot. John Randolph, an eyewitness of the group while in custody, stated, "The accused have exhibited a spirit, which, if it becomes general, must deluge the Southern country in blood. They manifested a sense of their rights, and contempt of danger. . . ."

Raimond, Julien

Journalist

Julien Raimond, mulatto journalist and advocate of civil rights from Santo Domingo, was an octoroon who was born free and wealthy in the latter half of the eighteenth century. In 1784, he was one of the three mulattoes chosen to go to France to appeal for better conditions for mulattoes of the island. The fortune inherited from his wealthy father was destined to be used by him in the cause of freedom. He was one of the 545 blacks from Santo Domingo who fought with the French Army in the American Revolution. He caught the spirit of revolt from the principles advocated by the American patriots.

In 1786, Raimond set forth the grievances of the mulattoes in the colonies and their demands for more recognition to the minister of the marine, the Marquis de Castries. With the slow means of communication at that time, nothing was achieved because the French Revolution erupted in Paris. Raimond joined forces with the group known as the *Amis de Noirs,* an organization to coordinate all of the efforts of Negroes and mulattoes in the American colonies for the abolition of slavery and for civil rights for the mulattoes.

As a journalist, Raimond published pamphlets during the American Revolution expounding the cause of the mulattoes, and his tone was that of the master class for he did not concern himself during this period over any espousal whatever of the cause of the slave. His fortune gradually ebbed away as he spent it on the publication of his caustic and sarcastic writings in the cause that was a burning flame in his heart. When he went to France, he had an annual income of 55,000 livres from his estates in Santo Domingo. By 1790, he had spent half of his fortune, yet he grandiosely offered the sum of 6 million livres to the Na-

tional Assembly as a gift from his fellow citizens of Santo Domingo. He had made a similar theatrical offer during the Revolution by providing the services of a brigade of mulattoes for the Continental Army.

Finally, in the Act of May 15, 1791, civil rights were granted to free mulattoes in the French colonies.

Ranger, Joseph

American Seaman

Joseph Ranger, seaman in the Virginia Navy during the American Revolution, was a free man of color from Northumberland County who enlisted in the service of the Commonwealth of Virginia in 1776. He rendered the greatest possible number of years of service, staying in the navy until Virginia disposed of its last vessel in 1787. He served on four of Virginia's man-of-war vessels, the *Hero,* the *Dragon,* the *Jefferson* and the *Patriot.* The ill-fated *Jefferson* was blown up by the British on the James River, but Ranger survived to join the *Patriot.* In October 1781, shortly before Cornwallis' surrender at Yorktown, Virginia, Ranger and the remainder of the ship's crew were taken prisoner by the British.

Official records show that, after Ranger's discharge from the navy in 1787, he received a pension and a land grant of 100 acres from the Commonwealth of Virginia, possibly in the Virginia Military Reserve of the Northwest Territory. Under the government established by the adoption of the Constitution, he received a pension of $96 a year.

During the Revolutionary War, naval service was far more attractive to Negroes than service in the army because they were able to work as equals with white seamen. Many acted as pilots, boatswain's mates and gunner's mates. Ranger helped establish a naval tradition for Negroes, and they enlisted extensively in the War of 1812.

Robinson, James

American Soldier

James Robinson (1753–1868), awarded a gold medal by Lafayette for military valor in the Battle of Yorktown, was born a slave in Maryland in 1753. He had been promised his freedom by his master upon the completion of his military service, but after the death of the master the heirs refused to honor the promise. Instead, they sold the fighter for America's freedom on the New Orleans slave market. In spite of this disappointment, he again answered the call to defend America in the War of 1812. General Andrew Jackson called upon the Negroes of New Orleans to help defend the city against the British. Robinson was one of the first to answer the call, but later he was returned to the life of a slave on a cotton plantation until the Civil War. After the War and his final reward of freedom, he migrated to Detroit, Michigan, where he died at the age of 115.

A newspaper account of his death and funeral pointed out the injustice that this veteran of the Revolutionary War and gold medal winner had suffered despite his service to the cause of freedom.

Salem, Peter

American Soldier

Peter Salem (?–1816), veteran of the Battles of Lexington and Concord and Bunker Hill, had been a slave but was awarded his freedom so that he could serve in the army. The Committee on Safety had agreed in May 1775 to use only free men in the armed forces of the Continental Army of the American Revolution because the use of enslaved men would be inconsistent with the principles for which they were fighting. Thus Peter Salem was freed by his owners, a fam-

PETER SALEM

ily in Framingham, Massachusetts, to fight for his country's independence.

Some accounts of the Battle of Bunker Hill claim that it was Salem who fired the shot that mortally wounded the British commander, Major John Pitcairn. This story cannot be substantiated, but there is no doubt that Peter Salem, like many other Negroes of his time, fought for the freedom of America, convinced that liberty was to come to all who proved themselves worthy of it.

Sancho, Ignatius

Scholar

Ignatius Sancho (1729–1780), brilliant scholar of eighteenth-century England, was born on board a slave ship between Guinea in Africa and the Spanish West Indies in 1729. His mother died soon after his birth. The child was baptized by the Catholic Church, and at the age of two he was carried to Greenwich, England, where he was given to three maiden ladies. At an early age, he displayed unusual intelligence through his reaction to books, fine paintings and music. His mistresses, however, had no appreciation for the unusual talent of their young slave and punished him whenever they found him in the library.

The Duke of Montague, who often visited the household, was the first to notice the boy's alertness. He frequently took the boy home on visits and thus began his education. Sancho's mistresses resented his training and threatened to sell him on the slave market if he pursued his studies. Having learned the fundamentals from the Duke, he continued to read and learn in spite of the threat of his mistresses. Upon the death of the three sisters and the Duke of Montague, the Duchess took Sancho into her services as a butler. When the Duchess died, she gave him his freedom plus an annuity of 30 pounds.

Through careful management, he was able to open a grocery store to earn a sufficient living for himself and his family of seven, while he continued to develop his interest in music, art and literature. He wrote many tracts, pamphlets and essays. One of his chief themes was the evils of human slavery. His letters were more outstanding in literary form than his essays. They were published in 1803 by his son, William Sancho. He loved the theater and wanted to become an actor; but instead, he contributed plays and enjoyed the association of David Garrick, the greatest English actor of his time. He associated with the famous English painter Gainsborough, who painted his portrait in 1768. His musical criticism and analysis were sought by composers. He composed many musical selections himself, but was more widely recognized for his publication of *A Theory of Music*.

Saunders, Prince

Statesman and Diplomat

Prince Saunders (*c.* 1775–1839), a free Negro, served Haiti as a diplomat-statesman. Born possibly in 1775 in either Lebanon, Connecticut, or Thetford, Vermont, he is listed in church records of Lebanon as baptized on July 25, 1784. His parents, Cuff and Phyllis Saunders, were free Negroes of Lebanon. Prince was educated at Thetford Academy and at one time taught at a colored school in Colchester, Connecticut, where he was the owner of some property in 1805. In 1807–08, he was a student in Moor's Charity School of Dartmouth College. He taught at the African School in Boston until 1812. While in Boston, he became a member of the African Lodge of Masons and served as secretary in 1811. Interested in literary and cultural pursuits, Saunders, along with a

IGNATIUS SANCHO

group of young white men, founded the Belles Lettres Society.

In 1812 or 1813, he attended the British Grand Lodge of Freemasons in England. It is not quite clear whether Saunders went to Haiti first or whether he left England for Haiti. In Haiti he obtained the favor of King Henri I (Christophe) and returned to England, where he was described as a "lion of the first magnitude in fashionable circles." Christophe, who was anxious to establish an educational system in his island empire, had called upon William Wilberforce for help in this effort. Wilberforce sent his suggestions by Saunders and two others, who organized a school system in Haiti.

As an advisor to the dictator-king, Saunders was able to introduce vaccination on the island; the royal family was the first to submit to vaccination. He was instrumental in persuading the King to establish the Church of England in Haiti in place of the Catholic Church. Christophe was wise enough to use the services of Saunders as his special envoy to England as he lived in constant fear of the French attempting to retake the island. Fortified with his official appointment, Saunders returned to England in 1816, where he published his "Haitian Papers." This was a translation of the laws of Haiti into English, with comments by Saunders. His comments indicate that he was familiar with the basic principles of jurisprudence and was a skillful linguist.

When King Henri I recalled Saunders from England, he declined to return; instead, he came to America and became a resident of Philadelphia. He became active in the abolitionist movement and included in his lectures a plea for sympathy and support of Haiti. In 1820, when King Henri I committed suicide and his regime was overthrown, Saunders returned to Haiti. The establishment of a republic under President Boyer brought Saunders the appointment of attorney general; and

he is credited with the authorship of Haiti's criminal code. He died in Port-au-Prince in February 1839.

Sisson, Tack

American Soldier

Tack Sisson, prime participant in executing commando raids against the British forces during the American Revolution, was one of the abductors of Major General Prescott, the commander of British troops at Newport, Rhode Island, in 1777. In order to effect an exchange of prisoners with the British who had captured Major General Charles Lee, it was necessary to capture a British officer of equal rank. Lieutenant Colonel William Barton, in command of the Rhode Island militia, undertook the dangerous mission on July 9. With a hand picked group of some 40 or so men, he embarked in five small boats to within a distance of three-quarters of a mile of General Prescott's quarters. Arriving at this point around midnight, Colonel Barton took Tack Sisson and another soldier with him to complete the mission. Under the cover of night, they evaded the guards and subdued a sentry; and Sisson smashed down the doors of the general's bedroom.

Prescott surrendered meekly but with a feeling of confidence that his abductors would not be able to pass his array of troops. The Americans adroitly slipped out of the camp as they had entered, with their prize prisoner. Colonel Barton and Sisson, according to an account in the *London Chronicle,* had spirited the British general away "without his breeches."

Solimann, Angelo (Mmadi-Maki)

Soldier and Scholar

Angelo Solimann, or Mmadi-Maki, linguist, historian, and soldier of the Holy Roman Empire under Emperors Joseph and

Francis I, was the son of an African prince. He was captured by an invading tribe of Africans and sold into slavery. The nationality of his first master is unknown, but he was next sold to a Sicilian noblewoman at Messina, Sicily. She treated him kindly, instructing him in the language in hope of his accepting the Christian faith. During his convalescence after a serious illness, the boy asked for baptism in the Catholic Church. His mistress was so pleased she provided a very elaborate scene for the ill boy's baptism into the church. It was on this occasion that he adopted the Christian name of Angelo Solimann.

The boy was eventually given to Prince Lobkowitz, who frequently visited Sicily in the service of Emperor Joseph of the Holy Roman Empire. While serving under the Prince, he became fluent in languages. He was given a teacher who taught him all of his subjects: history, literature, math and languages. He accompanied the Prince on the battlefield and was instructed in military tactics. On one occasion, when the Prince was wounded, he rescued his master and took over the command of the troops. For this act of bravery and leadership, he was offered command of a company of troops. Emperor Francis I invited him to enter his service, but he refused as he wished to remain with Prince Lobkowitz. Later, he taught the son of Francis I.

After the death of Prince Lobkowitz, he served Prince Wenceslas of Liechtenstein, the uncle of Francis I. His picture may be seen today in the art gallery of Liechtenstein.

Sunni Ali Ber

Ruler of Songhay

Sunni Ali Ber (1464–1492), one of the most effective conquerors and organizers in West African history, founded the kingdom of Songhay. He was one of the sons of Dia Assibai, who had been taken as a hostage by Mansa Musa in 1425. Sunni Ali escaped from Mali, returning to Songhay, where he established himself as ruler and launched his program of conquest.

He was the first empire builder in West Africa to recognize the importance of controlling the Niger River. For this purpose, he built a navy and systematically developed a plan to ensure the success of his conquest and later defense of the river. His armies were equally well organized and trained. He conquered the city of Timbuktu, and after a long siege, the city of Djenne. He was reported to have been ruthless and unmerciful to the Moslem scholars and merchants of Timbuktu; but when he entered Djenne in triumph in 1483, he was as merciful to them as he had been harsh to the people of Timbuktu.

Although Sunni Ali had outwardly accepted the Islamic faith, he ignored the question of religion in building his empire. Islamic schools and mosques which were loyal to him were protected and supported, while those centers expressing hostility to his rule were ruthlessly destroyed.

Sunni Ali realized that adequate transportation was a vital instrument in holding his empire together. Thus he conceived of and started construction of a canal that would connect Walata with Timbuktu, a distance of nearly two hundred miles. It was never completed because his attention was directed against the Mossi, who were invading Songhay. On the way to fight the Mossi in 1492, Sunni Ali drowned while crossing a flooded stream.

Tarrant, Caesar

American Seaman

Caesar Tarrant (?–1796), valiant seaman during the American Revolution, was a slave, probably from Elizabeth City. He served as a pilot in the Virginia Navy for over four years. He entered the service in 1776 or 1777 and served until the British captured the *Patriot* on the eve of the battle at Yorktown. Tarrant was the pilot of the *Patriot*, which was under the command of Commodore Taylor when the ship was engaged in fighting against a British privateer south of the Cape of Virginia. He steered the ship with great skill during the encounter and was commended by his commodore for having behaved gallantly.

On November 14, 1786, after the close of the war, the Virginia legislature passed a resolution for his emancipation stating that "he had entered very early into the service of his country, and continued to pilot the armed vessels of this state during the late war." After his emancipation, Tarrant accumulated a sizeable estate and became a man of influence in his community. Virginia saw fit to make a large land grant to his heirs in the 1830's in the disposal of the military reserve lands of Ohio which had been set aside for veterans of the Revolution.

Toussaint L'Ouverture

Haitian Revolutionist

Toussaint L'Ouverture, or François Dominique Toussaint (1743–1803), led the slaves' revolt on the French half of the island of Santo Domingo that began in 1791. Born on the island, he was about fifty years old when he joined the revolutionists. The complications of the situation in Haiti arose out of the three different groups involved: the French planters, the mulattoes and the slaves. When the Revolution occurred in France, both the mulattoes and the slaves responded to the cause of the Paris revolutionists against the royalists. The French planters of Haiti made some concessions to the mulattoes to win them over to their side, only to betray them in a new

TOUSSAINT L'OUVERTURE

turn of events. Then the Colonial Assembly issued a decree granting equal rights to the mulattoes if they helped in restoring order, but the blacks were to be returned to the chains of slavery again. This apparent union of the whites and mulattoes on the island caused the government in France to issue a counter decree to free the slaves and send an army to enforce the decree. Thus, Toussaint, the leader of the blacks, joined forces with the French army to fight against the planters and mulattoes.

Events in Europe further complicated the Haitian struggle. News of the French-Spanish War caused Toussaint to join forces with the Spanish half of the island. The area was ravaged by political and military strife. The French commissioners found it expedient to proclaim a general emancipation of the blacks and to invite them to return to the French colors. Toussaint and his followers accepted the invitation only to be tricked again by the fickleness of the French Revolutionists.

By his genius and extraordinary ability, Toussaint gathered fresh forces and drove the English and Spanish from the island. Next, the struggle turned into one between the mulattoes under Rigaud, and Toussaint. He won a series of victories over the mulattoes which gave him control of the bulk of the area. His control over the island was not destined to last, as Emperor Napoleon was determined to recapture the possession for his empire. The French expedition under the command of Leclerc was dispatched to Haiti. Fighting ensued again, with the forces of Toussaint difficult to defeat. Leclerc decided upon a strategy to trick the blacks into submission. He promised liberty and equality to all if they would cease fighting. Toussaint accepted the truce, only to be arrested and sent to France, where he died in prison of starvation in 1803.

Varick, James

Church Founder and Bishop

James Varick (1750–1828), one of the founders and first bishop of the African Methodist Episcopal Zion Church, was born in Newburgh, New York. In 1796, Varick and some of the other blacks who had been attending the Methodist Episcopal Church in New York requested of Bishop Francis Asbury permission to hold meetings by themselves. The group hired a house on Cross Street and converted it into a church. In 1801, the congregation organized the A.M.E. Zion Church according to the laws of the state of New York and were to be subject to the government of the Methodist Church.

A church building was completed, and the congregation was led by a regularly appointed white minister. This arrangement lasted until 1820, when the congregation under Va-

JAMES VARICK

rick's leadership adopted resolutions to break with the Methodist Episcopal organization and to declare its independence. As chairmen of a committee to draft the Discipline of the new organization, Varick and Abraham Thompson were granted the power of performing as elders until they could be ordained by constituted authorities. They expected this ritual to be approved by the Methodist organization, but the bishops refused to recognize them. In the meantime, several other all-Negro Methodist congregations from Philadelphia, New Haven and Long Island met in a conference on June 21, 1821, with Varick and elected him as district chairman, or presiding elder. Finally, in 1822, he was made bishop of the A.M.E. Zion Church.

Vassa, Gustavus (Olaudah Equiano)

World Traveler

Gustavus Vassa, or Olaudah Equiano (1745–1801), was a world traveler and a colonizer who was kidnapped at the age of eleven from his homeland in Benin, West Africa. He was transported to the slave market in Barbados, where he was sold to a Virginia planter. Shortly thereafter, he was sold again, this time to a roving sea captain by the name of Pascal, who owned a ship, the *Industrious Bee.* A young American boy, Richard Baker, became friendly with the African lad and taught him how to speak English on the voyage across the Atlantic to England. The two boys became inseparable friends for the two years that they were being trained as seamen. Baker died in 1759, leaving his African friend in grief.

Gustavus was again kidnapped and was placed on a man-of-war, where he served for a year along the coast of France and across the Atlantic to America. Finally, he was returned to England, where he was taught to read and write. His sea-roving master, Pascal, was made lieutenant of his majesty's ship the *Namur,* which was assigned to the Mediterranean. Gustavus accompanied him on the voyage, but he continued to study and to apply all of his spare time in seeking information. Upon their return to England, he approached his master for the purchase of his freedom, but Pascal became enraged over the boy's request and threatened to send him to the West Indies slave market to be sold. True to his word, Pascal sent the boy to the West Indies in 1762. He was fortunate in that he was purchased by Robert King, a Quaker of Philadelphia, who trained the boy in math and bookkeeping so that he could become a clerk. He worked diligently and saved his money to purchase his freedom; and his Quaker master honored his request.

Gustavus wanted to return to England, but Mr. King prevailed upon him to remain in his service. He was sent on a voyage to Montserrat with Captain Doran, who was killed by an enraged steer. The ship was taken over by Gustavus upon the death of the captain. Only twenty years of age, he piloted the ship to the island of Antigua and back to Montserrat with skill and earned the title of Captain Vassa. In order to earn money to return to England, he accepted work with Dr. Irving in 1773, on an expedition to find a northwest passage to India.

The trip was almost disastrous to the explorers, but Vassa and Dr. Irving became good friends. Dr. Irving prevailed upon Vassa to go to Jamaica and take over the management of his plantation there. He accepted the offer, but in 1776 he asked to be relieved of the job. When he booked passage on a sloop to England, he almost lost his freedom at the hands of a greedy slave-trader. He managed to escape and finally reached England in 1777. He continued to serve as a seaman for the next eight years; but in 1785, when the British government

GUSTAVUS VASSA

was engaged in the project of sending Africans back to their native land, he was asked to superintend the expedition to Africa. He was shocked to find that there was so much cheating and corruption among the commissary agents, and he reported the conditions to the naval authorities. He was dismissed for his efforts, but he was so deeply concerned that he drafted a brilliant and very scholarly appeal to Queen Charlotte, imploring her to investigate the commissary agents. Describing the miserable conditions of the Africans, he pleaded ". . . that they may be raised from the condition of brutes to which they are at present degraded to the rights and situation of free men . . . ."

Vassa remained in England for the remainder of his life and published his autobiography, *The Interesting Narrative of the Life of Olaudah Equiano, or Gustavus Vassa, the African*, in 1789.

PHILLIS WHEATLEY

Wheatley, Phillis

Poet

Phillis Wheatley (*c.* 1753–1784), an early American poetess, was brought from Senegal as a child and was sold as a slave on the docks at Boston in 1761 to a tailor by the name of John Wheatley, who gave the slave girl his family name. Mrs. Wheatley taught Phillis to read and write. She began writing verses in her early teens and published a collection of her poems under the title *Poems on Various Subjects* in 1773. The Wheatleys gave her freedom and a trip to London, where the lord mayor presented her with a copy of *Paradise Lost*. Her fame as a poetess grew, and she became known throughout the New England colonies. General George Washington wrote her a letter of commendation for her verses.

Whipple, Prince

American Soldier

Prince Whipple was born at Amabon, Africa, and was sent to America at the age of ten to obtain an education. Instead of this, however, he was sold by a treacherous sea captain into slavery at Baltimore, Maryland.

Whipple earned his freedom by serving in the American Revolution. When Washington pushed across the jagged cakes of ice and chilling spray of the Delaware River on Christmas of 1776 to surprise the British garrison at Trenton, New Jersey, Prince Whipple was among the soldiers who accompanied him. He had entered the services of the army as bodyguard to General Whipple of New Hampshire, who was an aide to Washington. The surprise attack on the British at Trenton was complete, and the patriots suffered only five casualties. The success of the attack depended on the skillful men who rowed the boats across the half-frozen Delaware River.

PART II

The Nineteenth Century

Introduction

THE high hopes and aspirations of mankind for the inalienable rights of man to life, liberty and the pursuit of happiness had been kindled in the last quarter of the eighteenth century. This was expressed in the American Revolution of 1776 and reached its peak in the French Revolution of 1789, with the slogan "Liberty, Equality, Fraternity." This philosophy had touched off isolated sparks around the world, wherever oppressed peoples were seeking a new concept of individual rights. The men who gave their lives fighting for these principles died without knowing the disappointments that were to follow. Those who survived, like James Forten, Paul Cuffee, Richard Allen, Absalom Jones, and many others who were presented in Part I, soon realized that the high ideals that had inspired them with hope and patriotism were meaningless symbols, whether by design or fate. The rewards of victorious revolutionary armies in America, France and Haiti were not to be enjoyed by all.

Other unforeseen forces had been unleashed by the wars, and another type of revolution had been set in motion. The commercial revolution of the sixteenth century had brought the Europeans into contact with the peoples of Africa, Asia and the Americas. The Industrial Revolution, two centuries later, coincided with the social and political revolutions of America and France.

The Industrial Revolution, originating in England, unleashed new economic forces which played a decisive role in the events of the last twenty-five years of the eighteenth century. The growth of industrial processes was highly stimulated by the French Revolution and the Napoleonic Wars; and when Eli Whitney invented the cotton gin in 1792, the yoke of slavery was clamped on the Negro of the Americas for the following century. It appears, then, that fate contributed to the designs of men in bringing about a denial of the noble social and political principles arising from the revolutionary philosophy of 1776. The leaders of the American Republic evidenced their change in attitude as early as the Constitutional Convention of 1788–89. Napoleon made the French Republic into a dictatorial empire by 1800. The Haitian revolution turned ever more rapidly into a despotic empire under Dessalines and into a divided nation, in 1806, under the republic of Pétion and the absolute monarchy of King Henri Christophe.

In America, slavery was abolished in the Northern states, but equality was not to be included in this gain. Instead, the policy of segregation, separation and discrimination became the pattern. The Southern half of the nation was affected by the needs of the English textile mills for more cotton. "The peculiar institution of slavery" was to become the new design of the agrarian planters of the South and the fate of the Negro. Reaction on the part of the Negroes of America, who had shared in the discovery, exploration and settlement of the land and had fought for the ideals of the Revolution, was crushed ruthlessly.

The new century opened with the unsuccessful revolt of Gabriel Prosser in Virginia in 1800. The heroic effort of Thomas Jefferson to control the expansion of slavery in the Northwest Territory was achieved in the Ordinance of 1787, which prohibited slavery in the future states of Ohio, Indiana, Illinois, Michigan and Wisconsin. Stubborn resistance to the prohibition of slavery developed after 1800. The African slave trade was outlawed in 1808, but this was ignored by those who smuggled Negroes into America after horrible, inhumane voyages across the Atlantic. In addition, "slave breeding plantations" were developed in the South.

As a result of the Civil War, the Thirteenth, Fourteenth and Fifteenth Amendments were passed, and Negroes were able to participate actively in the governments of Southern states. The biographical sketches in this section reveal the contributions of those who struggled to achieve the abolition of slavery, the Reconstruction of the South, and the full recognition of their citizenship.

Abraham, Negro

Diplomat of the Seminoles

Negro Abraham, a fugitive slave adopted by the Seminole Indians, was born in Pensacola, Florida, in the early 1800's. Around 1826, he escaped from slavery and sought shelter with the Seminole Indians of the area. Among the Indians, he was referred to in many different roles, such as "prophet," "principal counselor of his master, Chief Micanopy," and "high chancellor and keeper of the king's conscience." Although he was uneducated, he was a persuasive and gifted speaker. One writer described him as "a perfect Talleyrand of the Savage Court of Florida."

As the spokesman for the chief in the period when the United States was moving the Indians from Florida across the Mississippi River to Oklahoma and Kansas, Abraham opposed this relocation. He feared that, in the process of traveling across the Southern states, many of the Negroes who had fled from slavery would be recaptured by their former masters. He agreed to investigate the proposed site of their new home in Oklahoma, but refused to move until he was assured of everyone's freedom. A diplomat of skill, he delayed until he secured his terms. He also opposed the settlement of the Seminoles with the Creeks because the latter were known to enslave Negroes. In a treaty signed at Fort Dade in 1837, he demanded a guarantee against future domination by the Creeks.

NEGRO ABRAHAM

The Seminole Indians finally moved West in 1839, but were deluded by U.S. government agents who broke the Fort Dade treaty. Favored by the government, the Creeks dominated the Seminoles and enslaved the fugitive Negroes or else handed them over to agents who returned them to their former

43

owners. After 20 years of suffering at the hands of the Creeks, the Seminoles were recognized as an independent nation.

Chief Micanopy died in 1848; the new chief became a tool of the Creeks. To escape this situation, many Seminoles and Negroes moved to Mexico in 1850. It is not clear whether Abraham went to Mexico or remained in the Indian Territory. The majority of the Negroes of the tribe, however, remained in Mexico until after the Civil War ended, when they returned to the United States.

Aldridge, Ira Frederick

Actor

Ira Frederick Aldridge (1807–1867), star of Shakespearean dramas and an eminent tragedian, spent his early years in Maryland.

IRA FREDERICK ALDRIDGE

He received his early education at the African Free School in New York, where he made his first stage appearance when he portrayed the character Rolla in Sheridan's *Pizzaro*. As a stage hand at the Chatham Theater, he had the opportunity to observe various interpretations of the drama. He was encouraged to return to the African Free School and to attend Schenectady College, where he discovered his potential as an actor. However, because he realized that there was little opportunity for him to develop his talent in America, he entered the University of Glasgow (Scotland), where he won several prizes and a medal for excellence in Latin.

His dramatic career in London was assured when, at the age of 19, he appeared in the role of Othello in 1826. He appeared in the same role in Ireland, with the famous Edmund Kean as Iago. This marked the beginning of a lasting friendship between the two actors. Aldridge's portrayal of Othello was so fine a work of art that he was immediately acclaimed as a great actor. He played such leading roles as King Lear, Shylock, Oroonoko, O'Rozembo, Mungo and many others, throughout Europe.

Aldridge's critics could never agree as to which performance was the best, as he interpreted each one as if it were the highlight of his career. Many tributes were paid to him by the crowned heads of Europe: he received awards from the King of Prussia and the Emperor of Austria, and the Medal of Merit from the city of Bern. Today, at Stratford-on-Avon there is an Ira Aldridge Chair designated in his honor at the Shakespeare Memorial Theatre.

America lost the opportunity of seeing this great actor perform, as he died in Lodz, Poland, on the eve of his return to his native country.

Alvés, Castro

Brazilian Poet and Abolitionist

Castro Alvés (1847–1871), poet and abolitionist of Brazil, was born and educated in Bahia. One of the outstanding literary figures of his nation, he died at age 24, but not before he had had a productive literary life. His activities as well as his poetry were devoted to the cause of freedom. Although he received training at the law school in Recife, Castro Alvés' genius flowered in all of its emotional intensity in his protests against the ugly institution of slavery, which had blackened the cultural development of the New World. His most powerful and heart-rending poetic efforts on the evils of slavery are "Poema dos escravas," "Voges d'Africa" and "Navio negreiro." Speaking for the degraded slave crying out for freedom, he vividly describes the polluted holds of the slave ships, the misery and suffering, the tortures; all are depicted in the melodic verse of "Navio negreiro." His works are held in high esteem by the Negroes in Brazil.

His works include poems not only of social protest but also of romantic love and devotion to women. His early works reveal an ardent and headstrong youth obsessed with intense passions and romantic fancies.

Besides the three previously mentioned poems, Alvés' major works are "Espumas fluctuantes," "Gonzaga" and "Manuscriptos de Stenio." The remainder of the poet's unpublished works were collected under the direction of Afranio Peixoto and published as *Obras completas de Castro Alvés.*

Americo, Pedro

Brazilian Artist

Pedro Americo (1845–1905), outstanding painter of historical themes, was born in Paraíba, Brazil. His unusual artistic talent was revealed at the age of nine, when he drew an array of household objects and animal figures. Because of this early display of talent, he was sent to Rio de Janeiro to begin the formal study of art. Later, he journeyed to Europe to study further and to become acquainted with the leading art centers and masters of the continent. Returning to Brazil, Americo painted a veritable gallery of national heroes and scenes of his native land. The heroic theme became a distinguishing feature of his work.

Pedro Americo's best-known productions are "The Proclamation of Independence," "The Battle of Avahi" and "The Battle of Campo Grande." This artist's concern for the history of Brazil indicates that Negroes, after the abolition of slavery, became accepted members of the Brazilian community.

Anderson, Caroline Virginia

Physician

Dr. Caroline Virginia Anderson (1848–?), woman pioneer in the field of medicine, was born in Philadelphia, Pennsylvania. The daughter of William Still, the well-known abolitionist and conductor of the Underground Railroad, she received her early education at the private school of Mrs. Henry Gordon, at the Friends' Raspberry Alley School and at the Institute for Colored Youth of Philadelphia. She received her college training at Oberlin College, Ohio. Graduating at the age of 19, she was the youngest in a class of 45. After teaching school for one year, in 1875 she entered the Howard University School of Medicine, where she also taught drawing and speech. The following year, she transferred to the Women's Medical College in Philadelphia, where she successfully completed the work for her medical degree in 1878.

The first time she applied for an internship at the Boston New England Hospital for Women and Children, she was turned down because she was a Negro. Later, she was accepted by a unanimous decision of the board of directors. In time, Dr. Anderson established her practice in Philadelphia.

She participated in many civic and educational activities not connected with medicine. She taught in the Berea Church School for 30 years and served as assistant principal. A member of the Women's Medical Society, she served as treasurer of the Women's Medical Alumnae Association. She was president of the Berea Women's Christian Temperance Union for several years and a member of the board of the Home for Aged and Infirm Colored of Philadelphia. She was one of the organizers of the first Colored Young Women's Christian Association of that city.

Dr. Anderson first married an Oberlin classmate, E. A. Wiley, who died in 1874. Her second marriage, in 1880, was to the Reverend Matthew Anderson.

Asbury, John Cornelius

Businessman and Civic Leader

John Cornelius Asbury (1862–1932), outstanding businessman and politician, was born in Washington County, Pennsylvania. He received his education at Washington and Jefferson College and obtained his Bachelor of Laws and Master's degrees from Howard University in Washington, D.C. From 1887 to 1891, he served as the commonwealth's attorney in Norfolk County, Virginia.

Returning to his native state, Asbury settled in Philadelphia, where he entered politics and established his law office. In 1902, he organized the Keystone Aid Society, an insurance organization. He served as the editor-in-chief of *The Odd Fellows' Journal* and opened the Eden Cemetery, where Negroes could purchase burial plots. One of his most lucrative investments, its stockholders have earned dividends each year. However, the opening of the Keystone Bank in 1922 was a disastrous business venture—

JOHN CORNELIUS ASBURY

it was forced to close during the depression years of the thirties. Nevertheless, Asbury proved his business integrity by not allowing a single depositor to lose money. Instead, he worked diligently to balance the books and drew upon some of his private capital to meet the needs of the defunct bank.

As an active politician, he was elected to the lower house of the state legislature of Pennsylvania. He served as deputy attorney general, as assistant city solicitor and as a member of the Republican city committee.

In spite of his involvement in these business operations and political offices, he was concerned with the development of community projects. In particular, he made jobs and careers possible for young Negroes by having them trained and employed in the Odd Fellows' publishing house and in his Keystone Insurance Agency. He helped to organize the Mercy Hospital for Negroes, served as president of the Bureau for Colored Children, and was responsible for the Farm and Vocational School for Boys at Pomeroy, Pennsylvania. As chairman of the board of trustees of the Donnington Industrial School, which was supported by the Negro Baptists of Philadelphia, he obtained financial aid from the state and worked for the accreditation of the institution.

Bannister, Edward M.

Artist

Edward M. Bannister (1828–1901) achieved distinction as a landscape painter. In 1876, he was awarded a medal at the Centennial Exposition in Philadelphia for his painting "Under the Oaks." When the judges of the competition discovered that the winning painter was a Negro, they wanted to reconsider their choice, but the other competitors demanded that Bannister receive the award. It had been racial prejudice that had

made Bannister resolve to become an artist and to disprove the thesis of an article in the *New York Herald* in 1867, which declared that the Negro seemed to appreciate art but was incapable of producing it.

A poverty-stricken orphan with an indomitable will to develop his talent, Bannister, born in New Brunswick, Canada, migrated to Boston, where he worked at odd jobs. Sketching without any instruction from the age of 10, he later was able to have private lessons with Dr. William Runner and some instruction from the Lowell Institute in Boston.

The New England landscape attracted his interest, as did scenes of waterfront life; in fact, Bannister never painted Negro types, only landscapes. In 1870, he moved to Providence, Rhode Island, where he made a comfortable living as a painter. He was a founder of the Providence Art Club, which is still the leading art organization of the city and which preserves Bannister's works. Other works by Bannister can be found at Atlanta University, the Rhode Island School of Design and Howard University.

Barbosa, José Celso

Puerto Rican Leader

José Celso Barbosa (1857–1921), an ardent supporter of independence from Spanish domination, was born in Puerto Rico. In the period of adjustment following the Spanish-American War in 1898, Barbosa, an eminent leader of the colored middle class, opposed the perpetuation of Puerto Rico's colonial status. Unlike his opponent Muñoz Rivera, the white leader of the Federal Party, which advocated full autonomy, Barbosa wanted statehood for his island or incorporation into the United States on an equal basis with the other states.

Founder of a political party which advocated statehood, Barbosa served as a member of Puerto Rico's executive council five times, each time being nominated, regardless of his party affiliation, by a United States President. As a spokesman for Puerto Ricans, Barbosa favored use of the English language rather than Spanish in the school system. In addition, he opposed plantation owners' having more than five hundred acres of land. Barbosa also used his influence to obtain college scholarships for Puerto Ricans who wished to study on the mainland.

As a graduate of the University of Michigan, Barbosa was honored by his alma mater with an honorary Master of Arts degree in 1903; he was the recipient of an honorary Doctor of Laws degree from the University of Puerto Rico in 1917.

Barnett, Ida B. Wells

Civil Rights Worker

Ida B. Wells Barnett (1869–1931), militant civil rights fighter of the 19th century, was born of free parents in Holly Springs, Mississippi. As a child, Ida showed unusual aptness by learning to read at an early age. She established a fine record at Rust College, located in Holly Springs. Since the majority of the Negro adults who patronized her father's store could not read, Ida's father would sit on a cracker barrel with the newspaper to read to the customers. At the age of 14, Ida lost both of her parents in a yellow fever epidemic. A courageous and determined young woman, she took on the responsibility of raising seven children by obtaining a job as a schoolteacher.

The conditions of the Negroes around her were so appalling that the young school mistress wrote articles to newspapers citing the injustices that Negroes had to endure. Although she won national recognition for her forceful articles, she was dismissed from her teaching job because her articles displeased the members of the school board.

IDA B. WELLS BARNETT

Moving to Memphis, Tennessee, in 1892, Ida devoted herself to fighting racial discrimination. When three of her associates were lynched in Memphis and she voiced her protest loud and strong, she was compelled to flee the city. In Chicago, she launched a campaign against lynchings in the South, using her pen and the platform as a means of focusing attention on this injustice. She gathered the first statistical records on lynchings in the United States and used these facts in her speeches in America and in England.

In connection with the campaign for civil rights for the Negro in the South, she saw the similar needs of the poverty-stricken Negroes of the slums of Chicago. She opened a social center for Negro youth and was the first Negro probation officer appointed in Chicago. In addition, Mrs. Barnett was a cofounder of the National Association for the Advancement of Colored People.

Bassett, Ebenezer D.

Diplomat

Ebenezer D. Bassett (1833–1908), first Negro diplomat to represent the United States government abroad, was born in 1833 in Connecticut. Immediately after his inauguration in 1869, President Grant appointed Bassett as minister-resident to Haiti, a position he held with honor and distinction from 1869 to 1877. At the time of his appointment, he was principal of the Institute for Colored Youth, a Quaker school in Philadelphia. He had attended the Wilbraham Academy in Wilbraham, Massachusetts, and the Connecticut State Normal School, and had studied at Yale University.

Bassett served the United States in Haiti during a period of tense relations with her neighbor Santo Domingo. At this time, the Haitian government was aware that America was considering annexing many of the islands in the area. Bassett, whose duty it was to keep the American government informed of developments on the island, was still able to ease the strong anti-American feeling in Haiti.

When he completed his assignment in 1877, the Haitians expressed their confidence in his integrity by appointing Bassett as their consul general to the United States for 10 years. Upon his retirement from this post, he returned to live as a private citizen in Haiti. He published his *Handbook of Haiti* in French, English and Spanish; this was a valuable contribution to the geographical knowledge of the island. The American Geographical Society and the Connecticut Historical Society named him a member of their organizatons in recognition of his contributions.

EBENEZER D. BASSETT

Beckwourth, James P.

Explorer and Pioneer

James P. Beckwourth (1798–1867), colorful adventurer and explorer, was the son of a mulatto mother and a white father. He was born in Virginia but moved to St. Louis. Before he was 20, he had become a nomadic adventurer. He accompanied General William H. Ashley on a fur-trading expedition to the Rocky Mountains in 1824–25. Leaving the white traders, he went to live for six years with the Crow Indians. He soon became a famous warrior, and then a chief. As scout and explorer, he traveled with both John C. Frémont and Kit Carson. He discovered present-day Beckwourth Pass, in California. He also fought in the Cheyenne wars in 1864. Three years later, he died near Denver, Colorado.

The life of this colorful pioneer is evidence of the fact that Negroes were a part of the history of America's westward expansion. To T. D. Bonner, a biographer, Beckwourth dic-

JAMES P. BECKWOURTH

tated an account of his life entitled *Life and Adventures of James P. Beckwourth, Mountaineer, Scout and Pioneer, and Chief of the Crow Nation of Indians.*

Behanzin

Ruler of Dahomey

Behanzin (?–1906), last king of Dahomey, made a courageous stand against French aggression in 1890 at the Battle of Poguessa. The leader of Dahomey had rallied his troops to defend the land of his people against an army that was well organized and equipped with weapons far superior to those of the Africans. The French forces under the mulatto General Dodds had met defeat in battle after battle against troops led by Behanzin. However, the superior forces of the French pushed Behanzin into retreat, no matter how courageously he and his men resisted. In the end, the native forces were defeated at Djokone, which was the last

obstacle to the French drive to the capital. Following the defeat, Behanzin fled from the capital with as many supporters as he could rally, resolving to continue harassing the French invaders as long as he could.

The French had been successful in taking the capital and the country, but Behanzin, the ruler and symbol of authority to his people, remained uncaptured. The French realized that, until they disposed of Behanzin,

BEHANZIN

France could never peacefully rule Dahomey. Behanzin's attempts to negotiate with the French failed or were not honored; and, when the king surrendered, he was sent into exile. Humiliated and brokenhearted, he died in Algeria in 1906. Behanzin's last request was that his remains be returned to his native soil of Dahomey; but the French were so fearful that the return of his body would rekindle the flames of nationalism that they did not comply with his wishes until 1927.

Bell, James Madison

Poet

James Madison Bell (1826–1902), poet of protest, was born in Gallipolis, Ohio, then moved to Cincinnati, where he worked at the plasterer's trade and attended night school for his education. In 1854, he relocated in Canada and, as a supporter of John Brown, recruited men for his raid. At the outbreak of the Civil War, Bell migrated to California, where he assumed an active role in the struggle for the recognition of the black man's civil rights. Returning to Ohio in 1865, he settled in Toledo and became a Republican delegate-at-large.

Bell's potential literary talent remained undeveloped because of his preoccupation as a crusader for abolition and civil rights. His poetry, which evoked considerable interest, was not published as a collection until 1901, when the author was near the end of his life. Some of his best works are: "Emancipation," "The Dawn of Freedom," "Lincoln," "The Future of America in the Unity of the Races," "Song for the First of August," "The Blackman's Wrongs," "The Progress of Liberty" and "The Triumph of the Free."

Bethune, Thomas Greene

Blind Musician

Thomas Greene Bethune (1844–1905), musical prodigy and composer, of pure African descent, was born without sight in Columbus, Georgia. He was sold as a very young child, with his mother, to Colonel Bethune. "Blind Tom," as he was later to be called, displayed his musical genius at sounds of a heavy storm. First playing the piano at the age of four, he mastered the instrument so rapidly that soon he surpassed his teachers. His master, who eventually accumulated a fortune from Tom's playing, added to the young boy's repertory by

THOMAS GREENE BETHUNE

hiring professional musicians to play for him. Colonel Bethune later boasted that, at the peak of his career, Tom was able to perform more than 5,000 numbers.

For years, Tom was cruelly driven and exploited by his master, who shrewdly claimed that Tom was actually an idiot whose musical ability was the result of occult powers. When Tom and his mother became free after the Civil War, Bethune persuaded the mother to appoint him as Tom's guardian; and he continued to profit from the young man's talent.

In concerts throughout Europe and America, Tom received acclaim for both his technique and memory, winning special praise for his interpretation of Beethoven's "Pathétique Sonata." A composer as well as a performer, Tom wrote several popular marches.

When Colonel Bethune died, his son continued to drive Tom, whose musical genius, as a result, all but vanished. Blind Tom, his health broken by years of overwork and living in poverty, died when he was 61 years old.

Blackwell, George Lincoln

Bishop

George Lincoln Blackwell (1861–?), Bishop of the African Methodist Episcopal Zion Church, was born in Henderson, North Carolina, of parents who were slaves of the well-known William Blackwell of Granville County. Because the father could read only a little from the Bible and the mother could neither read nor write, George's parents were determined that their children be educated. Since the public schools were in session only three to five months of the year, George was tutored by the son of his father's ex-master. He later acquired enough education to teach school himself, but continued to study in order to be admitted to the North Carolina Conference of the African Methodist Episcopal Zion Church. Enrolling in Livingstone College in 1882, he completed the preparatory and collegiate courses in 1888.

After graduating from Livingstone, he was appointed to pastorates in Cambridge and Boston, where he was able to attend the theological seminary of Boston University, from which he received the degree of Bachelor of Sacred Theology in 1892. Returning to be professor of theology at Livingstone for three years, he was appointed by the church to manage the A.M.E.Z. publishing house in Charlotte in 1896. In this position, he edited the literature which was prepared for the Sunday school.

In 1900, Reverend Blackwell was sent to the Wesley A.M.E.Z. Church in Philadelphia as its pastor. He served also as general secretary of the denomination, in the office of the missionary secretary. During this time, he published a book of discipline for the church organization. In 1908, he was elected bishop in recognition of his many contributions to the church.

Bland, James A.

Musician

James A. Bland (1854–1911), composer of minstrel songs, was born in Flushing, New York, but was sent to Philadelphia for his education. When Bland was 12, his father was appointed an examiner in the United States Patent Office in Washington, D.C., and James completed his high school education in the District of Columbia. During these years, he discovered the banjo, spending more time trying to pick out tunes on this popular minstrel instrument than he did on his studies. By the time he entered Howard University, he was earning money playing and singing his tunes on downtown street corners. The management of a large hotel, attracted by his music, hired him to entertain the guests.

Because Bland's music closely resembled that of the beloved Stephen Foster, his compositions were readily accepted by the American public. When he was 24 years old, he had composed his greatest melody, "Carry Me Back to Old Virginny," which was an immediate success and was used by George Primrose in his famous minstrel show. Today, it is the official state song of Virginia.

When Haverly's Colored Minstrels appeared in Baltimore, James Bland joined the show, to the disgust of his teachers at Howard and his parents, who wanted him to become a lawyer or a doctor. Even though Bland did not look like a traditional minstrel character, he was successful; eventually, he was booked as "The World's Greatest Minstrel Man." The numbers he composed and performed, such as "Oh, Dem Golden Slippers" and "In the Evening by the Moonlight," became popular in America. In the 1880's, the company took the show to England, where Bland's popularity reached its peak. He remained in England for 20 years, performing as an independent artist and accumulating considerable wealth. However, when he returned to the United States in 1900, he was poverty-stricken and, like Stephen Foster, died penniless, in Philadelphia.

Blyden, Edward Wilmot

Liberian Scholar

Edward Wilmot Blyden (1832–?), linguist, author, diplomat and scholar, was born in the Virgin Islands but attained eminence in Liberia, Africa. A native of St. Thomas, he

EDWARD WILMOT BLYDEN

came to the United States as a youth; but, in 1851, he and his brother went to Liberia, where he attended the Alexander High School in Monrovia. After mastering Latin and Greek, he studied Arabic and the languages of the African tribes of the West Coast. As an educator, he was principal of the Alexander High School, then a professor at Liberia College and, in 1881, president of the college.

From his study of African languages, he developed an interest in the religions of the people, particularly the Moslem religion, which he believed contained far more sincerity than he found in Christianity. He traveled extensively in Africa, the Middle East and Europe. An account of his visits to Palestine and Egypt, published in 1866, was entitled *From West Africa to Palestine.*

He was sent as envoy from Sierra Leone to the King of the Sooluna country, a journey later reported in the journal of the Royal Geographical Society. He was sent on another mission in 1873 to visit a Moslem chief in the interior of West Africa. He served as Liberian minister to England from 1877 to 1881 and was accepted as a member of the Athenaeum Club there.

His major publications are: *Our Origin, Dangers and Duties* (1865); *Liberia, Past and Present and Future* (1869); *The Negro in Ancient History* (1869); *Philip, the Eunuch, or the Instruments and Methods of Africa's Evangelization* (1882); *The Aims and Methods of a Liberal Education for Africans* (1882); *An African Problem and the Method of Its Solution* (1890); *Africa and the Africans* (1903); *West Africa before Europe* (1903); *Three Needs of Liberia* (1908); *African Life and Customs* (1908); *Problems before Liberia* (1909); and "Islam in Western Sudan" and "The Koran in Africa," published in *The Journal of the Royal African Society.*

Booth, Edward

Gold Miner

Edward Booth (1810–1900), pioneer in the gold fields of California and Alaska, was born in Baltimore, Maryland. His father, who was free, had obtained freedom for Edward's mother and had provided a comfortable home for the family. Edward, the eldest son, venturing to the West Indies in the early forties, made a considerable fortune in trading. Returning as news of the discovery of gold in California reached Baltimore, he headed West and reached the Coast in 1849.

After staking his claims to gold mines near Sacramento and mining them successfully for a year, he decided to bring the entire family to California. On the return trip to Baltimore, he stopped at Oberlin, Ohio, to enroll his nephew James H. Hubbard at Oberlin College, and made a generous bequest to the school. In November 1851, he completed the arrangements for his family's departure to the West. Before he and five of his sisters and brothers could leave Baltimore, however, they had to prove that they were free persons.

Tribulations filled their journey as they traveled by boat from Maryland, by mule train across the Isthmus and by steamer to San Francisco. They were forced to discard most of their belongings on the way to Panama City, where they waited three weeks for a steamer. Because only Booth and the sisters could be accommodated on the steamer, the brothers had to book passage on a cargo vessel. Furthermore, the captain of the steamer lost his route, the drinking water ran low, and the crew mutinied. Finally reaching San Francisco in 1852, they went on to Sacramento, which was overrun by large river rats forced out by the raging flood of the American River.

After settling his family, Booth returned to his mining interests and made a fortune. But the desire to travel obsessed him. When he heard of the gold strike in Alaska, he went in quest of it, filed a claim, and remained there until his death.

Bowen, John Wesley E.

Scholar and Minister

John Wesley E. Bowen (1855–1933), outstanding scholar and minister in the Methodist Episcopal Church, was born of free parents in New Orleans, Louisiana. His father,

a prosperous carpenter, could afford the best educational training possible for his son. After the Civil War, Bowen studied at New Orleans University and became a teacher at Walden College in Nashville, Tennessee. After two years of teaching, he entered Boston University, where he received his Bachelor of Divinity degree in 1885. Continuing his studies, particularly in Hebrew, philosophy and metaphysics, he received his doctorate from this same university.

In Boston, he had his own congregation, and after graduating, he served Methodist churches in Newark, New Jersey, Baltimore, Maryland, and Washington, D.C. As secretary, he served the Methodist Episcopal Foreign Mission Society and later the Stewart Missionary Foundation for Africa. Bowen was appointed professor of historical theology at the Gammon Theological Seminary in Atlanta, Georgia, where he taught for 40 years, serving as its president for a four-year term and as its vice-president for several years. A fluent speaker and fine scholar, he was in demand as a popular lecturer.

Boyd, Richard Henry

Minister and Publisher

Richard Henry Boyd (1843–1922), outstanding Baptist minister and founder of the National Baptist Publishing Board, was born a slave in a log cabin in Mississippi. His master moved his entire establishment, family and slaves, to Texas in 1849. During the Civil War, his master, fighting in the Battle of Chattanooga, was killed, leaving his trusted slave, Richard Boyd, to manage his estate. During the Reconstruction period, Boyd was ordained a Baptist minister and became active not only in establishing Negro Baptist churches in Texas but also in serving as superintendent of missions and as educational secretary of the Negro Baptists in Texas.

Citizens' Savings Bank and Trust Company; the founder and president of the Nashville Globe Publishing Company and of the National Baptist Church Supply Company, which furnished pews, benches and other church equipment. In 1879, he was a special delegate to the World Baptist Alliance meeting in London, England.

Bridgetower, George Polgreen

Violinist

George Polgreen Bridgetower (1779–1860), celebrated violinist of Poland, was born in Biala (or Viala), Poland. He was the son of John Frederick Bridgetower, an African, and Marie Ann, of German-Polish descent. This violin prodigy became known throughout Europe as the "Abyssinian Prince." Recognition as a master of the violin came to him at the age of 10, when he made his first concert appearance in

RICHARD HENRY BOYD

Boyd, a self-educated man, mastered the alphabet at the age of 22 and later was influential in founding such educational institutions as Bishop College in Marshall, Texas, and Hearne Academy and the National Baptist Theological and Missionary Training Seminary at Nashville. Furthermore, he was responsible for establishing Baptist missionary centers abroad, particularly in the Panama Canal Zone, where he founded a school and four Baptist churches.

Recognizing the scarcity of literature available to the Baptist churches, he founded the National Baptist Publishing Board in Nashville, which issued the first series of Baptist literature for Negroes in the United States in the 1890's. Boyd himself wrote 14 volumes of this material.

Among his other achievements, he was the founder of the National Negro Doll Company; the organizer and president of the

GEORGE POLGREEN BRIDGETOWER

Paris on April 13, 1789. In February of the following year, he appeared in London at the Drury Lane Theatre, where he played a violin solo during intermission at a performance of Handel's *Messiah*.

He studied under Haydn; and he was a close friend of Beethoven, who was encouraged by Bridgetower to complete his sonatas for pianoforte and violin. Bridgetower played the "Theme and Variations in F" from Beethoven's manuscript in the Hall Augarten. He was once a violinist at the establishment of the Prince of Wales. The virtuoso enjoyed successful concerts in Vienna, Dresden, London, Paris and Rome.

Among manuscripts found in the British Museum which bear his signature, are these compositions: "Henry," a ballad; 41 pianoforte studies; and *Minuets for Violin, Mandolin, German Flute and Harpsichord.*

Brown, William Wells

Historian

William Wells Brown (*c.* 1816–1884), mid-nineteenth-century historian, was born in Lexington, Kentucky. His mother was a slave and his father was a plantation owner. He received his inspiration and education in St. Louis, where he served as an apprentice to the antislavery editor Elijah P. Lovejoy. Brown wrote *The Black Man* (1863), *The Negro in the American Rebellion* (1867) and *The Rising Son* (1874). After visiting France and England in 1850, he wrote *Three Years in Europe* and *Clotel: Or the President's Daughter,* a narrative of slave life in the Southern states. He was a regular contributor to the London *Daily News, The Liberator, Frederick Douglass' Paper* and *The National Antislavery Standard.* In 1854, he published *Sketches of Places and People Abroad,* in which he gave his impressions of such personalities as Richard Cobden, Victor Hugo and Alexis de Tocqueville.

WILLIAM WELLS BROWN

During the course of his life, he served on the Underground Railroad, and from 1843 to 1849, he was a lecturer for the American Anti-Slavery Society. Brown was also active in the temperance movement and worked for the extension of suffrage to women and for prison reform.

Bruce, Blanche Kelso

United States Senator

Blanche Kelso Bruce (1841–1898), Senator from Mississippi during the Reconstruction period, was probably one of the state's most astute politicians. Born a slave in Farmville, Virginia, he was given a rudimentary education by his master's son. Before the War, he moved to Missouri, where he worked in a printing office and served as a teacher in Hannibal. He began special training at Oberlin College in 1866. In 1868, he migrated to Mississippi to become a planter in Bolivar County; and soon after establishing himself in the area, he was appointed conductor of elections for Tallahatchie County by the military governor, General Adelbert Ames. Immediately, Bruce became a political leader in the state.

He became sergeant-at-arms in the state senate in 1870. After attending the national Republican convention in 1872, he was sponsored for the United States Senate by James Hill, the most powerful Negro politician in the state. When the Mississippi legislature met in 1874, the white and the black Republicans first held separate, then joint, meetings; the Negroes were unyielding in their demands for Bruce's election to the Senate. Successful, he took his seat in March 1875, and when the outgoing Senator, James L. Alcorn, refused to escort him to the swearing-in ceremony, Senator Roscoe Conkling of New York stepped forward to perform the service.

BLANCHE KELSO BRUCE

He was a member of the Senate committees on manufactures, education and labor, pensions, and the improvement of the Mississippi River and its tributaries. He tried to protect the depositors of the defunct Freedmen's Savings and Trust Company. Serving as chairman of the investigating committee, he and his fellow members were successful in eliminating graft from the bank commissioners' salaries, but they were unable to reimburse the depositors. He was opposed to the exclusion of Chinese from America and fought for citizenship rights for the American Indian.

At the close of Bruce's Senate term in 1881, President Garfield made him Register of the Treasury; President Harrison appointed him recorder of deeds for the District of Columbia, and President McKinley appointed him for another term as Register of the Treasury in 1897. He died the following spring. During the periods when he was not in office, he was greatly in demand as a lecturer. He was chairman of the Negro exhibit at the World Cotton Exposition in New Orleans in 1884 and served as a trustee of Howard University for many years.

Burleigh, Harry T.

Musician

Harry T. Burleigh (1866–1949), baritone, arranger and composer, was born in Erie, Pennsylvania. His musical talent was encouraged by the mother of composer Edward MacDowell, who obtained a scholarship for Burleigh to study at the National Conservatory of Music in New York. While pursuing his studies, he came in contact with Anton Dvořák, the Bohemian composer, and Victor Herbert, American composer of light operas. Singing in various churches in New York, he was appointed baritone soloist at St. George's Episcopal Church as a result of a competition in which he won over many white candidates. Some of the congregation objected, but, with the support of J. P. Morgan and other outstanding members, his appointment was upheld, and he served as soloist for over 50 years.

He had the opportunity to tour the United States and Europe and became a trailblazer for other Negro artists by appearing before mixed audiences. On one occasion, he sang a Paderewski composition while being accompanied by the distinguished pianist himself. In 1900, Burleigh was selected baritone soloist at Temple Emanu-El, one of the wealthiest synagogues in New York.

One of Burleigh's greatest achievements was the arrangement of Negro spirituals for concert singers. Described as art songs, some of his compositions are "The Prayer," "Down by the Sea" and "In the Wood of Finvara." Foremost among these art songs is "The Young Warrior," inspired by World War I, which became a marching song of the Italian

HARRY T. BURLEIGH

Army. Other war songs by Burleigh were "One Year—1914–1915" and "The Soldier."

In 1917, he received the Spingarn Award for his outstanding contributions to the progress of the Negro in music.

Bush, George W.

Pioneer

George W. Bush (*c.* 1790–1863) helped lead the first group of American settlers to the shores of Puget Sound. Born free in Pennsylvania, Bush began his pioneering with the French trader Robideau, who had trading posts as far west as the Rocky Mountains. After the purchase of the Louisiana Territory in 1803, the people of the area became citizens of the United States. Wishing to travel, Bush joined Andrew Jackson at the Battle of New Orleans in the War of 1812. Later, because of his knowledge of Rocky Mountain trails, he joined the Hudson's Bay Company, in whose service he reached the Pacific Coast in 1820. Moving to Missouri in the 1830's, he settled for some 12 years as a cattle rancher.

In the winter of 1843–44, George Bush, deciding to leave Missouri, led his family and seven white companions, with their families and a large train of wagons and livestock, over the old Oregon Trail to the Columbia River valley. He carried with him more than $2,000 in silver, which he used to purchase the first saw- and grist-mill on Puget Sound. The hard-pressed little party, reaching the area in 1845, survived with the aid of Bush's friends, Frenchmen who were employees of the Hudson's Bay Company. These were the first Americans to settle on the Sound; their colony served as the basis of the United States' claim to the land south of the 49th parallel.

Being a Negro, Bush was not entitled to the land on which he had settled, but the first Washington legislature asked the Federal government for special permission for this pioneer to have clear title to his land. Instead of selling his crops to the new settlers who came into the area, Bush shared his produce with the newcomers. His son, William Owen Bush, carrying on the tradition of his father, was an influential member of the first Washington state legislature.

Cain, Richard H.

United States Congressman

Richard H. Cain (1825–1887), bishop of the African Methodist Episcopal Church and congressman, was born of free parents in Greenbrier County, Virginia. With his father, he moved in 1831 to Gallipolis, Ohio. Here his educational opportunities were limited until he entered the ministry. At the age of 35, he entered Wilberforce University, where he studied for two years before serving as a pastor to several churches in New York. He

RICHARD H. CAIN

was sent by the A.M.E. Church council to Charleston, South Carolina, in 1865, to aid the freed slaves. From this headquarters, he traversed the state, making converts and establishing new churches.

He was at the South Carolina constitutional convention in 1868; he was elected to the state legislature, and later to the state senate for two years. He served two terms in the United States House of Representatives, from 1873 to 1875 and from 1877 to 1879. Joining the debate on the civil rights bill, he stated: "What we desire is that our civil rights shall be guaranteed by law, as they are guaranteed to every other class of persons; and when that is done all other things will come in as a necessary sequence, the enforcement of the rights following the enforcement of the law."

After his retirement from Congress, Cain was elected 14th bishop of the African Methodist Episcopal Church. In 1885, he established *The Missionary Record,* which became the most influential medium of communication for Negroes in the state. Educator as well as churchman, he was president of Paul Quinn College in Waco, Texas.

Campbell, James Edwin

Poet and Educator

James Edwin Campbell (*c.* 1860–*c.* 1905), one of the first poets to employ the black dialect, was born in Pomeroy, Ohio, where he graduated from the local academy in 1884. He taught school for two years at Buck Ridge, Ohio, near the West Virginia border. Campbell found West Virginia an inviting field for rapid advancement because the development of the coal mines and oil resources had opened the area to economic expansion. He accepted the editorship of the *Pioneer,* a newspaper owned by Christopher Payne. Next, he was principal of the Langston School in Point Pleasant; then he was selected by the West Virginia board of education as principal of the new West Virginia Colored Institute at Charleston, now West Virginia State College.

Although he was not a college graduate, Campbell had attended Miami College in Oxford, Ohio, and had furthered his education by reading extensively. He was

JAMES EDWIN CAMPBELL

able to guide the restless Negro coal miners and direct them toward helping their children acquire an education.

When he resigned from the institute, he moved to Chicago, where he was a staff member of the *Chicago Times-Herald*. It was as a newsman that he made his chief contribution in the literary world. Earlier in his career, he had written simple poems in the Negro dialect; some of them had been published in newspapers and magazines. In 1887, he pub-

lished his first book of poems, *Driftings and Gleanings,* and in 1895, his second book, *Echoes from the Cabin and Elsewhere.* Richard Linthicum, editor of the *Chicago Sunday Times-Herald,* wrote the introduction to the second volume. He said that Campbell had "caught the true spirit of the ante-bellum Negro and in characteristic verse has portrayed the simplicity, the philosophy and the humor of the race." Richard B. Harrison, the actor who gained fame for his role of "De Lawd" in *Green Pastures,* often used Campbell's poems when he gave dramatic readings.

Cardozo, Francis L.

Reconstructionist

Francis L. Cardozo (1836–1903), South Carolina secretary of state from 1868 to 1872 and treasurer from 1872 to 1876, was born in Charleston, South Carolina. He remained in school until he was 12, when he was apprenticed to a carpenter. Working as a carpenter for nine years, he was able to save enough money to continue his education abroad. With the aid of a generous scholarship, he was able to study at the University of Glasgow in Scotland for four years and then at Presbyterian seminaries in Edinburgh and London. At the University of Glasgow, he won prizes for outstanding achievement in Latin and Greek.

After returning to the United States in 1864, he accepted the pastorate of the Temple Street Congregational Church in New Haven, Connecticut. The American Missionary Association appointed him director of its newly created normal school in Charleston in 1865. During the Reconstruction era, he was a member of the South Carolina constitutional convention of 1868 and then was elected secretary of state. Fourteen months prior to the end of his term, he was offered a professorship in Latin at Howard University. He was permitted to appoint a deputy to complete his term of office while he taught at Howard.

His associates in South Carolina prevailed upon him to return in 1872. He was elected state treasurer that year and re-elected for a second term in 1876; however, with the return of "home rule" to the state in 1877, he was unable to assume any public office. As treasurer of the state, Cardozo's superior training and personal integrity kept him from

FRANCIS L. CARDOZO

being tainted with the corruption that was so prevalent in many of the post-War governments, both Northern and Southern.

He was appointed by Secretary John Sherman in 1878 to serve in the Treasury Department in Washington, D.C. From 1884 to 1896, he was principal of the District's Colored High School. Cardozo was recognized, even by his most bitter enemies, as one of the best-educated men, regardless of race, in the political affairs of South Carolina.

Carney, William Harvey

Civil War Hero

William Harvey Carney (1840–?), famed for the words "The Old Flag never touched the ground!" and hero of the 54th Massachusetts Regiment in the Civil War, was born in Norfolk, Virginia, and attended a private school that was conducted secretly by a minister. His home, which is now officially called the "Sergeant Carney Memorial House," has become a shrine. Carney himself is depicted in the Saint-Gaudens monument which immortalizes Colonel Robert Gould Shaw and his intrepid colored troops. Carney's features are represented on the face of one of the soldiers following his commander. The flag rescued by Carney is enshrined in Memorial Hall, Boston.

Early in 1863, William Carney, then 23 years old, enlisted in the Morgan Guards, which became part of the 54th Massachusetts Regiment. In July, 1863, the regi-

WILLIAM HARVEY CARNEY

ment was engaged in the disastrous battle at Fort Wagner. When Carney saw that the color sergeant, the soldier who carried the flag, had been wounded, he rescued the flag, going through a volley of enemy bullets. Delivering it to a squad of his own regiment, he shouted, "The Old Flag never touched the ground!" Then Carney fell to the ground in a dead faint, weak from the wounds that he had received. Mustered out of the army in 1864, he went to New Bedford, Massachusetts before going to California. In 1870, he returned to New Bedford and became one of the four men employed as letter carriers. After 31 years in the postal service, he retired in 1901, then spent his last years as an employee at the state capitol, in Boston.

Carney was in great demand as a leader of Memorial Day parades and as a speaker at patriotic events. In 1904, he was the Memorial Day orator at the Shaw Monument on Boston Common.

CHAKA

Chaka (Tshaka)

Zulu King

Chaka, or Tshaka (1787–1828), chieftain of the Zulus, made himself known in Europe and in South Africa by his military tactics, which enabled him to bring the majority of the tribes of Natal under his rule. In 25 years, he conquered vast numbers to make himself master of Natal. He had an absolute system of discipline and loyalty: if Chaka gave an order, it was carried out, even if it meant death to hundreds; a warrior returning home from battle without his weapons was executed without a trial. No one dared to remonstrate or to question the will of Chaka. Despite Chaka's ruthless methods, the Zulus developed a sense of security through their unity. He was assassinated in 1828, just as the onrush of whites was penetrating South Africa. Because his reputation became identified with that of the Zulu people, the Europeans moved with caution against them.

Chaka's birth and his childhood are shrouded in legend and folklore, out of which can be gleaned some facts. He was an illegitimate child who was abandoned by his father, Zenzangakona, and he brooded over this and the taunts of other children who called him a coward. Thus, he wandered from tribe to tribe, trying to find acceptance. When he reached manhood, he conditioned himself to be a great warrior and to display the courage that would eradicate his childhood fears. Through the aid of his father's rival, Dingiswayo, Chaka became the leader of the Mtetwas tribe. As leader of this tribe, he developed the military skill and discipline that he used to unite the remaining tribes of Natal.

Chavis, John

Teacher and Minister

John Chavis (1763–1838), teacher of whites and Negroes in North Carolina, was born in Oxford, Granville County, North Carolina. As a student at Washington Academy, later Washington and Lee University, he demonstrated an unusual intelligence, which attracted the attention of some of the liberal citizens, who sent him to Princeton for further study. There, he studied Latin and Greek, and theology under the guidance of Dr. Witherspoon. Granville County was populated by a group of liberal Scotch-Irish Presbyterians who looked upon Negroes as human beings. They gave John Chavis, a black man, the opportunity to prove his capabilities as a Presbyterian minister. When he fulfilled the requirements satisfactorily in 1800, he was licensed to preach. He served a church in Lexington, Virginia, until 1805, when he returned to North Carolina to join the Orange presbytery. He preached for more than 20 years in Orange, Wake and Granville Counties.

After the Nat Turner Rebellion in 1831, it was unlawful for a Negro to preach or teach in North Carolina. However, Chavis owned and directed a select preparatory school for children of prosperous white citizens of the state. Some of his pupils became outstanding in both local and national affairs. Among them were W. P. Mangum, later a United States senator; P. H. Mangum, his brother; Archibald and John Henderson, sons of Chief Justice Henderson; and Charles Manly, who later served as governor of the state.

In 1830, the editor of the Raleigh *Register*, Joseph Gales, visited Chavis' school. Speaking of the free Negro children, he claimed he "had seldom received more gratification from any exhibition of a similar character."

Cinque, Joseph

Leader of the Amistad Revolt

Joseph Cinque (1811–1879), an African who was sold into slavery in Havana, Cuba, executed one of the most daring attempts to return to Africa ever to be recorded in the history of Negro slavery. In 1839, Cinque and a group of 52 other slaves had been purchased from the Havana market by two Spaniards and were being transported to Puerto Prıncipe on the schooner *Amistad*. Four days out at sea, after the crew had exhausted themselves keeping the vessel afloat in a raging storm, Cinque and his companions escaped from the hold and murdered the captain and the cook. The two Spaniards' lives were spared because neither Cinque nor the other Negroes knew anything about navigation.

Cinque directed Señores Ruiz and Montez to steer the ship eastward toward Africa; but,

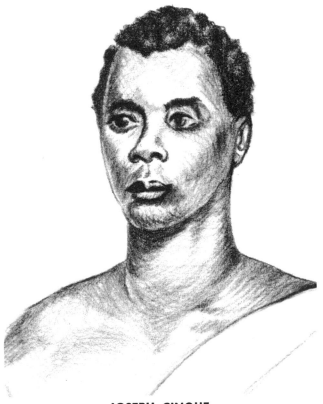

JOSEPH CINQUE

instead, the Spaniards set the *Amistad* on a northerly course. The ship was sighted off Long Island and brought to shore at Connecticut. The Spaniards told the United States authorities of the revolt and the murders committed on the ship, and the Negroes were imprisoned. There was an immediate public reaction in favor of punishment.

The New England abolitionists reacted differently and formed a committee to defend the rights of the prisoners. The famous case of the *Amistad* revolt, with the slaves being defended by John Quincy Adams, began its long journey through the courts of the nation. Finally, the U.S. Supreme Court ruled in favor of the enslaved Africans by declaring them free to return to Africa. While the case was being carried through the courts, Cinque and some of his companions were given a rudimentary education by the abolitionists. Cinque, a man of considerable intelligence, soon became a skillful speaker.

PETER HUMPHRIES CLARK

Clark, Peter Humphries

Educator

Peter H. Clark (1829–c.1895), a prominent leader in establishing public school education in Ohio, was the natural son of Michael Clark and grandson of the great explorer of the Northwest, William Clark. Peter Clark was born in Cincinnati, Ohio. His grandfather, fearing that his Negro family in the South might be enslaved while he was on an exploring assignment, had moved them to Ohio for safety in early 1800.

There were no public schools in Cincinnati for Negro children, but Peter Clark was able to attend a private school and Gilmore's High School. He was sent to Oberlin College to complete his training. At the close of the Civil War, Peter Clark was the leader of a movement in Cincinnati to establish new

schools and improve the existing ones. As principal of Gaines High School, he strengthened the course of study and placed all 12 grades in one building. Academically strong, his school served as a model for visiting observers. When Clark retired from the school system in 1886, he was the highest paid principal in the city.

More than just an educator, Clark concerned himself with the problems of the laborer and became a leader in the Workingman's Party, which was a forerunner of organized labor.

During the years before the Civil War, Clark was active in the Underground Railroad. Spending many nights conducting runaway slaves to safety and freedom through Ohio into Canada, he was familiar with all of the stations along the route.

Coleridge-Taylor, Samuel

Composer

Samuel Coleridge-Taylor (1875–1912), noted English composer of African descent, was born in Holborn, London, the son of a West African physician from Sierra Leone who was a member of the Royal College of Physicians and the Royal College of Surgeons. His mother was an Englishwoman, Alice Hare, who raised the young musician in Croydon after his father returned to Africa.

When he was five, Samuel Coleridge-Taylor received his first musical instrument, a violin. Because he possessed a sweet, pure voice, he sang in the choir at St. George's Presbyterian Church. Joseph Beckwith, an orchestra conductor, recognized the musical talent of the young boy and gave him lessons. In 1890, Samuel entered the Royal College of Music, where he studied violin, piano, harmony and composition. He won the Lesley Alexander Prize in composition in 1895.

His talent as a composer had shown itself when he was nine years old; he had made an original arrangement of the national hymn. In 1891, his anthem "In Thee O Lord" was published by Novello and Company. He gave his first chamber music concert in 1893, playing three of his own compositions. He received recognition as a serious composer in 1898, after his concert at Shire Hall in Gloucester and the performance of *Hiawatha's Wedding Feast* by the orchestra and choir of the Royal College of Music, under the direction of Sir Charles Stanford.

He became the conductor of the Royal Rochester Choral Society in 1902 and the Handel Society in 1904. In 1906, he founded the String Players' Club. During this period, he was professor of composition at Trinity College of Music. After hearing the Fisk Jubilee Singers in 1899, the composer became interested in musical themes based on the folk music of the Negro.

SAMUEL COLERIDGE-TAYLOR

His compositions were becoming popular in America. In 1900, the Cecilia Society of Boston performed "The Wedding Feast." The Coleridge-Taylor Society, a group of musicians in Washington, D.C., invited him to America in 1901 to conduct a performance of his *Hiawatha* trilogy. The composer, however, could not accept the invitation until two years later. In 1909, he made another trip to the United States as the guest of Carl Stoeckel of Connecticut. During this visit, he conducted the first two parts of *Hiawatha* and *Bamboula*.

Among his outstanding works are *Twenty-Four Negro Melodies Transcribed for the Piano, A Tale of Old Japan,* "Overture to Songs of Hiawatha," *African Suite,* "Symphonic Variations on an African Air," *Violin Concerto* and *African Romances.* This last work is a setting of six poems by Paul Laurence Dunbar.

Cook, John Francis, Sr.

Educator and Minister

John F. Cook (?–1855), a co-founder of the Fifteenth Street Presbyterian Church and Negro school in Washington, D.C., was born in the District of Columbia of parents who had purchased their freedom in the 18th century. Since there were no schools for Negroes in the newly built capital, the Cook family opened a school for Negro children. As a boy, their son John attended this school; as a man, he became its principal. In 1835, as the result of rioting in Washington, many Negroes left the city, including John Cook, who moved to Lancaster, Pennsylvania, where he taught for two years before returning to the District to reopen his school.

Recognizing the need for religious institutions for Negroes in the District, he helped organize the Metropolitan A.M.E. Church. Then, as a minister in the Presbyterian Church, he helped to organize the Fifteenth Street Presbyterian Church and its school. He served this church as its pastor from 1841 until his death. His two sons, John Francis, Jr., and George F. T. Cook, continued his work in the church and the school. The latter, a graduate of Oberlin College, was assistant superintendent of schools in charge of Negro schools in the nation's capital.

Cook, Will Marion

Composer

Will Marion Cook (1865–1944), outstanding composer of musical comedy, was born in Washington, D.C. A musical genius, he was the son of well-educated free parents who had moved from Fredericksburg, Virginia, in search of more security and liberty. He was educated at Oberlin Preparatory School, then studied violin at Oberlin College. After a year there, he went to Berlin

WILL MARION COOK

to study under Joachim, the famous violinist. On his return, he studied at the National Conservatory of Music in New York, under Dvořák, the Bohemian composer. Intrigued with the cakewalk and ragtime rage of the period, Cook worked with a number of Negro comedians and, at the suggestion of George Walker, wrote some of the musical scores for popular lyrics. His first important composition was the operetta *Clorindy, the Origin of the Cakewalk,* which created a sensation when it opened at the Casino Roof Garden in New York. Two popular songs, "On Emancipation Day" and "That's How the Cakewalk's Done," influenced the popular music of the period.

Cook organized and directed a group of musicians known as the American Syncopated Orchestra, which appeared on the theatrical circuit throughout the United States and Europe in 1919 and 1920. Under Cook's influence, the cakewalk reached its highest artistic expression. He was also well equipped to transcribe primitive jazz and to interpret it through a group of well-trained musicians. Some of his most popular compositions are "Swing Along," "Rain Song," "Exhortation" and "Wid de Moon, Moon, Moon." He completed the musical drama *St. Louis Woman* in 1935.

Coppin, Fanny M. Jackson

Educator

Fanny M. Jackson Coppin (1836–1913), principal of the Institute for Colored Youth, now the Cheyney Training School for Teachers, was born a slave in Washington, D.C. She owed her liberation to a self-sacrificing aunt, Sarah Orr Clark, who purchased Fanny's freedom for $125 although she earned a mere $6.00 a month. The young girl was sent to relatives in New England to attend school. When she was 14 years old, she worked for the George H. Calvert family in Newport, Rhode Island. Mrs. Calvert took an interest in training the young girl. Fanny worked, studied and saved her earnings so that she could enroll in the Rhode Island State Normal School in Bristol.

While attending the normal school, she resolved to become a teacher. On completing the normal course, she entered Oberlin College with the generous aid of her Aunt Sarah. Entering Oberlin in 1860, she spent over five years at the college, working and studying Greek, mathematics and French. When the freedmen poured into Ohio during the closing months of the Civil War, she formed a class for them. Teaching adult men and women to read and write convinced her that she had

chosen the most worthwhile way to serve her people.

When a request for a teacher came from the Institute for Colored Youth in Philadelphia, Fanny Jackson was highly recommended. She began her work at the institute in 1865; four years later, she was the principal. Aware

FANNY M. JACKSON COPPIN

of the needs of young Negroes for industrial training, she enlarged the curriculum of the school.

She married the Reverend Levi J. Coppin in 1881, but continued her work at the institute for 19 more years. When her husband became a bishop and was assigned to Africa in 1900, she joined him to assist in the missionary work.

Mrs. Coppin published her autobiography, *Reminiscences of School Life,* and *Hints on Teaching,* in 1913.

Cornish, Samuel

Antislavery Journalist

Samuel Cornish (1790–1859), talented journalist of the antislavery crusade, was born free in Delaware; later, he migrated to Philadelphia, where he was able to attend school. In 1822, he settled in New York, where he organized the first Negro Presbyterian congregation. With John B. Russwurm in 1827, he founded the first Negro newspaper, *Freedom's Journal*. When Russwurm became involved with the colonization movement, Cornish continued to publish the paper as *The Rights of All*.

Freedom's Journal played a major role in shaping a social and economic philosophy for the Negro. Such gifted persons as James McCune Smith, Alexander Crummell, Martin R. Delany and David Ruggles used it to express their opinions. Cornish, as the editor, fought relentlessly for full rights of citizenship and equality for the Negro.

As a trustee of the free schools for Negroes in New York, he energetically promoted higher education for Negroes. Participating in many reform movements, he was an active member of the American Anti-Slavery Society. On one occasion, he voiced his contempt for a group of prominent Philadelphia Negroes who urged the free people of color to drop the adjective "colored" and use the term "oppressed Americans."

Councill, William Hooper

Educator

William H. Councill (1849–1909), educator, clergyman, lawyer and Reconstructionist, was born of slave parents at Fayetteville, North Carolina. His father, a fugitive slave in Canada, had hoped to earn sufficient money to purchase the freedom of his family, but had never succeeded. The mother and children went from one owner to another un-

til William finally lost his mother, who died in Huntsville, Alabama. During the Civil War, he followed the Union soldiers and entered one of the freedmen's schools at Stevenson, Alabama. By 1868, he had sufficient education to take charge of a school where he taught only fundamentals; however, he recognized his need for further training.

With the rise of the Ku Klux Klan in northern Alabama, he found it increasingly difficult to obtain further training, as well as to maintain his school. Studying privately, he decided to enter politics. Participating in the Reconstruction politics of the 1870's, he was rewarded with a job as enrolling clerk in the legislature of the state. Serving as associate editor of the Republican newspaper *The Negro Watchman,* he was nominated by the party for the legislature in 1874. President Grant appointed him tax collector of the northern district of Alabama in 1875, but he refused the offer in order to be the principal of the Colored School of Huntsville. When the state created the Alabama State Agricultural and Mechanical Institute in 1875, he was elected president.

William Hooper Councill was not only a devoted champion of education but also a minister in the African Methodist Episcopal Church, who concerned himself more with the development of the Sunday school for children than with instruction for the adult members of the congregation. He studied law and was admitted to practice before the supreme court of Alabama in 1883.

Couvent, Mme. Bernard

Philanthropist

Mme. Bernard Couvent (?-1837), a philanthropist interested in the welfare of Negro orphans, was born in Africa but was transported to New Orleans as a slave; very little is known of her life. It is known that in her will she provided for the founding of a school for Negro orphans. When the executor of her will did not honor her request, Father Manehaut and others formed a society, in 1848, for the establishment of the School for Negro Orphans. They demanded that the executor account for the property, which consisted of several small houses situated on the corner of Union and Grands Hommes Streets, and that he turn it over to the society. As a result of their settlement with the executor, the École des Orphelins de Couleur was established in the third district of New Orleans.

Mme. Couvent's will placed the orphanage under the supervision of the Catholic clergy. Father Manehaut enlisted others to contribute to the original bequest so that the school could build a larger plant. Before the Civil War, the board of directors obtained grants from the state legislature and from the city of New Orleans. The school was the best of its kind during the ante-bellum period.

According to the death record in the archives of the Cathedral of St. Louis, Mme. Couvent's name was Justine Firvin Couvent; she was the widow of Bernard Couvent.

Craft, William and Ellen
Fugitive Slaves

William and Ellen Craft, heroes of the autobiography *Running a Thousand Miles to Freedom* (London, 1860), were fugitive slaves from a Georgia plantation. Though both were illiterate, they succeeded in their escape from bondage. Ellen Craft, who was fair enough to disguise herself as a white man of means, pretended to be ill, and her husband William masqueraded as the devoted slave of the young master. Her disguise protected them until they reached Philadelphia, where they were befriended by anti-slavery workers. They were advised to move to Boston, where both William and Ellen were given employment.

WILLIAM CRAFT

ELLEN CRAFT

Because of the Fugitive Slave Act of 1850, the Crafts were in jeopardy, and a warrant had been issued for their arrest. Their anti-slavery friends hid them and staged meetings in Faneuil Hall protesting the attempt to return the Crafts to Georgia. To make their freedom secure, arrangements were made for the Crafts to sail for England, where they were received by friends of the abolitionists. Later, William Craft, employed by a London business house, was sent to Africa to establish branch houses for the firm.

When the Civil War was over, the Crafts returned to Georgia, purchased a plantation and established an industrial school for Negro youth, near Savannah.

Crogman, William H.

Educator

William H. Crogman (1841–1931), teacher and college president, was born on an island in the Danish West Indies. Orphaned at the age of 12, he went to sea at 14. For 11 years, he sailed from one port to another, but, fortunately, he developed a friendship with a Mr. Boomer of Massachusetts, who took Crogman to Boston to live with his family. During the first 25 years of his life, Crogman had received no formal education, but his travels and experiences had provided him with a good knowledge of people and places. Encouraged by Boomer, he entered Pierce Academy in 1868, and upon completing the academy's courses, he moved to the South to teach. He accepted a job at Claflin University in South Carolina and enrolled at Atlanta University for the four-year classics course, which he completed in three years. After graduating, he was appointed professor of Latin and Greek at Clark University in Atlanta, in 1880. After 23 years of service at the university, he became its president. He was the first Negro to be president of Clark University, and when

WILLIAM H. CROGMAN

he retired from the presidency, he resumed his professorship until 1921.

His greatest contribution was in the classroom, where, for more than 50 years, he influenced hundreds of students by training them in the arts and humanities. He strongly opposed the concept of training Negroes solely for industrial vocations—a philosophy popularized by Booker T. Washington. Instead, he was more in accord with W. E. B. Du Bois' theory of educating the talented upper one-tenth of students in the liberal arts.

Cuney, Norris Wright

Reconstructionist

Norris Wright Cuney (1846–1898), active in politics in Texas after the Civil War, was born in Waller County, Texas, and attended local schools. Reaching manhood at the time of the passage of the Fourteenth Amendment, Cuney entered politics. Involved with contemporary movements and issues, he theless was made collector of customs at Galveston in 1889, a position he held until the party lost the election of 1892.

Day, Thomas

Cabinetmaker

Thomas Day, skilled craftsman of Milton, North Carolina, was a free Negro who created his own designs and taught his apprentices the art of cabinetmaking. Greatly in demand among the wealthy Southerners along the Atlantic seaboard, Day designed special emblems so that the furniture might remain in sets in one family for many generations. Governor Reid, later United States senator, bought several sets of furniture from Day.

This creator of fine furniture was inspired by a handsomely furnished house when he was a child. His mother had sent him, when he was 10, to deliver some farm produce to one of the prominent families of the community. The lady of the house took the boy to the parlor to hear the melodeon played. He became so absorbed with the richly carved antiques from the Old World that he hardly heard the music. When Thomas returned home, he reproduced a footstool that he had seen in the room, carving it in walnut with a small knife. When it was finished, his mother showed the stool to the family. They recognized the boy's ability and saw that he was trained in the fundamentals of cabinetmaking. For three years he was sent to school in Boston and Washington.

By 1818, he was producing the first mahogany furniture for sale in the community. His first shop was on his mother's farm, but he moved into town in 1823 and purchased an old yellow brick tavern, which he converted into a factory. For 30 years, he had a flourishing trade in finely carved furniture and trained both Negro and white boys as apprentices.

NORRIS WRIGHT CUNEY

fought for racial equality and human rights. Serving the Texas Republican Party, he was largely responsible, in 1879, for bringing the Negroes back into the party after they had aligned themselves with the Populist movement.

During the Reconstruction era, as many as eight Negroes were elected to the 16th legislature of Texas; but, on each of his attempts to be elected, in 1876 and 1882, Cuney was defeated. However, he was appointed sergeant-at-arms of the 17th legislature and also held various positions in the Republican Party.

Cuney was known for his honesty and integrity, qualities which undoubtedly caused him to lose votes in his elections. He stood for the principle of right rather than for partisanship when he opposed the removal of the daughter of Sam Houston from the job of postmistress of Abilene, Texas. He resisted the state's spoils system, but never-

Delany, Martin R.
Physician and Colonizationist

Martin R. Delany (1812–1885), Harvard University-trained physician and advocate of colonization, was born in Virginia, the descendant of Gullah and Mandingo grandparents.

One of the spokesmen in the great debate following the passage of the Fugitive Slave Act of 1850, he turned his interest to the American Colonization Society because he felt that America was too inhospitable for persons of African descent. Following the meeting of the society in Chatham, Canada, in 1859, he traveled to the Niger Valley in Africa, where, with eight African kings, he concluded a treaty which offered inducements to Negroes to emigrate to that area.

In 1843, he published a newspaper called *The Mystery* and, in 1852 and 1879, produced two major books: *The Condition, Elevation, Emigration, and Destiny of the Colored People of the United States, Politically Considered,* and *Principia of Ethnology: The Origin of Races and Color.* He presented a scientific paper to the International Statistical Conference in London in 1860. He practiced medicine in Chicago and Canada but spent most of his time in traveling and speaking on abolition and colonization.

During the Civil War he was a major in the 104th U.S. Colored Troops. In Charleston, after the War, he worked with the Freedmen's Bureau. In 1874, he ran for lieutenant governor of South Carolina, but lost.

DeLarge, Robert Carlos
United States Congressman

Robert Carlos DeLarge (1842–1874), member of the House of Representatives from South Carolina, was born at Aiken, South Carolina, and was largely self-educated. However, he not only learned the tailor's trade but also became a skilled parliamentarian. When the Republican Party was organized at Columbia and a state committee was formed to select delegates for the constitutional convention in 1867, DeLarge was a prominent leader and a delegate to the convention, which also met at Columbia in 1868. He was elected to the state legislature, and in 1870 ran for the United States Congress as representative for the second district.

He was elected to the 42nd Congress, where he actively supported enforcement of the Fourteenth Amendment. However, he took a conciliatory stand on restoring Southerners to governmental activities. During this period, he admitted that the Republicans had deceived many Negroes. No doubt because of his criticism of the Republicans, his seat was contested by C. C. Bowen in the election of 1872. DeLarge was given an indefinite leave of absence; Bowen, however, was not seated.

MARTIN R. DELANY

ROBERT CARLOS DeLARGE

DeLarge, like many black Reconstructionists, was a victim of circumstances. While serving as land commissioner for the state, DeLarge was charged with corruption, but he had inherited the corruption in the land office from C. P. Leslie, a white Republican. In spite of this charge, congressional records reveal that he voted for the investigation of Crédit Mobilier and for the repeal of the test oath against Southerners. He was a magistrate in Charleston when he died.

Dennis, George Washington

Businessman

George Washington Dennis, successful business pioneer in California, was the son of Green Dennis, a slave trader and gambler from Mobile, Alabama, who took his son and a group of gamblers to California in 1849. While en route to San Francisco by steamship from Panama, George Dennis was lost and rewon three times by his father during an extended gambling game. The captain of the steamship had charged Green Dennis $350 for the fare of his Negro son because the law prohibited the steamship line from carrying slave passengers.

When these gamblers reached San Francisco, they erected a large tent on the corner of Kearny and Washington Streets. This temporary shelter, named the Eldorado Hotel, housed 10 gambling tables, which were operated by men during the day and by women at night. When a permanent structure was erected, George Dennis became porter and caretaker at a salary of $250 per month. His father-master encouraged him to save his money to purchase his freedom. In a short time, George paid Green Dennis $1,000 for his own freedom and $950 for the freedom of his mother, who had come to San Francisco to join her son.

For a sum of $40 a day, George Dennis rented one of the gambling tables, on which his mother served hot meals. Even though the expenses were heavy, it was reported that she averaged about $225 a day. George joined the Frazier River Mining Company. Though he staked three claims, he was unsuccessful and so returned to work at the Eldorado Hotel until he had enough money to purchase property in a partnership with Mifflin Gibbs. Holding the property for six months, they then sold it for $32,000. In 1856, George Dennis purchased another block of property for $1,550. Later, he extended his real estate holdings and made large profits on the resale of land.

Owning the first livery stable in San Francisco, he secured a contract from the British government for 500 cavalry horses. Even though a white employee poisoned 90 horses, Dennis fulfilled the contract; but, after this experience, he decided to open a wood and coal yard. The poisoner was convicted and sentenced to 14 years in the penitentiary.

Dennis suffered losses each time San Francisco was destroyed by fire, but still managed to restore his fortune. The father of 11 children, he gave them all the best education obtainable in California. Winning honors in school, they later became distinguished citizens of the state.

Douglass, Frederick A.

Abolitionist

Frederick A. Douglass (1817–1895), born in Tuckahoe, Maryland, escaped from bondage in 1838. From his experience as a slave, he wrote *Narrative of the Life of Frederick Douglass,* a classic. After joining the abolitionist movement, he published the *North Star* in Rochester, New York, in 1847. Through this, later called *Frederick Douglass' Paper,* he relentlessly fought slavery in the United States; he also lectured in Great Britain on slavery and its abolition. During the

FREDERICK A. DOUGLASS

Civil War, he advised President Lincoln on the possible role of the Negro in the War.

Besides being an abolitionist, he was involved in business and political affairs. In 1874, he was elected president of the Freedmen's Bank and Trust Company. After 1877, he was appointed to numerous offices: marshal of the District of Columbia, recorder of deeds for the District, minister-resident and consul general to Haiti, and chargé d'affaires to Santo Domingo. Douglass' leadership and militant role as an abolitionist earned him the title of "spokesman for his race."

Downing, George T.

Youth Leader

George T. Downing (1819–1903), pioneer youth leader, was a militant leader in the struggle not only for justice for the Negro troops who fought in the Union armies but also for equality of educational opportunities for Negro youth. Born in New York City of a father who was a successful businessman, he was educated at the Mulberry Street School. Early recognizing the plight of the city's Negro youth, Downing, then 14 years old, and a group of schoolboys formed a society to discuss questions pertaining to the social and economic condition of the Negro people.

When the Civil War divided the nation, he enlisted in the Union Army and organized several regiments of Negro soldiers in New York. He was constantly vigilant, however, in seeing that the Negro regiments were granted the same rights as the white troops.

Because of the persistent and valiant efforts of Downing and his wife, the Rhode Island school system was completely and permanently integrated in 1866. When the nationwide movement for separate schools had developed earlier, he had besieged the Rhode Island legislature for 12 years for the integration of Negro children.

GEORGE T. DOWNING

A rather interesting feature of Downing's philosophy is illustrated in his admonition to Negroes, during the peak of the post-War years, not to cast all their votes for the Republican Party. Instead, he strongly advised that the Negro community would fare better politically if there was a division of the Negro vote.

Dozier, John

Minister and Legislator

John Dozier (1800–?), Baptist minister and Reconstructionist politician, was born a slave in Richmond, Virginia. He was self-educated—even to the extent of learning Greek—because, as a slave of a college president in Virginia, he was reared in an environment conducive to study. Liberated before the War, he migrated to Perry County, Alabama, where his enslaved wife and sons had been sold to an Alabama slaveowner.

John Dozier founded the First Colored Baptist Church of Uniontown, Alabama, and served as its pastor for 20 years. As a leader in the community after the Civil War, he joined the Reconstruction forces in the county. He was elected to the Alabama house of representatives in 1872 and served for two sessions. A fellow politician who was associated with Dozier in the legislature reported that he was a man of high ethical and moral standards. He passed through the period of political corruption in the state without becoming tainted by it.

Dumas, Alexandre
(Dumas père)

French Author

Alexandre Dumas (1802–1870), prolific French Romantic novelist and playwright of the 19th century, was born in Villers-Cotterets, the son of Haitian-born General Thomas Alexandre Dumas, a mulatto, and Marie Labouret, a Frenchwoman. Although Dumas' father died when the child was three years old, his ambitious mother secured the services of Abbé Grégoire, who tutored her son. Because of the family's poverty, Dumas had to work as a clerk in a notary's office. Later, moving to Paris in search of employment, he was hired as a copying-clerk in the office of the Duke of Orléans. To improve his meager education, he studied the sciences, languages and literature. In particular he studied the works and techniques of the French masters of drama. His earliest play, *Hunting and Love,* was a failure, as were other early works. However, his drama *Henri III and His Court* was a great success, bringing overnight popularity to the young playwright and an appointment as assistant librarian in the Palais Royal.

Dumas, a most prolific writer, is credited with introducing, through his plays, the Ro-

ALEXANDRE DUMAS (PÈRE)

mantic movement to the French stage. He produced over 300 volumes of novels, memoirs and travel books and 25 volumes of drama. Of his famous plays, *Christine, Antony, Kean, Mlle. de Belle Isle* and *Henri III* are the greatest. His famous novels *The Count of Monte Cristo, The Three Musketeers* and *The Black Tulip* have been popularized by the movie industry and can still be seen on television.

Because he was an ardent supporter of the French Republic, he had to take refuge in Switzerland during the Revolution of 1848. Dumas was a friend of the greatest French writers, such as Victor Hugo, Alfred de Musset and Alfred de Vigny, who greatly respected his genius.

Dumas spent the last years of his life wandering through Europe in search of new ideas. Although he had earned a great deal of money from his works, his extravagance left him very poor in his old age.

Dumas, Alexandre (Dumas fils)

French Author

Alexandre Dumas (1824–1895), noted son of the elder Dumas, became famous as a philosopher and reformer, whereas his father was a writer of Romantic literature. The son's writings were revolutionary in combating prejudice and in trying to secure more consideration for the unfortunate. As his illustrious father had done, he first wrote poetry and then turned to drama and the novel. Having seen his father's career end because of dissipation, he turned his attention to the social and moral questions of a decadent French society.

With his early publication, *The Sins of Youth,* he gained recognition as a reformer; in his famous work, *La Dame aux Camélias,* he analyzed the life of a rehabilitated courtesan who had lived a life of passion. His preoccupation with philosophy and reform

ALEXANDRE DUMAS (FILS)

appears in his most outstanding works: *Money Question, The Demi-monde, The Natural Son, The Ideas of Madame Aubray, The Wedding Visit* and *Denise.*

The works of both father and son are still popular on the French stage. The younger Dumas was made a member of the French Academy of Arts and Sciences in 1874, an honor that had been denied his father, who was a greater writer.

Dunbar, Paul Laurence

Poet

Paul Laurence Dunbar (1872–1906), famous poet, was born in Dayton, Ohio, and attended Central High School there. He wrote his first poems as a young child; but when he graduated from high school, he was unable to go to college and began working as an elevator operator. Dunbar continued writing poetry and soon became known as a "poet of the people." He is best known for his poems in Negro dialect, such as "When Malindy Sings."

In 1893, Dunbar published his first volume of poems, *Oak and Ivy.* With the publication of his third volume, *Lyrics of Lowly Life,* which contained a preface by William Dean Howells, Dunbar became a national literary figure. In addition to his poems, Dunbar published four collections of short stories and four novels. He died at the age of 34, at the height of his popularity.

Duncanson, Robert

Artist

Robert Duncanson (*c.* 1817–1872), one of the ablest ante-bellum painters, was born in New York State of Scotch, Canadian and Negro parentage. He received his early training in Canada, and later, having won the admiration of prominent Cincinnati artists, the Freedmen's Aid Society of Ohio sent him to England and Scotland, where he studied for three years. His first painting to gain recognition, "The Lotus Eaters," is an allegorical interpretation of Tennyson's poem.

Two of Duncanson's most famous works, "Blue Hole" and "Trial of Shakespeare," are owned by the Cincinnati Museum of Art. During his stay in Europe, Duncanson became famous for his landscape paintings. He had many admirers in Great Britain, and it is said that Queen Victoria bought one of his paintings.

Dunn, Oscar James

Reconstructionist

Oscar James Dunn (1826–1871), lieutenant governor of Louisiana, was born a slave in New Orleans. At the age of 15, he ran away from his cruel master; and later, he purchased his freedom. He was sufficiently skilled as a plasterer and house painter to earn a comfortable living.

When the Federal troops occupied Louisiana at the close of the Civil War, Dunn

OSCAR JAMES DUNN

worked with the Freedmen's Bureau as a traveling agent, checking employment policies of plantation owners who were hiring Negro laborers. Often the Negroes were cheated of their $15.00-a-month wage; Dunn uncovered many of the abuses of this system. Previous to his service with the Freedmen's Bureau, he had opened an employment service in New Orleans to guide the former slave-laborers in their role as free laborers. His services involved drawing up contracts and interpreting the conditions of work and the wages to be received by the Negro. At the same time, he opened a bakery with a capital stock of ten thousand dollars. He was able to demonstrate to the newly freed Negroes the nature of their new status as free laborers because he employed a large number of them in his bakery.

Actively participating in the Reconstructionist politics of the state, Dunn was one of 49 Negroes to attend the convention to draft the Louisiana constitution of 1868. In 1868, he was elected lieutenant governor on the conservative Republican ticket. Presiding over the senate with courage and firmness, he was regarded as being incorruptible, even by the Democrats. He placed honesty above personal gain, and was outspoken in his distaste for graft and corruption in office.

At the peak of his struggle for honesty and equality, Dunn died suddenly, after serving only three of his four years as lieutenant governor of Louisiana.

Durham, John Stephens

Journalist and Diplomat

John Stephens Durham, journalist and United States diplomat to Haiti, was born in Philadelphia, attended the local public schools and graduated from the Institute for Colored Youth. Serving as a teacher in Delaware, New Jersey and Pennsylvania during the early part of his career, but desiring to improve his work, he attended the Toune Scientific School of the University of Pennsylvania, graduating with his Bachelor of Science degree in 1886. He received a degree in civil engineering in 1888.

While studying at the university, he became interested in writing and was editor of the *University Journal,* later a free-lance reporter for the *Philadelphia Times* and, finally, assistant editor of the *Philadelphia Evening Bulletin.* His writings were indicative of his keen interest in the social and economic conditions of the colored people of the city. He demonstrated his concern by organizing and sponsoring bureaus and associations to educate and direct the city's Negroes and teach them the importance of industry and self-development.

In 1891, he was appointed by President Benjamin Harrison to serve as United States minister to Haiti. This was a difficult assignment because the country was in a state of revolution and each political faction wanted the recognition of the United States government. Durham's diplomatic skill in handling the interests of the United States was meritorious.

Elliott, Robert Brown

United States Congressman

Robert Brown Elliott (1842–1884), brilliant lawyer and congressman from South Carolina, served in the 42nd and 43rd Congresses of the United States. He was born in Boston of West Indian parents and was educated in England at Eton, where he graduated with high honors in 1859. He then studied law with a London barrister. Upon returning to the United States, Elliott decided to establish a law practice in South Carolina, where the Negro population exceeded that of the white and where opportunities existed for rapid political advancement in the post-War Republican Party.

ROBERT BROWN ELLIOTT

In 1868, Elliott was elected to the South Carolina legislature, and in 1870 and 1872, he was elected to the United States House of Representatives, but before he completed his tenure, he resigned to return to his law practice and political role in his state.

During his tenure in Congress in 1874, Elliott challenged Alexander Stephens to debate the civil rights bill, which was designed to implement the Fourteenth Amendment. He accused Stephens of "seeking to break up the Union of their states and to blot the American Republic from the galaxy of nations." His speech, a triumph for the Republicans, carried Elliott to the pinnacle of his fame. Shortly afterwards, he resigned to return to South Carolina, where he ran unsuccessfully for attorney general in 1876. He served as speaker of the state house of representatives and continued to wield extensive political power for several years before he moved to New Orleans, where he died.

Ferguson, Catherine

Pioneer in Welfare Work

Catherine Ferguson's work with destitute children began in her Sunday school, the first in New York, and gave impetus to the movement to found homes for orphaned children. Her work reached the attention of a well-known minister, Dr. John M. Mason, who recognized the usefulness of her project and assisted in its expansion.

Katy was born a slave on board a schooner en route from Virginia to New York City. When she was eight, her mother was sold, and Katy never saw her again. As this had happened to her at an impressionable age, she matured with compassion for all motherless children, regardless of their race. However, the small slave girl did have a kind mistress who permitted her to attend church services; another sympathetic woman purchased Katy's freedom for two hundred dol-

CATHERINE FERGUSON

lars when she was 16 years old. No doubt it was a very lonely freedom. She married at the age of 18 and had two children, who died young. The lonely woman then dedicated herself to assisting orphan children as a means of filling the emptiness in her life.

At her little house on Warren Street, on Sundays she gathered all of the neglected children, both black and white, to instruct them in religious matters. It was at this household that Dr. Mason appeared one morning to find Katy with the children. Seeing that she needed assistance, he made arrangements for her to transfer her Sunday school to the basement of his Murray Street Church. This was the beginning of the Murray Street Sabbath School, which Katy conducted for over 40 years. She continued to have the children come to her house on Warren Street on Fridays and on Sunday afternoons.

From the poorhouse or from destitute parents, she collected 48 children, 20 of them white, caring for them until she could place them in good homes. In tribute to Catherine Ferguson's welfare work in New York, a home for unmarried mothers was named in her honor. The Katy Ferguson Home was founded in 1920.

Flipper, Henry Ossian
First Negro Graduate of West Point

Henry Ossian Flipper (1856–1940), first Negro to graduate from the United States Military Academy at West Point, was born in Thomasville, Georgia. After the liberation of slaves in 1865, the Flipper family moved to Atlanta, where Henry was educated at a school conducted by the American Missionary Association and at Atlanta University. He won the appointment to West Point while he was studying at Atlanta University. His graduation from the Military Academy in 1877 attracted the attention of the nation's leading newspapers. The *New York Herald*

HENRY OSSIAN FLIPPER

said that Cadet Flipper was the only one to receive cheers at the graduation exercises.

As early as 1877, there was some concern about Second Lieutenant Flipper's request for cavalry service because there were reports of an army regulation which forbade black officers in white regiments. Because of this controversy, Flipper was assigned to the 10th Cavalry at Fort Sill, one of two black regular army cavalry regiments authorized by Congress in 1866. In Fort Davis, Texas, Flipper was arrested on two charges and tried by a general court-martial in 1881. He was found not guilty of the charge of embezzlement, but he was found guilty of the second charge of conduct unbecoming an officer and a gentleman and was dismissed from the service. He contended for years for another review of his case because it stood to reason that, if he was not guilty of embezzlement, then there was no basis for the charge of misconduct. In view of discriminatory policies in the armed services throughout the history of the United States, Flipper was no doubt justified in contending that the charges were trumped up.

After leaving the army, he became an engineer, and in 1890, the chief engineer of the Altar Land Company. He was then employed as a surveyor of public lands in Sonora, Mexico. While in Mexico, he also was an agent of the United States Department of Justice, from 1893 to 1901. He remained in Mexico until 1912, when he accepted employment with the Sierra Mining Company in Duluth, Minnesota. However, by 1919, recognized as an authority on Mexican affairs, he was called upon by the Senate Committee on Foreign Relations for information on Mexico. In 1923, the Secretary of the Interior employed him as an assistant advisor.

From 1923 to 1930, he was employed by the Pantepec Oil Company in Venezuela. By the time of his retirement in 1930, he had opened a new field and was recognized as an outstanding petroleum engineer. He died in his native state of Georgia.

Fortune, T. Thomas

Crusading Journalist

T. Thomas Fortune (1856–1928), fearless, able, and most sarcastic of Negro journalists, waged a relentless fight in the press against corrupt politicians and those who denied the Negro his full rights of citizenship. This militant crusader was born in Florida of slave parents who, after the liberation of slaves, moved to Jacksonville, where Fortune attended the Stanton High School for Negroes and was employed in the local newspaper offices. He was appointed special inspector of customs for the eastern district of Delaware in 1875, but soon resigned to continue his education at Howard University in Washington, D.C. After two years of study, he returned to Florida to teach, but, because the classroom held no interest for him, he moved to New York City in 1879.

In New York City, Fortune started a newspaper, *The Rumor,* which became *The New York Globe;* but, because of a disagreement between Fortune and his partner in the newspaper, the *Globe* died in 1884. A week later, Fortune produced another paper, *The New York Freeman,* which became one of the most militant Negro newspapers in the United States. With Jerome Peterson as partner, he changed the name of the paper to the New York *Age.*

Fortune published three books, *Black and White, The Negro in Politics* and *Dream of Life,* and in the late 1880's worked as an editorial writer for the New York *Evening Sun,* a leading daily newspaper.

T. THOMAS FORTUNE

Garnet, Henry Highland

Antislavery Minister

Henry Highland Garnet (1815–1882), scholar, lecturer, minister, was born a slave in Maryland, but escaped with his parents in 1824 to New Hope, Pennsylvania. The following year, the family, taking a new name, moved to New York City, where Henry devoted his attention to acquiring an education. Although he graduated from the Oneida Institute in 1840, he had already gained recognition as a public antislavery speaker by 1837. The peak of his antislavery crusade was reached in 1843, when, delivering an inflammatory address to the Convention of Free Colored People in Buffalo, he proposed that the convention should broadcast his message to all of the slaves of the United States. His radical speech for slaves "to strike for their lives and liberties" aroused the convention to the extent that Frederick Douglass intervened and secured an adjournment until the afternoon session, when the proposal was tabled. Six years later, John Brown had the address published at his own expense.

While serving as pastor of the Fifteenth Street Presbyterian Church in Washington, D.C. (1864–1866), Garnet was invited to preach to the House of Representatives. He was minister to the Shiloh Presbyterian Church in New York and, afterwards, was president of Avery College in Pittsburgh. At the time of his death, he was serving his government as minister to Liberia.

Gaunt, Wheeling

Philanthropist

Wheeling Gaunt (1812–1894), farmer and real estate dealer, was born a slave in Kentucky. However, he worked to earn nine hundred dollars to purchase his freedom and a subsequent five hundred dollars for his wife's freedom. Although he learned the fundamentals of reading and writing, his wife was illit-

erate. In the 1860's, the Gaunts migrated to Yellow Springs, Ohio, where he bought property and farmed. The profits earned from his farming were invested in real estate in Yellow Springs and Xenia, Ohio.

At his death, he left a will which reflected his concern and sympathy for his fellow men. An estimated estate of thirty thousand dollars was given to Wilberforce University as an endowment for worthy students. During his lifetime, Gaunt was a devout man; therefore, he made a substantial contribution to the Central Chapel African Methodist Episcopal Church, which was founded in Yellow Springs in 1866. Wheeling Gaunt also expressed his concern for the welfare of unfortunate widows in a supplementary will which deeded to the city government a tract of nine acres which was to be rented each year. The money obtained was to be used to purchase flour at Christmas for all the widows of the community.

Over the years, this request has been honored, even though the land is no longer rented as farm land, for the city council converted it to the Wheeling Gaunt Recreational Park. Income from the swimming pool is used to maintain the park, and a certain amount is set aside to give the needy widows their Christmas flour; but it is in the form of bread, fruits and sugar, since today flour is no longer consumed in large quantities.

The obituary of Wheeling Gaunt, published in the *Xenia Gazette,* referred to him as "an old wealthy pioneer colored man." Regardless of their race or color, the citizens of Yellow Springs enjoy the swimming pool and recreational facilities of Wheeling Gaunt Park.

Gibbs, Mifflin W.

Judge and United States Consul

Mifflin W. Gibbs (1823–1918), who began as a bootblack in San Francisco and became a member of the judiciary in Arkansas, was born in Philadelphia, Pennsylvania. Migrating to San Francisco in 1850, he operated a bootblack stand in front of the Union Hotel, where the old city hall now stands. Later, he formed a partnership with John Lester in a shoe firm on Clay Street. A restless man, Gibbs migrated in 1858 to Victoria, British Columbia, Canada, where he established the first general merchandise house that was not connected with the Hudson's Bay Company. Becoming an influential person in Victoria, he was not only a councilman from the James Bay district but also a contractor who built a railroad from the coal mines of Queen Charlotte to Skidgate Harbor in 1867. When the line was completed, he shipped the first cargo of coal mined on the Pacific Coast to San Francisco.

Again moving on, he left British Columbia in 1869. While in Canada, he had studied law with an English barrister, and before he settled in Little Rock, Arkansas, he studied at Oberlin College. In Arkansas, he was admitted to the bar and was elected city judge in 1873. Not merely a local politician, Gibbs was chosen by President Hayes as register of the United States Land Office at Little Rock, Arkansas, in 1877. Under President Harrison, Judge Gibbs served as receiver of public moneys; later, he was the United States consul at Tamatave, Madagascar, from 1897 to 1901.

In his declining years, he published several articles and his autobiography, which detailed his many experiences and travels. At the age of 72, he again visited Victoria and San Francisco. During his visit in Canada, he not only was escorted by the speaker of the provincial house of parliament to a seat in that body but also received many marks of distinction from the Canadians. In San Francisco, Judge Gibbs' visit was given publicity by the leading newspapers of the city.

MIFFLIN W. GIBBS

Greener, Richard Theodore
Educator and Political Leader

Richard Theodore Greener (1844–1923), university professor, lawyer, diplomat and politician, was born in Philadelphia, but spent most of his childhood in Boston. His college preparatory work was done at Oberlin in Ohio and Phillips Academy in Andover, Massachusetts. At age 26, he became the first Negro to graduate from Harvard University. An excellent student in classical literature and the ancient languages, Greener was principal of the Institute for Colored Youth in Philadelphia for two years and then of Sumner High School in Washington, D.C. In 1873, he was professor of metaphysics and logic at the University of South Carolina, serving until the legislature adopted the segregation policy of the Hampton legislature of 1877. As a librarian at the University of South Carolina, Greener delivered a paper on the

RICHARD THEODORE GREENER

university's rare books at the meeting of the American Philological Association at Johns Hopkins University in 1877. Some of the scholarly articles he published are: "Socrates as a Teacher," "Benjamin Banneker," "Academic Life" and "John Milton."

Besides teaching, Greener studied law and served on a state commission to develop the public school system in South Carolina. After leaving the state, Greener settled in Washington, where he practiced law and served as an instructor in the law department of Howard University; he became dean of the law school in 1879. As a practicing lawyer, he was a clerk for the first comptroller of the United States Treasury in 1880 and an attorney in a case involving the brutality complaint of the Negro Cadet Whittaker against the United States Military Academy at West Point.

Although Greener did not run for political office, he participated in the national con-

ventions and campaigns of the Republican Party. Because he spoke in many campaigns in support of the presidential candidates, he was rewarded by various appointments; the most outstanding of these were as United States consul at Bombay (India) and Vladivostok (Siberia).

Greenfield, Elizabeth Taylor

Concert Singer

Elizabeth Taylor Greenfield (1809–1876), "the Black Swan of the concert stage," was born in Natchez, Mississippi, but was taken as a child to Philadelphia by Mrs. Greenfield, a Quaker lady who discovered that Elizabeth had a gifted voice. In 1844, Elizabeth went to Buffalo, where she achieved recognition. Her voice had flexibility as well as an unusual range; and her control was phenomenal for an untrained vocalist.

She appeared in Boston in 1852 and

ELIZABETH TAYLOR GREENFIELD

was highly praised by the critic of the Boston *Evening Transcript*. Subsequent tours of the Northern states brought her into contact with many people who extolled her artistry.

She appeared in London in 1853 at the same time Harriet Beecher Stowe was in the city. Mrs. Stowe and the Duchess of Sutherland arranged a concert for Elizabeth which was quite successful. The following year, she sang at a command performance at Buckingham Palace for Queen Victoria; she was accompanied by Sir George Smart, the organist and composer of Her Majesty's Chapel Royal.

When she returned to America in 1854, the New York *Herald* wrote, "The Swan now sings in true artistic style and the wonderful powers of her voice have been developed by good training." Although Elizabeth Greenfield received the coveted praise of the critics, her earnings were never sufficient for her to live comfortably. Her talent and the critics' commendations substantiated the claim of the abolitionists that the Negro was capable and gifted.

Grimké, Archibald H.

Lawyer, Editor and Diplomat

Archibald H. Grimké (1849–1930), lawyer, crusading editor, and consul to Santo Domingo, was born in Charleston, South Carolina, the son of Henry Grimké, a prominent planter, and Nancy Weston, a beautiful slave. He attended Lincoln University and graduated with a law degree from Harvard in 1874. From 1883 to 1885, he not only edited the *Hub*, a weekly paper in Boston, where he had established his law office, but also was a special writer for the *Boston Herald* and *Boston Traveler*. He was appointed United States consul to Santo Domingo, serving from 1894 to 1898.

For 10 years, Grimké, as president of the Washington, D.C., chapter, was one of the

ARCHIBALD H. GRIMKÉ

ablest and most persistent officers of the National Association for the Advancement of Colored People; he also was president of the American Negro Academy from 1903 to 1916. He was the author of biographies of both William Lloyd Garrison (1891) and Charles Sumner (1892). The NAACP awarded him the Spingarn Medal in 1919 for his outstanding achievements.

His father was the brother of the famous abolitionist sisters, Sarah and Angelina Grimké. When Angelina Grimké Weld, a resident of Washington, D.C., read a newspaper account of Archibald Grimké's triumphs at Lincoln, she shocked Washingtonians by acknowledging her kinship with the young Negro. She welcomed him as a house guest and assisted him in pursuing his law degree at Harvard.

Grimké, Charlotte L. Forten
Abolitionist and Teacher

Charlotte L. Forten Grimké (1838–1914), teacher of freedmen at Port Royal, South Carolina, during the Civil War, was as dedicated to the advancement and freedom of the Negro as her celebrated grandfather James Forten. She was born in Philadelphia, the daughter of Robert Bridges Forten, who sent her to New England for her education. She graduated from the Higginson Grammar School in 1855, and after completing a course at the Salem Normal School, she taught at the white Epes Grammar School of Salem. Her appointment was accepted by both parents and pupils without any type of incident, but ill health forced Charlotte Forten to return to Philadelphia in 1858.

During her stay in New England, Miss Forten lived at the home of the abolitionist Charles Lenox Remond, where she became acquainted with William Lloyd Garrison, Wendell Phillips, William Wells Brown, Lydia Maria Child and John Greenleaf Whittier. In this atmosphere, she resolved to dedicate her life to the struggle against slavery and discrimination. After the outbreak of the War, on being informed of the situation near Port Royal, where some ten thousand illiterate slaves had been left destitute by fleeing masters, Miss Forten was eager to contribute her services, and arrangements were made for her to travel to Port Royal. With an elderly Quaker friend and his daughter, she sailed from New York in October 1862, hoping to educate these ex-slaves. After the War, she married the militant Reverend Francis J. Grimké of Washington.

CHARLOTTE L. FORTEN GRIMKÉ

Grimké, Francis James
Minister

Francis James Grimké (1850–1937), outspoken defender of the rights of the Negro, was born in Charleston, South Carolina. His father was a member of one of the most prominent white families of the South; his mother was a slave girl. His famous aunts of the white side of the family, Sarah and Angelina Grimké, became abolitionists, freed their slaves and devoted the remainder of their lives to the cause of freedom for the Negro.

After the close of the Civil War, Grimké entered Lincoln University in Pennsylvania. After graduating as an honor student in 1870, he studied law and served as financial agent for the college. But, interested more in theology than in law, he graduated from Princeton Theological Seminary in 1878. He was assigned to the pastorate of the Fifteenth Street Presbyterian Church in Washington, where he distinguished himself as a scholarly and influential minister.

In an effort to expose the growing segregation movement in the Christian churches of

FRANCIS JAMES GRIMKÉ

Hall, George Cleveland
Physician and Educator

George Cleveland Hall (1864–1930), noted surgeon, one of the founders of Provident Hospital in Chicago, was born in Ypsilanti, Michigan. The family moved to Chicago, where Cleveland completed high school. After graduating from Lincoln University in Pennsylvania, he entered Bennett Medical College of Chicago, receiving his degree in 1888. Specializing in surgery, he opened an office in Chicago. With Dr. Daniel Hale Williams, he launched the founding of Provident Hospital so that Negro surgeons would have an opportunity to further develop their skills. While Dr. Williams became famous for heart surgery, Dr. Hall served as chief surgeon of the hospital. By organizing clinical demonstrations in surgery, Dr. Hall developed a program of continuing education for Negro doctors throughout the United States. In

the 1890's, Dr. Grimké delivered lectures and preached sermons denouncing the practice. He printed and distributed his message in pamphlets to clergymen of both races, urging them to support the cause of righteousness and never to compromise with any evil or system that did not accept the Negro as a Christian brother.

Early in his career, he was an ardent supporter and lecturer at Hampton and Tuskegee Institutes; but when these institutions committed themselves exclusively to the policy of special training for the Negro, Dr. Grimké had less to do with them. When Booker T. Washington, president of Tuskegee, refused to speak out for the civil rights of the Negro and called a meeting of Negro leaders in New York in 1906, Grimké, along with W. E. B. Du Bois, opposed him and caused a schism at the meeting. He was drawn into the battle of human rights because, as a minister, he felt obligated to plead for equality and justice.

GEORGE CLEVELAND HALL

parts of the South, those doctors who could not afford to come to Chicago for these clinics were provided locally with a similar program each year.

Dr. Hall had many other interests besides his medical career. As an active and untiring leader in Negro national affairs, he served as vice-president of the National Urban League and was one of the devoted supporters of the Chicago chapter. As a member of the library board of Chicago, he made certain that the Negro community of that city was not neglected. In recognition of his service on the board, the branch of the public library located at 48th Street and Michigan Avenue was named after him.

His concern for the problems of Negroes in America made him one of the five founders who joined with Dr. Carter G. Woodson to organize the Association for the Study of Negro Life and History in Chicago in 1915. Dr. Hall not only helped Lincoln University obtain an endowment of a half-million dollars but also unhesitatingly gave support to other educational institutions, such as Fisk University, Meharry Medical College and Tuskegee Institute.

Many Negro and white leaders consulted Dr. Hall; Booker T. Washington and Governor Lowden of Illinois were among the outstanding leaders who sought his opinions on many of the issues of his time.

Harper, Frances Ellen Watkins
Abolitionist Poet

Frances Ellen Watkins Harper (1825–1911), antislavery lecturer and poet, was born free in Baltimore, Maryland. Reverend William Watkins, her uncle and a teacher of free Negroes, educated her. In 1851, after moving to Ohio, she taught domestic science. In 1853, she moved to York, Pennsylvania, where, for the first time, she observed the operations of the Underground Railroad;

FRANCES ELLEN WATKINS HARPER

later, living in Philadelphia, she witnessed the terrors of the pursued fugitive slaves. These episodes, which impressed her greatly, doubtless made her join the antislavery crusade as a full-time lecturer with the Maine Anti-Slavery Society, touring the North and Canada for six years. Her fame as a reformer and as an entertaining speaker was enhanced by her original poetry. Her pamphlets sold by the thousands at abolitionist meetings. Her first volume of poetry, *Poems on Miscellaneous Subjects,* was published in 1854.

After the death of her husband, Fenton Harper, in 1860, Mrs. Harper concentrated on writing verse and fiction; *Iola Leroy: Or Shadows Uplifted* (1892) was her best novel. She is remembered as the author of the following poems: "Eliza Harris," "The Slave Mother," "Bible," "Defense of Slavery," "The Freedom Bell" and "Bury Me in a Free Land."

Healy, James Augustine

Catholic Bishop

James Augustine Healy (1830–1900), first Catholic bishop of African descent in the United States, was born in Macon, Georgia. His father was a white planter, and his mother was a slave. His father sent him to a well-known Quaker School, located in New York, to be educated. He continued his education in Worcester, Massachusetts, at Holy Cross College, where he graduated with highest honors in the first class to complete the course, in 1849. After the death of his parents in 1850, friends of his wealthy father encouraged him and provided him with the necessary funds to continue his studies abroad. He studied at the St. Sulpice Seminary in Paris, and was ordained in Paris in 1854.

After returning to America, he served as pastor of St. James' Catholic Church in Bos-

JAMES AUGUSTINE HEALY

ton's southeast end, a predominantly Irish neighborhood. The Irish were reluctant to accept him at first, but, when the area was ravaged by epidemics of typhoid, influenza and tuberculosis, Father Healy administered the Sacraments to the victims with no thought of the danger to his own health. Soon, he was accepted and respected by the members of his congregation as a true priest.

As the assistant to Bishop John Fitzpatrick of Boston, he served as chancellor of the diocese, having charge of the account books, the official correspondence and the many contacts with various units of the diocese. When he was elevated to the bishopry, it was evident that he had been well trained for the post. As bishop, he presided for 25 years over the diocese of Maine and New Hampshire. During this period, 50 new church buildings were erected, 18 parochial schools and 68 mission stations were established, and the number of Catholic communicants more than doubled.

Bishop Healy's brother, Patrick F. Healy, was president of Georgetown University in Washington, serving in that capacity from 1872 until 1883.

Henson, Josiah

Conductor on the Underground Railroad

Josiah Henson (1789–1883), a fugitive slave who escaped by the Underground Railroad when he was 40 years old, served as an agent for the Underground Railroad in Canada. In 1842, he worked with Hiram Wilson to found the British-American Manual Labor Institute in Canada.

His abolitionist activities resulted directly from his bitter experiences as a slave. He was born in Maryland, where as a child he witnessed the brutal assault of his mother and the mutilation of his father for striking the overseer who was thrashing her. Both parents were sold, leaving the young boy an

JOSIAH HENSON

orphan. Unable to obtain an education as a child, Henson was taught to read by one of his own sons.

As Henson matured, he assumed the personality of an "Uncle Tom." Concealing his hatred for slavery, he won the trust of his master, who, making him an overseer, sent him to deliver other slaves to a kinsman in Kentucky. After he worked in Kentucky for three years, he attempted to purchase his freedom, but was badly cheated. When he learned that he was to be sold downriver to New Orleans, he escaped with his wife and two children to Ohio, and, late in 1830, he entered Canada, where he joined the Underground Railroad and labored in behalf of emancipation. On three occasions, he traveled to England, where he was presented as an example of the brutality of slavery because he was maimed by a beating that he had received in Maryland.

As an agent of the Underground Railroad, he freed 30 Kentucky slaves in 14 days and, on another occasion, helped 118 slaves to escape. The story of his life is reputed to have been the basis of Harriet Beecher Stowe's *Uncle Tom's Cabin*.

Houat, Louis T.

French Author

Louis T. Houat, French poet, novelist and physician, was born on the island of Réunion, a French possession in the Indian Ocean. He was a music teacher in 1835 at St. Denis when he was arrested on the charge of plotting to massacre the whites on the island. During his eight months in jail awaiting trial, the authorities further accused Houat of corresponding with the abolitionists in France. After the court of the island condemned him to deportation, he went to France, where he studied medicine, and traveled in Italy, Germany and Russia.

Houat was probably the first French Negro to write poetry. Four of his poems were published during the time of his imprisonment on Réunion in the *Revue des Colonies*, 1836–37. His first poem, "Poésie à mon ami," celebrates the beauties of nature; another, "Le pêcheur," describes the dangers of the fisherman at sea; the fourth poem, "Le bengali," is a comparison of his imprisonment with that of a caged bird.

Upon his return to Réunion in 1844, he wrote his novel *Les marrons,* which is a highly melodramatic story of four slaves who planned to escape bondage. It portrays the beauty of nature and the cruelty of man.

Returning to France, Houat did not produce any further work until 1863, when he published *Etudes et sciences spirites*, subtitled *Morale, philosophie, médecine, psychologie,* showing his affiliation with an organization of physicians who followed the homeopathic ideas of Dr. Samuel Hahnemann of Germany. He read a paper before the Society of Homeopathic Medicine in 1867 and published medical treatises in the society's journal. He spent his last years as a physician in the town of Pau, in southern France.

Ikard, Bose

Cowboy

Bose Ikard (1847–1929), a cowboy who rode with such men as Charles Goodnight, Oliver Loving, John Chisum and John Slaughter, was born a slave in Mississippi, but, at the age of five, was taken to Texas by his master's family, the Ikards, who settled near Weatherford. Growing up on the frontier, Bose learned to ride, rope and fight—skills that made him a valuable cowboy. After the War, he joined Oliver Loving and Charles Goodnight on their cattle drives from Texas through New Mexico northward to Fort Sumner.

Bose Ikard and Charles Goodnight became nearly inseparable. Goodnight said of him: "He was my detective, banker, and everything else in Colorado, New Mexico, and the other wild country I was in. The nearest and only bank was at Denver, and when we carried money, I gave it to Bose, for a thief would never think of robbing him." Often, when Goodnight was exhausted from the terrible trials of the trail, he called upon Bose to take over. A superb rider, Bose saved Goodnight's life on more than one occasion.

According to J. Evetts Haley, the author of *Charles Goodnight: Cowman and Plainsman,* Bose Ikard "added life, friendship, and color to the Goodnight Trail." Ikard, returning to Texas, lived there the rest of his life.

Johnson, Harvey

Church Leader

Harvey Johnson (1843–1923), distinguished Baptist leader of Baltimore, was born in Fauquier County, Virginia, and educated at the Free Negro School of Alexandria and at a Quaker school in Philadelphia. With the help of some friends in Massachusetts, he attended Wayland Seminary and graduated in 1872. He was asked to take over the leadership of the Union Baptist Church in Baltimore, Maryland.

In 1872, there were only 250 members in the congregation; but, by 1885, Johnson had increased the membership to 2,200. As a leader of the community, he waged a struggle against racial discrimination and particularly against the denial of rights to the Negro. He was successful in the fight to admit Negroes to the state bar in Baltimore.

HARVEY JOHNSON

When a member of Johnson's congregation was refused first-class passenger service on the steamer *Sue,* a ship out of Baltimore, he helped sue the steamer company. The case was decided in favor of the Negro; thereafter, Negroes were never denied first-class accommodations on a passenger ship out of that port.

Harvey Johnson, a strong advocate for an educated and enlightened ministry, encouraged young men to study before assuming leadership in a pulpit. His ideas concerning racial separatism were similar to those of Booker T. Washington, and he was a staunch promoter of Negro schools taught by Negro teachers.

Jones, J. McHenry

Educator

J. McHenry Jones (1859–1909), fraternal leader, minister and first president of West Virginia Colored Institute, was born in Gallipolis, Ohio, and completed high school at Pomeroy, Ohio, in 1882. He was both a minister in the African Methodist Church and a teacher near Pomeroy in 1882; but the following year, he moved to Wheeling, West Virginia, where he served as principal of the Lincoln School, developing it into a good secondary school. A gifted orator, Jones was well known as a speaker on the Chautauqua circuit in Ohio and West Virginia.

In 1898, the state of West Virginia created the Colored Institute near Charleston and appointed Jones president of the school. Holding this position until his death, he developed the institution into a fine vocational and teacher-training school. As a leading educator in the state, he was a strong advocate of equal rights for Negroes, fighting the introduction of separate seating for Negroes in railroad cars and other public accommodations. As an associate editor of the militant newspaper *The Charleston Advocate,* he at-

tacked measures which he considered dangerous to the welfare of the Negro. Though a staunch supporter of the Republican Party program of the state, he never ran for public office or accepted any appointments.

As a fraternal leader, Jones joined the Grand United Order of the Odd Fellows and represented the group in England in 1897. He was grand master of the order in 1902. His forceful speeches appeared in print, and he wrote a book entitled *Hearts of Gold.*

Jones, John

Businessman and Antislavery Leader

John Jones (*c.* 1817–1879), a prominent citizen of Chicago and one of the wealthiest Negroes in America, was born free in North Carolina. He taught himself to read and write while serving as a tailor's apprentice. In 1845, with only $3.50, he and his octoroon wife migrated to Chicago. With his skill, he opened a tailoring business from which he amassed a fortune; this enabled him to finance and lead the fight to repeal the "Black Laws" of Illinois. He worked with John Brown and Frederick Douglass in the abolitionist movement and used his home as an Underground Railroad station. A militant reformer, Jones made speeches, wrote pamphlets, organized meetings and lobbied in the legislature—his activities in the years before, during and after the Civil War. For two terms, he served as a Cook County commissioner and was instrumental in abolishing segregated schools in Cook County, Illinois.

Lafon, Thomy

Philanthropist

Thomy Lafon (1810–1893), philanthropist, was born in New Orleans of a black Haitian mother and a French father. After an education that qualified him to be a school teacher, he became a merchant and invested his money in real estate. His father having deserted him in childhood, Lafon learned the thrifty habit of saving and investing early in life. He became one of the richest men in New Orleans; but, having experienced the sting of poverty, he spent the remainder of his life helping the needy, regardless of their race, color or creed. He made large contributions to the American Anti-Slavery Society and the Underground Railroad. At his death, he left an estate valued at $600,000—a sum that was willed to charity.

Despite the racial discrimination which prevailed in Louisiana in 1893, the state legislature voted to honor him in memoriam. His bust was commissioned in recognition of his broad humanitarianism—the first testimonial by a state to a man of color. Grace King, a noted white author, wrote "Thomy Lafon, seeing no color nor sect in his love for mankind, distributed his life's earnings indiscriminately among black and white, Protestant and Catholic alike."

A devout Catholic and lover of the arts, he lived in semi-seclusion. Fluent in French and Spanish, he was constantly mistaken for a European, for his skin was white and his manner polished. Because he had considerable wealth, the city of New Orleans, on one occasion, borrowed money from him.

Lane, Isaac
Bishop and Educator

Isaac Lane (1834–1937), bishop of the Colored Methodist Episcopal Church and founder of Lane College in Jackson, Tennessee, was born of obscure parentage on an isolated plantation in west Tennessee. However, he managed to learn the rudiments of reading and writing. Even though he was 30 years old at the time of emancipation, he did not let his age deter him from further study. He was licensed to teach while a slave, but the Southern Methodist Church

ISAAC LANE

permitted him to preach only as a lay minister. During the Civil War, the church recognized him as a minister. Because he had 11 children, he supplemented his income from preaching by raising cotton and supplying firewood for the local market. His salary as a minister, even after his consecration as a bishop in 1873, was well under two hundred dollars a year. After many years of poverty and self-denial, in 1882 the dedicated bishop succeeded in raising funds to build Lane College, which stands today as a monument to a man who came from a lonely, obscure childhood of slavery to freedom and accomplishment.

Langston, John Mercer
Educator and United States Congressman

John Mercer Langston (1829–1897), the first Negro elected to the U.S. Congress from Virginia, was born in Virginia of a slave mother and a plantation master, Ralph Quarles, who made liberal provisions for his

JOHN MERCER LANGSTON

children. Langston was sent to Cincinnati and later to Oberlin College for his education. He studied law and, in 1854, won his first jury trial in Chillicothe, Ohio. After gaining a voting residence, he was elected on the Liberty Party ticket as clerk of the township.

Langston's career touched upon many areas of life. He was a member of the city council of Brownhelm, Ohio (1855–1860), president of the National Equal Rights League (1865), member of the Oberlin, Ohio, board of education (1867–1868), school inspector general of the Freedmen's Bureau (1868–1869), dean of the law school of Howard University (1869–1876), minister-resident to Haiti (1877–1885) and president of Virginia Normal and Collegiate Institute (1885–1888). Among the last of the Negroes elected to Congress during the 19th century, he was a United States congressman for Virginia from 1890 to 1891.

Before the Civil War, John Langston was an active leader in the various free Negro conventions, speaking at meetings of the American Anti-Slavery Society and advocating the extension of the areas of freedom for the American Negro; he opposed the movement for the relocation of Negroes by the American Colonization Society. After the War, he was active in the movement to organize the freedmen, for their economic security, in the Negro National Labor Union.

Leary, Lewis Sheridan

Fighter with John Brown

Lewis Sheridan Leary (1835–1859), heroic fighter at Harpers Ferry, was born of free parents in Fayetteville, North Carolina. Even as a child, he hated slavery. Once, as a young man, he witnessed a white man beating a slave; interceding, he beat the white man. As would be expected, his action caused so

LEWIS SHERIDAN LEARY

much excitement in the community that he was forced to escape across the Cape Fear River under cover of darkness. The youth traveled in a northwesterly direction until he reached Oberlin, Ohio.

Fortunately, in Oberlin he was able to support himself, for not only had he been trained under private tutors in his father's home and sent to the free colored people's school in Fayetteville, but he was a skilled designer and decorator of saddles—a trade which his father had taught him. He displayed unusual musical talent and learned to play several instruments, but he showed no interest in reading.

Even though he was miles from Fayetteville, the question of slavery still haunted him. He made trips to Cleveland, where he was friendly with a group of John Brown's admirers; eventually, he met the great liberator himself. When John Brown called for volunteers to help in his daring enterprise, Leary was ready to join the group, though he never informed his family of his plans. A nephew, John A. Copeland, volunteered also, and the two joined John Brown's raid on Harpers Ferry. After the failure of the raid, Copeland was captured, tried and hanged. Leary died of wounds the day after the raid. Both men gave their lives in the cause of freedom for all men.

Leidesdorff, William Alexander
Millionaire and Diplomat

William Alexander Leidesdorff (1810-1848), millionaire, was born at St. Croix, in the Virgin Islands, the son of a Danish planter and an African mother. Later, he and his two brothers were sent to New Orleans to work in their father's cotton business. When his brothers died, Leidesdorff inherited the capital from the business and, on the 160-ton schooner *Julia Ann,* sailed for California in 1841.

In only seven years, Leidesdorff played an exciting and influential role in the political struggles between Mexico and the United States for possession of California. Because the land he desired for a home and a store was owned by Mexico, he applied to the Mexican government for two lots in San Francisco. Wishing to acquire more land, he became a Mexican citizen in 1844 and obtained 35,000 acres on the American River from the government. During the United States' war with Mexico, in 1846, the last Mexican mayor of San Francisco gave him another grant which, now located in the city's center, bears the name "Leidesdorff Street."

In July 1846, the United States Marines under Captain Montgomery took over the city. Leidesdorff immediately entertained the conquering Americans. Already a member of the city council, he became the American consul in California and city treasurer of San Francisco.

Not only a politician but also a sportsman, he introduced horse racing to California. When he died, at the age of 38, he left an estate that was valued at about $1,500,000. His great wealth came primarily from the land he owned on the American River, one of the sites of the gold strike in 1849.

Lewis, Edmonia
Sculptor

Edmonia Lewis (1845–1890), first Negro sculptress of note, was born of mixed Negro and Chippewa Indian parentage in New York. Her parents died when she was quite young. It is not known whether Edmonia grew up with her mother's tribe, but she did obtain an education at Oberlin College, where she was friendly with many abolitionists. Through the efforts of William Lloyd Garrison, who had heard of her ambition to study art, she was introduced to a Boston sculptor, Brackett, who taught her the rudiments of sculpture.

EDMONIA LEWIS

Her first piece was a bust of John Brown. Her bust of Robert Gould Shaw, the famous colonel of the first Negro Civil War regiment, attracted the attention of the Story family of Boston. They not only helped to sell her work but also encouraged her to study in Italy.

In Rome, where she worked directly in marble, Miss Lewis mastered the exacting techniques of sculpture. Some of her works are "Death of Cleopatra," "The Marriage of Hiawatha," "Madonna with the Infant" and "Forever Free." This last portrays a muscular, scantily clad Negro freedman greeting emancipation—his left arm upraised and his fist clenched; with his other arm he protects his wife; he seems to embody the freed slaves' conflicting emotions of doubt and confidence.

Her best works are portrait busts done in the classical style of the Romans, particularly those of Charles Sumner, John Brown, Abraham Lincoln, Henry Wadsworth Longfellow and William Story. Miss Lewis remained in Italy, returning to America only for rare visits to execute commissions and to show her work. One of her important exhibitions was at the Philadelphia Centennial in 1876.

Lewis, James

Civil War Hero and Reconstructionist

James Lewis (1832–1914), Civil War hero and Reconstructionist, was the son of a white father and a mulatto mother. Soon after his birth in Woodville, Mississippi, his mother moved to Bayou Sara, Louisiana. At the outbreak of the Civil War, he served a Confederate officer for a few months and then became a steward on a Confederate troop transport. When the Federal troops occupied New Orleans, he abandoned the Confederate ship to answer the call of General Benjamin Butler of the Union Army for free Negroes to enlist in the United States Army. Lewis

JAMES LEWIS

was among the first to raise two companies of Negro soldiers. As captain of the 1st Regiment of the Louisiana National Guard, he lead his group during the famous battle for Port Hudson.

At the close of the War, he worked for the Freedmen's Bureau as a traveling agent who established schools and training centers for freedmen. Life as an agent was quite dangerous at times, particularly in the northern section of the state, where he was once seized by obstructionists who resented the teaching of Negroes. In 1867, he was appointed United States customs inspector for two years. Joining the metropolitan police force of New Orleans in 1869, he was promoted rapidly from sergeant to captain of the fifth precinct; by 1870, he was administrator of police; in addition, he was a colonel in the 2nd Regiment of the state militia. As administrator of public improvements for the city in 1872, Lewis is reputed to have saved the city more than a half-million dollars during his first year in office. This was an unusual achievement since he was the only Republican official on a city council controlled exclusively by the Democrats.

Lewis attended the national Republican conventions as a delegate from Louisiana. He was rewarded for his service by appointments: first, as naval officer of the port of New Orleans; later, as superintendent of the United States bonded warehouse; and finally, as surveyor-general of the state, in 1884.

Loguen, Jermain Wesley

Minister and Antislavery Leader

Jermain Wesley Loguen (c. 1813–1872), noted for his stand against the Fugitive Slave Law of 1850, was born in Tennessee of a Negro mother who had been kidnapped in Ohio. He escaped from slavery in his early youth and settled in Canada, where he learned to read. He later moved to Rochester, New

JERMAIN WESLEY LOGUEN

York, and then to Oneida, New York, where he studied with Beria Green. Afterward, he became a minister of the African Methodist Episcopal Zion Church and served as a pastor in Ithaca, Syracuse and Troy, New York.

He was a pastor in Syracuse when the Fugitive Slave Law of 1850 was passed. Loguen was outraged over the law, which jeopardized his freedom because he had been a slave of Mrs. Sarah Loguen of Maury County, Tennessee. However, rather than go into hiding, flee the country or try to purchase his freedom, as many other fugitives did, he took an adamant stand against the law. He called upon the citizens of Syracuse "to proclaim to the despots at Washington whether the Act shall be enforced here— whether you will permit the government to return me and other fugitives who have sought asylum among you to the hell of slavery."

In 1860, Mrs. Loguen had the effrontery to write Loguen requesting one thousand dollars in "hush money" to cancel his obligation to her. Filled with scorn for his former owner, he replied with an indignant letter, vowing that he would never pay for what was his birthright. He attacked those fugitives who paid "insurance" against re-enslavement on the basis that they had recognized the property right of slave ownership. Because he and 23 others had rescued a fugitive slave, the Reverend Loguen was arrested and charged with treason. The citizens of Syracuse, as well as Gerrit Smith and William Seward, signed the note authorizing their bond. Eventually, the charges of treason were dropped; and citizens of Syracuse commemorated the incident with an annual celebration known as "Jerry's Day."

In 1859, the daring Loguen published his autobiography, *Reverend J. W. Loguen as a Slave and as a Freeman: A Narrative of Real Life.* He was elected bishop in 1868.

Lynch, John R.

United States Congressman

John R. Lynch (1847–1939) was born in Louisiana of a slave mother and a white planter, who wished to free the mother and son but died before arrangements were completed. His relatives sold the mother and child in Natchez, Mississippi. Lynch received some tutoring in his youth and spoke fluently, without the customary accent of the slave quarters. Aristocratic and handsome, he was a celebrated Negro political leader for many years.

He served as United States congressman from Mississippi to the 43rd, 44th and 47th Congresses but served only two full terms. His third term was at first contested in a disputed election, after the Republican Party had returned the South to Democratic control. In defending his seat in the 47th Congress, Lynch said of the Democrats: "They cannot disfranchise the poverty-strick-

JOHN R. LYNCH

en Republican voter without disfranchising at the same time and in the same way the poverty-stricken Democratic voter."

Lynch continued to serve the party as chairman of the Mississippi Republican state executive committee up until 1889. For his loyalty, he was awarded two offices: he was appointed fourth auditor of the treasury in the Navy Department and, later, was made a paymaster in the army.

In 1917, Lynch published in the *Journal of Negro History* an article entitled "Some Historical Errors of James Ford Rhodes," in which he stated that the generalizations about the Reconstruction era made by this historian were groundless. He concluded his critique with the hope that some other scholar, rather than basing his work on unreliable gossip, gross exaggerations and campaign slogans, would investigate and record the true nature of the Reconstruction period.

Matzeliger, Jan Ernst

Inventor

Jan Ernst Matzeliger (1852–1889), a shoemaker, was born in Paramaribo, Dutch Guiana, the son of a Negro woman and a Dutch engineer, in whose machine shop he began working at the age of 10. Although he could speak little English, young Jan earned his passage to the United States as a sailor. He found work in Philadelphia and later moved to Lynn, Massachusetts, where he learned shoemaking, a trade in which he worked for the remainder of his life. Before he died, he had invented the lasting machine which revolutionized the manufacture of shoes and helped make Lynn the shoe capital of the world.

Mechanization of shoemaking had been applied to the cutting and stitching of leather, but the final problem of shaping and attaching the upper portion of the shoe to the leather sole still remained. This slow, tedious task, which was done by the shoemakers working by hand, produced a bottleneck: the men could not finish a shoe as rapidly as the machine produced its parts.

Matzeliger recognized the problem as he worked at his bench, stretching, shaping, and attaching each shoe to its sole. In secret, he experimented with a crude wooden machine and then with an iron model, on which he worked for 10 years, until he had perfected it. He sent his diagrams to Washington, D.C., for a patent and on March 20, 1883, received his grant for the "lasting machine." He had invented a machine which held the shoe on the last, gripped and pulled the leather down around the heel, set and drove in the nails and then discharged the completed shoe.

JAN ERNST MATZELIGER

Menard, John Willis

United States Congressman

John Willis Menard (1838–1893), first of the Reconstruction politicians to be elected to Congress, was born of French Creole parents in Kaskaskia, Illinois. He was educated in Sparta, Illinois, and at Iberia College in Ohio. During the Civil War, he was a clerk in the Department of the Interior in Washington, D.C. At that time, President Lincoln and others were considering seriously the advisability of colonizing the emancipated slaves. A large tract of land in Belize, Central America, was given to the government, and Menard was selected by the commissioner of emigration to investigate the proposed colonization plan. He was officially received by the governor of Belize, but his report was not acted upon by the U.S. government.

At the close of the War, he moved to New Orleans to work for the Republican Party's

JOHN WILLIS MENARD

Menelik II
(Sahala Mariem)

Ruler of Ethiopia

Menelik II (1844–1913), by uniting the warring tribes of Ethiopia, defeated the Italians in 1896 and forced them to withdraw and recognize Ethiopia as an independent nation.

In his struggle to gain control of the country, Sahala Mariem had been imprisoned in 1865 by Kassai, the governor of Shoa, whose authority was recognized by many tribes. When Kassai died in 1868, the Ras of Tigre took the throne, as John IV. The marriage of Sahala's daughter to the King's son placed him close to the royal family. Three years later, John IV was killed by a stray bullet during a campaign against the Mahdi. With the unwitting help of the Italians, who hoped to seize the country themselves, Sahala ascended the throne as

Reconstruction policies. Nominated for a vacant seat in Congress in 1868, he ran against a white man and received the greater number of votes in the election; but, when he claimed his place in Congress, the defeated man contested the seating of a black. Both contestants were granted permission to speak in defense of their rights, on the floor of Congress. The case was referred to the committee on elections, where it was decided that it was "too early" to admit a Negro to the United States Congress. The seat was again declared vacant, but Menard was awarded the full salary that was normally paid to its holder. In 1869, after Congress had refused to seat Menard, he served as inspector of customs for the port of New Orleans and, later, commissioner of streets.

In addition to his political activities, Menard was the editor of a newspaper, *The Free South,* which was later renamed *The Radical Standard.*

MENELIK II

Menelik II. Pacifying the hostile tribes, he made them recognize him as king.

The Italo-Ethiopian conflict, which occurred in 1896, resulted from conflicting interpretations of a clause in the treaty between the two nations. Menelik II insisted that the clause meant not that Ethiopia was dependent on Italy for its foreign policy but that it "might avail [itself] of the good offices of Italy." The Italians insisted that the Ethiopians were "obligated to consult Italy." The issue was settled on the battlefield, and Ethiopia emerged with her independence.

Merrick, John

Businessman

John Merrick (1859–1921), businessman and one of the founders of the North Carolina Mutual Life Insurance Company, was born in Clinton, North Carolina. Though he was originally trained as a bricklayer, he became a barber and eventually built and operated five barber shops in Raleigh. As a barber, he came into contact with numerous enterprising businessmen, including J. B. Duke, the tobacco industry magnate, who encouraged Merrick in his ambitions to succeed in the business world.

Receiving advice from this successful businessman, Merrick saved his profits with the intention of investing them in various business enterprises. In 1899, Merrick and Dr. A. M. Moore established an insurance company and employed C. C. Spaulding as agent and manager. The office of the company was located in a room of Dr. Moore's office. Spaulding sold his first policy for sixty-five cents but had to pay forty dollars soon afterwards on the death of the policyholder. The news of the payment spread; and by the end of the first year, the company had collected around eight hundred dollars in premiums.

JOHN MERRICK

From this meager, unpretentious beginning, the North Carolina Mutual Life Insurance Company became one of the largest, most successful businesses exclusively owned and controlled by Negroes.

Reinvestment of the profits was skillfully handled by Merrick, who was now president of the company as well as of the Mechanics and Farmers Bank, an affiliate of the insurance company. The company officials began a policy of leadership and helped provide civic and educational services for Negroes in Durham. They sponsored the construction of Lincoln Hospital, which included Merrick as the president of the board of directors, and encouraged educational opportunities, particularly by hiring a rural school supervisor. Merrick, in association with Dr. Moore, did much to encourage the social, business and educational progress of North Carolina Negroes.

Morris, Elias C.

Minister

Elias C. Morris (1855–1922), organizer and first president of the National Baptist Convention of the United States, was born in northern Georgia. He was reared by a brother-in-law, who was a minister in Stevenson, Alabama. Though he had been trained as a shoemaker, he entered the ministry after he had been converted, when he was 19. As pastor of the Centennial Baptist Church in Helena, Arkansas, from 1879 to 1922, he established the first religious paper for Negroes in the state and founded, in 1884, the Arkansas Baptist College. As chairman of the board of trustees for many years, he developed a program of self-help for impoverished students.

In 1895, Reverend Morris brought together three separate Baptist organizations to create a national group. The American National Convention joined the Foreign Mission Convention and the National Education Convention to form the National Baptist Convention of America. Elected president, he held that position until his death.

Moshesh

Basuto Ruler

Moshesh (1790–1870), South African ruler of the Basuto, was a progressive, enlightened ruler who exercised his intellectual gifts and diplomacy in dealing with the encroaching Europeans during the 19th century. During the troublesome years of 1821–1825, he drew together the remnants of the decimated Bakivena and Zulu tribes, who had broken away from Chaka's despotic rule, and settled them in the impregnable mountain area of Basutoland, which had served as a natural fort for the Basuto. When the Matabele tribes tried to dislocate them, Moshesh and his people drove them back in defeat. Compassion-

MOSHESH

ately, he gave the Matabeles cattle so that they could survive on their return home.

Other tribes came to him for peace and protection. Many of them were Zulus, but most were Bechuanas, who happily conformed to the customs and mores of the Basuto. Thus, he was able peacefully to unite this group into a nation. During the years of peace, Moshesh formed an industrious and progressive people. However, the new nation was not to enjoy peace for long, for migrating Boers eventually harassed them beyond endurance. Moshesh, who was very aware that the British were the enemies of the Boers, diplomatically made overtures to the British. The latter, however, failed to accept the friendly gesture.

A series of wars occurred from 1841 to 1851, between the Boers and the Basuto. In 1852, the British were humiliatingly defeated by Moshesh, but he dealt with them generously in the hope that they would refrain from further encroachment. Conflict with the Boers continued until Moshesh's death, in 1870.

Murphy, John Henry

Publisher

John Henry Murphy (1840–1922), founder of the *Baltimore Afro-American* newspaper, was born a slave in Baltimore, Maryland, but was emancipated in 1863. Enlisting in the Union Army, he served as a non-commissioned officer during the last years of the Civil War. Murphy learned the printing trade late in life—until he was 50 years old, he worked at many menial trades. But a turning point in his life came when he launched the *Baltimore Afro-American* newspaper, for which he set the type himself and delivered the first issues.

JOHN HENRY MURPHY

At the time of his death, this venture had developed into one of the largest Negro newspapers in America printed in a plant manned and operated entirely by Negro employees. Equipped with a modern typesetting machine and a 32-page rotary press which could print a paper in three colors, the paper gained the reputation of being a reliable medium of communication for Negroes because its founder insisted on efficiency and maintained an independent policy of supporting only the best men, regardless of their political affiliations.

Murphy exemplified the type of leader who firmly believed in the ability of the Negro people to succeed, as he himself had done, even after many years of disappointment and frustration.

Myers, Isaac

Labor Organizer

Isaac Myers (1835–1891), shipyard owner and pioneer in organized labor, was born in Baltimore, Maryland, of free parents. After being educated by the Reverend John Foster in his private school, Myers, then 16 years old, was apprenticed to a ship caulker. In four years, he had mastered the trade enough to become a supervisor, responsible for the caulking work on some of the largest clipper ships built in Baltimore in that period. However, by 1865, the Negroes employed as longshoremen and mechanics were facing discrimination; in fact, a strike was led by Joseph Edwards to force the firing and banning of future employment of Negroes in the industry.

Isaac Myers countered Edwards and his men by raising ten thousand dollars to invest in a shipyard which was to be owned by Negroes and which was to hire only Negro workmen. With a down payment of ten thousand dollars on property costing forty thousand dollars, Myers opened the yard and

ISAAC MYERS

employed three hundred Negroes. After receiving a government contract for fifty thousand dollars, he was able to pay the balance of the note within five years.

The struggles of labor became intense in this period; the National Labor Union adopted a political program under the leadership of Travellick, whose objective was to divide the colored vote in the South and to divert it from the Republican Party. Myers, strenuously objecting to this plan, called for a national labor convention of all Negro workers so that they could organize nationally. The purpose of the organization of which Myers was president was to educate Negroes so that they could form their local unions. Union agents traveled throughout the nation organizing and aiding the unions on a state level and directing Negroes to cast their votes for the Republican Party. At the National Labor Union Congress in Cincin-

nati in 1871, Myers delivered a speech in favor of President Grant and the Republican Party, which caused resentment among the members and created disorder in the convention.

In 1870, Myers was appointed special agent-at-large for the Post Office Department and was instrumental in bringing about the arrest of the famous English swindler Dr. William Parker. Among his other endeavors, he began the weekly newspaper *Colored Citizen* (1882), organized the Maryland Colored State Industrial Association (1888) and sponsored the organization of a home for aged ministers of the African Methodist Episcopal Church.

Nell, William Cooper
Historian and Antislavery Leader

William C. Nell (1816–1874), author of *Colored Patriots of the American Revolution,* was a native of Boston who, by collecting and preserving important data on the American Negro, made himself the best-informed individual on the Negro of the antebellum period. His book, containing much material on the early personalities of the antislavery movement, was the sole authority for the history of the Negro before the time of emancipation, when William Wells Brown began to produce his historical works.

Nell, an active worker, was responsible for arranging the place and time of many antislavery meetings. A successful speaker himself, he had conflicts with Frederick Douglass. In a reply to an editorial in *Frederick Douglass' Paper* in 1853, Nell wrote: "What I have said and done, touching this controversy, has been prompted solely by that fidelity which I have cherished for the anti-slavery cause since its advent in Boston in 1831. I have borne allegiance to *principles,* rather than to *men.*"

Omar, El-Hadj

Conqueror of West Africa

El-Hadj Omar (1797–1864), Moslem warrior and empire builder of the 19th century, built an empire across West Africa, but his exploits weakened the people of the area to such an extent that they were left vulnerable to the French and English conquerors who were penetrating the region.

Although Omar was successful in conquering the people, he was by no means a successful political ruler, for the rigorous rule that he imposed on the suppressed peoples caused the expanded Tukular empire to disintegrate as rapidly as he had put it together. In each of the kingdoms, he placed a relative as governor. Furthermore, petty strife and jealousy made it impossible for the animists and the Moslems to unite against El-Hadj Omar's forces. These internal revolts gave the Europeans an opportunity to intervene as "friends and liberators."

EL-HADJ OMAR

Omar, after waging two battles on the Niger River to conquer the Mossina and the Fulani capital at Segu in 1861, went on to take Timbuktu, but withdrew from the city after looting it. Blocked in his efforts to take Hamdallahi, he retired. He was later trapped by some of the disgruntled Fulani in a cave, where he died. The majority of his vast empire was occupied by the French.

Payne, Christopher

Minister and Diplomat

Christopher Payne (1848–1925), United States consul general of the Danish West Indies, now the Virgin Islands, was born in Monroe County, Virginia, which was later a part of West Virginia. Learning to read and write from his mother, he taught school in his neighborhood until he entered the ministry. Attending the Richmond Theological Institute, he graduated with honors. While serving several churches in Virginia, he read law and, after passing the bar examination, was admitted to the practice of law. Continuing as a minister, he served the First Baptist Church of Huntington and, for many years, was president of the West Virginia Baptist State Convention.

Participating in state Republican Party politics, Payne was elected to the lower house of the state legislature in 1896 and, on three occasions, went as a delegate to the national Republican convention. In 1903, to reward his efforts for the Republican Party, President Theodore Roosevelt appointed him consul general to the Virgin Islands, where he remained until 1917, when the United States purchased the islands from Denmark. Remaining in the islands after they were United States possessions, Payne resumed his law practice and was appointed assistant prosecuting attorney and then judge advocate of the islands, a position he held until his death.

In West Virginia, Christopher Payne had been not only a minister but also an editor of several newspapers: *The West Virginia Enterprise, The Pioneer* and *The Mountain Eagle*. These papers generally supported the Republican Party, which most Negroes believed championed their best interests.

Payne, Daniel Alexander

Bishop and Educator

Daniel Alexander Payne (1811–1893), African Methodist Episcopal bishop and first Negro president of Wilberforce University (Ohio), was born of free parents in Charleston, South Carolina. Because both parents died before he was 10 years old, he was left in the care of a great-aunt, who placed him in the Minor's Moralist Society in Charleston, where he was able to continue his education. After two years at this school, he went to work for a relative to learn carpentry and

DANIEL ALEXANDER PAYNE

then tailoring. While he was working at both these trades, he studied the classics and read the histories of Greece, Rome and England.

In 1829, Payne began teaching free colored children, but, in 1834, the state of South Carolina passed a law against the Negroes being educated. The closing of his school forced him to leave the area, a departure which he expressed in the poem "The Mournful Lute or the Preceptor's Farewell." Payne first decided to go to Canada, where he could teach unhampered, but, during a short visit in New York City, he met Alexander Crummell and Lewis Tappan, the well-known abolitionists, who persuaded him to enter the ministry.

Following their advice, he entered the Lutheran seminary at Gettysburg, Pennsylvania. After two years at the seminary, he accepted the pastorate of a Presbyterian church in East Troy, New York. Losing his voice as a minister, he relinquished preaching and went to Pennsylvania to recuperate. In Philadelphia, he taught again and met Bishop Morris Brown and other leaders of the African Methodist Episcopal Church. He joined the Bethel A.M.E. Church in 1841 and was licensed as a preacher by the Philadelphia conference in 1843. Later, Payne accepted the pastorate of the Israel A.M.E. Church in Washington, D.C.

Once identified with the A.M.E. Church, Payne not only wrote articles on the necessity of an educated ministry but was chairman of a committee on education for the general conference and incorporated instrumental music in the church service. In 1845, he was appointed to the Bethel A.M.E. Church in Baltimore, where he remained for five years. Serving as historian of the church for three years, he traveled throughout the country collecting his materials. He was elected bishop in 1852, though it was said that this election was against his wishes. In 1863, he was responsible for the purchase of Wilberforce University, an institution for Negro youth that had been established by the Methodist Episcopal Church in 1856; he paid ten thousand dollars for this property. He served as president of the institution for 16 years. The theological seminary, a part of the university, bears his name.

At the close of the Civil War, Bishop Payne not only built a fine educational institution at Wilberforce but also continued in his capacity as a bishop to organize new conferences for the church. In 1865, he returned to his native state of South Carolina to organize the South Carolina Conference and to extend the A.M.E. Church into Georgia, Florida and Alabama.

Pelham, Benjamin and Robert
Newspaper Pioneers

Benjamin and Robert Pelham, sons of a free family of Petersburg, Virginia, founded in 1883 one of the nation's leading Negro

ROBERT PELHAM

newspapers, the *Plaindealer,* in Detroit, Michigan. The Pelham brothers came from a distinguished and prosperous Negro family who were forced to leave Virginia because of harassment by envious townspeople. Their decision was caused by an incident concerning an unlicensed pet dog. When the Pelhams went to purchase a license, the authorities refused to sell the license because only whites and slaves could purchase dog licenses. Selling their farm and moving to Columbus, Ohio, the family discovered that discrimination was there, also; Philadelphia was just as unsatisfactory. After they finally settled in Detroit, the children received the best education available.

Benjamin and Robert attended the public schools and the fashionable Barstow private school, where they maintained high scholastic records, particularly in mathematics. While delivering the daily Detroit *Post,* they became interested in the mechanical aspects of typesetting and later became apprentice typesetters. Ben joined the staff of the *Post*

BENJAMIN PELHAM

and later the *Tribune*. Robert launched his own paper, the *Venture*. When Ben joined Robert on his paper, they changed the name first to the *National Era* and later to the *Plaindealer,* which had the second best-equipped plant in Michigan.

For 11 years, the *Plaindealer* with its widely read editorials, was a leading Negro newspaper. The Pelham brothers gained political influence on the national level because they gave wide coverage to Negro affairs. In 1884, they raised to a national level the colored men's state convention and, hence, formed a channel for the political voice of the Negro throughout the Midwest. Ben Pelham, recognized as an expert on county government administration, received appointments to local offices in Michigan and rose to the position of chief accountant of the board of supervisors of Wayne County. Robert Pelham's career took him to Washington, D.C., as an agent in the Interior Department.

Pennington, James W. C.
Minister and Civil Rights Worker

James W. C. Pennington (1809–1870), a fugitive slave who received his Doctor of Divinity degree from the University of Heidelberg (Germany) in the 1840's grew up in Washington County, Maryland. As a young man, he was trained as a blacksmith and a stonemason; but, because of the cruelty he had endured, he fled around 1830, aided in his escape by a Pennsylvania Quaker who sent him to Long Island, New York. There he acquired enough education to teach in the Negro schools. After studying theology in New Haven, Connecticut, he served as pastor of the African Congregational Church in Hartford. Because he was an effective platform speaker, he was invited to speak before aristocratic audiences in Paris, Brussels and London while he was attending various conferences in Europe.

JAMES W. C. PENNINGTON

In 1849, Pennington published his autobiography, *The Fugitive Blacksmith*, in which he recorded his experiences of slavery and described his escape and flight to the free North. With William Still, he fought against discrimination on public conveyances. As a prominent antislavery leader, he not only denounced every affront to first-class citizenship but studiously worked on programs outlining ideology and tactics for the Negro protest movement.

Pinchback, Pinckney Benton Stewart
Lieutenant Governor

Pinckney Benton Stewart Pinchback (1837–1921), lieutenant governor of Louisiana during Reconstruction, was born free in Georgia but was sent to Cincinnati, Ohio, to continue his education at Gilmore High School. From 1854 to 1861, he worked as a cabin boy and then as a deck hand on a riverboat. He settled in New Orleans.

PINCKNEY BENTON STEWART PINCHBACK

During the early stages of the Civil War, Pinchback recruited and organized two regiments of Negro soldiers for the Union Army. However, because of the discriminatory policies of the army, Pinchback resigned in 1863.

After the War, he was an inspector of customs for the port of New Orleans and a delegate to the state constitutional convention in 1868 and to the national Republican convention in 1868. Elected not only as a state senator but also as lieutenant governor, he served for a brief period as acting governor of Louisiana. In 1873, he was elected to the United States Senate, but he was not permitted to take his seat. However, for his loyal support of the Republican Party, he was appointed by President Chester A. Arthur as surveyor of customs for the port of New Orleans.

Pleasants, "Mammy" E. (Mrs. Alexander Smith)
Financial Supporter of John Brown

"Mammy" E. Pleasants (?–1904), controversial figure in the history of San Francisco and the episode of John Brown's raid, was born a slave in Georgia. A planter named Price purchased her for six hundred dollars, freed her and sent her to Boston to be educated, but the family who was to supervise her while she studied failed to carry out the agreement. Later, she married Alexander Smith, who was active in the Garrison Anti-Slavery Society. Anticipating his death, he made her promise to use her legacy of fifty thousand dollars in gold for the abolition of slavery.

Moving to San Francisco in 1849, she loaned the money at 10 per cent per month and, hence, accumulated a fortune. When the news of John Brown's efforts to free the slaves in the South reached "Mammy" Pleasants, she fulfilled her husband's wish by aiding this abolitionist. She is reported to have met him in Chatham, Canada, where she gave him thirty thousand dollars to finance the raid on Harpers Ferry. After Brown's capture in 1859, a note signed "M. E. P." was found on him, but the detectives read the rough signature as "W. E. P." The search for "Mammy" Pleasants was foiled by the letter "W." In the meantime, taking an assumed name, she escaped by sailing to California in a ship's steerage.

Upon her return to San Francisco, she began her career as a financial adviser to distinguished white gentlemen of the city. Her home on Octavia Street, known as the "House of Mystery," was the scene of the death of Thomas Bell, a white man who had fallen over the bannisters. "Mammy" Pleasants was accused of killing him to inherit his money. Neither the motive nor the state's case was substantiated, because she was not mentioned in his will. On another occasion, as the backer of the wife to the extent of sixty-five thousand dollars, she figured in the famous divorce case of Sharon vs. Sharon.

After the death of Thomas Bell, "Mammy" Pleasants, locked out of the "House of Mystery," died in poverty in a little house on Baker Street. An article appearing in the *San Francisco News-Letter* stated: "So ended the old colored woman who for years was a power in San Francisco's affairs and who so largely aided in precipitating the crisis that started the Civil War by furnishing John Brown with the funds to start his historical raid at Harpers Ferry."

Powell, William Frank

Educator and Diplomat

William Frank Powell (1844–1921), advocate of a teacher-training program in public schools and United States diplomat to Haiti, was born in Troy, New York. Moving to New York City, he attended the local public schools, the New York City School of Pharmacy and Lincoln University in Pennsylvania; finally, he graduated from the Collegiate Institute of New York in 1865. His first employment was with the Home Mission Board of the Presbyterian Church as a teacher of freedmen at Leesburg, Virginia. The state, which opened a school at Alexandria for the same purpose, selected Powell to be its director. Remaining with the school until 1881, he became a bookkeeper in the United States Treasury during 1882.

However, still desiring to teach, he became principal of the fourth district school in Camden, New Jersey. Finally obtaining the requisite position, he experimented with the theory of training teachers to present subject matter in the classroom by having normal school students participate in a classroom situation. Practice teaching is today a basic requirement for teacher certification.

President William McKinley appointed William Powell the United States minister to Haiti in 1897. The turbulent situation in Haiti generated for American diplomats many sensitive problems, one of which involved giving asylum to Haitian revolutionists. When his tenure in that country was completed in 1905, he retired to his New Jersey home until his death.

Purvis, Robert

Abolitionist

Robert Purvis (1810–1898), businessman and abolitionist, was born in Charleston, South Carolina, of a wealthy white father and a free mulatto mother. Educated in Philadelphia, he was a graduate of Amherst. Although he was heir to his father's fortune, and he appeared to be white, he identified himself with the Negroes. He married a daughter of James Forten, with whom he had worked in the antislavery movement. Two years after William Lloyd Garrison founded the *Liberator,* Purvis helped organize the American Anti-Slavery Society and the Pennsylvania Anti-Slavery Society, but he devoted the majority of his time and effort to the Underground Railroad.

Purvis defied the Federal Fugitive Slave Law by belonging to state vigilance committees which aided escaping slaves. And as a prominent member of the Negro convention movement, he fought for the extension to free Negroes of suffrage and the right to serve on juries and to join the militia. In spite of the many sacrifices Purvis made for the cause of freedom, he was attacked by Frederick Douglass, who made many insinuations about Purvis' fair complexion.

Purvis went to London in 1834, where he was introduced as an American gentleman to the Irish patriot Daniel O'Connell, who refused to shake hands until he was assured that Purvis was not only an abolitionist but also a Negro.

Pushkin, Aleksander

Russian Author

Aleksander Pushkin (1799–1837), Russia's greatest poet, was the great-grandson of the African slave Abram Hannibal, who was a high-ranking military engineer under Tsar Peter the Great. Pushkin's mother, Nadezhda Osipovna, married Sergey Lvovich Pushkin, a member of the Russian nobility. Born in Moscow, Aleksander was humiliated by his family because he was a fat, shy, awkwardly unattractive child. It was nurse Arina, a freed serf in the Pushkin household, who gave affection to the neglected child. Her influence on the young poet was as important as the formal education that he received, for she taught him about Russian folklore, the cadences and deep significances of the Russian language and the destitute conditions of the troubled peasants.

He had a series of tutors and also read everything available in his father's library. He attended a private school for six years,

but did not attract any attention until the day of final examinations. On that occasion, when young Pushkin was called upon to recite his original verses, the amazed and delighted Dershavin, foremost of Russian poets, predicted that some day Pushkin would replace him in Russian literary circles.

With youthful enthusiasm, the young poet took the Russian language and shaped it into a beautiful and powerful medium of expression. Heretofore, French had been the language of Russian literature. Placing the language of his people among the world's important languages, Pushkin cried out for freedom and protested bondage and serfdom. He became the spokesman for the poor and oppressed, to the alarm and concern of the Tsar and the nobility. His poem "Ode to Liberty" created so much uneasiness among the ruling powers that Pushkin was exiled from St. Petersburg to southern Russia where, ironically, he wrote some of his finest works. After writing *The Conversation between the Bookseller and the Poet* and *The Gypsies,* he began *Eugene Onegin,* his masterpiece. After six years, Tsar Nicholas pardoned him and allowed him to return to St. Petersburg, on condition that all of his works be approved before publication.

Even though Pushkin was restricted, he continued to produce poetry, plays, stories and novels. Two of his novels were converted into operas: *Boris Godunov* by Mussorgski and *Eugene Onegin* by Tchaikovsky.

His most popular poem, "The Fisherman and the Fish," appears in many primary school readers in English; *The Golden Cockerel* is a fairy tale of beauty and fancy; the lengthy historical novel *The Captain's Daughter,* considered by some critics to be his greatest work, is the story of the peasants' revolt. On the 100th anniversary of the poet's death, the Soviet government found it expedient to publish the complete works of Pushkin in *The Literary Heritage of Pushkin.*

Rainey, Joseph Hayne
United States Congressman

Joseph Hayne Rainey (1832–1887), the first Negro representative from South Carolina to the House of Representatives, was born in Georgetown, South Carolina, of free parents. Growing up with a limited education, he became a barber, which gave him an opportunity to learn from observing and listening to his educated customers. When the Civil War began, he was conscripted to work on fortifications for the Confederate Army, but he escaped to the West Indies, where he remained until after the end of the War.

Returning to South Carolina, he entered the post-War politics of Reconstruction. He was sent to the state constitutional convention in 1868 and entered the state senate in 1870. He also served in the 41st, 42nd, 43rd, 44th and 45th United States Congresses,

JOSEPH HAYNE RAINEY

with a favorable record. Generally, his speeches were devoted to the advancement of the oppressed and to the procurement of education for the Negro as a means of rapid transition toward economic and social acceptance.

After his retirement from Congress in 1879, Rainey served as an internal revenue agent in South Carolina until 1881. Next, he engaged in the banking and brokerage business in Washington, D.C., then finally retired in 1886 to Georgetown, South Carolina, his birthplace.

Rapier, James Thomas
United States Congressman

James Thomas Rapier (1837–1883), distinguished member of Congress from Alabama, was born at Florence, Alabama. He was one of the best-prepared of the representatives from his state since he had been educated by private tutors and had studied law in Canada, where he was admitted to the bar. While a student in Canada, he had the opportunity to speak before future King Edward VII, who was visiting North America at the time. After the Civil War, he returned to the South as a correspondent for a Northern newspaper. He gave up this career in order to purchase a farm and to remain in his home state of Alabama as a cotton planter.

A delegate to the first state Republican convention, he served on the committee that framed the platform. He was a member of the constitutional convention held in Montgomery in 1867. Aspiring to become secretary of state, Rapier waged an unsuccessful campaign in 1870 against Nicholas Davis, a white opponent; however, he was appointed assessor of internal revenue to lessen the sting of his defeat. Later, he was successfully elected as a Republican representative to the 43rd Congress; but he failed to be re-elected

JAMES THOMAS RAPIER

in 1874 because he had aligned himself with members of an unsuccessful Republican faction that caused a split in the ranks of the party.

After his defeat in 1874, Rapier returned to farming and became quite successful. In 1878, however, the Republicans again gave him an appointment, this time as collector of internal revenue for the second district of Alabama, a capacity in which he served until his death.

Rayner, John B.

Populist Leader

John B. Rayner (1850–1918), populist organizer, was born a slave in North Carolina, the son of a plantation owner and a slave woman. Following the Civil War, Rayner's father sent him to St. Augustine Catholic School, where he obtained a rudimentary education. He became a teacher and, later, a Baptist minister. In 1881, Rayner left North Carolina and moved to Texas, where he continued teaching.

In North Carolina, he was not only a teacher but also a deputy sheriff, having been elected on the Republican ticket. In Texas, however, Rayner, disillusioned with the state Republican Party, did not become involved in politics until a movement developed for a third party—the People's Party, or the populist movement.

The populist movement of the 1890's, an offspring of the Farmers' Alliance, was directed at monetary deflation, railroad abuses and monopoly practices. Although Negro farmers had been active in the populist movement as early as 1892, Rayner did not associate with it until two years later. He was an untiring and faithful party worker, even after the populists had excluded the Negroes from the movement in order to gain the support of the Southern whites. In the rough and tumble of Texas politics, Rayner was known as being quick-witted and sharp-tongued in debate. His criticisms were sharp and bold. He said of the white Republicans that ". . . they are mephitic vaporings from cadaverous carpetbagism."

Even though he was a member of the state executive committee of the People's Party and a regular lecturer who campaigned throughout the state, he received no salary. Often the *Southern Mercury* newspaper carried requests for contributions to pay his expenses because he did not have money enough to buy postage stamps, much less to pay his traveling expenses.

After the political campaign of 1896, his name appeared less and less in the *Southern Mercury*; the last account of John B. Rayner appeared in 1898, when he, as captain, and two others were named as organizers of a colored military company. However, he continued working for Negro rights until his death. In the first year of World War I, he requested government officials to enlist Negroes in the military services. Following this activity, he lapsed into virtual retirement and wrote a series of opinions concerning his philosophy of the Negro's role in society.

Reason, Charles L.

Educator and Poet

Charles L. Reason (1818–1898), educator and poet, was born in New York of parents who had fled the Haitian revolution of 1793. A promising student at the African Free School by the age of 14, he instructed the other students so that with the extra money he could employ a private tutor in mathematics. His reputation as a scholar won him an appointment in 1849 as professor of belles lettres at the New York Central College in McGrawville, New York. He resigned in 1852 to accept an appointment as director of the Institute for Colored Youth in Philadelphia, which, after being moved to Cheyney, was reorganized as a state teachers' college.

CHARLES L. REASON

The school was originally established by a bequest from Richard Humphreys, a Quaker, in 1839. The bequest stipulated that the students should be trained for manual labor, but the school's program failed to prosper based on this narrow approach. When Reason took on his new post, he added an appreciation of both the practical and the cultural to the students' mental development. His program gave new meaning and new life to the institution.

Reason was a successful educator, lecturer and poet. Although he did not write much poetry, he did produce some verse meriting attention. His long poem entitled "Freedom" is regarded by some critics as the best antebellum poem written by a Negro. Some of his other significant poems are "The Spirit Voice," "Silent Thoughts" and "Hope and Confidence."

Rebouças, André

Brazilian Engineer

André Rebouças (1855–?), Brazilian engineer and abolitionist, was born near Santo Amaro of a black woman and an educated white gentleman who took his son to Rio de Janeiro to attend school. André obtained his secondary schooling in the Collegio de São Salvador and a civil engineering course at the Escolar Politecnica, which he completed in 1876. He taught for two years before beginning his career as an engineer. A skilled mathematician, he designed the plans for a number of important engineering projects, one of which was the waterworks for Rio de Janeiro. He was responsible not only for the construction of the customhouse but also for the design of the docks of Rio.

Rebouças was invited to join a commission directed by an American engineer to study the navigability of certain rivers. After the commission members had met with a minister to discuss the project, the newspaper

Diário Official published a report of the meeting but omitted Rebouças' name because he was a man of color.

Rebouças became the foremost authority on water power and its utilization in Brazil. His reports are of considerable scientific value. He also contributed many articles to scientific and technical journals in Europe. However, his ruling passion in life was his devotion to the abolition of slavery.

Rebouças, the abolitionist and scientist, was also a distinguished contributor to the military efforts of Brazil in the Paraguayan war. Assigned to the engineering corps, he assisted in planning the technical aspects of the campaign.

Reed, William L.
Lawyer and Legislator

William Reed (1866–1938), lawyer, politician and legislative representative of Massachusetts, was born in Danville, Virginia, but his family moved to Boston around 1872, where Reed was educated in the public schools and attended Bryant and Stratton Commercial College. Afterwards, he studied law and was admitted to the Massachusetts bar.

Entering state politics as a staunch supporter of the Republican regime, he ran for the state legislature and was elected to the lower house in 1896. After a single term as a legislator, Reed was appointed deputy collector of internal revenue in 1898 and deputy tax collector of the city of Boston in 1900. Next, he became messenger to the chief executive of the state and, finally, clerk and executive secretary to the governor and council of Massachusetts.

Active in community affairs, Reed served on the board of directors of the Boston Urban League and was a member of the Bostonian Society. He received an honorary degree from Lincoln University in Pennsylvania in 1933.

Remond, Charles Lenox
Abolitionist and Orator

Charles Lenox Remond (1810–1873), the first Negro to appear as a regular lecturer for the Massachusetts Anti-Slavery Society, was born in Massachusetts of free parents. He was well educated and developed into an eloquent speaker. As an agent of the society, he traveled throughout New England, New York and Pennsylvania and, in 1840, was selected as a delegate to the World Anti-Slavery Convention in England, where he remained for 18 months. Upon his return, in 1841, he brought back a petition signed by 60,000 Irish citizens in support of the antislavery movement. In 1842, Remond appeared before the legislative committee of the Massachusetts house of representatives in support of petitions against segregation in traveling accommodations.

He had the reputation of being the most effective Negro speaker until Frederick Doug-

CHARLES LENOX REMOND

lass arrived in 1842. In his appearances before the Northern public, Douglass, with his experience as a former slave as well as his greater oratorical skill, relegated Remond to second place in public esteem. Although the competition between the two orators led to intense rivalry, together they remained powerful opponents of racial prejudice and worked to keep the American Anti-Slavery Society alive after the close of the Civil War.

Revels, Hiram

Educator and United States Senator

Hiram Revels (1822–1901), educator and Reconstructionist, was born free in Fayetteville, North Carolina. Because there was little opportunity for obtaining an education there, he moved to a Quaker settlement in Indiana, where he acquired a rudimentary education at the Quaker seminary in Union County; later, he attended Knox College in Galesburg, Illinois. With this training, Revels became a minister in the Methodist Episcopal Church and had pastorates in several of the border states. At the outbreak of the Civil War, he helped organize the first of two Negro regiments raised in Maryland. After the successes of the Union Army in the West, Revels taught former slaves in St. Louis during 1863 and 1864.

From Missouri he moved to Vicksburg, Mississippi, where he assisted in the reorientation of the freedmen. In Jackson, he organized churches and schools. Work with the Freedmen's Bureau led to his participation in the state's Reconstruction activities. He was appointed alderman by General Ames, the military governor of the area. He was elected to the senate of Mississippi in 1869 and the following year was appointed to the United States Senate to fill the term vacated by Jefferson Davis. For a few months, Revels served as secretary of state under Governor Powers.

After his term in the Senate, he returned to Rodney, Mississippi, to serve as president of Alcorn College, a new institution to which he devoted his remaining years, forming a creditable educational center for Negroes. Later, he served as an African Methodist Episcopal minister in Indiana.

Richards, Fannie M.

Teacher

Fannie M. Richards (1840–1923), first Negro school teacher in Detroit, was born of free parents in Fredericksburg, Virginia. When the Southern states began restricting the free Negroes of the South, the Richards family moved to Toronto, Canada, and later to Detroit, Michigan. Fannie received her early education in Canada. An outstanding scholastic record in Detroit earned her an appointment as a teacher in the public schools of the city in 1868. For the Negroes, the city maintained separate schools, usually manned by one or two teachers, until 1870. Three

HIRAM REVELS

FANNIE M. RICHARDS

Rillieux, Norbert

Engineer and Inventor

Norbert Rillieux (1806–1894), engineer and inventor, was born in Louisiana. His white father sent him to France to be educated. Upon his return to New Orleans, he became interested in finding a solution to the problem of refining sugar, because the old "Jamaica train" method was slow and costly. In 1846, Rillieux patented a vacuum pan that revolutionized the method of refining sugar and reduced the production cost of granulated sugar, which still retained its sweetness but now lost its crude, dark color.

Although other scientists had developed similar vacuum pans and condensing coils, they had failed to utilize the heat properly during the evaporating process. Rillieux solved this problem by enclosing the condensing coils in a vacuum chamber and by adding a second chamber for evaporating the juice under greater negative pressure. Be-

Negro schools of the city were conducted by white teachers; one was taught by Fannie Richards. In their effort to integrate the schools, the Richards family took an active role against the school board. Their case against the board went through the local courts to the supreme court in Lansing, guided by John Bagley, who later became governor of Michigan.

Although Fannie Richards had fought against the board for the integration of the schools, she was retained as one of the three Negro teachers in the mixed schools of the city and rendered 47 years of service.

Miss Richards was well known by the thousands of youngsters who attended the Everett School. She was an active worker in the community and served as the first president of the Phillis Wheatley Home for Aged Women, established in Detroit. She was retired in 1915, with a pension from the city.

NORBERT RILLIEUX

cause this revolutionary process was not immediately accepted by the sugar industry of France, the inventor returned to Louisiana, where his machinery came into widespread use, as it also did in Cuba and Mexico. Rillieux returned to France, where he turned to deciphering hieroglyphics and to writing scientific papers on steam engines. Finally, Europeans with sugar plantations in the West Indies began to experiment with Rillieux's method of sugar refining and adopted it. Because of this renewed interest, he continued improving the process and successfully adapted it to the processing of sugar beets.

Rillieux also designed a method for handling sewage which could have removed the menace of yellow fever from New Orleans, but his scheme was not adopted.

In 1934, the large sugar manufacturers of the United States placed, in honor of Rillieux, a bronze tablet in the state museum in Louisiana.

Rodgers, Moses

Mining Engineer

Moses Rodgers (?–1890), mining engineer and owner of several mines in California, was born a slave in Missouri. He seized every opportunity he could to obtain an education, giving special attention to mathematics and engineering. Arriving in California in 1849 at the peak of the gold rush, he was highly successful in working his claims. With this gold, he was able to purchase mines at Hornitos, Mariposa County, California. One of the first carloads of machinery to arrive in the state was consigned to the mines at Mount Gains in Mariposa County; Moses Rodgers, as the superintendent, guaranteed that the mine would be worked on a paying basis.

To establish his family where the children could be educated, he built an attractive house in Stockton, where, boring for a gas

well, he spent thousands of dollars until he finally reached the source.

Moses Rodgers almost lost his fortune when he acted as a bondsman for a bank cashier in Merced. This man, accused of having a discrepancy in his accounts, committed suicide before his trial. Rodgers had to make good the shortage in the account and lost as much as $30,000 in the case. Despite this loss, he left his family comfortable because he still had a few of his mines intact. The *Merced Star,* carrying an account of his death, stated: "He was an expert in his line and his opinion was always sought by intending purchasers of mines. He was a man of honor and his word was as good as his bond."

Ruffin, George Lewis

Judge

George Lewis Ruffin (1834–1886), a district judge in Massachusetts, was born of free parents in Richmond, Virginia. The family moved to Boston, Massachusetts, in 1853, after the state of Virginia had enacted laws prohibiting free Negroes' learning to read and write. George Ruffin, an excellent student, was educated in the Boston public schools and worked in a barber shop to earn enough money to continue his training. He was fortunate in favorably impressing two prominent lawyers of Boston, who accepted him as an apprentice. He learned rapidly, and in a few years, he entered the Harvard Law School, where he completed the course in one year, receiving his Bachelor of Laws degree in 1869.

In the meantime, since he was an enterprising young man, he had entered local politics; he was elected to the Massachusetts legislature in 1869 and re-elected the following year. He was elected to the common council of the city of Boston from 1875 to 1879.

At the age of 49, this brilliant lawyer was nominated by Governor Benjamin Butler as

GEORGE LEWIS RUFFIN

judge of the district court of Charlestown, Massachusetts. The nomination was unanimously confirmed by the Republican executive council. He held this position until his death at the age of 52.

Ruggles, David
Conductor on the Underground Railroad

David Ruggles (1810–1849), one of the first men of African blood to escape slavery, was a daring conductor on the Underground Railroad. He was reported to have helped more than 600 slaves to escape from the Southern states to the North and Canada. As secretary of the New York Vigilance Committee, Ruggles worked with Isaac T. Hopper, Lewis and Arthur Tappan, Samuel Cornish and other antislavery advocates. Frederick Douglass stated in his autobiography that Mr. Ruggles was the first officer on the Underground Railroad whom he met after coming North and was the only one with whom he associated until he became such an officer himself.

Along with his work on the Underground Railroad, Ruggles struggled for the moral, social and political elevation of the free Negroes of the North. He published in 1838 the quarterly magazine the *Mirror of Liberty,* which advocated the rights of the Negro. This magazine was the first to be edited by a Negro.

Ruggles demonstrated unusual logic and wit in his essays. In a pamphlet entitled *The "Extinguisher" Extinguished! Or D. M. Reese, M.D. "Used Up!"* he expressed his opposition to the American Colonization Society, which was active in returning Negroes to Africa. Ruggles also owned a bookstore and had a reputation as a hydrotherapist. He had his own establishment for water cures at Northampton, Massachusetts.

DAVID RUGGLES

Russwurm, John B.
Publisher and Abolitionist

John B. Russwurm (1799–1851), the founder of the first Negro newspaper, *Freedom's Journal,* was also the first Negro to receive a degree from a college in the United States. Born in Jamaica of a white American father, Russwurm went to Canada, where he received his early training, and then to Bowdoin College (Maine), where he graduated in 1826. The following March, 1827, he established the first black newspaper, *Freedom's Journal,* together with the writer Samuel Cornish. The antislavery societies used the columns of this paper as a forum, and the editor became a staunch advocate of immediate emancipation.

At first, the editors directed their paper toward a program of abolition, of equal rights for blacks in America. But within a short time, Russwurm, in the pages of *Freedom's Journal,* published an article that praised the work of Paul Cuffee, the colonizationist who had taken 38 Negroes to Sierra Leone. This article destroyed Russwurm's influence among the various groups of free Negroes in the North. Furthermore, he himself finally believed that it was hopeless "to talk of ever enjoying citizenship in this country." Subsequently joining the colonizationists, he went to Liberia, where he served creditably as superintendent of schools and as governor of the Maryland Province before it became a part of Liberia.

JOHN B. RUSSWURM

Samory
Ruler of the Wassulu Empire

Samory (*c.* 1837–1900), in eight years of conquest, established the powerful Wassulu Empire in Western Africa in the latter half of the 19th century. Adopting the Islamic faith, he took the title of Almany, or Anthanty from God. To win the respect of his subjects, he promoted a program of religious reform by teaching the principles of the Koran. He made Islam the state religion and had mosques built in each city. Further, to ensure the entrenchment of the faith, Samory had the chiefs' sons master the principles of the religion at the mosque schools.

His financial policy, a rather simple one, was not much of a burden on the people. Each village cultivated a field for the ruler, who also collected one-tenth of the empire's gold yield.

The well-organized army was maintained by the king's revenues. The guard of Samory consisted of about 500 young men chosen for their intelligence and physical superiority. With this army equipped with rapid-firing weapons, Samory withstood the French for a generation. At one time the French, fearing that Samory would bottle them up in the Bkoy Valley, maneuvered and cut him off

SAMORY

from his base of supplies. In 1898, Samory tried to commit suicide rather than surrender to the French; but, being unsuccessful, he was exiled to Gabon, where he died two years later.

Sampson, James Drawborn
Carpenter and Educator

James Drawborn Sampson (1801–?), son and slave of a rich planter of Sampson County, North Carolina, was freed by his father and established as a carpenter in Wilmington, North Carolina. Under the sponsorship of his white father, James trained other slave boys apprenticed to the carpentry trade and treated them with integrity until they developed sufficient skill to be set free. Even though the law forbade training slaves to read and write, Sampson instructed the apprentices in these rudiments, as well as in religion.

As a free man of color, Sampson was so well liked that he was permitted to possess a gun for hunting and was allowed to preach before slave audiences. Marrying a free woman, Minerva Kellogg, he imported a teacher from Massachusetts to educate their 10 children, as well as the apprentices. Two of his daughters became teachers; two, dressmakers. The sons were sent to Northern cities for further training: Benjamin Sampson went to Oberlin College and became a teacher at Wilberforce University; John was educated in Boston and became a prominent minister.

The unpretentious little school which Sampson established on his property became one of the first schools for Negroes in North Carolina. Other free Negro children were permitted to attend, as well as a few slave children whom Sampson unobtrusively brought in. However, when the authorities discovered the school for "free Negroes," they immediately closed it.

James Sampson, dying near the close of the Civil War, had accumulated a fortune through his carpentry business. However, in the upheaval of the War, the sons who were in the North were prohibited from returning to Wilmington. Ruthlessly, the whites persecuted the remainder of the family in Wilmington by confiscating their property and sending the sons threats decorated with skulls and crossbones, so that they would not return. Mrs. Sampson and the daughters were also threatened, but their lives were spared.

After the War, one of the daughters, Franconia, taught school in Robeson County, where she gave many future notables their start. Among them were the Spauldings, Arthur Moore and George H. White. Moving to Washington, D.C., Susie taught in the new schools of the District, but later returned to Greensboro as the wife of James B. Dudley, president of the Agricultural and Technical College.

Scarborough, William Saunders
Linguist and Educator

William Saunders Scarborough (1852–1926), the first Negro classical scholar of note, was born a slave in Macon, Georgia, but achieved eminence as a scholar and linguist. He learned to read and write at the age of six and, during the Civil War, forged passes for his fellow slaves. His father was a freedman who had declined an offer of as much as $3,000 to leave the South, in order to remain with his enslaved family. Young William studied music at the age of 12 and graduated from the Lewis High School at the age of 15. He studied at Atlanta University and Oberlin College, graduated in 1875 and earned his M.A. degree in 1878. He was awarded the LL.D. degree from Liberia College (Africa) in 1882.

Gifted and proficient in languages, Scarborough taught Latin, Greek and mathematics at Lewis High School. In 1877, he became professor of Greek at Wilberforce University. In 1881, he wrote a Greek textbook, and in 1886, he published *Birds of Aristophanes*. Besides being expert in Latin and Greek, he was also proficient in Hebrew, Sanskrit and the Slavic languages. He was elected to the American Philological Association in 1882, the American Spelling Reform Association in 1883, the Modern Language Association in 1884 and the American Social Science Association in 1885. In 1908, he was elected president of Wilberforce University. He was an ordained African Methodist Episcopal minister, a gifted lecturer and an able college administrator. He retired in 1920, at the age of 68.

WILLIAM SAUNDERS SCARBOROUGH

Séjour, Victor
Dramatist

Victor Séjour (1817–1874), dramatist, was christened Juan Victor Séjour Marcon et Ferrand. He was born in New Orleans, Louisiana, the son of François Marcon, a Negro from Santo Domingo, and Eloisa Phillipe Ferrand, a quadroon. His father owned a dry-cleaning establishment on Charles Street in New Orleans. Victor was educated at the Saint Barbe Academy, which was conducted by Michel Seligny, an intelligent colored man. At the age of 17, Victor read one of his original poems in French before La Société des Artisans, a social and benevolent organization of Creoles. His family sent him to Paris to continue his formal education. He made his debut as an author in 1841 with the publication of his heroic poem, "Le Retour de Napoléon."

Being a writer, he was accepted in the literary circles of Paris, where he became acquainted with Alexandre Dumas and Emile Augier. Because of these friendships, he became intrigued with drama. His first stage play, *Diegarias,* was produced in 1844 at the Théâtre Français and was followed in 1849 by *La Chute de Sejan*. His greatest plays were *Richard III* (1852); *Les Noces Véni-tiennes* (1855); *Le Fils de la Nuit* (1856); *Les Grands Vassaux* (1859); *Les Fils de Charles Quint* (1864); and *Les Volontaires de 1814* (1862), which is his only work based on an American theme. His works were noted for the grandiose verse, the sump-tuous costuming and spectacular settings—all of which were popular in Paris during the mid-19th century. When the popular taste changed, his works were no longer in demand, and his last two plays, *Cromwell* and *Le Vam-pire,* were never fully accepted. He died in a charity ward of a Paris hospital.

Settle, Josiah T.

Reconstructionist

Josiah T. Settle (1850–?), Republican elector-at-large from Mississippi, was born a slave. When given their freedom before the Civil War, his family resettled in Hamil-ton, Ohio. Since only mixed schools existed in this community, Negro children suffered from discrimination by both teachers and pupils. However, one teacher took an inter-est in the lonely Josiah, encouraged him with her friendship and kindness, and in-spired him to continue his education at Oberlin College in 1868. He gained recog-nition there as an orator and was selected to represent his class in the various contests of the college. Even though lack of funds forced him to withdraw after the first year, he refused to give up his goal.

He continued his education at a school organized by the Freedmen's Bureau in Washington, D.C. He entered Howard Uni-versity and graduated in its first class in 1872. To defray his college expenses, he had various jobs, such as teaching in the high school and serving as a clerk for the Freedmen's Bureau. After graduation, he entered the law school of Howard University and participated in local politics.

JOSIAH T. SETTLE

Upon receiving his law degree, he was admitted to the bar of the District and to the Supreme Court, but he did not wish to remain in Washington. The lure of the Reconstruc-tion politics in his native state prompted him to establish his law office in Sardis, Missis-sippi. Entering politics there, he was unani-mously nominated by the Republican con-vention to serve as district attorney in the 12th judicial district.

In the political upheaval of 1875, when the Republicans lost control in Mississippi, the brilliant young politician was caught up in the circumstances. He remained active in the party, however, attending the national con-ventions in 1876 and 1880, and serving as Republican elector-at-large for the state on the Hayes-Wheeler and the Garfield-Arthur tickets. In 1883, Settle ran as an indepen-dent for a seat in the Mississippi legisla-ture. He won the election by more than 1,200 votes, defeating both the Democratic and Republican candidates.

By 1885, the reaction against Negroes forced Settle to give up politics and leave the state. He settled in Memphis, Tennessee, and concentrated on his law practice. Within two months, he was appointed assistant attorney general of the criminal court of Shelby County. He developed a lucrative law practice which he maintained for a number of years.

Simpson, William H.

Artist

William H. Simpson (1830–1872), early portrait painter, was born in Buffalo, New York. In school, instead of paying attention to the teacher or working his arithmetic problems, Simpson was constantly drawing and sketching. After a piecemeal formal education, he became an errand boy for Matthew Wilson, a local artist who recognized the boy's talent and proceeded to train him. Both Wilson and Simpson moved to Boston in 1854, where the young artist developed into a popular portrait painter.

Simpson's portraits of Charles Sumner and John L. Hilton are rich in color and depth of feeling. He was especially gifted at painting children and family groups. Many of his paintings became scattered throughout New England, Canada and California. It appears that Wilson's teaching was based on the techniques of the European Old Masters, as Simpson's style reflected the influences of Titian, Murillo and Raphael.

This early painter of Negro descent showed unusual talent that was equal to any other of his day and time in America.

Singleton, Benjamin "Pap"

Colonizationist

Benjamin "Pap" Singleton (1809–1892), post-Civil War colonizationist, was born a slave in Tennessee. He escaped, however, and lived in Canada until after the Emancipation Proclamation. He was an unlettered mulatto who advocated separate racial communities because he believed that the Negro could only rise in an environment where there was no white competition. With these views, "Pap" Singleton, returning to the South after the War, and led the movement for the migration and colonization of Negroes from the cotton states to Kansas.

In the turbulent years following the Civil War, when the Ku Klux Klan destroyed the newly gained political rights of the Negroes, and as others exploited Negroes economically, Singleton traveled in the South, advertising Kansas as a haven of refuge. Tens of thousands of Negroes moved into Kansas and Missouri. With about 300 Negroes, he founded the town of Singleton's Colony in 1873, in Cherokee County, Missouri. Within 20 months, more than 19,000 Negroes moved into Kansas. The great exodus from the South halted in 1881, when a congressional committee investigated the movement. During the hearings, Singleton testified that he had been instrumental in starting the exodus.

Singleton, a carpenter by trade, could barely read, but he was a persuasive talker and a skilled promoter. Educated Negroes opposed his colonization schemes; and he, in turn, was hostile to them.

Smalls, Robert

Naval Hero and United States Congressman

Robert Smalls (1839–1915), a Reconstructionist, was born a slave in Beaufort, South Carolina. By secret self-instruction, he learned to read and write. In 1851, to learn the skills of a seaman, he worked as a rigger in Charleston. During the War, he was assigned to a Confederate transport, the *Planter,* which was stationed in the Charleston harbor. In the spring of 1862, Smalls smuggled his family on board the ship while

ROBERT SMALLS

the Confederate officers were ashore. At dawn, he raised the Confederate flag and sailed into the open sea toward the vessels of the Union Navy that were maintaining the blockade of Charleston. Upon being discovered by United States naval officials, he immediately surrendered the *Planter*.

This daring escape brought Smalls into national prominence. He was granted a sizeable sum of money for his contraband and was appointed a pilot in the United States Navy. Later in the War, he was promoted to captain for saving one of the Union vessels.

During Reconstruction, Smalls returned to South Carolina and was elected a member of the constitutional convention. He served in the state government in both the house and the senate and was elected to the United States House of Representatives, serving five terms.

In spite of his lack of formal education, Smalls enjoyed a fine reputation; he was intelligent, moderate and even-tempered. When

home rule was re-established in South Carolina, Smalls and the Republican Party furiously fought the rising tide of Negro disfranchisement in the constitutional convention of 1895.

Smith, James McCune
Physician and Abolitionist

James McCune Smith (1813–1865), a dignified and highly trained physician, was educated at the University of Glasgow (Scotland), where he received the A.B., M.A. and M.D. degrees. His mother was self-emancipated; his father was freed by a New York law passed in 1827. A successful physician and the proprietor of two drugstores in New York City, Dr. Smith became well known for his pioneering work in the scientific study of race and for his scholarly treatment of the slavery question. He was a prolific writer on the subject of racial equality and an able speaker who fought against the deportation of the

JAMES McCUNE SMITH

Negro. With the skills of a scholar and a knowledge of history, the sciences, languages and literature, he wrote on a remarkable range of subjects concerning the Negro. By his essays and articles, he sought to change attitudes toward the Negro and to direct sober thought to the question of the physical and moral equality of Negro and white.

Dr. Smith was a member of the Committee of Free Colored Citizens that sent a petition to the United States Senate in 1844. This document, which contained facts about the social conditions of Negroes in eleven states of the North, was a scientific protest against derogatory remarks about Negroes that Secretary of State John C. Calhoun had made to the British minister to the United States.

Smythe, John Henry

Minister to Liberia

John Henry Smythe (1844–1908), United States minister to Liberia, was born the son of a slave father and a free mother in Richmond, Virginia. Although his mother purchased the freedom of his father, she could not free him because the laws of Virginia prohibited it; she willed the elder Smythe to their son John. The family moved to Philadelphia, where John attended the Institute for Colored Youth and was the first Negro student to attend the Pennsylvania Academy of Fine Arts. He worked as a clerk in a Federal bureau in Washington in order to attend the Howard University Law School. Upon his graduation, he was made cashier of the Wilmington, Delaware, branch of the Freedman's Bank. After the bank failed, he opened his law office and became active in the Republican Party.

In the controversial election of 1876, Smythe exerted all of his efforts in behalf of the Hayes ticket and was rewarded with a diplomatic appointment to Liberia. He was reappointed by President Chester A. Arthur

JOHN HENRY SMYTHE

in 1882. In Liberia, he also served as representative of several European governments. His official summaries on conditions in Liberia are perhaps the most comprehensive of the period. After his return to the United States in 1886, he resumed his law practice in Washington, D.C.

Sousa, João da Cruze

Brazilian Poet

João da Cruze Sousa (1862–1898), a distinguished poet of the Symbolist movement in Brazil, was born in Florianopolis in the state of Santa Catarina. The intellectuals and literary figures in the Symbolist movement protested the coldness of the Parnassian school in Europe by reflecting in their works a spiritual reaction to life. In tones of grief and discontent, Sousa expressed the despair, humiliation and isolation which he suffered because he was a Negro. He rejected the Darwinian theory of social evolution, which was interpreted as signifying the racial inferiority of the African peoples.

He published two volumes during his lifetime: his first volume, *Missal,* was a combination of prose and poetry; *Broqueis,* the second work, contained highly emotional poems. The three volumes published after his death, *Farōis, Evocaço* and *Ultimos Sonetos,* are a monument to his character and talent.

Still, William
Director of the Underground Railroad

William Still (1821–1902), secretary of the Pennsylvania Society for the Abolition of Slavery, aided 649 slaves to freedom and documented the activities of the society in a book entitled *The Underground Railroad* (1872). William was the youngest of 18 children of an ex-slave father and a fugitive slave mother. His mother escaped from Maryland to join her husband in New Jersey, where William was born. Still learned to hate slavery because of the hardships it wrought upon his parents. In 1844, he moved to Philadelphia, where he taught himself to read and write. A small group of white abolitionists welcomed him because they needed someone who knew the Negro community. Within three years, the society elected him chairman. As director of the Underground Railroad, he kept meticulous records of the fugitives so that relatives and friends might locate them.

One of the most dramatic episodes of a slave's escape which he recorded is the story of Henry "Box" Brown. The name "Box" was given to Brown because he was sealed in a box containing biscuits and water by a sympathetic merchant in Richmond, Virginia, and shipped to Still in Philadelphia. After a rugged, two-day journey by steamboat, wagon and rail, Brown arrived, unharmed by the ordeal.

Energetic and vigorous, Still participated in many activities to aid his people. He helped to organize and finance a society to collect information on Negro life and was responsible for the establishment in Philadelphia of an orphanage for fatherless children of colored soldiers and sailors. Interested in the welfare of Negro youth, he was inspired to organize a Young Men's Christian Association for Negroes.

WILLIAM STILL

Talbert, Mary Burnett
Worker for Civil Rights and the Red Cross

Mary Burnett Talbert (1886–1923), patriotic worker during World War I and a Red Cross nurse with the American expeditionary forces in France, was born and educated in Oberlin, Ohio. She received her Bachelor's degree from Oberlin College at the age of 19 and earned her Ph.D. from the University of Buffalo. When the United States entered World War I in 1917, Mrs. Talbert assisted

MARY BURNETT TALBERT

As president of the Frederick Douglass Memorial Association, Mary Burnett Talbert was responsible for the restoration of the Frederick Douglass Home at Anacostia in 1922. She also served as a delegate to the International Council of Women in Christiania, Norway, in 1920. She traveled throughout Europe, lecturing on race relations and woman's rights.

Tanner, Henry Ossawa

Artist

Henry Ossawa Tanner (1859–1937), noted painter, was born in Pittsburgh, Pennsylvania. Son of A.M.E. Church Bishop Benjamin Tucker Tanner, he was des-

in the war loan drives, personally soliciting the purchase of thousands of dollars' worth of Liberty Bonds. Further heeding the call to serve her country, she enlisted as a Red Cross nurse and saw active service in France. Returning home at the close of the war, she found that the idealistic slogan of fighting to make the world safe for democracy was false for the American Negro.

As president of the Colored National Association of Women's Clubs from 1916 to 1920 and as vice-president and a director of the National Association for the Advancement of Colored People, Mrs. Talbert joined the struggle for first-class citizenship for Negroes. As chairman of the Anti-Lynching Committee, she launched a crusade for passage of the Dyer Anti-Lynching Bill. She traveled thousands of miles throughout the United States, speaking to mixed audiences to gain support for the bill.

HENRY OSSAWA TANNER

tined, because of family wishes, to study theology to maintain the ministerial tradition in the family. The young man preferred art, but received little encouragement from his family. He managed to enter the Pennsylvania Academy of Fine Arts, where he studied under Thomas Eakins and William Chase. After graduation, he wanted to study in Europe; instead, his family sent him to Atlanta, where one of his brothers was pastor of a prominent church. He tried to earn a living by teaching art at Clark University and by selling his paintings and photographs. He made the acquaintance of Bishop Hartzell, who arranged an exhibit of Tanner's work in Cincinnati with the hope of selling enough paintings to finance the young artist's trip to Europe. Since no one purchased the paintings, Bishop Hartzell bought the entire collection and canvassed friends to raise enough money to make it possible for Tanner to study in Paris.

In 1892, Henry Tanner became a student at the Académie Julian, where he studied under Paul Laurens and Benjamin Constant. After four years of study, he attracted attention with his "Music Lesson" and his "Young Sabot-Maker"; he also became well known for his interest in peasant types and, later, Biblical subjects. In 1897, his dramatic painting "The Resurrection of Lazarus" won him recognition as an artist of great ability, and the French government purchased the work for the Luxembourg Gallery. Earlier, Tanner had visited Palestine, with financial help from Rodman Wanamaker; the outcome of this visit was the great Biblical series that earned him fame and fortune.

There followed "Christ on the Road to Bethany," "Christ at the Home of Mary and Martha," "The Return of the Holy Women," "Christ and Nicodemus on the Housetop," "The Five Virgins," "The Annunciation" and many others. These paintings are in prominent American museums. Tanner received the Lippincott Prize of 1900, the silver medal of the Paris Exposition, the gold medal at the San Francisco Exposition and the French Legion of Honor. He was recognized as exhibiting the technique of a master of the art of painting.

America was a lucrative market for his works, but, because the sensitive artist resented publicity which emphasized his race instead of his talent, he remained in Paris until his death.

Tolton, Augustus

Catholic Priest

Augustus Tolton (1834–1897), first Negro to be ordained in the Catholic priesthood, was born in Ralls County, Missouri. As a fugitive slave, his mother took him to Quincy,

AUGUSTUS TOLTON

Illinois, where the child was reared in the Catholic faith. In order to survive, he worked in a tobacco factory at an early age. When he attended Mass and confession at St. Boniface's parish, the priests not only noted his devotion and piety but also quickly recognized his intelligence and native talents. He was encouraged to study by the local clergy, and when he made the decision to enter the priesthood, they obtained his admission to a seminary in Rome in 1880.

He mastered the languages rapidly; and upon meeting the requirements in theology in 1886, he entered the priesthood on April 24 of that year. When the young priest returned to America, he was assigned to a small parish in Quincy, Illinois: St. Joseph's Catholic Church for Negroes. A wealthy Catholic contributed $10,000 in 1889, for the erection of St. Monica's Church for Negroes, in a heavily populated area of Chicago. Father Tolton served as its pastor until his death.

SOJOURNER TRUTH

Truth, Sojourner
Civil War Heroine and Abolitionist

Sojourner Truth (1797–1883), one of the most notable and unusual antislavery speakers, was born Isabella, a slave, in Hurley, Ulster County, New York. Although she was illiterate, she possessed a keen insight into men and their motives and seemed to have an endless storehouse of wit and wisdom. One of 12 children, she was owned by a succession of masters in New York State. She was the mother of five children, but was separated from her husband before slavery was outlawed in the state in 1827. At that time, she was owned by John J. Dumont, who wanted to retain her services for another year, but she left early one morning with her youngest child, Peter. After walking for miles, she stopped at the home of Isaac S. Van Wagener, who gave her shelter and agreed to pay Dumont for her services. Over

a year later, she went to New York City, where she was employed by a religious fanatic named Pierson. She became deeply engrossed in the activities of Pierson's cult, only to be disillusioned by the group later.

One morning, she announced to her employer that she was leaving and that her name was no longer Isabella, but Sojourner. In June 1843, beginning her pilgrimage, she said that "the Lord gave me *Truth,* because I was to declare the truth to the people." Likely to appear anywhere, at any time, she spoke whenever the spirit moved her or an opportunity was available.

On an occasion when Frederick Douglass was the main speaker at Faneuil Hall in Boston, he said that the Negro could not find justice in America; his salvation lay in his own right arm. Sojourner, rising, asked,

"Frederick, is God dead?" The pessimistic tone of the meeting changed to optimism and assurance. At the second National Woman Suffrage Convention, held in Akron, Ohio, in 1852, Sojourner saved the convention when she challenged the extensive praise given to the male intellect by the visiting ministers. The women officers had been hesitant about permitting her to speak because they did not want to confuse their cause with that of the abolitionists, but Sojourner used an awkward situation to win a splendid victory for the cause of woman suffrage.

During the Civil War, she helped to care for the wounded soldiers and the newly emancipated slaves. When President Lincoln gave her an audience, she urged him to call to arms the free Negroes of the North to fight for the Union. She urged the freedmen to develop land ownership and to obtain an education. She advocated rehabilitating former slaves on the public lands of the West.

Crippled and old, she retired to a little home, acquired with the aid of friends, in Battle Creek, Michigan, where she died.

Tubman, Harriet
Conductor on the Underground Railroad

Harriet Tubman (*c.* 1820–1913), daring woman conductor on the Underground Railroad, escaped from slavery and then dared to return to her former master's plantation to help others escape to freedom. One of 11 children, she was born in Dorchester County, Maryland. In 1857, at great personal risk, she helped three of her brothers and sisters escape from slavery. Later, she liberated her mother and father.

Harriet's early life on the slave-breeding plantation in Maryland was a typical one, with the exception of an incident which made her incapable of being a "breeder." As a young girl, when she had been hired out as a

HARRIET TUBMAN

fieldhand, she received a severe blow on the head from a weight that had been thrown at another slave by an enraged overseer. The damage from the blow caused her to suffer from "sleeping seizures."

Around 1844, she married a free Negro named John Tubman, but she remained a slave. When the master of her plantation died in 1849, the rumor spread among the slaves that they were to be sold in the Deep South. Harriet and two of her brothers decided to escape. Always in dread of recapture, the brothers returned, but Harriet fixed her gaze on the North Star as guide. With sheer determination, walking by night and hiding by day, she finally arrived in Philadelphia.

Two years later, she returned to Maryland for her husband, but he had married another woman. This disappointing news gave her increased determination to help others to escape bondage. She had already rescued a sister and a brother in December 1850, and in December 1851, she had successfully led a party of 11 into Canada. By now, Harriet had developed the hard and dauntless characteristics of a "trail boss." If the fugitive became faint-hearted and wanted to return, she did not hesitate to level her pistol at the victim, saying, "You go on or die." Her reputation as a conductor on the Underground Railroad is best expressed in her own words: ". . . I nebber run my train off de track and I nebber los' a passenger."

It was in 1857 that she brought her aged parents to freedom and settled them in Auburn, New York, where she had purchased a modest home from William H. Seward. The antislavery workers of New England and New York helped her raise the funds for the home, which she turned into a home for elderly Negroes after the War. She remarried, and some authorities speak of her as Harriet Tubman Davis.

William H. Seward tried to get her a government pension from Congress for her heroic and dauntless courage in the cause of freedom. A tablet commemorating her work was unveiled in Auburn on June 12, 1914, by the Cayuga County Historical Association. Harriet Tubman trusted in God on her many journeys into and out of the South. Prayer was her constant companion and consolation whenever she was in danger.

Turner, Benjamin Sterling
United States Congressman

Benjamin S. Turner (1825–1894), member from Alabama of the House of Representatives in the 42nd Congress, was born a slave in Halifax, North Carolina. His master moved his establishment to Alabama in 1830, and the boy obtained a passable education by studying secretly. After the War, Turner, developing a prosperous business in Dallas County, was elected tax collector of the area in 1867. He became a

BENJAMIN STERLING TURNER

responsible citizen and leader through service on many local committees. He was elected a member of the Selma city council in 1869.

Nominated by the Republican Party for the 42nd Congress in 1870, Turner was elected; but he failed to be re-elected to the 43rd Congress. The division in the power structure of the Republican Party in Alabama at this time forced most of the Negro politicians into retirement. After his defeat, Turner confined himself to his business and to local affairs.

Turner, Henry MacNeal
Bishop and Colonizationist

Henry MacNeal Turner (1833–1915), bishop of the African Methodist Episcopal Church and colonizationist, was born free in Abbeville, South Carolina, of European and royal African ancestry. Following his father's death, he was hired out at the age of 12 to work in the fields with slaves. First learning

HENRY MAC NEAL TURNER

the alphabet from a white playmate, Turner mastered the art of reading with the aid of a speller, a Bible and a hymnal.

He ran away at 15 and became a messenger boy to an attorney. Surrounded by books, magazines and intelligent men, Turner absorbed as much education as possible. In Baltimore, he worked as a handyman at a medical school, where he had access to books on medicine, law and theology. Later, the eager pupil was tutored by an Episcopal bishop. Turning to the church, he became an African Methodist Episcopal minister and was appointed by President Lincoln as chaplain to a Negro regiment during the Civil War.

While working with the Freedmen's Bureau in Georgia, he became an active leader in the Republican Party. He defended the rights of Negroes when the legislature in 1868 attempted to bar them from holding state offices. From these experiences in Georgia, Turner, concluding that "the Negro had no manhood future in the United States," became

a colonizationist. He was one of the sponsors of the ill-fated expedition of 206 colonists to Liberia in 1878. In spite of this disastrous venture, Bishop Turner continued his support of colonization until 1895.

Bishop Turner received an honorary degree from the University of Pennsylvania; he compiled a catechism and a hymnal while serving as the manager of the A.M.E. publishing house. He was chancellor of Morris Brown University in Atlanta, Georgia, and founded several denominational periodicals.

Turner, James Milton

Educator and Diplomat

James Milton Turner (1840–1915), founder of Lincoln University in Missouri, was born a slave in St. Louis County, Missouri. He received his freedom at the age of four, when his father purchased him for $50. As a child he was apt in learning, and at 14, he enrolled in the preparatory department of Oberlin College. During the Civil War, he served as a Northern officer's valet. Returning to Missouri after the War, he took advantage of the new state constitution, adopted in 1866, and advocated educational facilities for Negroes. He urged the people of the state to provide adequate schools as rapidly as possible. In the meantime, Turner became one of the first Negro teachers to be hired in Missouri.

To establish an educational institution for Negroes, Turner helped the state board secure the funds by personally soliciting contributions. It was by his determined efforts that Lincoln University in Missouri was founded. During the Reconstruction period, he was immediately considered a leader and was drawn into the sphere of politics. After the Missouri politicians bolted from the radicals and formed the Liberal Republicans, President Grant and the radicals found it expedient to offer as many political plums as

JAMES MILTON TURNER

possible to the Negroes of Missouri to keep them in the party. Hence, in 1871, James Turner was appointed minister resident and consul general at Monrovia, Liberia. He served from July 1871 to May 1878, the turbulent years of native uprisings and frequent changes in the governmental administration. His experiences in Liberia caused him to take a firm stand against any future movements in America to place American Negroes in the equatorial regions of Africa. Seeing the conditions of the native tribes of Africa, he urged American philanthropists to help them.

Upon his return to America, Turner took up the cause of the American Indian and, in 1886, urged President Cleveland to press Congress into appropriating $75,000 for the claims of Cherokee freedmen.

Turner, Nat

Insurrectionist

Nat Turner (1800–1831) believed that he was chosen by God to lead his people out of bondage. By wearing a cloak of religious fervor, he was successful in executing his plot to revolt in 1831. He was born in Virginia, the son of African-born slaves. His father escaped and returned to Africa, and his mother, hating enslavement, attempted to murder her infant. He received some education as a boy, but this was interrupted several times because he was sold and resold by his masters.

As an adult in Southampton County, Virginia, he was looked to by his fellow slaves for advice and direction. His mysticism brought him awe and respect as he quoted his theory of revolt from the Scriptures. In 1831, Nat Turner, concluding that the day of judgment was at hand for slaveowners, chose to strike on August 21. At ten o'clock, Turner and his followers murdered the entire Joseph Travis family and then moved from plantation to plantation in Southampton County, killing 51 whites within 36 hours.

When the slaves' revolt became known, more than 3,000 whites came to the county to put down the insurrection. A massacre of Negroes by the enraged whites followed, but Turner eluded capture by hiding out in the neighborhood for almost two months. Turner and 52 followers were finally caught, and 17, including Turner, were hanged; 12 slaves were convicted and sent out of the state; and 24 insurrectionists were acquitted.

The Turner insurrection terrorized the slaveholding states of the South and led to the passage of the restrictive Black Codes, which were intended to prevent slaves from attempting other revolts.

Tyler, Mansfield

State Legislator

Mansfield Tyler (1829–1904), minister and a member of the Alabama house of representatives during the Reconstruction era, was born a slave near Augusta, Georgia. At the age of 18, he was taken from Augusta by his master to Alabama, where he was reared by the Reverend Jacob Walker, a Baptist preacher who converted Tyler in 1855. Shortly after his conversion, Tyler began to preach, even though it was against the law for slaves to hold religious meetings without the presence of a white person. Before emancipation, he was blocked by many obstacles in his effort to function as a preacher.

He had learned the rudiments of reading, and at the close of the Civil War, he moved to Loundesboro, Alabama, where he immediately organized a church. Ordained a minister in 1868, he helped to organize the Alabama Colored Baptist State Convention in Montgomery. As a charter member of the organization, he was influential in establishing a Baptist training center in 1878. It later became Selma University, and in 1890, conferred the degree of Doctor of Divinity upon Tyler.

Participating in the political affairs of the county, Tyler ran for the Alabama house of representatives from Loundes County, and serving from 1870 to 1872, he supported the establishment of the free public school system and the adoption of civil rights and Reconstruction legislation.

Valdés, Gabriel de la Concepción ("Plácido")

Cuban Poet

Gabriel de la Concepción Valdés (1809–1844), Cuban poet of liberation, was abandoned at birth by his Spanish mother but was later adopted by his mulatto father, D. F. Matoso. Valdés grew up in Mantanzas, Cuba, where the Spanish authorities were fearful of the spread of the Haitian revolution. As a child, he suffered because he bore the taint of illegitimacy and knew the frustrations of being free, but a mulatto. Valdés was envied by the blacks because he was free and spurned by the whites because of his mixed ancestry.

When he was 14, Valdés was sent to work in a printing office, but, because he received no pay, his father apprenticed him to a comb-trader. In this trade, he developed an artistic skill for making tortoise-shell combs and portrait frames. Despite a limited elementary school training, he developed a love for literature, supplementing his lack of formal education by reading avidly the works of many great authors.

His interest in literature continued to develop, aided by his selling subscriptions for new books during his spare time. This activity brought him into contact with writers and literary critics. At the age of 11, he experimented with expressing in verse his pent-up emotions. When he was 16, he began writing seriously, using the pseudonym "Plácido." His works appeared in the periodicals of the major cities of Cuba and South America.

The sensitive young poet fell in love with a beautiful slave girl in 1831. They met secretly and planned their marriage, but Fela died, victim of a cholera epidemic. Her death was a great shock to the young poet, and he turned to his poetry to express his suffering. His poems to Fela represent his deepest and most beautiful love poetry. The year after Fela's death, he entered a contest in honor of Martinez de la Rosa, prime minister of Spain. At the contest banquet, he recited from his "La Siempreviva" ("The Evergreens"), and won the coveted prize. His success grew rapidly, and Plácido found himself in great demand as a writer of extemporaneous and festive verse.

His great popularity as a writer, however,

made the authorities suspicious of him. In the turbulent years of 1840–1843, the captain-general of Havana feared a changed attitude among the Negroes of Cuba. Captain O'Donnell regarded all writers as agitators and all intelligent Negroes as dangerous. Plácido was arrested, released, kept under surveillance and finally charged with being the leader of a movement to revolt among the Negroes. At his trial, he was accused of being the author of a poem called "My Oath." Along with 11 others, he was sentenced to die before a firing squad.

During the 12 days before the execution, Plácido wrote four of the most beautiful poems in Cuban literature: "Despedida a Mi Madre" ("Farewell to My Mother"), "A la Fatalidad," "Adios a Mi Lira" and "Plegaria a Dios." The last poem, "Prayer to God," written the night before his execution, is described as one of the most eloquent prayers in world literature. In a clear decisive voice, Plácido recited the prayer as he faced the firing squad. The poet died for the cause of Cuban liberty—not merely for Negro freedom from slavery, but more to protest the tyranny of the Spanish rulers.

Valdés, José Manuel

Peruvian Surgeon and Poet

José Manuel Valdés, Peruvian poet, philosopher, physician and Latinist, was born of a Negro slave mother and a free Indian, Baltazar Valdés. The child was destined to suffer the social restrictions of the 18th-century sanctioning of slavery by the Christian Church, even though the humanizing flames of the French Revolution had ignited the hope of many Peruvians that slavery would be abolished and all individuals would be treated as equals. The Spanish pharmacist who owned Valdés' mother supervised and trained the child, who showed evidence of unusual ability. Because he had

acquired a high school education from the Order of St. Augustine in Lima, the boy hoped for a university career; but he was shocked and frustrated to learn that, as a mulatto, he should not have expected such a privilege.

In his disappointment, he turned to the Church for solace and for acceptance into the priesthood, but the beloved priests who had taught him were bound by the Royal Order of 1765 not to accept a Negro as a priest. Desiring to utilize his fine liberal arts training, he turned his attention to medicine. Valdés entered the San Andrés Hospital, where he studied under Cosme Bueno and Hipolito Unanue. Finding a new outlet, he worked hard to prepare himself for a medical career. Even after he received his degree of "Latin Surgeon," he continued to study, to observe and to experiment. Having dexterous and sensitive fingers for surgery, he was granted the right to practice medicine by the Proto-Médico. In the 15 years of his practice, he became famous, and prosperous enough to buy the most expensive books and surgical instruments from Europe.

Writing medical treatises, Valdés shocked the scientific scholars of Peru when he published an article against the prevailing theory that uterine cancer was contagious. When his theory was substantiated by European physicians, Valdés was accepted in the university, where he received his Bachelor's degree; later, he received his doctorate after the requirements were waived. Four years later, he joined the university as examiner in surgery and professor of clinical medicine and was elected to membership in the Royal Medical Academy of Madrid for his treatise on the use of a drug for treatment of children's convulsions.

In spite of the great success of his medical career, Valdés was taunted by insults about his color, and, unfortunately, he never married. In his frustration, he turned to the

Church again. The Pope granted a special dispensation for his color so that he might take Holy Orders, but the local priests refused to accept him.

Rejected, he began to write poetry as an outlet for his suffering. When news of the liberation of Latin America by Bolívar and San Martín reached Peru, he wrote stirring odes to the liberators, inspired by his reading of the French philosophers. He became identified with the revolutionary forces, and after the establishment of the Republic of Peru, he was honored as a citizen and sent to the congress as a deputy from Lima. Many honors and much recognition came to him: he was the first official physician of Lima and director of the Independence Medical College. This famous Peruvian at last became an integral part of the social, political and national life of the republic.

Vesey, Denmark

Insurrectionist

Denmark Vesey (1767–1822), antislavery insurrectionist, organized an unsuccessful slave revolt in Charleston, South Carolina, in 1822; he and 34 other Negro conspirators were hanged. Télémaque (his real name) was born on the island of Hispaniola. He was purchased by a Charleston slave agent, Captain Vesey, who traded between the islands of St. Thomas and Hispaniola. In 1800, Denmark purchased his freedom with money won in a lottery and settled in Charleston as a carpenter. As a lay reader in the newly organized African Methodist Episcopal Church, he was able to speak to large numbers of Negroes without being questioned by the white plantation owners. His deep-seated hatred for slavery inspired him to spread dissatisfaction and revolt among the slaves. Toussaint L'Ouverture's revolt in the islands deeply impressed him and became his pattern for a detailed, well-organized plot.

For five years, he organized and planned, hoping to ensure the success of his revolt.

His chief assistant, Peter Poyas, a ship's carpenter, was placed in charge of recruiting slaves and organizing them into cell units in which only the leaders were trusted with the details of the plot. Weapons were made and stored; wigs and false beards were made. The cell leaders recruited approximately 9,000 slaves over a radius of about 100 miles around Charleston. The date for the revolt was set for mid-July of 1822, but two weeks before, the insurrectionists were betrayed by a house servant. The whites of the city rounded up hundreds of blacks and eventually forced one of the slaves to reveal the names of some of the leaders. Vesey and 36 of his men were hanged; the second informer was also hanged. Vesey and Peter Poyas refused to betray their followers; they admonished the others to die as they did, with sealed lips.

Walker, David

Abolitionist and Author

David Walker (1785–1830), author of the radical book *Walker's Appeal,* was born in Wilmington, North Carolina, of a free mother and a slave father, which entitled him to freedom. By 1827, he lived in Boston, where he operated a second-hand clothing store. He read extensively on revolutions and resistance to oppression. The first edition of *David Walker's Appeal; . . . with a Preamble to the Colored Citizens of the World, but in Particular, and Very Expressly, to Those of the United States of America,* was published in 1829. Following the publication of the third edition, in 1830, the author died under mysterious circumstances.

He admonished the enslaved of America: ". . . it is no more harm for you to kill the man who is trying to kill you, than it is for you to take a drink of water." This bold and radical proclamation, by a Negro writer against slavery, confounded both the North and the South. Abolitionist leaders rejected the appeal to violence, while the South considered its circulation a capital offense. When the officials of Massachusetts refused to suppress the publication of the book, a reward amounting to $10,000 was offered for the deliverance of Walker alive, or $1,000 for his corpse, by a group of Georgia citizens. In spite of the attempt to suppress the book, it passed through three editions at Walker's expense and became one of the most widely circulated books of the antislavery movement.

After the Civil War, the image of David Walker as a hero in the cause of freedom increased. His *Appeal* had been reissued in 1848 by the Reverend Henry Highland Garnet, along with Garnet's own appeal to the slaves to resist their bondage. In 1866, his son was elected to the Massachusetts legislature.

"MADAME" C. J. WALKER

Walker, "Madame" C. J.

Cosmetic Manufacturer

Sarah Breedlove Walker (1869–1919), millionaire cosmetic manufacturer, was born a pauper in Louisiana. Her ex-slave parents died when she was six years old. She married C. J. Walker at the age of 14 and was a widow at 20. Taking in laundry to make a living, she experimented in her spare time with a concoction of oils to condition her hair so that she could remove the typical Negro curl. The oil softened the hair but did not remove the excessive curl. It was in 1905 that she developed a hot iron, or straightening comb, which would remove the tight curls.

For millions of women of African descent the straightening comb was an answer to their major cosmetic problem; and Madame Walker found herself in business. She opened a school of cosmetology to train her oper-

ators, employed agents to sell her products and built a factory to produce them. Before her death, she had more than 2,000 agents selling and demonstrating the "Walker System" of hair styling and cosmetics. She maintained an annual payroll of more than $200,000 and reaped a sizeable fortune from her large factory and school in Indianapolis. She advertised in all of the Negro publications and made headlines herself because of her social activities.

At a cost of about $250,000, she built a mansion at Irvington-on-the-Hudson, New York, and furnished it with the most expensive items available. Despite this display of her wealth, she was deeply concerned with the poverty of others and, like other American millionaires, became a philanthropist. She bequeathed $100,000 toward the establishment of an academy for girls in West Africa and donated large sums of money to Negro institutions and charities in America.

Walker, Maggie Lena

Banker

Maggie Lena Walker (1867–1934), organizer and founder of the St. Luke Bank and Trust Company of Richmond, Virginia, was born in a poverty-stricken family in Richmond. The family lived in an alley, where her widowed mother earned only a meager living as a laundress. A gifted child, Maggie completed high school at the age of 16 and began a teaching career. After taking a course in business, she left teaching in 1889 to become the executive secretary of the Independent Order of St. Luke. Within 10 years, she had become secretary-treasurer, and she held this position for 35 years.

The purpose of the Order of St. Luke was to provide assistance to its members in sickness, in old age and in meeting funeral expenses. Mrs. Walker's duties were to collect the dues, verify the claims and keep the books. She conceived of the idea of training the members to save and invest their money. When she assumed the job of secretary-treasurer, the order had only 3,408 members, no reserve funds and no property. By 1924, she had increased membership to 100,000, had also acquired a home-office building valued at $100,000, had organized an emergency fund of $70,000 and had established a newspaper, the *St. Luke Herald*.

In 1902, she had proposed the plan for the founding of the St. Luke Penny Savings Bank, of which she later became president. In time, the bank became the St. Luke Bank and Trust Company, a depository for gas and water accounts and for city taxes.

Mrs. Walker, well known for her interest in individuals, had been influential in helping those who first helped themselves. For instance, she once encouraged a one-legged bootblack to save his pennies. When he had accumulated $50, the order helped him first to rent, then to purchase, a place of his own. Children, encouraged to deposit their meager earnings in a savings account, were taught by the order to save with the definite purpose of using their earnings wisely.

MAGGIE LENA WALKER

Walls, Josiah T.

United States Congressman

Josiah T. Walls (1842–1905), Republican member from Florida of three Congresses, was born at Winchester, Virginia. Born of very poor parents, he had little opportunity for schooling, but, because of his determination, he managed to receive the fundamentals of an education in the common schools of the area. Moving to Florida at the close of the Civil War, he developed a truck-farming business and, in addition, joined the various Republican groups operating in Florida, to learn as much about politics as he could.

In 1868, he was a delegate to the state constitutional convention and, later the same year, was elected to the state house of repre-

JOSIAH T. WALLS

sentatives. After one year in the lower house, he ran for the state senate and was elected. In the national elections, Walls was elected to the 42nd and the 43rd Congresses. His third term of office, in the 44th Congress, was contested by Jesse J. Finley; for nearly a year, Walls fought unsuccessfully to maintain his seat.

After he lost the contested seat in Congress, he retired to his truck farm near Tallahassee but continued to participate in the activities of the state organization of the Republican Party by playing an important role in determining party nominations.

Ward, Samuel Ringgold
Antislavery Minister

Samuel Ringgold Ward, an eloquent, influential pastor of a New York Presbyterian church, spoke out defiantly against the infamous Fugitive Slave Law of 1850. He fearlessly denounced Mason of Virginia, the author of the bill, and criticized Daniel Webster for compromising the issue. In a speech delivered in April 1850, later published in the *Liberator,* Ward expressed his resentment: "That infamous bill of Mr. Mason of Virginia, proves itself to be like all other propositions presented by Southern men. It finds just enough dough-faces in the North who are willing to pledge themselves, if you will pardon the uncouth language of a backwoodsman, to lick up the spittle of the slavocrats, and swear it is delicious."

Ward was more a platform orator than a minister, for his aim appeared to be to preach the gospel of this world more than the gospel of heaven. He recommended that men calling themselves Christians should learn to respect the natural and political rights of their fellow men. In the interest of freedom, he traveled throughout the country, and visited England in 1852. He finally settled in Jamaica, where he resided until his death.

SAMUEL RINGGOLD WARD

Washington, Booker T.

Leader and Educator

Booker T. Washington (1856–1915), outstanding leader and builder of Tuskegee Institute in Alabama, was born a slave at Hale's Ford, Virginia. Because he lacked funds, he walked several hundred miles from his home to Hampton Institute, where he enrolled in 1872. After graduating from Hampton three years later, he taught in Malden, West Virginia, before entering Wayland Seminary in Washington, D.C. He later returned to Hampton to teach Indian boys; but, in 1881, he was appointed principal of Tuskegee Institute, which at that time consisted of two small frame buildings and thirty students.

Under Washington's direction, the institute achieved worldwide fame. Washington, as its principal, was invited to be the spokesman for the Negro at the Atlanta Exposition in 1895 and was consulted about the Negro in America by Presidents Theodore Roosevelt and William Howard Taft. In 1900, Washington organized the National Negro Business League; he participated in the organization of the General Education Board and of the Phelps Stokes Fund.

Speaking to the Negro people, Washington advised them to work out their salvation in the South by practical, patient self-help, which he felt would lead to the slow improvement of the condition of the masses and the gradual wearing down of white indifference and prejudice. His philosophy created a great rift between the conservative and liberal schools of thought concerning the race question. Further, he was never able to disavow the interpretation of his program as an acceptance of the principles of biracial segregation. New and interesting viewpoints are now being advanced about Washington's role as a leader.

Washington, George

Founder of Centralia, Washington

George Washington (1817–1905), pioneer in the Far West and founder of Centralia, Washington, was born in Frederick County, Virginia, of a white mother and a Negro slave father. The unwanted child was given to a white family named Cochran, who moved to Ohio and, five years later, to northern Missouri. The child developed skills necessary for frontier life and became an integral part of the Cochran family. In Missouri, the Cochrans erected a grist mill and a distillery, while Washington set himself up as a tailor and sawmill owner. His frustrations as a Negro started when he sold some lumber to Jeremiah Coyle, who refused to pay the bill because the law stated that Negroes had no rights in Missouri.

Moving to Illinois in hope of escaping discriminatory laws, Washington encountered a similar situation when he applied for a

BOOKER T. WASHINGTON

GEORGE WASHINGTON

license to make whiskey: Illinois had passed a law prohibiting Negroes from manufacturing, handling or selling alcoholic beverages. In 1850, he and his foster parents sold everything and migrated to the Oregon Territory. Washington cut timber for only $9.00 a month to keep the Cochrans fed and housed. He became seriously ill during this first year in Oregon and was taken to the hospital at the Vancouver barracks. While he was recuperating, the Cochrans brought a woman to visit him. After she left, he learned that she was his mother, but he never saw her again.

After recovering from his illness, he looked for a suitable place to stake out his claim; he found an ideal location on the Chehalis River, fenced it in and planted 12 acres in oats. Two white men who had stopped to enjoy Washington's hospitality hinted that they were going to file claims on the land because, as a Negro, Washington had no rights to the land. Discriminatory laws had

caught up with him again, even after he had trekked at least 3,000 miles to escape them. Rushing to the Cochrans, who were living at Cowlitz's Landing, he urged them to file the claim to the land in their name. Four years later, he bought it back from them for the sum of $3,000.

In 1872, when the transcontinental railroads were being built, the Northern Pacific Railroad purchased a right-of-way across his land. Washington planned the town of Centralia, and in order to attract settlers, he offered virtually free lots and moving services. Never pressuring the settlers for unpaid bills, he showed a paternalistic sympathy and understanding. When the economic depression hit the town in 1893, he carried out a relief program to keep his community alive.

Whipper, William
Early Advocate of Non-Violent Resistance

William Whipper (1805–1885), forerunner of the non-violent resistance movement in America, was born in Columbia, Pennsylvania, of a Negro house servant and her white employer. He was reared in his father's household along with his younger, white half-brother. He operated successful lumber businesses in Columbia and Morristown, which he inherited upon his father's death.

Whipper became active in the antislavery movement in Pennsylvania, using his wealth and influence to help slaves escape and to publish pamphlets and articles against slavery. One of the founders of the American Moral Reform Society, he was the editor of its official publication, the *National Reformer*.

The purpose of the society was to promote education, to be a truthful and informative outlet for news and to compile a history of the Negro. As the editor, Whipper wrote in a controlled, plain language that was bold and outspoken in the advocacy of truth. He was opposed to segregation and the building of separate churches and schools for Negroes.

In 1837, he published his famous article in the *Colored American* entitled "An Address on Non-Resistance to Offensive Aggression," in which he stated that "the practice of non-resistance to physical aggression is not only consistent with reason, but the surest method of obtaining a speedy triumph of the principles of universal peace."

His theory of non-resistance was written 12 years before Thoreau's famous essay, "Civil Disobedience." In this respect, Whipper was the forerunner of Thoreau, Gandhi and Martin Luther King. His son William J. Whipper was a Reconstruction politician in South Carolina after the War, and his grandson Leigh Whipper was a brilliant actor.

White, George Henry
United States Congressman

George Henry White (1852–1918), last of the Negro Reconstructionists to serve in Congress, was born in Rosindale, North Carolina. Educated in the state's public school system, he completed his training at Howard University in 1877. While teaching at the Presbyterian parochial school and at the normal school of North Carolina, he studied law and was admitted to the bar in 1879. As a lawyer, he participated in politics during the waning years of the Republican Party's power in North Carolina. He was elected to the state house of representatives in 1880 and to the state senate in 1884.

As a delegate, he attended the Republican national conventions in 1896 and 1900. Running for Congress in 1896 on the Republican ticket, White was elected to the 55th Congress and again, for a second term, to the 56th, but lost the election for the 57th. He was the last black to serve in Congress until the election of Oscar De Priest in 1928. A

GEORGE HENRY WHITE

persuasive and eloquent debater, Congressman White worked hard for the development of an adequate public school system in North Carolina and elsewhere in the nation. After losing his bid for Congress, he left North Carolina and moved to Philadelphia, where he practiced law.

White wished to establish an all-Negro community in New Jersey and obtained a large tract of land near Cape May. His success in attracting Negroes to his project was slow; and, finally, his inability to attract lucrative enterprises, which could provide job opportunities, proved financially disastrous.

Williams, Egbert Austin
Actor and Comedian

Egbert Austin ("Bert") Williams (1874–1922), outstanding comedian on Broadway, was born in Antigua, British West Indies. His parents migrated to California, where Williams first appeared as a singer and

EGBERT AUSTIN WILLIAMS

comedian, working in saloons and with touring musical companies. In 1893, he joined with George Walker to form the team of "Williams and Walker." Together they produced a show called *Policy Players* and, later, *Sons of Ham*. Neither of these two productions gained popularity, but the team gained experience. Their success dated from *In Dahomey,* which ran for some weeks on Broadway, where the New York critics praised it highly, particularly its lively musical score. After the New York run was over, the show was booked in London, where the actors appeared in a command performance at Buckingham Palace.

Williams and Walker had reached the peak of their popularity, but the pace exhausted Walker, who retired in 1909 and died in 1911. Williams tried to carry on alone in a show called *Mr. Lode of Koal,* but it failed. His reputation attracted the attention of Florenz Ziegfeld, who selected Wil-

liams to star in his famous *Ziegfeld Follies.* Williams remained with the *Follies* until 1920. He died in 1922.

Williams, George Washington

Historian

George Washington Williams (1849–1891), scholar and historian, was born at Bedford Springs, Pennsylvania. His family moved to Massachusetts, where he studied with a private tutor for two years and in the public schools. At 14, he ran away to join the Union Army under an assumed name. He advanced rapidly from private to sergeant-major of the regiment. After the Civil War, the adventurous youth enlisted in the Mexican Army and, in 1867, in the United States Army to fight against the Comanches.

Eventually, in 1868, Williams returned to Massachusetts and enrolled in the Newton

GEORGE WASHINGTON WILLIAMS

Theological Seminary to complete his studies. Graduating in 1874, he delivered his senior oration on "Early Christianity in Africa," a subject which generated Williams' interest in African history as a background to the history of the American Negro.

He served as a pastor in Boston for a few years, before moving to Washington and then to Cincinnati. While pastor of the Union Baptist Church, he studied at the Cincinnati law school and was admitted to practice in the supreme court of Ohio. In 1879, he was elected to the Ohio legislature.

During this time, the *Cincinnati Commercial* printed articles by Williams which were written under the pen name "Aristides." For his speeches and articles, he made use of the several libraries in the city and became convinced that there was sufficient material for him to write a definitive history of the Negro. Diligently, he carried on his research; and in 1883, Putnam's published his two-volume *History of the Negro Race in America from 1619 to 1880*. It was considered the most definitive work on black history written in the 19th century. In 1888, he published his *History of the Negro Troops in the War of the Rebellion, 1861–1865*.

A visit to the Belgian Congo, in 1883, resulted in his severe criticism of the Belgian rule of this colony. Williams was appointed, by the United States Department of State, minister resident to Haiti in 1885. He died in Blackpool, England.

Woods, Granville T.

Inventor

Granville T. Woods (1856–1910), inventor of electrical appliances, was born in Columbus, Ohio, where he worked in a machine shop while studying privately and attending evening school. In 1872, Woods was employed as a fireman and engineer on a railroad in Missouri, but he continued with

GRANVILLE T. WOODS

his studies in electrical and mechanical engineering. After being employed on a British steamship for two years, he was given a job as engineer on the Danville and Southern Railroad in 1880. Woods' imagination had been fired by these experiences with ideas for the improvement of the crude transportation and communications devices that were in current use.

After settling in Cincinnati, he opened a factory for the manufacture of telephone, telegraph and electrical equipment. He patented his first invention in 1884, a steam boiler furnace. His next productions were an amusement apparatus, an incubator and automatic air-brakes. He patented over 15 devices for electrical railways and a telegraphic device for transmitting messages between moving trains.

Eventually, Woods moved to New York, where he continued to produce devices for the large electrical manufacturers. His patents were sold to the General Electric Company, the Westinghouse Air Brake Company, the Bell Telephone Company and other electrical and engineering companies.

Work, John Wesley, Sr.

Musician

John Wesley Work, Sr. (1873–1925), collector and interpreter of Negro spirituals and director of the Fisk Jubilee Singers, was born in Nashville, Tennessee. After graduating from Fisk University in 1895, he studied Latin at Harvard University for one year and then returned to Fisk to teach Latin. But, because of his love of it, he began to study music seriously. He studied voice for five years, a period during which he manifested his love for Negro spirituals. He began to

JOHN WESLEY WORK, SR.

reorganize the Fisk Jubilee Singers, using Negro folk songs. For many years, he organized different quartets of Jubilee Singers and traveled with them in the interest of the university.

Work made a systematic study of the spirituals as he collected them for his quartets. With his brother Frederick Work, he published *Folk Songs of the American Negro* in 1907. Revisions and new volumes were produced by their own publishing firm. By 1910, John Work was publishing many of his own compositions, such as the "Negro Lullaby," "Negro Love Song," "If You Were Only Here" and "Song of the Warrior." He wrote an important treatise, *The Folk Song of the American Negro,* in 1915.

In 1916, Professor Work retired from a strenuous life of touring with the Jubilee Singers and concentrated his talents on directing the Fisk Mozart Society and teaching history and Latin. During this period, he organized each year a special chorus of some 300 voices to give concerts of spirituals.

Some of the better-known spirituals collected by Work are "I Couldn't Hear Nobody Pray," "Little David Play on Yo' Harp," "Shout All over God's Heaven" and "By and By."

He accepted the presidency of Roger Williams College in Nashville in 1923, just two years prior to his death.

Wormley, James

Hotel Proprietor

James Wormley (1820–1884), owner of the once-famous Wormley Hotel in Washington, was born of free parents in the District of Columbia. He acquired the rudiments of an education and the skills for business from his father, who was the proprietor of a livery stable. James Wormley, successful in his business enterprises, became the proprietor of a hotel.

It was partly in Wormley's hotel that the disputed election of 1876–77, between candidates Rutherford B. Hayes and Samuel J. Tilden, was settled. Hayes, the Republican, obtained Southern votes by promising to withdraw the Federal troops from the South. It is ironical that the sellout of the Negro by the Republican Party took place in an establishment owned and operated by a Negro.

Among the patrons of the hotel were many of the prominent figures of that day. The parlors and the dining room were the scene of many distinguished gatherings. One of the rooms was known as the "Sumner Parlor," because the furniture had been purchased from the residence of the late senator.

James Wormley had a national reputation as a caterer, having served as a steward on various naval vessels and at the famous Metropolitan Club. He is reputed to have accompanied Reverdy Johnson, the minister to the Court of St. James, to England, where his skill as a caterer contributed to Johnson's diplomatic success.

Wright, Jonathan Jasper
Jurist

Jonathan Jasper Wright (1840–1885), associate justice of the supreme court of South Carolina, was born in Pennsylvania. He obtained some college training in Ithaca, New York, and studied law in a private law office in Pennsylvania. In 1866, he became the first Negro to be admitted to the state bar. The American Missionary Society sent him to Beaufort, South Carolina, to organize schools for freedmen and to serve as their legal adviser. Entering politics, he became a member of the constitutional convention of 1868 and of the state senate in the election that followed the convention. In February

1870, he was elected to fill an unexpired term on the bench of the South Carolina supreme court and was re-elected in December 1870 for the full term. He resigned in 1877, when the Republican regime was overthrown by the return of "home rule" to the South.

Although Wright lisped when he spoke, he was regarded as an intelligent speaker as well as one of the best-trained Negroes in the state. Of the 425 cases heard by the state supreme court during his tenure, 87 of the decisions were written by Justice Jonathan J. Wright. In the debates on the economic situation during the constitutional convention, Wright expressed the opinion that, if they did not destroy all elements of the institution of slavery, the convention would be guilty of recognizing the right of men to own other men as property.

Wright, Richard Robert, Sr.
Educator and Banker

Richard Robert Wright, Sr. (1855–1945), outstanding in the fields of education and banking, was born in Georgia prior to the Civil War. He attended the newly established Atlanta University and, upon graduation, entered the field of education to help eradicate illiteracy among the freedmen of Georgia. In 1891, he founded Savannah (Georgia) State College, which he established with the firm conviction that the Negro race would rise no higher than its educated masses. His energies were given to the school from 1891 to 1921.

Richard Wright's struggle for his own education inspired his dedication to educating others. In 1866, he and his mother walked nearly 200 miles from Cuthbert to Atlanta to enroll him in a school being held in an old commissary car abandoned by the Con-

RICHARD ROBERT WRIGHT, SR.

federate Army. In the school, conducted by the American Missionary Association, were enrolled more than 400 freedmen ranging in age from six to sixty. When Wright could no longer afford to attend school, he worked as a houseboy in Atlanta, but a kindly white man sent him to Atlanta University, where he graduated with top honors in its first class.

His retirement from Savannah State College did not end his activities. Instead, he launched a highly successful career in Philadelphia as the founder and president of the Citizens and Southern Bank and Trust Company. Opening the bank in the prosperous twenties, Wright established a sound financial policy and, hence, was able to weather the depression of the thirties. At the age of 88, he was still directing the affairs of the bank as well as serving as president of the National Negro Bankers' Association.

Wright, Theodore Sedgewick
Abolitionist and Opponent of Colonization

Theodore Sedgewick Wright (1797–1847), the first Negro to receive a degree from the theological seminary of Princeton University (1828), was born in Providence, Rhode Island, of free parents. His father, R. P. G. Wright, was a delegate to the Convention of Free Colored People in Philadelphia in 1817. The son, following in the footsteps of his father, became an active leader in the free colored convention movement. Theodore Wright, one of the most outstanding ministers of the Presbyterian Church, did not hesitate to use his pulpit to challenge the pro-slavery groups in the Presbyterian Synod of America, especially when these groups came out in support of the colonization movement.

As pastor of the First Colored Presbyterian Church of New York City, he attracted many serious students of American social life. Having faith in the principles of American democracy, he denounced all advocates and programs of the "back-to-Africa" movement. He appealed to Negroes to remain and fight for their rights and liberties. Working with the Reverend Samuel E. Cornish, he skillfully analyzed the propaganda of the Colonization Society for many influential Presbyterians and won many of these individuals to the antislavery movement. Cornish and Wright challenged the community to prove the inferiority of the Negro and pressed the members of the synod to open the doors of schools to Negroes to prove their faith in the equality of man.

Wright served on many executive committees of religious and antislavery organizations and was one of the most active conductors on the Underground Railroad in New York. He was a quiet, unobtrusive worker.

PART III

The Twentieth Century

Introduction

NEGROES throughout the world witnessed the dawn of the twentieth century with bleakness and despair; the achievement of the abolition of Negro slavery in the previous century had not guaranteed the recognition of the ideal concept of equality. Instead, there was a steady negation of the philosophy that "all men are created equal." The Social Darwinist reversed the principle entirely and proclaimed that the Negro was inferior and incapable of contributing to the civilization and the culture of mankind. Operating on this thesis, Americans passed laws, rendered court decisions and instituted social and economic practices to relegate the Negro to the lowest possible point on the social scale. Professor Rayford Logan of Howard University called the period of the turn of the century the "nadir" of the Negro in American life and thought. Similar conditions prevailed in Africa, as European imperialists appropriated the land and the people for colonial exploitation. The Africans were subjected to the current idea that they were inferior and incapable of managing their own affairs. It was the "white man's burden" to bring the fruits of civilization to the so-called savages of Africa.

Out of the darkness, there arose those individuals who sought to counteract this misconceived notion through various movements and methods and by outstanding individual achievements. Leaders of religious and educational institutions dominated the scene, as the last American Negro political leaders practically disappeared. The reversals suffered from the lack of legal protection under the Fourteenth and Fifteenth Amendments brought forth a new group of leaders. The bloody race riots of the North and the increased number of lynchings in the South led to the founding of the National Association for the Advancement of Colored People in 1909. It was organized for the purpose of demanding equality before the law and the guarantee of civil rights for the Negro. Such personalities as W. E. B. Du Bois, James Weldon Johnson, Walter White, Charles Houston, Thurgood Marshall, Roy Wilkins and others rose as leaders in this movement. Concern over the destitute economic status of the Negro in the Northern cities inspired another group to organize the Urban League for the purpose of guiding and directing Negroes into more satisfactory employment opportunities. Eugene Kinckle Jones emerged as the leader of this movement, and Whitney Young continued the program in the challenging period of revolt in the 1960's.

While these organizations were fighting

for the rights of the Negro in America, Marcus Garvey reached down to the masses in his "back to Africa" movement in the 1920's. This movement contributed more toward developing race pride and consciousness than did any other racially oriented program. Booker T. Washington's founding of the Negro Business League during the early part of the twentieth century was another effort to develop the economic status of the Negro. Determined to counteract the prevalent concept of the inferiority of the Negro, Carter G. Woodson organized The Association for the Study of Negro Life and History for the purpose of preserving and publishing the record of the achievements and contributions of people of African descent.

In the mid-twentieth century, the impact of world affairs on the Negro in the United States was especially profound and significant. The American Negro had been affected by the emergence of the Asian and African peoples who had rebelled against the current theory of inferiority and thrown off the yoke of Western white domination. The end of white supremacy in Africa and the rest of the world inspired a new type of militancy in American Negro leadership. After the 1950's, new movements and organizations arose designed to use "positive mass action" for the immediate achievement of first-class citizenship. Paramount among the personalities involved in the revolt of the sixties were the Rev. Martin Luther King, James Farmer, A. Philip Randolph, James Forman and Floyd McKissick.

This section of biographical sketches contains only a partial listing of persons who have obtained recognition in the various fields of achievement. It was impossible to include all of the many outstanding athletes, entertainers, educators, ministers, scientists, artists, politicians, and entrepreneurs in this volume. An attempt has been made to select typical examples from each of the categories, with particular concern to include those who were pioneers in a given area. In pursuit of objectivity, controversial individuals are presented in the same manner as those who are more readily accepted by the general public. Elijah Muhammad and Marcus Garvey do not meet with the approval of the Negro intelligentsia, yet they have made an indelible impression on the masses of Negro Americans.

Certain personalities, such as Booker T. Washington and Mary McLeod Bethune, are not given extensive coverage because they are more widely known and information about them can be obtained easily from other sources. Men like Monroe Trotter, who was decidedly opposed to Washington's leadership, are less known and are therefore given greater coverage so as to present their views and contributions as fully as possible. The struggle for equality has not been confined to any one individual or any particular movement. What has been accomplished so far is a result of the sum total of all the contributions of those included in this volume, as well as the contributions of many individuals who are not included.

We can choose either to walk the high road of human brotherhood or to tread the low road of man's inhumanity to man. How we deal with this crucial situation will determine our moral health as individuals and our prestige as a leader of the free world. If America is to remain a first-class nation, it cannot have a second-class citizenship.

Martin Luther King, Jr.

Abbott, Robert S.

Publisher

Robert S. Abbott (1870–1940), founder and editor of the *Chicago Defender,* was born on St. Simons Island off the Georgia coast. He attended Hampton Institute in Virginia and, in 1903, earned a law degree from Kent College in Chicago. After practic-

ROBERT S. ABBOTT

ing law for several years in the Midwest, Abbott became convinced that he could better represent his people through the printed word than in the courtroom. He used his savings and borrowed money to establish his first newspaper office—in his landlady's dining room.

The first copies of the *Chicago Defender* appeared on May 5, 1905, when the climate of racial relations had reached the lowest possible depths. Abbott himself sold these copies, trudging the streets of southside Chicago, visiting homes, barber shops, pool rooms, drugstores and churches.

Abbott wrote strong editorials attacking injustice toward the Negro, and he encouraged Southern Negroes to migrate from the Deep South to the North in search of better living conditions. Under his guidance, the *Defender* became an articulate voice of Chicago's Negro population and reached a circulation of over 250,000 copies by 1929.

Adams, Robert

Actor

Robert Adams (1910–), athlete, actor and a leading Negro film star in Europe, was born in Georgetown, British Guiana. His remarkable ability earned him scholarships to attend high school and college. Upon graduation, he became a teacher in Georgetown; but he developed an interest in producing and directing amateur plays and wished to become an actor. Opportunities for such a career were limited in Guiana. In 1934, he used all of his savings for a trip to England, where he arrived with only sixpence-halfpenny in his possession. Consequently, he worked as a laborer, wrestler and private tutor, taking any job in order to live until he could reach his goal.

Before reaching stardom in British films, Adams used his athletic skill to become the champion heavyweight wrestler of the British Empire. This financial success enabled him to pursue his ambition of becoming an actor. He obtained a minor part in the production *Sanders of the River* and gradually worked his way up through the films *Midshipman Easy, Song of Freedom* and *King Solomon's Mines.* His London stage debut was in the production of *Stevedore,* at the Embassy Theatre. He was given the featured role in the stage play *Colony,* and parts in nine additional plays.

Adams organized a group of actors into the London Negro Repertory Theatre for the purpose of utilizing Negro talent in the presentation of racial themes on the stage. This group was highly successful in presenting O'Neill's *All God's Chillun Got Wings,* in 1946, at the Unity Theatre.

Continuing as a film actor, Adams was featured in *Old Bones of the River, An African in London, It Happened One Sunday, Dreaming* and *Caesar and Cleopatra.* His greatest role was as an African composer and pianist in the film *Men of Two Worlds.* The British critics praised Adams' performance in the role of Kisenga as a moving piece of acting. In his spare time, Adams has studied law and music and has written plays, articles and a book on the West Indies, entitled *Caribbean Hurricane.*

Albritton, David Donald
Athlete and State Legislator

David Donald Albritton (1913–), Olympic high jump star and a member of the Ohio General Assembly, was born in Danville, Alabama. As a member of the United States Olympic Team, he was elected to the Helms Foundation Hall of Fame; he distinguished himself as an ambassador of good will by representing the U.S. State Department in the Far East. Participating in all sports as a student at East Technical High School in Cleveland, he won the light-heavyweight boxing championship of Cleveland in 1933. While at Ohio State University, he was light-heavyweight boxing champion of the university in 1938. He won the national high school track title for the high jump and hurdle in 1933, as well as the state championships in 1932 and 1933. He set a world high jump record and won the national high jump championship 13 times.

Dave Albritton was first elected to the General Assembly of Ohio in 1960 and assumed the major responsibility for sponsoring and managing the most significant single piece of legislation that was passed by the 104th General Assembly: the extension of the jurisdiction of the Civil Rights Commission to include places of public accommodation. He combines the job of teacher and athletic director of Dunbar High School in Dayton with his service as representative to the Ohio General Assembly.

Alexander, Archie A.
Engineer

Archie Alexander (1888–1958), builder of tunnels, viaducts, bridges and heating and hydraulic plants, was born in Ottumwa, Iowa, and graduated from the University of Iowa with a Bachelor of Science degree in engineering in 1912. He had been discouraged by the head of the school about the limited opportunity for a Negro in this field. Alexander succeeded as an engineer in spite of his race, and the university gave him an honorary degree for his achievements, in 1925. After working as engineer for a bridge construction firm for two years, Alexander went into business for himself; and within 11 years, he completed contracts totaling $4,500,000. He is recognized as having been one of the most successful engineers in the country.

One of his most satisfying contracts came from the University of Iowa, where he constructed a million-dollar heating plant with a system of tunnels running under the Iowa River. He built the Tidal Basin bridge from the nation's capital across the Potomac River to Arlington, Virginia. In the early 1950's he was governor of the Virgin Islands.

Alexander, Raymond Pace

Judge

Raymond Pace Alexander (1898–1974), senior judge of the court of common pleas, Philadelphia, Pennsylvania, was appointed senior judge in 1970 after serving 11 years as judge of the court of common pleas. Judge Alexander, a native Philadelphian, was a graduate of the University of Pennsylvania (1920) and of Harvard University Law School (1923). Since passing the Pennsylvania bar examination in 1923, he had practiced in Philadelphia. He was a co-founder and editor of the *National Bar Journal* and served as president of the National Bar Association from 1934 to 1936.

In 1950, Judge Alexander received a citation from the American Jewish Congress for 25 years of outstanding contributions in the field of civil rights. He was elected to serve two terms on the city council prior to his appointment to the judiciary in 1958. He had been active in organizing the election campaigns of the Democratic Party in Philadel-

RAYMOND PACE ALEXANDER

phia in the two previous decades. In 1965, to lecture in the serious trouble spots of the Far East.

Anderson, Charles W., Jr.

State Legislator and UN Delegate

Charles W. Anderson, Jr. (1907–1960), first Negro to be elected to the legislature of a Southern state after Reconstruction, was born in Louisville, Kentucky. He was educated at Kentucky State College in Frankfort and Wilberforce University in Ohio. He received the LL.B degree from the Howard University Law School in 1931 and an honorary LL.D. from Wilberforce in 1936. After establishing his law office in Louisville, he entered politics and was elected to the house of representatives of Kentucky for six consecutive terms, serving a total of 12 years.

Since the state of Kentucky did not permit Negroes to study in the professional colleges of the state, Anderson sponsored the Anderson-Mayer State Aid Act, requiring the state to appropriate funds to assist Negroes to study in other states.

His career in the legislature was outstanding: he sought legislation to end segregation on common carriers in the state, and also to admit Negroes to the white universities and to increase facilities for rural schools. He was responsible for repeal of the Kentucky public hanging law. In 1946, he resigned from the legislature to become the assistant commonwealth attorney for the 30th judicial district of Kentucky. He was the first Negro to occupy this position in a Southern state.

Anderson received the Lincoln Institute Award in 1940 and the Howard University Alumni Award in 1945. Under the Republican administration of President Dwight D. Eisenhower, he was appointed alternate delegate to the United Nations General Assembly.

Anderson, Eddie ("Rochester")

Actor and Entertainer

Eddie ("Rochester") Anderson (1905–77), comedian of Hollywood, radio and TV, was born in Oakland, California, where he entered the entertainment field as a singer in the chorus of *Struttin' Along*. Afterwards, he joined a vocal trio and accepted engagements as one of the Three Black Aces. He toured the United States theatrical circuits for many years in different variety and vaudeville shows, and for three years was the featured dancer, singer and entertainer at Sebastian's Cotton Club in Los Angeles. Appearing on radio in Los Angeles, he eventually teamed up with Jack Benny and was featured on radio and television.

In the 1940's, Anderson appeared in the movies, his film credits reading "Rochester." He was featured in *Buck Benny Rides Again,* 1940; *Cabin in the Sky,* 1943; and *The Sailor Takes a Wife,* 1945.

In 1958, Anderson suffered a heart attack. Difficulties with both sight and speech have since curtailed professional engagements. He was last seen in *It's a Mad, Mad, Mad, Mad World,* 1963. His friendship with Jack Benny has continued. Eddie Anderson, to the delight of his many fans, still signs autographs "Rochester."

Anderson, Gertrude E. Fisher

Candy Manufacturer

Gertrude E. Fisher Anderson (1894–), originator, owner and manufacturer of Nanette Home-Made Candies, was born in Hamner, Alabama. She was educated at Spelman College and the University of Chicago, where she specialized in home economics. She taught at Parker High School in Birmingham, Alabama, until her marriage to Dr. Benjamin Anderson. Later, when he died, she was left with three children to support and educate. One child had already entered college, and the others were preparing to go. Mrs. Anderson could have returned to the profession of teaching, but the salaries of public school teachers in the 1930's were not sufficient to educate three children.

Without capital, she began making candy, using such crude equipment as she could find. She offered the candy for sale at churches, schools and organizations, and the returns were sufficient for her to invest in one piece of equipment after another. The demands for Nanette Home-Made Candies increased, and she expanded by building a special room on the back of her home; next, her business increased and she was able to hire other workers. Her employees are provided with modern equipment, and Mrs. Anderson supervises their preparation of the candy and manages sales promotion.

Anderson, Marian

Singer

Marian Anderson (1908–), one of the outstanding contraltos of our time, was born and educated in Philadelphia, Pennsylvania. She began her singing career at the age of six, in the choir of the Union Baptist Church. Recognizing her unusual talent, the members of the church started a trust fund, "Marian Anderson's Future," for the purpose of securing adequate musical training for the young girl. This fund made it possible for her to study under Giuseppe Boghetti. Miss Anderson made her professional debut in 1924, and in 1925 she was chosen from among three hundred competitors to sing with the New York Philharmonic Orchestra. Later, she was invited to appear as guest soloist with the Philadelphia Philharmonic Symphony Orchestra.

Miss Anderson received a Rosenwald scholarship, which enabled her to study in Germany. She made her European debut in Berlin and was invited to tour the Scandinavian countries, where she sang in both Swedish and Finnish. Returning to America, she traveled on the concert circuit from the Atlantic to the Pacific Ocean.

During her next tour of Europe, she sang in Sweden, Denmark, Finland and Norway, and was decorated by the King of Sweden and the King of Denmark. The famous Finnish composer Sibelius was so moved by her rich contralto voice that he dedicated a composition to her. The London Symphony Orchestra, under the direction of Sir Henry Wood, engaged her for two concerts; and Arturo Toscanini, after hearing her sing, expressed the opinion that a voice such as hers "comes once in a century."

In the United States, however, the Daughters of the American Revolution in 1939 denied Miss Anderson permission to sing in Constitution Hall, Washington, D.C. When, underlining the racial slur, she sang instead from the steps of the Lincoln Memorial in open air concert on Easter Sunday morning of 1939, 75,000 people gathered to hear her.

Miss Anderson has received many honorary degrees and awards for her achievements in the field of music. Some of them are: a request for a command performance by the British crown; a decoration from the government of Finland; the Spingarn Medal; the Order of African Redemption of the Republic of Liberia; and the Bok Award of $10,000. She was the first Negro to sing at the Metropolitan Opera; and in 1961, she was named one of the world's 10 most-admired women by the American Institute of Public Opinion poll. She was appointed United States delegate to the 13th General Assembly of the

MARIAN ANDERSON

United Nations and was sent on a good-will tour of the Far East by the State Department.

Miss Anderson is the author of an autobiography, *My Lord What a Morning,* published in 1956. Since retiring from the Metropolitan Opera Company in 1965, she has been active as a member of the National Council on the Arts and the Connecticut Council on the Arts. In 1972, she was named to the National Arts Hall of Fame. She is a resident of Danbury, Connecticut, and is listed in *Who's Who of American Women.* In 1974, she announced plans to participate, with 10 other women, in contributing to a new syndicated column, "One Woman's Voice."

Armstrong, Louis

Jazz Musician

Louis "Satchmo" Armstrong (1900–1971), pre-eminent jazz trumpeter, was born in New Orleans, Louisiana, of hard-working, but poor, parents. From the slums of New Orleans, Louis Armstrong rose to fame and international recognition as the foremost musician of popular jazz. His education was limited, because he had to leave school at the age of nine to go to work. His musical career began four years later, when he was placed in the Colored Waifs' Home. In the year and a half he spent at the home, he played in the band: first the tambourine, then the drums and the bugle. By the time he left the home, Louis was playing the cornet and leading the band.

He received his first professional opportunity in Henry Ponce's cabaret one night when the cornet player failed to report for work. Louis was permitted to use the player's horn because he did not own an instrument. Later, he met the famous King Oliver, who gave him one of his old cornets and sent him to play in some of the better clubs in New Orleans. Oliver also taught the young jazzman some of

LOUIS ARMSTRONG

his techniques; and by 1918, Louis was able to give up his coalman's job and devote his entire time to music. For a year, he sailed the Mississippi River on the riverboat *Sydney* with Fate Marable's orchestra; and David Jones, the band's melodeon player, taught him to read music. King Oliver invited Louis to join his band in Chicago, where he was allowed to sing in his deep, husky, half-growling voice, which won for him immediate popularity.

Armstrong (by then known as "Satchel Mouth," or "Satchmo") organized his own band in 1925; he toured the world with his orchestra. Armstrong made over fifteen hundred records, many of which are collectors' items. Armstrong composed many popular numbers, such as "Swing That Music," "Where Did You Stay Last Night," "Satchel Mouth Survey," "I've Got a Heart Full of Rhythm," "Wild Man Blues," "If We

Ever Meet Again" and "Sugar Foot Stomp." In the 1930's, he was in the films *Every Day's a Holiday* and *Going Places*. His technique pioneered the way for later jazz soloists and influenced such singers as Billie Holiday and Bing Crosby.

Baker, Josephine
Entertainer and Humanitarian

Josephine Baker (1907-1975), "the toast of Paris" and a humanitarian, was born of a poor family in St. Louis, Missouri. She began her career in the United States in the all-Negro musical *Shuffle Along,* and in the 1920's she was featured as a dancer of the "Charleston" and the "Black Bottom" at the Old Plantation Club in New York City. She was noted for her statuesque beauty and being an exciting entertainer on the stage.

After an appearance in the *Ziegfeld Follies* in 1936, she was featured in 1938 by Jack Goldberg in the film *Siren of the Tropics*. Miss Baker then departed for Paris, where she became a sensation as an exotic dancer at the Folies Bergère and the Casino de Paris. For 15 years, Josephine Baker was known as "the toast of Paris." In this period, she returned occasionally to make appearances in the United States, but the "Black Venus" of Paris preferred to become a French citizen. During World War II, she entertained the Allied soldiers in North Africa, worked as an ambulance driver on the Belgian front and fought with the Free French Resistance, for which she later received the Legion of Honor.

Hoping to show that children of different racial backgrounds could achieve equally when brought up with equal opportunity and treatment, Miss Baker and her French husband Jo Bouillon in 1947 purchased a 15th-century château in the Dordogne Valley, in France. The couple adopted 12 children. Expenses plus the stresses and strains of a large

JOSEPHINE BAKER

family contributed to the breakup of Miss Baker's marriage. She was forced into bankruptcy and was forcibly evicted from her château.

Princess Grace of Monaco then provided a house for Miss Baker and the children in Roquebrune, France, on the Riviera, near Monaco.

In 1973, Josephine Baker returned to the United States for a "comeback," to help support her 12 children, the eldest of whom has graduated from college. At 67, Miss Baker packed houses in Los Angeles and in major cities throughout the United States, and played to a completely sold-out house at Carnegie Hall.

A sign of Miss Baker's continued concern over racial discrimination was demonstrated when she flew to America to participate in the "March on Washington" in 1963. She wanted to display her belief that Negro celebrities should participate in the civil rights movement.

Baldwin, James

Author

James Baldwin (1924–), one of the "angry young men" of 20th-century literature, was born in Harlem and educated in the schools of New York City. He was given a Saxton Trust award when he was 21 to help him finish a novel, but this book was not published then. He turned to writing book reviews while waiting on tables in Greenwich Village. He did a book about storefront churches with photographer Theodore Pelatowski; it, too, was never published, but it won for him a Rosenwald Fellowship. Baldwin used the fellowship stipend to go to France, where he finished *Go Tell It on the Mountain,* published in 1953. Then came two books of essays; the second, *Nobody Knows My Name,* was a national bestseller and was selected by the Notable Books Council of the American Library Association as one of the outstanding books of the year.

Nobody Knows My Name comprises 13 essays covering Baldwin's 10-year self-exile in France, his return to Harlem and his first trip South during the battle over school integration. His book *The Fire Next Time* is an angry outburst that created a sensation; it is the author's philosophical interpretation of the Negro revolution of the 1960's. His play *Blues for Mister Charlie* appeared off-Broadway in 1964. Major journals have featured articles on Baldwin, and newsmen provided television coverage of his appearances in the major cities of the South where Negroes were demonstrating. A new novel is *If Beale Street Could Talk,* published in 1974. His first essays on the race question appeared in *Notes of a Native Son.* In this book, Baldwin wrote his famous conclusion on the racial problem in America: "People who shut their eyes to reality simply invite destruction. . . . This world is white no longer, and it will never be white again."

JAMES BALDWIN

Barnett, Claude Albert

Founder of the Associated Negro Press

Claude A. Barnett (1889–1967), the founder of the Associated Negro Press, was born in Sanford, Florida. He was educated at Tuskegee Institute in Alabama, where he came under the influence of Booker T. Washington. At that time, Washington was promoting the organization of Negro businesses and the economic independence of Negroes. Barnett spearheaded the founding of the Associated Negro Press (A.N.P.) in 1919 and afterward served as its director. He had his office in Chicago, where he was acknowledged as a powerful influence in the clearance of all news pertaining to the Negro. One of the main objectives in founding this organization was to counteract

CLAUDE ALBERT BARNETT

dent Hospital and Training School in Chicago and as special assistant to the U.S. Secretary of Agriculture.

Barthé, Richmond

Sculptor

Richmond Barthé (1901–   ), noted sculptor, was born in Bay St. Louis, Mississippi. He tried to satisfy his desire to study art in the South but was discouraged by the unequal educational facilities of the area. As a result, he moved to Chicago in 1924 and entered the Art Institute of Chicago. His first interest was in painting, but in 1928 he turned to sculpture and won Rosenwald Fellowships in 1931 and 1932, and later two Guggenheim Fellowships. He was cited by the American Academy of Arts and Letters and won the Audubon Artists Gold Medal in 1945. Most of his

the criticism of whites who were accusing Negro journalists of being anti-American.

The A.N.P. assigns reporters throughout the nation to keep aware of all items of interest regarding the Negro people and report them to the Chicago headquarters. During World War II, this organization put pressure on the government for the accreditation of Negro newsmen to cover the theaters of war for their papers. Barnett's attitude was that the Negro newspaper plays a vital role in focusing attention upon the injustices suffered by the American Negro.

In addition to his role as director of the A.N.P., Claude Barnett followed closely the new developments in Africa. He and his wife, Etta Moten, were exponents of African art and culture, and their Chicago home was a center for promoting understanding between Americans and Africans. Barnett served as president of the Provi-

RICHMOND BARTHÉ

citations were received on the basis of his theme of interracial justice. Some of his works are "West Indian Girl," "Toussaint L'Ouverture" and a bust of Booker T. Washington, which he did for New York University's Hall of Fame.

He is one of a small group of black artists successful enough to make a full-time living from his art work. Since the 1950's he has lived in Jamaica in the British West Indies.

Bates, Daisy Gaston

Civil Rights Worker

Daisy Gaston Bates (1922–), moving spirit behind the integration of Central High School in Little Rock, Arkansas, was born in Huttig, Arkansas. Her parents tried to instill in her the traditional attitude of submissiveness toward whites, but she rejected this

DAISY GASTON BATES

type of relationship early in life. She could not accept her parents' belief that Negroes must passively accept indignities, inequalities and degradation. Because of her rebellious attitude toward the social order of her local surroundings, her parents sent her on an extensive tour of the North and Canada, where she was able to observe that people in other places live together harmoniously in spite of the difference in the color of their skin.

After her marriage to C. L. Bates, a newspaperman, she settled in Little Rock, where her husband launched a campaign against segregation, police brutality and all forms of inhumanity. In the meantime, Daisy Bates, working with 22 organizations, searched for an instrument to use in attacking the barriers of discrimination. Active in the NAACP, she was elected president of the state organization in 1953. When the Supreme Court issued its desegregation decision in 1954, Daisy Bates was in an excellent position to enter the fight against segregated schools in Arkansas, and she brought organized pressure on the school board to admit Negroes to Central High School. In 1957, she helped initiate legal action against the "Little Rock Plan" of integration. The successful outcome of the case enabled the famous nine students to enter Central High School that fall.

When school opened that September, Governor Faubus ordered troops to the front of the school to block the Negro children. Eight of the seventeen withdrew in fear, and the remaining nine were turned back by the National Guard of Arkansas. The Little Rock struggle was in the national headlines, and on September 25, President Eisenhower ordered the 101st Airborne Division to escort the Negro children to school. Daisy Bates continued to offer them vital support during the trying days of taunts and torture. Because of her part in the struggle, the Bateses lost their newspaper, the *Arkansas State Press,* but Mrs. Bates was awarded numerous citations and awards for having spearheaded the desegregation of schools in the South.

When the NAACP awarded the Spingarn Award to the Little Rock Nine in 1958, the students refused to accept it until Mrs. Bates was included in the citation.

Bethune, Mary McLeod

Educator

Mary McLeod Bethune (1875–1955), who founded Bethune-Cookman College at Daytona Beach, Florida, in 1904, with one dollar and fifty cents and five pupils, was born in Mayesville, South Carolina. She received her education at the Scotia Seminary in North Carolina and studied further at Moody Bible Institute in Chicago. A person of foresight and dynamic leadership, she received many awards, such as the Medal of Merit from the Republic of Haiti and the NAACP's Spingarn Award. Under Frank-

MARY McLEOD BETHUNE

lin D. Roosevelt's administration, she served as director of the Negro affairs division of the National Youth Administration and as a consultant to the founding conference of the United Nations. After the President died, Mrs. Roosevelt presented his cane to Mrs. Bethune, who used it until her own death, in 1955.

Mrs. Bethune was the founder of the National Council of Negro Women and served as director of the American Red Cross in the state of Florida. In addition, she served for many years as president of the Association for the Study of Negro Life and History.

Binga, Jesse

Financier

Jesse Binga (1865–1950), aggressive financial-empire builder, was born into an enterprising Detroit family. After three years of high school training in Detroit, he read law for two years under a Negro lawyer; but he never took the bar examination. Moving to Chicago during the World's Fair of 1893, he became a vendor, selling wares to Negroes on the south side of the city. As his "peddling" business grew, Binga became well known to the people of the area. He met and married Eudora Johnson, the niece of a well-known sportsman, who willed his estate to his niece. Binga's wife's inheritance became the nucleus of his enterprises.

Investing in real estate on the fringe of the Negro area, he soon had under control over three hundred units of real estate, from which he collected rent on nearly twelve hundred apartments. His real estate office was the site chosen for the location of the Binga State Bank in 1908. Aggressively and defiantly, Binga built his financial empire, and in the postwar period of the twenties he was at the height of success. Deposits were made to the extent of 1.5 million dollars.

When the economic depression hit in 1929, Binga found it difficult to refuse loan applicants, allowing them extended payments on their contracts with the bank. Like other hard-pressed bankers of the period, he found himself in financial difficulty; and by May 1932, the Binga State Bank had closed its doors. Binga, sentenced to prison in 1933, was later pardoned by the President; but he was unable to rebuild his financial empire.

Bolin, Jane Matilda

Judge

Jane Matilda Bolin (1908–), justice of the domestic relations court of New York City, was born in Poughkeepsie, New York. She received her B.A. degree from Wellesley College in 1928, and her LL.B. degree from Yale University in 1931. Passing the New York State bar examination in 1932, she began the private practice of law in New York City. Within five years she was appointed assistant corporation counsel for the city; and, in 1939, Mayor Fiorello La Guardia appointed Jane Bolin as judge of the domestic relations court of the city.

Judge Bolin has served as a member of the board of directors of the Wiltwyck School for Boys, the Dalton School, the United Neighborhood Houses and the Neighborhood Children's Center; she has served also on the Committee on Children of New York City. Facing disrupted domestic relations in court and making judgments on the destinies of children, her activities on these committees have enabled her to follow their rehabilitation and adjustment. Her other activities include membership in the Scholarship and Service Fund for Negro Students, the Urban League of Greater New York and the New York State Committee Against Discrimination in Housing. In July, 1969, she was sworn in for her fourth term as judge of the family court, New York City.

JANE MATILDA BOLIN

Bontemps, Arna

Author

Arna Bontemps (1902–1973), formerly writer-in-residence at Fisk University, was born in Alexandria, Louisiana. He received his Bachelor's degree from Pacific Union College in California in 1923, and his Master's degree in library science from the University of Chicago. The *Crisis* Magazine Poetry Prize was awarded to him in 1927, and the Alexander Pushkin Prize in 1926 and 1927. He has also received Rosenwald and Guggenheim Fellowships.

Publishing his first novel, *God Sends Sunday,* in 1931, he has written histories, novels, children's books, biographies, poetry and a Broadway play. In 1969, he accepted a distinguished visiting professorship at Yale University as a lecturer and curator in Afro-American studies. He returned to Fisk in 1971. Some of his books are: *You Can't Pet a Possum,* 1934; *Black Thun-*

ARNA BONTEMPS

der, 1936; *Golden Slippers: An Anthology of Negro Poetry for Young People,* 1941; *Story of the Negro,* 1948; *George Washington Carver,* 1950; *Frederick Douglass: Slave, Fighter, Freeman,* 1959; *100 Years of Negro Freedom,* 1961; *American Negro Poetry,* 1963; and *Famous Negro Athletes,* 1964.

Braithwaite, William Stanley

Poet and Anthologist

William S. Braithwaite (1878–1962), a leader in the revival of interest in poetry in the United States, through his *Anthology of Magazine Verse,* was born in Boston, Massachusetts. He was the son of a university-trained father from British Guiana who migrated to the United States and married a mulatto woman who had fled from the South. Even though the father was of mixed blood, he did not associate with the Negroes of Boston, nor did he permit his children to at-

tend the public schools. He tutored the children at home until his death. William was eight years of age when his father died, leaving the family destitute. He then attended the public schools, but had to withdraw after four years to work. Obtaining a job as the manager of a book store, he had access to books and an opportunity to cultivate a love for poetry.

He assembled his first book of original poems in 1904, but had to pay for the publication himself; his second volume of poems came out in 1908. Afterwards, he began to concentrate on compiling anthologies of verse. From 1913 to 1929, he published each year the *Anthology of Magazine Verse,* in an effort to encourage American poets.

Braithwaite gained a good reputation as a critic and also worked as a free-lance writer for the Boston *Transcript.* He served as visiting professor of creative literature at Atlanta University and was responsible for discovering and encouraging young Americans with literary talent.

Brice, Edward Warner

Government Official

Edward Warner Brice (1916–   ), assistant secretary of education for the Department of Health, Education, and Welfare, was born in Hallboro, North Carolina. He graduated from Tuskegee Institute and earned his M.A. and Ph.D. degrees at the University of Pennsylvania. Dr. Brice is the third-ranking federal official in the field of education.

Prior to his promotion, he held a number of important positions in the federal government. He was chief of the education division of the United States Operation Missions to the Republic of Liberia, Africa, and the kingdom of Nepal in Asia from 1952 to 1958, and served as director of the adult education branch and specialist in fundamental and literacy education from 1958 to 1966.

EDWARD WARNER BRICE

From 1952 until 1962, Dr. Brice served as an assistant to Mennen G. Williams, secretary of state for African affairs, with a special assignment as public affairs officer at the United States Embassy in Monrovia, Liberia. Prior to entering government service, he was dean of education extension and professor of graduate education at South Carolina State College. During World War II, he was an artillery officer in the army. He was president of Clinton Junior College in Rock Hill, South Carolina, prior to the war.

Dr. Brice is the recipient of the Bronze Star and the George Washington Carver Distinguished Achievement Award, 1950. He is a frequent contributor to professional publications, is the author of eight books and was the chief architect of UNESCO's world experimental literacy program. He is listed in *Who's Who in the South and Southwest, 1974–75*.

Brooke, Edward W.

United States Senator

Edward W. Brooke (1919–   ), Republican senator from Massachusetts, is the first black to be elected to the United States Senate since Reconstruction. A native of Washington, D.C., Brooke attended local schools, receiving a Bachelor of Science degree from Howard University, 1941. He received his L.L.B. from Boston University Law School, 1948, and his Master of Laws in 1950.

During World War II he served with the "Partisans" in Italy as a Captain in the U.S. Army. He received the Bronze Star and Combat Infantryman's Badge.

Brooke was elected attorney general of the Commonwealth of Massachusetts, 1963. In 1966, he was elected U.S. Senator from Massachusetts. He was reelected in 1972.

Brooke received the Charles Evans Hughes Award, National Conference of Christians and Jews, 1967; and the Spingarn Medal, 1967. He is a member of four major commit-

EDWARD W. BROOKE

tees: Banking, Housing and Urban Affairs; Committee on Appropriations; Select Committee on Standards and Conduct; and Special Committee on Aging. In 1974 he served as ranking minority member of the Subcommittee on Foreign Operations. He is the author of *The Challenge of Change*, published in 1966, and the recipient of over 30 honorary doctorates. He is a Fellow of the American Bar Association and of the American Academy of Arts and Sciences.

Brooks, Gwendolyn

Poet

Gwendolyn Brooks (1917–), successful American poet, is a master of poetic technique and style. She has literary competence which enables her to use the medium of poetry with originality of style and point of view. Her first volume of poems, *A Street in Bronzeville*, won the Merit Award of *Mademoiselle* magazine. Her second volume, *Annie Allen*, portrays the universal experiences of a modern woman. She received the Pulitzer Prize for poetry in 1950 for this work.

Miss Brooks was born in Topeka, Kansas, but has lived in Chicago since childhood. She is a graduate of Englewood High School and Wilson Junior College of Chicago. Her poetry has appeared in *Harper's, Poetry, Common Ground* and the *Yale Review*. She was the recipient of a $1,000 prize from the Academy of Arts and Letters in 1946 and received a Guggenheim Fellowship for the years 1946 and 1947.

In 1968, Miss Brooks succeeded Carl Sandburg as poet laureate of the state of Illinois. Her recent publications include *Family Pictures*, 1970, and *Aloneness*, 1971. In 1974, she led a black awareness program at the University of Houston (Texas), where she urged young writers to submit work to black publishing companies. She personally presents prizes to Illinois youngsters who compete in her poet laureate contests. She is working on new material for publication and concentrates on visiting college campuses for speaking engagements.

Brown, Charlotte Hawkins

Educator

Charlotte Hawkins Brown (1883–1961), founder of Palmer Memorial Institute, was born in Henderson, North Carolina. Her family moved to Cambridge, Massachusetts, where she attended the public schools of the city. She graduated from the State Normal School in Salem in 1901, and returned immediately to North Carolina determined to start a "farm-life" school. Near Sedalia she found an unoccupied shack. With the cooperation of residents and area churches, she opened a school and completed a year of teaching.

She returned to Massachusetts in the summer, organized a Sedalia Club to support the work of the school, and interested two families who underwrote the work for one year

GWENDOLYN BROOKS

CHARLOTTE HAWKINS BROWN

after her birth. Her talent as an elocutionist was noted while she was studying in the Ontario schools, and, to give her further training, the family returned to the United States to settle at Wilberforce, Ohio, where she enrolled at Wilberforce University. After graduating from the university, Miss Brown taught at Allen University and Tuskegee Institute, but she soon returned to her alma mater as professor of elocution.

Utilizing her talent as a speaker and a dramatic reader, she spread the name of Wilberforce throughout the United States and Europe. Her repertory consisted of such diversified subjects as: "The Progress of Negro Education and Advancement in America since Emancipation," "The Status of the Afro-American Woman before and after the War," "Negro Folklore and Folksong," "My Visit to Queen Victoria" and "Windsor Castle." In addition to lecturing, she recited

and donated a large tract of land for future growth and development.

Disaster struck the institution in December 1917, when a fire destroyed the wooden building. This loss opened the way for a series of new brick buildings, since staunch friends of Mrs. Brown, in both North Carolina and New England, raised money for the school. By 1920, the Julius Rosenwald Fund contributed to the maintenance and building program. Charlotte Brown continued to study while building and directing Palmer Memorial Institute. She received her college degree at Wellesley.

Brown, Hallie Quinn

Teacher and Elocutionist

Hallie Quinn Brown (1849–1949), well-known teacher and elocutionist, was born in Pittsburgh, Pennsylvania, but her parents moved to Chatham, in Ontario, Canada, soon

HALLIE QUINN BROWN

the works of Paul Laurence Dunbar in Germany, France, Switzerland and Great Britain, where she appeared before Queen Victoria in 1899.

Miss Brown participated in many national and international movements of her day. She was a member of the Royal Geographical Society of Scotland and the International Woman's Congress of London and served as president both of the Ohio State Federation of Women's Clubs and of the National Association of Colored Women. She was the author of several books: *Bits and Odds; First Lessons in Public Speaking; Machile, the African; Tales My Father Told;* and *Homespun Heroines and Other Women of Distinction.*

Also active in politics, she campaigned throughout Ohio, Pennsylvania, Illinois and Missouri in behalf of Warren G. Harding in 1920 and spoke at the Republican Party convention in Cleveland in 1924.

Brown, James Nathaniel

Athlete

James Nathaniel Brown (1936–), the king of football's running backs, was born on St. Simons Island, Georgia. His parents separated during his infancy, and he was left in his grandmother's care until he was seven years old, when his mother, who was employed as a maid in Manhasset, Long Island, sent for him to join her. There, he attended elementary and high school with the well-to-do children of the community and developed into an outstanding athlete who attracted the attention of college coaches and recruiters. He received about 45 offers of scholarships but did not accept any of them. Instead, he selected Syracuse University, even though he was offered no scholarship, because a committee of Manhasset citizens had encouraged him to choose Syracuse and offered him financial assistance.

JAMES NATHANIEL BROWN

Brown failed the Syracuse entrance examination but was allowed to enroll "on condition," which meant that he had to concentrate on his studies during his freshman year. The Syracuse coaches were slow to recognize his extraordinary talents, and he might have given up, had he not encountered Lieutenant Colonel Ernest L. Meggs of the R.O.T.C. staff, who took an interest in him. After making average grades his first year, he decided to remain, even though he had not impressed the coaches. His performance during his last two years at Syracuse was spectacular. And after the Cotton Bowl contest against Texas Christian University, he was named the most outstanding back of the game.

When he graduated from Syracuse, Brown selected professional football as his career and joined the Cleveland Browns in 1957. The United Press voted Jim Brown the

"Rookie of the Year" at the close of his first season. In 1958, he was presented the Jim Thorpe Trophy as the National Football League's foremost star. United Press International named him American Athlete of the Year and Player of the Year. He has left football to pursue a movie career.

Bunche, Ralph Johnson

United Nations Official

Ralph Johnson Bunche (1904–1971), Nobel Peace Prize winner in 1950, was born in Detroit, Michigan. His father, a barber, and his mother, an amateur musician, died before he completed school. He graduated from high school in California while living with his grandmother. He entered UCLA, where he won many sports trophies and graduated *summa cum laude;* won the Tappan Prize at Harvard for the best doctoral dissertation in the social sciences in 1934; and continued his academic post-doctoral studies at Northwestern University, the London School of Economics and the University of Capetown in South Africa.

This brilliant scholar assumed the chairmanship of the political science department at Howard University in 1937. During World War II, he was employed by the Office of Strategic Services as a specialist on information pertaining to Africa. At the close of the war, he had advanced to the position of associate chief of dependent areas in the State Department. His next appointment was to the trusteeship division of the United Nations. In this division, he was selected to represent the United Nations' secretary-general in the explosive Arab-Israeli crisis. He became the acting mediator of the crisis when Count Folke Bernadotte was assassinated in 1948.

Dr. Bunche directed the U.N. peacekeeping efforts in the Suez, 1956; the Congo, 1960; and Cyprus, 1964. His most spectacu-

RALPH JOHNSON BUNCHE

lar success at the U.N. is acknowledged to be the negotiation of the 1949 armistice between the newly born state of Israel and its Arab neighbors. He was awarded the Spingarn Medal in 1949.

In October, 1971, Dr. Bunche retired because of failing health from the U.N. position of under secretary-general for special political affairs. He died in December, 1971, eulogized by U.N. Secretary-General U Thant as "the most effective and best-known of international civil servants."

Butler, John Henry Manning

Educator

John Henry Manning Butler (?–1944), founder of the school at Alanimos in the province of Pangasinan in the Philippines, was at one time in his career a provincial superintendent of schools in the Islands. Butler was born in Elizabeth City, North Carolina, and was educated at the Plymouth Normal School. Teaching first in his native city in 1891, he next was vice-principal of the Normal and Industrial School until 1894, and served at the North Carolina Agricultural and Technical College in Greensboro from 1896 to 1900.

In 1902, he accepted an appointment to serve in the Philippine Islands as an organizer and inspector of schools. The successful establishment of the school at Alanimos resulted in his appointment as acting superintendent of schools in the province of Isabela. In 1927, the Cagayan schools were added to his district. Reaching retirement age in 1933, he accepted an appointment in the department of education at the privately owned National University of Manila.

When the Japanese Army took control of the Philippine Islands in 1942, Manning was interned by the Japanese military. He died in January 1944.

Caliver, Ambrose

Educator

Ambrose Caliver (1894–1962), senior specialist in the education of Negroes in the United States Office of Education from 1930 to 1946, was born in Saltville, Virginia. His father died when he was 11, and he was forced to work in the coal mines to help support his family. Eventually, he was sent to his grandmother in Knoxville, Tennessee. He graduated from Knoxville College in 1915, attended trade school at Tuskegee, and in 1918, received a diploma in personnel management from Harvard University. He earned his M.A. degree at the University of Wisconsin in 1920 and his Ph.D. from Columbia University in 1930.

After a successful teaching career in the public schools of Rockwood, Tennessee, and El Paso, Texas, he was appointed dean of Fisk University. In 1930, Caliver was granted a leave from Fisk to serve as senior specialist in the education of Negroes in the United States Office of Education. He was promoted in 1946 to specialist for higher education of Negroes and adviser on related problems in the Office of Education. While in this position, he also lectured at many Negro colleges. He initiated and directed the FERA and WPA emergency education programs under the New Deal, and was chairman of a special committee with the National Vocational Guidance Association from 1938 to 1942. This was followed by the directorship of a program for adult education for Negroes.

In 1941–42, Dr. Caliver created and directed Freedom's People, a series of nationwide radio broadcasts on the participation of Negroes in American life. He was a member of the Committee of the White House Conference on Children in a Democracy in 1941 and the Citizens' Committee on Integration of Negroes into the National Defense Program. Dr. Caliver published at least 18 books and bulletins and more than 50 articles in leading periodicals.

Campbell, Elmer Simms

Cartoonist

E. Simms Campbell (1906–1974), master cartoonist of sophisticated humor for *Esquire* and *Playboy* magazines, was born in St. Louis, Missouri. He attended Englewood High School in Chicago and the Chicago Art Institute. In St. Louis, he had been discouraged and advised not to expect a career in commercial art, but he was determined to try to break down the barrier of discrimination in this area. After completing the course at the Chicago Art Institute, he went to New York, where he became a free-lance cartoonist. In 1926, in his Armistice Day sketch, he attracted national attention with his cartoon summing up the debt of the nation to those who died in World War I.

During the 1930's and 1940's, Campbell was employed by *Esquire* under a long-term contract. His cartoons were of the harem of an Arabian potentate, of a business tycoon and of a young newlywed couple. His art appeared also in hundreds of newspapers and magazines as a syndicated feature; and commercial advertising agencies employed his talent in the composition of their ads. He had contributed cartoons and other art work to the following: *Cosmopolitan, Redbook, New Yorker, Collier's, Saturday Evening Post, College Humor, Opportunity, Esquire* and *Playboy.*

Carver, George Washington

Scientist

George Washington Carver (*c.* 1861–1943), recipient of the Roosevelt Medal for his service to science in 1939, was born during the Civil War at Diamond Grove, Missouri. After earning the degree of Master of Science from Iowa State College, he joined

GEORGE WASHINGTON CARVER

the faculty of Tuskegee Institute in 1896. In the rural environment of Tuskegee, Alabama, he began his studies of soil conservation and crop diversification. Using the native produce of the area, he developed more than 100 different products from the sweet potato and more than 300 different products from the peanut. In 1917, he was named a Fellow of the Royal Society of Arts, and, in 1923, he was awarded the Spingarn Medal by the NAACP.

He left his life's earnings to Tuskegee Institute for the establishment of the George Washington Carver Foundation to assist in the education of young Negro scientists.

Cassell, Albert J.

Architect

Albert J. Cassell (1895–1969), former head of the architecture department at Howard University, was born in Baltimore, where he completed his early training at Douglass High School. Entering the School of Architecture of Cornell University on the eve of America's entry into World War I, he left to serve in the army as a second lieutenant in France. After the war, he worked as an architect with W. A. Hazel on the construction of five buildings at Tuskegee Institute. As a draftsman, he worked in the office of Howard J. Weigner in Bethlehem, Pennsylvania, in 1920. He was responsible for designing an industrial plant for the manufacture of silk.

Associating again with Hazel in 1921, he began his career at Howard University during its building expansion program. They were responsible for the construction of the Home Economics Building. Then Cassell, operating alone, served as the architect for the gymnasium and athletic field, 1924; the College of Medicine, 1926; three women's dormitories, 1931; the chemistry building, 1933; and his most outstanding project at Howard, the

ALBERT J. CASSELL

Founders Library, 1946. His largest project was Mayfair Mansions, a $5 million apartment complex in Washington, D.C. His work appears elsewhere in this country, and also in Africa.

Chamberlain, Wilton Norman

Athlete

Wilton Norman Chamberlain (1936–), outstanding basketball star, was born in West Philadelphia, Pennsylvania. While attending Brooks Elementary School, he preferred the rougher sports of football and boxing and considered basketball a "sissy" game; but when he entered Shoemaker Junior High and learned to play basketball, he was impressed by the ruggedness and skill required by the game.

Because of his B average as a student, as well as his athletic career, professional basketball team owners began manipulating provisions in their rules in an effort to obtain Chamberlain for their professional teams while he was still in high school. By the time he graduated, he had received scholarship offers from more than 200 colleges. In May 1955, he decided to attend Kansas University because certain members of the faculty showed an interest in him as a prospective scholar, instead of limiting their interest to his athletic career. During his first year on the varsity team, the students began calling him "The Big Dipper." He led Kansas University to the finals of the NCAA basketball tournament but, after two years on the college varsity team and selection for All-American both years, he decided to drop out of college.

In June of 1958, Chamberlain was hired by the Harlem Globetrotters and joined the

WILTON NORMAN CHAMBERLAIN

team in Europe for an exhibition tour. By then known as "Wilt the Stilt," he had reached the unusual height of seven feet, which made him the center of attention in the European cities. Upon his return, he was offered a contract with the Philadelphia Warriors.

During his career, Chamberlain, who is now retired as an active ballplayer, has broken almost every scoring record in American professional basketball. At the end of his first season, he was given the basketball writers' Hy Turkin Award for rookie of the year, and the Sam Davis Award as the most valuable player. He accounted for eight of the eleven new marks set during the season.

Chesnutt, Charles Waddell

Educator and Author

Charles Waddell Chesnutt (1858–1932), lawyer, writer and educator, was born and educated in Cleveland, Ohio. After the Civil War, Chesnutt went to North Carolina, where he taught for nine years in the new public school system. Eventually, he became principal of the State Normal School, now Fayetteville State Teachers College. However, when the Solid South re-emerged in the 1880's and living conditions became precarious for the colored man, Chesnutt moved to New York, where he worked for a few months on a newspaper. Next, he returned to Cleveland and entered the law profession. He was admitted to the bar in 1887 and became a court reporter.

Recognition in the literary field came to Chesnutt in 1887, when his first short story, "The Goophered Grapevine," appeared in the *Atlantic Monthly*. His years of experience in the South enabled him to describe vividly and in depth the Negro's culture. Encouraged by the response to his magazine stories, he published a volume of stories in 1899 entitled *The Conjure Woman*. It was followed

W. MONTAGUE COBB

by *The Wife of His Youth* (1899), *The House behind the Cedars* (1900), *The Marrow of Tradition* (1901) and *The Colonel's Dream* (1905). In 1928, Chesnutt received the Spingarn Medal awarded by the National Association for the Advancement of Colored People.

Cobb, W. Montague

Spokesman for Negro Rights in Medicine

W. Montague Cobb (1904–   ), champion of national health insurance legislation, is known as the spokesman for black rights in medicine. He is professor of anatomy at Howard University Medical School, Washington, D.C., and editor of the *Journal of the National Medical Association*. He has served as president of the National Medical Association, the American Association of Physical Anthropologists, and the Anthropological Society of Washington.

Dr. Cobb received his A.B. degree from Amherst College, 1925; his M.D. from Howard University, 1929; and a Ph.D. from Western Reserve University, 1932.

Dr. Cobb pioneered efforts to ensure equal treatment for black physicians. His pamphlet *Old Clothes to Sam* pointed out the denial of membership privileges to black doctors by the American Medical Association. As a leader in the National Medical Association, he pressed for resolutions to hold annual meetings in cities in which blacks would not meet with discrimination.

Dr. Cobb believes that "the quality of teachers is much more important than anything else in imparting a good education." He is the author of more than 500 monographs, abstracts, editorials, scientific articles, and biographical sketches.

MERCER COOK

Cook, Mercer

Scholar, Author and Diplomat

Mercer Cook (1903–), distinguished linguistic scholar and author, was born in Washington, D.C. After graduating from Dunbar High School, he entered Amherst College, where he graduated with honors in 1925. The college awarded Cook, a member of the Phi Beta Kappa society, the Simpson Fellowship prize of $1,800, which made it possible for him to study the French language and literature at the Sorbonne in Paris for one year. After a brief period of teaching at the Agricultural and Technical College in Greensboro, North Carolina, and at Howard University, he entered Brown University and obtained his Master's degree and finally his Doctor of Philosophy degree in 1936.

On resuming his career as a teacher, he became head of the department of Romance languages at Atlanta University. In 1943, he was called upon by the Office of Inter-American Affairs to direct the English-teaching project in Haiti. In 1945, he returned to Howard University as professor of Romance languages. Dr. Cook has published a number of

scholarly books which have attracted international attention and has served on the editorial board of the *Journal of Negro History*. Dr. Cook served as United States ambassador to Nigeria from 1961 to 1964 and as ambassador to Senegal and Gambia from 1964 to 1966.

In May, 1973, Dr. Cook joined 12 other ambassadors and 2 under secretaries of state from the Kennedy and Johnson administrations in issuing a statement deploring the Nixon administration's increased contacts with minority governments in Southern Africa. The statement said these contacts "convey a sense of collaboration and retard the eventual independence of black Africans."

Crosthwait, David N., Jr.

Engineer

David N. Crosthwait, Jr. (1898–), specialist in the engineering of heating and ventilating systems, was born in Nashville, Tennessee. He was educated in Kansas City, where he graduated from high school in

1916. He received his Bachelor of Science in mechanical engineering and Master of Engineering degrees from Purdue University, and was employed as a heating specialist and consultant by the C. A. Durham Company of Michigan City, Indiana. He progressed in this firm from draftsman to checker and supervisor. As supervisor, he not only designed heating systems but also served as a diagnostician by inspecting and analyzing heating installations. By 1919, while still in college, Crosthwait had attained the position of engineer with a research laboratory developing experiments and inventions.

Some of his inventions and patents are: the automatic waterfeeder, 1920; automobile indicator, 1921; thermostat-setting apparatus, 1928; vacuum heating system, 1929; and the vacuum pump, 1930. Since 1925, he has been director of the research department of the company and has served as technical advisor and consultant to utility companies of large metropolitan areas. He helped develop the apparatus and method of heating for the 70-story structure of Radio City Music Hall in New York City.

Cullen, Countee Porter

Poet

Countee Porter Cullen (1903–1946), poet and writer of the "lost generation" and of the Negro Renaissance of the 1920's, was born in New York City and, after the death of his grandmother, was adopted by the Reverend and Mrs. Frederick A. Cullen. He received his early education in the city's public schools, where he produced his first poem, "To the Swimmer," which was published in the *Modern School Magazine* in 1918.

As a student at New York University in 1925, he was elected to the Phi Beta Kappa honor fraternity. He was the recipient of several prizes, among them the Witter Bynner Poetry Prize. He also won the John Reed Memorial Prize, awarded by *Poetry* magazine, for his poem "Threnody for a Brown Girl." He received his Master's degree in English from Harvard in 1926, and received a Guggenheim Award for study in France in 1928. He taught French at the Frederick Douglass Junior High School in New York City from 1934 to 1945.

His poems, though somewhat uneven, show a superb lyric quality; and throughout his lifetime, Cullen stressed his desire to be known as a lyric poet, rather than as a Negro poet. *On These I Stand,* his last book of poetry, was published posthumously in 1947.

Dailey, Ulysses Grant

Physician

Ulysses Grant Dailey (1885–1961), outstanding physician in the field of anatomy and surgery, was born in Donaldsonville,

COUNTEE PORTER CULLEN

Louisiana. After graduating from Northwestern University Medical School in 1906, he was appointed a demonstrator in anatomy at the college; and from 1908 to 1912, he was associated with Dr. Daniel Hale Williams at Provident Hospital as a surgical assistant.

ULYSSES GRANT DAILEY

After studying in Paris, London and Vienna, he established his own hospital and sanitarium in 1926. He was associate editor of the *Journal of the National Medical Association* for 38 years and was editor-in-chief of the *Journal* in 1948–49.

In addition, he was corresponding editor of the *Medics* journal of Karachi, Pakistan, and served as health advisor for the Department of State in India, Pakistan, Ceylon and Africa from 1951 to 1953. When he retired from active practice in 1954, he made his residence in Haiti, where he was named honorary consul for the United States government.

Davis, Benjamin Oliver
Officer in the United States Army

Benjamin O. Davis, Sr. (1877–1970), first black to attain the rank of brigadier general in the United States Army, was born in Washington, D.C., was educated in the District schools and attended Howard University. His 50 years of outstanding service to his country began in 1898, during the Spanish-American War, when he entered the army as a temporary first lieutenant in the 8th United States Infantry. He was mustered out on March 6, 1899, and in June of the same year, he enlisted as a private in the 9th Cavalry of the regular army. On February 2, 1901, he was commissioned a second lieutenant of cavalry in the regular army.

Promotions in the army were rare for Negroes, regardless of their service record. Davis proved his ability in the Philippine Islands and at Fort Washakie, Wyoming, before receiving his promotion to first lieutenant in 1905; and 10 years elapsed before he was made a captain. Because of the emer-

BENJAMIN OLIVER DAVIS

gency of World War I, he was given two rapid but temporary promotions: to major in 1917 and to lieutenant colonel in 1918. After the close of the war, he returned to his former rank of captain but was returned to the rank of lieutenant colonel in 1920.

In the interim, he had served as professor of military science and tactics at Wilberforce University and as military attaché to Monrovia, Liberia. In 1920, he was professor of military science and tactics at Tuskegee Institute in Alabama, and in 1924, he became instructor of the 372nd Infantry of the Ohio National Guard in Cleveland.

It was not until 1930 that he received his next promotion, when he was made a full colonel; and he was destined to wait another 10 years for his promotion to brigadier general (temporary) in 1940. He was retired on July 31, 1941, but was recalled to active duty in the grade of brigadier general the following day.

In World War II, Davis was assigned to the European Theater of Operations as an advisor on problems relating to Negro servicemen. He was responsible for implementing the policy of integration of facilities for these men.

General Davis was given the following awards and decorations: Distinguished Service Medal, 1944; the Bronze Star Medal, 1945; French Croix de Guerre with Palm; Grade of Commander of the Order of the Star of Africa, Liberian Government; and an honorary LL.D. degree from Atlanta University. When he retired in 1948, he was assistant to the inspector general, Washington, D.C.

Davis, Benjamin Oliver, Jr.
Officer of the United States Air Force

Lieutenant General Benjamin Oliver Davis, Jr. (1912–   ), retired Air Force officer, is assistant secretary of the U.S. Department of

BENJAMIN OLIVER DAVIS, JR.

Transportation, director of civil aviation security. Gen. Davis received the presidential appointment in 1971. He retired from the Air Force in 1970.

Born in Washington, D.C., Davis graduated from the United States Military Academy in 1936, the fourth black to graduate from West Point. In 1942, he received his wings and transferred from the Infantry to the Army Air Corps.

In World War II, he served as commander of the 99th Fighter Squadron and the 332nd Fighter Group stationed in Europe and Africa, 1943–45.

General Davis' post-World War II commands included chief of staff, United States Forces, Korea; chief of staff, United Nations Command, 1965–67; commander of the 13th Air Force at Clark Air Force Base in the Philippines; and deputy commander-in-chief of the U.S. Strike Command at MacDill Air Force Base, Tampa, Florida.

He has served on the President's Commission on Campus Unrest and, in 1970–71, as director of public safety for the city of Cleveland, Ohio. He holds honorary degrees from Morgan State College, Wilberforce University and Tuskegee Institute. His military medals include the Silver Star; Legion of Merit with two oak leaf clusters; Air Force Commendation Medal; the Croix de Guerre; and the Star of Africa.

In 1944, following a successful bombing raid against a German installation deep in occupied France, he received the Distinguished Flying Cross, which was pinned on by his father, the late Brigadier General Benjamin O. Davis, Sr.

Davis, John Warren

Educator

John Warren Davis (1888–), special director of the Teacher Information and Security Program of the NAACP Legal Defense and Educational Fund, was born in Milledgeville, Georgia. He received his B.A. degree from Morehouse College in Atlanta, Georgia, in 1911 and his M.A. in 1920, and studied at the University of Chicago from 1911 to 1913. He began his teaching career at Morehouse College. In 1919 he became president of West Virginia State College, where he remained until 1953. Upon his retirement, he was elected president emeritus of the college.

Dr. Davis guided the growth and development of the college from a student body of 27 to its peak enrollment of 1,850 and secured its accreditation by the North Central Association of Colleges and Secondary Schools in 1927. The college became one of the leading land-grant institutions in America, as Dr. Davis set the stage for it to become an integrated institution. White students entered the predominantly Negro college in increasing numbers; in 1965, they accounted for 71 per cent of the enrollment.

Dr. Davis combined a wide range of activities with his leadership of the college. He

JOHN WARREN DAVIS

served as a member of President Hoover's Organization on Unemployment Relief and as a member of the National Science Foundation for six years. Upon his retirement in 1953, he was sent to Liberia to direct the United States' technical assistance program. Since 1955, he has been special director of the Teacher Information and Security Program of the NAACP Legal Defense and Educational Fund. In this capacity, he uses his long experience as an educator to fight for the protection of Negro teachers in communities making the transition to integrated schools.

Dr. Davis has participated in the economic and educational progress of the Negro for the past five decades. He received numerous honorary degrees and was decorated by the governments of Haiti and Liberia. Since undertaking his present activities with the NAACP Legal Defense and Educational Fund, he has worked as a consultant to the Peace Corps and to the United States Department of State.

Davis, Sammy, Jr.

Entertainer

Sammy Davis, Jr. (1925–), who became a professional entertainer at the early age of three, is one of the nation's most famous song-and-dance men, as well as a successful actor on Broadway and the film screen. When he was born, in Harlem, his father was the lead dancer in Will Mastin's vaudeville troupe *Holiday in Dixieland.*

For years, Sammy toured with his father as a member of the Will Mastin Trio. In 1930, he appeared with Ethel Waters in the film *Rufus Jones for President.* His later film successes included *Anna Lucasta,* co-starring Eartha Kitt; the American folk opera *Porgy and Bess,* in which he played Sportin' Life; *Ocean's Eleven;* and *Sergeants Three,* which co-starred Dean Martin, Peter Lawford and Frank Sinatra. His career on Broadway began with his role in *Mr. Wonderful*; and he starred in the musical *Golden Boy.*

SAMMY DAVIS, JR.

Sammy Davis has appeared as both host and as a guest on many television shows, notably, Hollywood Palace, the Nat King Cole Show, the Dean Martin Show, and the Eddie Cantor Comedy Hour. In personal appearances before audiences in the best-known hotels and nightclubs, this small but powerfully talented entertainer continues to be vigorously applauded. In 1954, Davis lost his left eye in an automobile accident. He made a dramatic comeback at Ciro's the following year.

In 1960, Sammy Davis was requested by Queen Elizabeth of England to appear at the annual Command Performance at the Victoria Palace. After the performance, he received a rare honor when he was personally congratulated by the Queen. During his stay in England, he gave a special pre-opening show at the Pigalle, where his two and one-half hour performance was followed by twenty solid minutes of applause.

His biography, *Yes I Can,* published in 1965, became a best seller. In 1968, Davis received the Spingarn Medal from the NAACP for his achievements. In 1973, he flew to London to tape a television special for General Electric.

Dawson, William

Musician

William Dawson (1898–), composer and retired director of the Tuskegee Institute Choir, was born in Anniston, Alabama, and ran away from home at age 13 to attend Tuskegee Institute. Given the opportunity to work on the school's farm to finance his education, he accepted. He graduated seven years later and went on to obtain a bachelor's degree in music at the Institute of Fine Arts, Kansas City, and a degree of Master of Music at the American Conservatory of Music in Chicago.

He was first trombonist of the Chicago Civic Symphony, the first black to play in the orchestra. He organized and directed the School of Music at Tuskegee Institute and traveled throughout the United States and Europe conducting choral groups under the sponsorship of the State Department.

During his 25-year tenure as head of the Tuskegee Institute Choir, the choir sang before two Presidents. In 1933, they sang at the White House at the invitation of President Herbert Hoover. In 1932, the choir sang under Dawson's direction at the birthday party of President-elect Franklin D. Roosevelt. His choirs have performed at Carnegie Hall.

Dawson resigned as conductor in 1955. He is known for choral compositions and for his *Negro Folk Symphony* premiered in 1934 and performed by the Philadelphia Symphony Orchestra conducted by Leopold Stokowski. Although retired, Dawson remains active in music circles. In 1974, he was guest artist at a workshop on Afro-American music in Atlanta, a workshop devoted almost entirely to his works.

Dawson, William L.
United States Congressman

William L. Dawson (1886–1970), congressman from Illinois, was born in Albany, Georgia, and worked his way through Fisk University, graduating with honors in 1909. In Chicago, he attended Kent College of Law and, in 1920, graduated from Northwestern University with his LL.D. His law studies were interrupted by his war service (1917–19). He began practicing law in Chicago in 1920; and as a precinct worker in the Republican Party, he progressed in ward politics. He was elected for five terms (1933–1943) to the city council; and on the Democratic New Deal tide, he went to Congress in 1943.

WILLIAM L. DAWSON

His long tenure in Congress placed Congressman Dawson high on the seniority list. He was chairman of the House Committee on Government Operations and served on the Democratic National Committee. He kept tight control over the five Chicago wards that form the 1st Illinois district, which he represented. He also served as vice-chairman of the Cook County Democratic organization. Through his mild manner and vigorous attention to details, without a desire for fanfare or publicity, he won the respect of both government leaders and his fellow congressmen.

De Priest, Oscar
United States Congressman

Oscar De Priest (1871–1951), congressman from Illinois, fulfilled the prophecy made in 1901 by George H. White of North Carolina that a Negro would return to the United States Congress. It was the election,

OSCAR DE PRIEST

a delegate to the Republican national conventions from 1928. He was formerly assistant commissioner of the Illinois Commerce Commission and was a member of the board of directors of the Binga State Bank.

As the only black in Congress from 1929 to 1935, he was a courageous fighter for every legal guarantee of civil rights and against every aspect of racial bias. His blunt and outspoken speeches caused some of the intellectuals to look upon him as a "hack" politician. Despite his lack of social polish or formal educational training, however, De Priest denounced both timid "Uncle Tom" blacks and race-baiting whites, insisting that he was of the "common herd"; and as a symbol of the black man in Congress he wore his mantle well. He was deeply convinced that it is the duty of the black man to learn practical politics and to enter into the activities of political campaigns.

in 1928, of Oscar De Priest as representative of the voters from the 21st congressional district of Illinois that blazed the trail for the return of blacks to the legislative branch of the federal government. He was elected as a Republican to the 71st, 72nd and 73rd Congresses but, after serving three terms, lost his seat when the majority of blacks turned to the Democratic Party in 1934.

De Priest was born in Florence, Alabama, to former slave parents who moved to Salina, Kansas, when he was a boy. After attending the public schools of that city, he took a business course at the Salina Normal School and opened a painting and decorating business of his own. He moved to Chicago, where he developed his own real estate business and entered politics. Starting as a ward worker in Chicago, he was elected county commissioner in 1904 and 1906. In 1915, he was elected to the Chicago city council, and was

Dett, Robert Nathaniel

Musician

Robert Nathaniel Dett (1882–1943), conductor and composer of musical works, was born in Drummondsville, Ontario, Canada. Displaying talent in music, he was sent to the Halsted Conservatory of Music located in Lockport, New York, in 1901, and received his Bachelor of Music degree in musical composition from Oberlin College in 1908. He studied also at Columbia University, the University of Pennsylvania, the American Conservatory of Music in Chicago and at Harvard. He was the recipient of the Harvard Bowdoin Prize in 1920, for an essay entitled "The Emancipation of Negro Music," and he also won the Francis Boott Prize.

Although Dett was a brilliant conductor, his greatest achievements were as a composer. His "Danse Juba," which was played by the Australian pianist Percy Grainger, focused attention on Dett as a composer of

ROBERT NATHANIEL DETT

unusual ability. Some of his most outstanding compositions are in choral form and have been performed by such noted musical groups as the Syracuse University Chorus under the directorship of Professor Howard Lyman, the Church of the Ascension, the Columbia University Chorus and the Elgar Choir. His best-known compositions are: "Listen to the Lambs," "The Chariot Jubilee," "Enchantment," "Negro Folk Songs," "A Thousand Years Ago or More" and "Folk Songs of the South."

This gifted musician served as director of music at Lane College, Jackson, Tennessee; Lincoln University, Jefferson City, Missouri; and at Hampton Institute in Virginia. In recognition of his contributions to the world of music, Oberlin College awarded him an honorary Doctor of Music degree in 1926. His opera, *The Ordering of Moses*, was performed at Carnegie Hall in 1951 and was

recorded for distribution overseas by the Voice of America.

Diggs, Charles C., Jr.
United States Congressman

Charles C. Diggs, Jr. (1922–), veteran lawmaker now serving his tenth term as representative from the 13th district in Michigan, is a native of Detroit. Diggs was elected Michigan's first black Congressman in 1954, after serving for three years as the youngest member of the Michigan state senate. He was elected to the state body while still a student at Detroit College of Law.

The inspiration to organize efforts of black congressmen came from Diggs who, with the late William Dawson and the late Adam Clayton Powell, led nine representatives in formation of the Congressional Black Caucus in mid-1970. The Caucus boycotted the 1971

CHARLES C. DIGGS, JR.

State of the Union Address by President Nixon. Mr. Nixon subsequently agreed to meet with the Caucus. In March, 1971, the President met with a 13-person delegation led by Charles Diggs, first chairman of the Black Caucus.

Diggs, dean of the Michigan Democratic delegation, is chairman of the House Foreign Affairs Subcommittee on Africa. He has served as a full delegate at the 26th session of the United Nations General Assembly. He is chairman of the House Committee on the District of Columbia, the House Foreign Affairs Subcommittee on Africa and heads the National Black Political Assembly. He is serving his 10th term for Detroit's 13th District.

A licensed mortician, Diggs is president of the Detroit area mortuary corporation, House of Diggs, Inc. He is a graduate of Wayne State University and holds honorary degrees from Central State University and Wilberforce University, both in Ohio. He is a veteran of World War II.

DEAN DIXON

Dixon, Dean

Musician

Dean Dixon (1915–1976), conductor of the Frankfort Radio Symphony in West Germany, was born in New York City and was graduated from the Juilliard School of Music and from Columbia University. In 1941, Dixon made his debut as conductor of the New York Philharmonic Orchestra. He was the first black to conduct this prominent orchestra.

Dixon received the Alice M. Ditson Award for Outstanding Contributions to American Music in 1948. In 1949, he was invited to conduct the Radio Symphony Orchestra of the French National Radio in Paris.

After a 21-year absence from the United States, Dixon returned in 1970 to conduct the New York Philharmonic.

He has conducted most of the major symphony orchestras on the Continent and in Israel, introducing many American compositions, particularly the works of William Grant Still, to European music audiences. He received the Award of Merit from the American Society of Composers, Authors and Publishers for his encouragement and education of American youth in music.

Drew, Charles

Physician

Charles Drew (1904–1950), pioneer in blood preservation and founder of the blood bank, was chief surgeon and head of the staff at Freedmen's Hospital in Washington, D.C., at the time of his fatal automobile accident in 1950. A native of Washington,

CHARLES DREW

D.C., he attended Dunbar High School and won an athletic scholarship to Amherst, where he was captain of the track team and a football halfback. He received the Mossman Trophy at Amherst for having brought the most honor to the college over a four-year period. He excelled in scholarship and continued to attract notice as an athlete while studying medicine at McGill University in Canada. At McGill, he was awarded first prize in physiological anatomy. Chosen for special training under a General Education Board Fellowship at the Columbia Medical School in New York, he began his research into the properties of blood plasma.

Drew discovered ways and means of preserving blood plasma in blood banks for emergency needs. During World War II, he organized a blood-collecting service for the British government that saved the lives of thousands of injured servicemen. He direct-

ed the Red Cross blood bank, thus aiding the United States in 1942, when wounded American soldiers began receiving front-line transfusions. However, when "segregated" blood was called for (a policy that was later dropped, as blood differs only by type and not by "race"), Drew resigned and returned to Howard and Freedmen's.

Drew received the Spingarn Medal for his outstanding contributions to human welfare. As chief surgeon of the Howard Medical School, he strengthened the reputation of the school through his diligent attention to the emergency cases that came to the Freedmen's Hospital. Besides developing the blood bank, he studied the problems of fluid balance in surgery and surgical shock.

Du Bois, William Edward Burghardt
Leader in the Civil Rights Movement

William E. B. Du Bois (1868–1963), outstanding among Negro intellectuals and a militant civil rights leader, was born in Great Barrington, Massachusetts. His childhood in New England was a happy one until he experienced his first rejection because he was a Negro, when he was sharply snubbed by a newcomer at a school party. This incident helped set the course of the gifted youth's life. He became determined to establish a record of excellence in all of his school activities. At the age of sixteen, he graduated from college preparatory school with honors. Because of the influence of his mother and one of his teachers, he went to Fisk University instead of Harvard, where he had planned to study.

In 1888, Du Bois entered Harvard, where he won the Boylston oratorical contest and was one of the six commencement speakers. After two years of study in Germany, he returned to America, receiving his Ph.D. in 1895. He accepted appointments to teach at Wilberforce University and the University

WILLIAM EDWARD BURGHARDT DU BOIS

nomic exploitation of the Negro, Du Bois published books, articles, and poems to set forth his views. Some of his works are: *The Suppression of the African Slave Trade,* 1896; *John Brown,* 1909; *Darkwater,* 1920; *Black Reconstruction,* 1935; *Black Folk Then and Now; Color and Democracy,* 1945; and *The World and Africa.* At the time of his death, he was living in Ghana and serving as editor-in-chief of the *Encyclopedia Africana.*

Du Bois was generally recognized as one of the most incisive thinkers and effective platform orators in the United States, as well as one of the most profound scholars of his time and generation.

of Pennsylvania before moving to Atlanta University to head the department of history and economics for 13 years. Here he wrote, for the *Atlantic Monthly, World's Work* and other magazines, articles that later were collected in *The Souls of Black Folk,* a sociological study of the Negro people.

Infuriated by the compromising leadership of Booker T. Washington at the turn of the century and by the denial of protection to Negro citizens as race riots spread throughout the North, Du Bois backed the Niagara movement, advocating civil rights for Negroes. When the Springfield, Illinois, race riot shocked a group of liberal whites into forming a civil rights group, which later became the NAACP, they invited the participants of the Niagara movement to join them. With the establishment of the NAACP, Du Bois became the editor of its *Crisis* magazine.

In 1919, he launched the Pan-African Congresses in Paris, to focus world opinion on the conditions and status of black men. In his fight against discrimination and eco-

Dudley, Edward R.

State Supreme Court Justice

Edward R. Dudley (1911–), first Negro to be elevated to the diplomatic post of American ambassador, was born in Boston,

EDWARD R. DUDLEY

Virginia, and was educated at Johnson C. Smith University in Charlotte, North Carolina, and at Howard University in Washington, D.C. He taught in the rural schools of Virginia before moving to New York City, where he became associated with the Edward A. Johnson real estate firm. Meanwhile, he studied law at St. John's Law School in Brooklyn and earned his LL.B. degree in 1941. After one year of private practice in New York, in 1942 he was elected assistant attorney general for the state of New York. He served as an attorney on the legal staff of the NAACP, 1943–45.

It was not until 1948 that the post in Liberia was raised from a ministership to an ambassadorship. The policy of the State Department until this period was to limit the appointment of Negroes in the foreign service to ministerships, consulates and vice-consulates. The tenure of Dudley as ambassador to Liberia was from 1948 to 1953. He started the first Point 4 program in Africa. He had previously served as legal counsel to the governor of the Virgin Islands, 1945–47.

In 1965, he became an associate justice of the New York State supreme court. He was designated administrative judge of the criminal court of New York City in 1967 and administrative judge of the New York State supreme court (first district) in 1971. He is a trustee of the Fund for the City of New York and a life member of the NAACP.

Duncan, Todd

Singer and Actor

Todd Duncan (1903–   ), famous for his portrayal of Porgy in the musical drama *Porgy and Bess,* was born in Danville, Kentucky. He received his education at Butler University in Indianapolis and at Columbia University in New York. He received his L.H.D. from Valparaiso University in 1950

TODD DUNCAN

and the degree of Doctor of Music from Central State College in Ohio.

After appearing in the opera *Cavalleria Rusticana* in New York in 1934, he accepted the role of Porgy, the crippled character, in the Broadway stage production of *Porgy and Bess* in 1935.

After playing the role of Porgy twelve hundred times in the United States and abroad, Duncan went to London in 1939 to play a leading role in *The Sun Never Sets,* at the Drury Lane Theatre. He gave a concert at the White House for President and Mrs. Roosevelt in 1935 and has been a frequent soloist with leading symphony orchestras. Regular concert tours have taken him to Europe, South America, Australia and New Zealand. He starred in the Maxwell Anderson-Kurt Weill musical adaptation of Alan Paton's *Cry the Beloved Country,* which was given the title *Lost in the Stars.*

One of Duncan's most memorable concerts was his rendition of the baritone part in Beethoven's *Ninth Symphony* with the New York Philharmonic Orchestra in 1946. He had played Tonio in *Pagliacci* and Escamillo in the opera *Carmen* during the New York City Center opera season in 1945. He was awarded the Medal of Honor and Merit by the President of Haiti in 1945; the Critics Award, 1950; and the Donaldson Award for the best male performance in a musical for 1950.

Duncan, now retired as a performer, maintains a full-time teaching schedule at his Washington, D.C., studio. He teaches professional singers and also master classes at Temple University in the summers. In 1974, he was chairman of the jury for the International Arts Competition.

Dunham, Katherine

Dancer and Choreographer

Katherine Dunham (1910–   ), pioneer in introducing African and Caribbean dances to American audiences, was born in Joliet, Illinois. She attended the University of Chicago where she studied anthropology and became increasingly more interested in the dance. In 1935, she received a Rosenwald

KATHERINE DUNHAM

Fellowship for a year of field study in anthropology. She spent the year in the West Indies, studying the Haitian people and their dances.

Returning to the United States, she danced with the Chicago Opera Company and, in 1945, founded the Katherine Dunham School of Cultural Arts, New York City.

Miss Dunham is director of the Performing Arts and Training Center and Dynamic Museum at Southern Illinois University in East St. Louis, Illinois. She is also technical adviser on intercultural affairs at the John F. Kennedy Center for the Performing Arts, Washington, D.C.

In 1972, she directed *Treemonisha*, a ragtime opera by Scott Joplin, at Wolf Trap Farm for the Performing Arts in Virginia. She has staged plays, films, television specials and operas, including *Green Mansions*, and, for the Metropolitan Opera Company, *Aïda*.

Miss Dunham is the author of *Touch of Innocence*, 1959, and *Island Possessed*, 1969. She has a Ph.B. from the University of Chicago and an honorary L.H.D. from MacMurray College.

Ellington, Edward Kennedy (Duke Ellington)

Musician

Edward K. "Duke" Ellington (1899–1974), eulogized by President Nixon as "America's foremost composer," was born in Washington, D.C., just a few blocks from the White House. In April, 1969, the "Duke" celebrated his 70th birthday by playing at the White House, where he received the first Presidential Medal of Freedom awarded by President Nixon.

Nicknamed the "Duke" because of his impeccable attire, Ellington was popular in Washington as a dance band leader while still in school. He composed his first song at age 14. In 1922, he took his small group of musicians to New York. The group had some

EDWARD KENNEDY ELLINGTON

minor successes. In 1927, his band expanded almost to the size of the full swing band it in time became, Ellington was booked into Harlem's famed Cotton Club. He composed a completely new show each week, rarely missed a deadline, and became a musician of international stature. "Mood Indigo" is from the Cotton Club period.

In his 50-year-plus career, Ellington composed over 2,000 musical pieces. Some, such as "Mood Indigo," he composed in 15 minutes. Others were extended, major works: *Black, Brown and Beige, A Tone Parallel to Harlem.*

Ellington wrote songs for his musicians, suiting the music to their individual talents. His musicians stayed with him and played well for him. By the 1940's, his band had grown to become what is considered the greatest Ellington band.   It included Johnny Hodges, singer Ivie Anderson, Jimmy Blanton and Ben Webster.

After World War II, the Ellington band went into something of a decline. Musicians drifted away as bop replaced swing as the dominant jazz mode. The "Duke" himself continued to make one-night stands.

In 1956, the Ellington band, in a surprise to the music world, took over the Newport Jazz Festival, climaxing with a new Ellington composition, *Diminuendo and Crescendo in Blue.* With a career on the upswing, Ellington toured the world and was elected to the Royal Swedish Academy of Music. He received honorary degrees both in the United States and abroad.

The Smithsonian honored him with a birthday concert of his works in April, 1974, performed by a New England Conservatory of Music band. The "Duke," hospitalized, could not attend. One of his last appearances was in Washington, D.C., in February, 1974, playing for children at Hawthorne School.

Farmer, James
Leader in the Civil Rights Movement

James Farmer (1920–   ), head of the Council on Minority Planning and Strategy, a corporation affiliated with Howard University, Washington, D.C., is known as a pioneer of the non-violent sit-ins, freedom marches and freedom rides. He was one of the founders and the first national chairman of the

JAMES FARMER

Congress of Racial Equality (CORE, founded 1942).

In 1942, Farmer and a group of students from the University of Chicago staged the first non-violent sit-in in a Chicago restaurant. It was successful. In 1947, Farmer led freedom rides into the South. By the 1960's, the non-violent direct confrontation methods used by Farmer in the 1940's were in common use by many civil rights organizations.

In 1966, Farmer left CORE to look for other ways to effect black liberation. Plans for a new organization failed because of lack of funding. In 1966, he accepted a Presidential appointment as assistant secretary of Health, Education and Welfare. He resigned in 1970, citing disillusionment "with the idea of me working within the system."

Farmer envisions the Council on Minority Planning and Strategy as a black "think-tank," designed to find out where blacks are as a people, where they want to go and ways to get there. Farmer's interests have evolved through his years as a self-styled activist, from sit-ins to concern with reading scores and income gaps.

Father Divine
(George Baker)

Founder of the Peace Mission Movement

George Baker (c. 1865–1965) assumed the name Father Divine when he began his Peace Mission Movement in Sayville, Long Island, in the early 1920's. During the Great Depression, he entered Harlem and persuaded people to pool their earnings and possessions and put them in his care, promising his followers a "heaven on earth."

Father Divine practiced "faith healing," and his followers believe he was able to cure the physically and mentally ill. He refused to tolerate stealing, evading debts, indulging in liquor, smoking, gambling and promoting racial prejudice and hate of any kind. Members of his cult do not use a Bible; dur-

FATHER DIVINE

ing the lifetime of Father Divine, the sacred text was the *New Day,* a weekly newspaper dealing with contemporary issues as interpreted by him.

The Peace Mission Movement became interracial as early as 1926, and, by the mid-1960's, at least one-fourth of its members were white, including many non-Negro followers in foreign countries, such as New Zealand, Germany and Switzerland.

Fisher, Rudolph

Physician and Author

Rudolph Fisher (1897–1934), gifted medical doctor and writer of fiction, was born in Washington, D.C., and attended Brown University in Rhode Island, where he excelled in English literature and biology. Completing his Bachelor of Arts degree in 1919, he received his Master of Arts degree from Brown the following year. An outstanding student, he was a member of three honor societies:

Phi Beta Kappa, Sigma Psi and Delta Sigma Rho. He taught biology for a year before entering medical school at Howard University. Completing his internship at Freedmen's Hospital, he established his office for medical practice in New York City. He did further medical studies at Columbia University and was affiliated with the X-ray division of the department of health in New York City.

The young physician was also talented in the fields of music and literature. Dr. Fisher arranged a number of songs for Paul Robeson when the latter gave his first concert in New York. As a novelist, he depicted Negro life: his first book, *The Walls of Jericho,* is a skillful satire on Harlem society. *The Conjure Man Dies,* his second novel, placed Fisher in the group of Negro writers who were realistically capturing urban life in semi-satirical stories. His short stories "The City of Refuge" and "Blades of Steel" were published in the *Atlantic Monthly.*

RUDOLPH FISHER

Forman, James
Leader in the Civil Rights Movement

James Forman (1929–), former executive director of the Student Non-Violent Coordinating Committee (SNCC), was born in Chicago. He was 33 years old when he took over the leadership of SNCC. Although he was a Chicagoan, he had spent many of his summers visiting his grandparents in Marshall County, Tennessee. A graduate of Englewood High School, he earned his college degree at Roosevelt University and served in the army as a personnel classification specialist. After his tour of duty, he returned to Chicago as a public school teacher. He was enrolled in the Institute of African Affairs at Boston University when the conditions of Negro sharecroppers in Fayette County, Tennessee, were given prominent publicity in the nation's newspapers.

Forman saw no logic in studying conditions in Africa when the situation in Tennessee and Mississippi was an equally serious problem. He left Boston for Fayette County, Tennessee, where he performed a mammoth job raising money and collecting clothes for the tent-city victims who had been put off their land because they had attempted to register as voters. When the post of executive director of SNCC was vacated by Edward King, Jr., the job was offered to Forman. He brought both maturity and experience to the organization and a determination to end segregation in all areas; and SNCC emerged in competition with the other civil rights organizations. Despite the meager funds available to SNCC, it has had a powerful impact, not only in its fight against segregation but also in registering its dissatisfaction with the established Negro leadership.

In 1969, Forman walked into Riverside Church in New York City, took over the service by reading, instead of the expected Gospel, a Black Manifesto. In response, the Rev. Dr. E. T. Campbell, minister of Riverside, conceived the idea for a fund to aid the disadvantaged living in Manhattan. In 1972, the fund became a reality as Riverside Church began a $450,000 3-year fund-raising campaign called Riverside Fund for Social Justice. Among the first to receive a grant was the Puerto Rican Family Institute, which helps individuals find homes, jobs and medical care. The Institute also helps to bridge language and cultural barriers.

Franklin, John Hope

Historian

John Hope Franklin (1915–   ), professor of history at the University of Chicago and former head of the history department, was born in Rentiesville, Oklahoma. He has a B.A. degree from Fisk University and M.A. and Ph.D. degrees from Harvard University. In 1950–51, he was a Guggenheim Fellow. He also received a grant for post-doctoral re-

JOHN HOPE FRANKLIN

search from the Social Science Research Council.

He is the author of *The Free Negro in North Carolina, 1790–1860,* 1943; *From Slavery to Freedom: A History of Negro Americans,* 1947; *The Militant South,* 1956; *A Fool's Errand,* 1961; *Reconstruction after the Civil War,* 1961; and *The Emancipation Proclamation,* 1963.

Before joining the University of Chicago faculty in 1964, Dr. Franklin taught at Fisk, St. Augustine College and Howard University and several other colleges in the United States. He is a Fellow of the University of Chicago's Center for Policy Study and serves on the editorial board of the *Journal of Negro History.*

Frazier, Edward Franklin

Sociologist

Edward Franklin Frazier (1894–1962), author, scholar and outstanding sociologist, was born in Baltimore, Maryland, where he is reported, as a youth, to have spat upon buildings of Johns Hopkins University because he knew he could not attend school there. His father, having had no opportunity for an education, instilled in his son a vigorous drive to obtain a college education. Frazier obtained his first degree at Howard University with honors, in 1916, and his Master's degree in sociology from Clark University in Worcester, Massachusetts, in 1920. He was a research fellow at the New York School of Social Work in 1920–21; and as a fellow of the American-Scandinavian Foundation (1921–22), he studied the folk high schools in Denmark. From 1927 to 1929, he was research assistant in the department of sociology at the University of Chicago, from which he received his Doctor of Philosophy degree in 1931.

In 1940, he was granted a fellowship by the John Simon Guggenheim Foundation;

and in 1949, he completed an independent research project on race and culture contacts in the West Indies. An authority on the sociology of the Negro race, he published 7 books, chapters in 10 other volumes and 72 articles in professional journals. The books include: *Negro Youth at the Crossways,* 1940; *The Negro in the United States,* 1949; *Black Bourgeoisie: The Rise of a New Middle Class,* 1957; and *The Negro Church.* In his *Black Bourgeoisie,* Frazier created a sensation with his views on the frustrations and insecurities of the middle class Negroes influenced by Booker T. Washington. This Washingtonian influence, he said, had created a collective inferiority complex, which in turn created a world of make-believe centered around the myths of "Negro business" and "Negro society." He received the McIver Award of the American Sociological Society when he was completing *Black Bourgeoisie.*

Frazier was professor and chairman of the department of sociology at Howard University, president of the American Sociological Society and chairman of a committee of experts on race, with UNESCO, in Paris in 1949.

Gaither, Alonzo Smith

Athletic Coach

Alonzo Smith (Jake) Gaither (1903–   ), athletic director, head football coach, and director of the department of physical education at Florida A. and M. University, was born in Dayton, Tennessee. He graduated from Knoxville College in 1927 and received his Master's degree in 1937 from Ohio State University. He has studied also at the University of Michigan, Northwestern, Yale, and the University of Illinois.

His lengthy record as coach at Florida A. and M. includes many wins and few losses. His football teams have won the league title every year since 1945, with the exception of 1951, 1952, and 1966. On the basis of this outstanding record, Coach Gaither was elected in 1961 to the Helms Foundation Hall of Fame and in 1962 was presented the Small College Coach of the Year Award by the American Football Coaches Association.

In 1955, the city of Tallahassee named a recreation center and park after him, and the 100 Per Cent Wrong Club of Atlanta cited him as Coach of the Decade in 1960. In 1970 he retired from A. and M.

Garvey, Marcus

Colonizationist

Marcus Garvey (1887–1940), the best-known advocate of the "back to Africa" movement, was born in Jamaica, West Indies. After leaving the Wesleyan Methodist denominational school at the age of 16, he worked as an apprentice in the printing plant of

MARCUS GARVEY

Austin Benjamin in Kingston. He soon discovered his ability to influence people through his oratory and organizational skill and began to agitate for political rights for the blacks of the island, who, although in the majority, were on the lowest level of the economic and social scale.

From 1911 to 1914, he attended London University and traveled in Europe and North Africa, observing social conditions. Upon his return, he organized the Jamaica Improvement Association, with himself as president. Two years later, he came to America.

His first audience in Harlem was unresponsive; but as he traveled southward to New Orleans, he began to attract attention and to arouse American Negroes by offering them an escape from despair—a return to Africa, where the black man would be his own man. He organized the Universal Negro Improvement Association and raised the banner of black-race purity. In the short span of a few years, Marcus Garvey had hundreds of thousands of followers; in 1920, he claimed four million dues-paying members and, by 1923, six million.

Garvey organized the Black Star [shipping] Line, which was to provide blacks with the transportation to Africa, the promised land; but each ship that he purchased met with one disaster after another, and Garvey's empire began to crumble as quickly as it had arisen. Most of the money collected from his followers was lost in the steamship line venture; then, in 1923, he was convicted of using the mails to defraud. In 1925, he was sent to the Federal penitentiary in Atlanta. Garvey might have won the case, had he let his lawyer defend him; but the flamboyant and egotistical "Provisional President of Africa" dismissed his lawyer and served as his own defense counsel. In 1927, he was pardoned and left America.

Garvey's momentous rise to power over the depressed blacks of America created controversies of all kinds. He became an international figure, in that European colonial powers in Africa became concerned with his agitation to take Africa for the blacks. Educated Negroes in America were concerned because they felt that Garvey's movement was defeating their struggle for equal rights in America, particularly when Garvey made public his common cause with the Ku Klux Klan's white racism and the Klan approved his move to take the blacks back to Africa.

Negro leaders of the 1920's attacked Garvey and his movement, but in recent years there have been new interpretations of Garvey's significance to the mass of American Negroes. He persuaded them to recognize that black is not synonymous with evil and that there might be advantages in retaining the purity of Negro blood. Thus, Garvey gave the Negroes of America a feeling of self-respect that they had never known.

Gibson, Althea

Athlete

Althea Gibson (1927–), Wimbledon and Forest Hills tennis champion of 1957, was born in Silver, South Carolina. She grew up in the rough and tumble of Harlem, graduated from junior high school in 1941, and was transferred to the Yorkville Trade School. She was bitterly disappointed when she failed to be transferred to one of the downtown high schools along with her classmates. She played hooky more than ever at Yorkville and finally was given a stern warning by her parents and the truant officer. This sobered her to a certain extent, but it was the magic of tennis that really captivated her attention. On her block of 143rd Street, she had learned to play paddle tennis, playing the game so well she had won medals in competition with others.

Buddy Walker, a musician who had observed her playing, thought of introducing

ALTHEA GIBSON

Althea to the game of tennis; he bought her a cheap tennis racket and took her to the Harlem River Tennis Courts at 150th Street to learn the game. There, she justified Walker's expectations and also had the opportunity to meet Juan Serrell, a schoolteacher who took her to his tennis club for lessons. Learning the fine points of the game from Fred Johnson in 1941, within a year she competed in her first tournament, the girls' singles in the New York State Open Championship at Lincoln University in Pennsylvania. Althea went to the finals, where she was defeated by Nana Davis.

The American Tennis Association (A.T.A.) tournaments were cancelled for the duration of World War II; but, when they were resumed in 1944, Althea won the girls' championship, winning it again in 1945. In the 1946 tournament, held at the College of Education, Wilberforce, Ohio, she was eligible for the women's singles. She reached the finals and lost to Roumania Peters, a teacher from Tuskegee Institute. Two of the officials of the A.T.A., Dr. Hubert A. Eaton of Wilmington, North Carolina, and Dr. Robert W. Johnson of Lynchburg, Virginia, became interested in Althea's career and brought her to live in their homes until she completed high school, encouraging her to continue her

tennis in the summer season. In the summer of 1946, she won the A.T.A. championship, which she held for 10 years; and in 1949, Dr. Eaton proposed competition at Forest Hills to Althea.

She gained experience in the Eastern Indoor Championship and the National Indoor Championship tournaments, but it was not until 1950 that she reached the finals at the National Indoor meet. Meanwhile, she had enrolled at Florida A. and M. College in Tallahassee, where she was coached by Walter Austin and Jake Gaither. The gradual climb up the ladder to Forest Hills was finally achieved; but she lost the match to Louise Brough, the Wimbledon champion and former United States title holder.

Invited by the State Department to tour Southeast Asia with a team of American tennis players, she gained an international reputation; and, finally, 1957 was the Althea Gibson year. She won the championships at both Wimbledon and Forest Hills; and Vice-President Richard Nixon presented the trophy to Althea at Forest Hills.

In 1972, Miss Gibson became program director of the North Vale Racquet Club in North Vale, New Jersey. A golfer as well, she is a member of the Ladies Professional Golf Association and was named Woman Athlete of the Year, 1957–58. In 1971, she was elected to the National Lawn Tennis Hall of Fame. She is the author of *I Always Wanted To Be Somebody*.

Granger, Lester Blackwell
Leader of the National Urban League

Lester Blackwell Granger (1896–), former director of the National Urban League, was born in Newport News, Virginia. He was one of the outstanding Negro leaders of the 1940's. During World War II, he was a special adviser to Secretary of the Navy James Forrestal.

LESTER BLACKWELL GRANGER

The son of a medical doctor who left Virginia in 1904, when the state instituted its segregation laws, Granger settled with his family in New Jersey, where he entered the integrated schools of the community. Of the six Granger sons, three were enrolled at Dartmouth at the same time. They operated a clothes-pressing establishment under the name of "Granger, Granger, and Granger," earning their college fees and spending money. The subtle but effective lines of segregation at Dartmouth excluded the Granger brothers from several of the activities of the college, but they carefully avoided self-segregation. After college, Lester Granger was a lieutenant in the army during World War I; and after his discharge, he taught for one year at St. Augustine's before entering graduate school at New York University and the New York School of Social Work.

After World War II, Granger was appointed by President Truman to the five-man Committee on Equality of Treatment and Opportunity in the Armed Services. The efforts of this committee were implemented in the 1950 desegregation program of the armed services, and Granger was awarded the Navy's "Distinguished Civilian Service Medal" and the President's "Medal of Merit."

He became affiliated with the National Urban League in 1934 and served as executive director, 1941–61. In 1962–66, he was the Edgar B. Stern distinguished visiting professor, Dillard University, New Orleans. Since 1966, he has been visiting professor of urban sociology at Dillard. He was named honorary president of the International Council of Social Welfare, 1964. He now serves on the board of directors of the Council of Social Work Education.

Graves, Lemuel E., Jr.

War Correspondent

Lemuel E. Graves, Jr. (1915–), newspaper correspondent in World War II, was born in Tallahassee, Florida. During World War I, when Lemuel was two, his father was assigned to a post at Tuskegee. The family later settled permanently in Raleigh, North Carolina, where he was educated in the public schools and graduated from St. Augustine's College in 1934.

Graves' first newspaper job was with the *North Carolina Times* in Raleigh; in 1935, he joined the staff of the *Norfolk Journal and Guide,* where he served successfully as a general reporter, assistant city editor, news editor, sports editor, war correspondent and war news editor.

During the Second World War, Graves was assigned to cover the 332nd Fighter Group, which arrived in Italy in January 1944. From January until July, Graves covered the activities of the ground troops in the Italian theater of operations for the *Norfolk Journal and Guide.* He returned to the United States by way of England, which enabled him to give news accounts of the troops in that area.

Greene, Lorenzo Johnston

Historian

Lorenzo Johnston Greene (1899–), authority in the field of the Negro in colonial America, was born in Ansonia, Connecticut, where he completed his early educational training. He attended Howard University in Washington, D.C., where he received his Bachelor of Arts degree, and then Columbia University, to earn his Master of Arts. He returned to Washington as an assistant to Dr. Carter G. Woodson in investigating the conditions within Negro labor. The materials collected were published in *The Negro Wage Earner*.

In 1933, he accepted a position as instructor of history at Lincoln University in Missouri, having studied at Columbia University. During his years of advanced study, he had become interested in the history of the Negro in his native New England. He combined research with his duties as instructor at Lincoln, and, through his findings, he brought to light a mass of hitherto unknown facts about the role of the Negro in the colonial period of American history. Upon the completion of his dissertation in 1941, he received the Ph.D. degree from Columbia University. *The Negro in Colonial New England* is an authoritative treatment of this phase of Negro American history.

Dr. Greene has published many articles in scholarly journals and holds the rank of full professor at Lincoln University. He is a past president of the Association for the Study of Negro Life and History.

Haley, Alexander

Alexander Haley, Pulitzer Prize winning author, was born in Ithaca, New York, August 11, 1921. He was the son of well-educated parents who were living in Ithaca at the time while his father was studying for his master's degree at Cornell University. His mother, Bertha Palmer Haley who was an accomplished musician and teacher, had grown up in Henning, Tennessee, the daughter of a prominent local business man.

It was during the summers of his early youth that Alex's parents took him to Henning to spend time with his maternal grandparents. It was here that he learned about his heritage and the "furthest-back person" his grandmother talked about, Kunta Kinte. Haley says, "Grandmother would burst with pride about "Chicken George," Haley's great-great grandfather, but when talking about Kunta Kinte, her voice would fill with awe.

Haley spent twelve years researching and writing this family opus, and that quest in itself will be the subject of a future book. Financially for Haley the success of ROOTS has ended the days of not knowing where his next meal would come from. Over 1,500,000 copies of the hardbook edition had been sold before the paperback version appeared on the bookstands. "It really startles me that the last thing I think of now is money," says Haley.

The television adaptation of his book drew record audiences and captured the hearts of Americans as no previous television show had. It was nominated for 37 Emmy awards by the Academy of Television Arts and Sciences. His book has been translated into 24 languages and has become a best seller in many other countries.

Haley has also helped in the sequel to ROOTS which will be shown on ABC in early 1979. This segment will deal with his family's history from when they settled in Henning, Tennessee up until the present.

He is currently engaged in many projects related to his book; personal appearances, films, and lectures. In addition, he heads the Kinte Foundation and the Kinte Corporation in Los Angeles; and, he has established the Alex Haley Roots Foundation in New York which is to provide post-graduate scholarships and course materials for school children.

Handy, William Christopher

Composer and Musician

William Christopher Handy (1873–1958), bandmaster, cornetist and composer of jazz music and the blues, was born in Florence, Alabama. The son of a minister, Handy learned the rudiments of music in the public schools and began arranging choral parts for church choirs while he was in junior high school. At the age of 18, he ran away from home to Chicago and then to St. Louis, where he worked at odd jobs, often playing his trumpet to earn a decent meal. His fortunes turned in 1896, when he became the bandmaster of Mahara's Minstrels, touring the United States, Canada, Mexico and Cuba.

After a brief period of teaching music, Handy settled in Memphis, Tennessee, and organized a band. During a 1909 election, he wrote a selection entitled "Mr. Crump" for the political boss of Memphis; his band played the number with such vivacity that it caused dancing in the streets. Mr. Crump won the election, and Mr. Handy won the title of "Father of the Blues"—he had introduced a new form of syncopated music. The title of the song was changed later to the "Memphis Blues." In 1913, the composer formed the Pace and Handy Music Company, and the next year he published his famous number, the "St. Louis Blues."

In 1918, the popular demand for this new form of music caused Handy to move his publishing company to New York. The post-World War I period became the "jazz age," and Handy skyrocketed to fame. In 1928, he directed a concert at Carnegie Hall entitled "History of Music," using Negro artists to portray the history and development of Negro musical forms, from the importation of slaves from Africa to the evolution of jazz and the blues.

Handy wrote more than 150 secular and sacred musical compositions; even after the loss of his eyesight, he continued to produce. His autobiography is entitled *Father of the Blues,* and he founded the Handy Foundation for the Blind before his death in 1958. The city of Memphis named a park after him in 1931 and in 1947 opened the $200,000 W. C. Handy Theatre.

WILLIAM CHRISTOPHER HANDY

Harrison, Richard Berry

Actor

Richard Berry Harrison (1864–1935), famous for his portrayal of De Lawd in the stage-and-screen play *Green Pastures,* was born in London, Ontario, Canada. His parents, fugitive slaves from the United States, had made their escape to the free soil of Canada, but only the rudiments of elementary education were available to their son.

RICHARD BERRY HARRISON

With visions of becoming a great actor, the young Harrison migrated to Detroit, determined to study and hopeful that the opportunity to act in a theater in the big city would materialize. He studied dramatics and worked as an ordinary laborer until he completed his training. Since there were no openings for him in the theater, he toured the United States, Mexico and Canada giving dramatic readings. His receptive audiences were mainly Negroes, yet he made a living; and in time, he had increased their ability to appreciate dramatic art. His program consisted of poetry, famous orations and humorous literature and, occasionally, a one-man production of a Shakespearean drama.

The turning point in his career came when he accepted a part in *Pa Williams' Gal* at the Lafayette Theatre in New York. The producers of *Green Pastures* approached Harrison to find out if he would be interested in accepting the role of De Lawd, the play's leading character. At first, he hesitated because the play was based on the Bible and the Negro's concept of God, heaven and life after death. However, after studying the play, Harrison saw a great opportunity of using the stage to teach a religious lesson that the ministers in the churches were failing to impart.

With masterful acting by Harrison as De Lawd, the play was presented 1,568 times before full houses throughout the United States. Because of the popularity of *Green Pastures* as a stage production, the movie industry produced it, with Harrison doing a superb film interpretation of De Lawd. He was awarded the Spingarn Medal in 1930.

Hastie, William Henry

Judge

William Henry Hastie (1904–), judge of the United States third circuit court of appeals, was born in Knoxville, Tennessee. He graduated from Amherst College with honors in 1925 and earned his law degree at Harvard in 1930 and his Doctor of Jurisprudence degree there in 1933. After a brief period of teaching at Bordentown, New Jersey, he joined the Charles Houston law firm in Washington, D.C. When the School of Law at Howard University was upgraded under the leadership of Charles Houston, Hastie accepted a professorship at the institution in 1930 and became dean of the law school in 1939.

In the meantime, he had served as a federal district judge for the Virgin Islands from 1937 to 1939. After he served as dean of Howard Law School for one year, the Roosevelt Administration brought him into the War Department as a civilian aide. Judge Hastie resigned after two years to protest the slowness and evasiveness of the department in terminating its policy of segregation in the armed forces. He had urged the elimination

WILLIAM HENRY HASTIE

of discrimination from the Air Corps, but, because of the prejudice and fears of the incumbent Secretary Henry L. Stimson, nothing could be achieved. Judge Hastie, tired of the secretary's excuses and inaction, resigned in protest.

Two years later, Judge Hastie was appointed governor of the Virgin Islands by President Roosevelt. He served in this post from 1946 to 1949. In the presidential election of 1948, he campaigned energetically for President Truman. Later Hastie was appointed judge of the United States circuit court of appeals, third circuit, in Philadelphia. In 1972 Judge Hastie joined U.S. District Court Judge Joseph S. Lord III in overturning a Pennsylvania law reimbursing parents for non-public school tuition payments.

Hawkins, Augustus F.

United States Congressman

Augustus F. Hawkins (1907–   ), Democratic congressman representing the 21st district of California since 1962, was reelect-

ed to his fifth term in 1970 with the highest percentage of votes attained by any opposed candidate in that election—90 per cent of the total votes cast.

A member of the House Committee on Education and Labor and the Committee on House Administration, he has co-sponsored several bills, including the Economic Opportunity Act and the Equal Employment Opportunity section of the 1965 Civil Rights Act.

Hawkins was born in Shreveport, Louisiana. At 11, he moved to Los Angeles with his parents and attended local schools. He is a graduate of the University of California at Los Angeles, and did graduate work at the Institute of Government at the University of Southern California.

Before entering politics in 1934, Hawkins was in the real estate business. In 1934, he ran for the California State Assembly, defeat-

AUGUSTUS F. HAWKINS

ing a Republican incumbent who had held his post for 16 years.

Under legislation Hawkins sponsored, racial designation was removed from all state documents such as drivers' licenses and job orders. He also was involved in bringing about the appointment of the first California blacks as judges, as members of the highway patrol, and to various state commissions. Hawkins is a founder member of the Southeast Los Angeles Improvement Council.

Hawkins has been the author or co-author of more than 300 laws that are now on the statute books of the state. He has been active in the establishment of the law and medical schools at U.C.L.A., and has worked with various groups on plans to meet the threat of unemployment owing to automation.

Hayden, Palmer

Artist

Palmer Hayden (1893–1973), outstanding painter of marine subjects, was born in Virginia, where he received very little encouragement to develop his talent. After serving in the army, he settled in New York City, where he worked as a window washer and studied art. He entered his work in the Harmon competition in 1926 and won the gold medal award, which enabled him to study in Paris. After one year in France, he presented his works in a one-man show at the Bernheim Jeune Galleries and gained immediate recognition as a skilled artist. He was most interested in marine themes, which he executed in paintings of the Normandy coast.

After five years abroad, Hayden returned to America, and in the Harmon shows of 1931 to 1933, exhibited several paintings, including his prize-winning "The Schooners." His superior technique is displayed also in his striking skyscraper scene of New York City entitled "Theatre Alley." He became interested in African themes and types while

doing some sketches for the French Colonial Exposition in Paris; and, to develop his technique in this area, he toured the West Indies studying Negro models.

Hayes, Roland

Singer

Roland Hayes (1897–   ), famous lieder singer since the 1920's, was born in a cabin on a Georgia farm. His mother moved to Chattanooga to earn a living, and the young Roland was employed in a foundry. The inadequate three-month sessions of school were distasteful to him, but, when he met Arthur Calhoun, a Negro musician who gave him some lessons in music, he was eager to make up his lost time. He entered the preparatory department of Fisk University at the age of 18 as a sixth grade pupil.

Possessing a fine tenor voice, he joined the Fisk Jubilee Singers and toured New Eng-

ROLAND HAYES

land. He studied four years at Fisk, then went to Boston and studied with basso Arthur J. Hubbard. He also enrolled at Harvard University Extension School. By 1916, he was his own manager and had secured concert engagements in black churches and schools throughout the country. Using the funds earned on these self-managed tours, he presented a concert at Boston Symphony Hall.

In 1920, Hayes went to England and sang at a command performance in Buckingham Palace for King George V and Queen Mary. He then went to the continent to study German lieder. There he established a reputation as one of the world's great lieder singers.

In 1923 he returned to Boston, where his fame had preceded him. He gave a recital in Symphony Hall on January 7, 1923, and was rated by the Boston critics as the greatest tenor of the era. The doors of concert halls throughout America were opened to him, and he was universally recognized as one of the outstanding singers in the nation. His fame, however, did not protect him from racial bigotry. In 1942, he was struck by a policeman and jailed in Rome, Georgia.

For his achievements, Hayes received the Spingarn Medal in 1924; and in 1932, Fisk University awarded him the honorary degree of Doctor of Music. At the age of 70, when most vocalists retire, he was still making extended concert tours and recordings. He has appeared with most major orchestras and is a Fellow of the American Academy of Arts and Letters.

Henderson, Cornelius Langston

Engineer

Cornelius Langston Henderson (1887–), builder of bridges, factories and tunnels in Canada, the United States, Jamaica, Trinidad, Australia, New Zealand and many countries in South America, was born in Detroit, Michigan. His early training was received in the South, where his father was president of Morris Brown College in Atlanta, Georgia. Henderson was an apt pupil in mathematics and mechanics at Morris Brown College and Wayne University, from which he graduated in 1906. He received his Bachelor of Science degree in civil engineering from the University of Michigan.

In 1911, Henderson began working for the Canadian Bridge Company (a subsidiary of the United States Steel Corporation) in Windsor, Ontario, Canada. During World War I, when the company was manufacturing war materials, he was promoted to plant engineer and finally to structural steel designer. He contributed to the design and construction of the Quebec and Thousand Island Bridges, both over the St. Lawrence River; the Ambassador Bridge approach at Detroit; the vertical lift bridges across the Welland Canal and many other highway and railroad bridges throughout Canada.

Henderson is noted also for his construction of many factory buildings in Canada and the United States: for the Ford Motor Company of Canada, the General Motors Company, the Chrysler Corporation, the Dominion Forge and Stamping Company and the Dominion Iron and Steel Company. He has built for the Canadian government such structures as the Supreme Court building in Ottawa, the Royal Air Force hangars at Trenton and the Royal Canadian Mounted Police building. He revolutionized the building industry in 1929, when he constructed the first large, all-welded factory building for the General Electric Company at Peterborough.

The Canadian office of the United States Steel Corporation handles the company's foreign export work, and, as designing engineer, Henderson has traveled extensively throughout the world carrying out construction projects for the firm.

Henson, Matthew Alexander

Explorer

Matthew Alexander Henson (1866–1955), polar region explorer and companion of explorer Robert E. Peary, was born in Charles County, Maryland. Orphaned at age eight, he was reared by an uncle in Washington, D.C., where he attended the N Street School for six years. In search of employment and adventure, he joined the crew of a vessel sailing to China as cabin boy; later, he made trips to Asia, Africa, Europe and the South Pacific Islands.

In 1888, he became acquainted with Robert E. Peary, a civil engineer in the United States Navy. As Peary's personal attendant, Henson accompanied the engineer to Nicaragua and became his messenger at the League Island Navy Yard. When Peary made his second expedition to the arctic region in 1891, he took Henson along as a trusted aide and friend. Henson became expert in

MATTHEW ALEXANDER HENSON

handling the equipment, the dog sleds and the Eskimos, who thought he was akin to them because of his brown skin.

Again in 1895, 1898 and 1905, Robert Peary was accompanied by Henson on his expeditions to the North Pole in his search for the magical point. Finally, in 1908, the two explorers set out for their last venture to the top of the world. They left Cape Sheridan, Greenland, in February 1909. By April, exhausted and suffering from snowblindness, they were still 60 miles from their goal; but on April 6, 1909, Henson, sent forward by Peary, became the first man to reach the North Pole. He published his account of the expeditions in his book *A Negro Explorer at the North Pole* (1912).

Hinton, William Augustus

Physician and Educator

William A. Hinton (1883–1959), bacteriologist in the area of diseases of the blood, was born in Chicago, Illinois. As a serologist he originated the Hinton test, an authoritative test for syphilis, as effective as the Wassermann. He was a discoverer of the Davies-Hinton tests of blood and spinal fluid. As an authority in this area of medical science, Dr. Hinton's book, *Syphilis and Its Treatment* (1936), is a universally used professional reference work.

A Harvard University graduate, receiving his B.S. degree in 1905 and M.D. with honors in 1912, Dr. Hinton decided to restrict his practice and went to work in the laboratory of the Massachusetts General Hospital. There, he studied the effects of syphilis by examining children who had been fatally stricken by the disease. He became director of the laboratory department of the Boston Dispensary in 1915. At the same time, he was appointed chief of the Wassermann Laboratory by the Massachusetts Department of Public Health, while his alma mater, Har-

WILLIAM AUGUSTUS HINTON

vard, appointed him instructor in preventive medicine and hygiene. From 1921 to 1946, he was instructor in bacteriology and immunology; next, he was promoted to clinical professor. He retired from the Harvard Medical School in 1950, as professor emeritus.

Dr. Hinton accepted other responsibilities in the course of his profession, such as special consultant to the United States Public Health Service, consultant for the Massachusetts School for Crippled Children and lecturer at Simmons College in Boston. He has contributed many articles to nationally recognized medical journals and is a member of the American Medical Association, the American Society of Clinical Pathology, the Society of American Bacteriologists and the American Association for the Advancement of Science. In the late 1930's the NAACP awarded him the Spingarn Medal, but he declined to accept it then, as he felt that he had much more to accomplish.

Hope, John

Educator

John Hope (1868–1936), founder and president of the Atlanta University system, was a native of Augusta, Georgia, but was educated at Worcester Academy in Massachusetts. Although he had to work during his years at the academy, he was active in the life of the school, assuming the editorship of the student monthly, the *Academy,* and graduating with honors in 1886. The headmaster of Worcester secured a scholarship for him to enter Brown University, where he graduated with honors in 1894. He received his M.A. degree from Brown in 1907; and, 12 years later, he was elected to Phi Beta Kappa for his achievements after graduation.

He began his teaching career at the Roger Williams University in Nashville, then was transferred by the American Baptist Home Mission Society to the Atlanta Baptist Col-

JOHN HOPE

lege, or Morehouse College, as a teacher of Latin and Greek. He became the assistant to the president and, upon the resignation of Dr. George Sale in 1906, was appointed acting president, and a year later, president.

As early as 1904, in an article published in *Voice of the Negro,* John Hope voiced his concern over the number of schools trying to operate in Atlanta as separate units. His dream of bringing these colleges—Morehouse, Spelman, Clark, Morris Brown and Gammon Theological Seminary—into a unified system of education in Atlanta was partially realized in 1929. Morehouse, Spelman and Atlanta University agreed to affiliate and function as members of the Atlanta University system. Each college kept its own administration, but facilities were shared. Atlanta University became the center of graduate study, while Spelman and Morehouse concentrated on developing excellent undergraduate training. Later, Clark University and Morris Brown became affiliated.

John Hope, along with W. E. B. Du Bois, objected to the theories of compromise of Booker T. Washington and became one of the most active supporters of the National Association for the Advancement of Colored People. He served on the Commission on Interracial Cooperation and the Georgia State Council of Work among Negro Boys. He was also an active member of the Association for the Study of Negro Life and History, serving as one of its officials. In 1929, he received the Harmon Award in education; he was awarded the Spingarn Medal, posthumously, in 1936.

Horne, Lena

Singer

Lena Horne (1917–), talented, attractive singing star of Hollywood, was born in Brooklyn, New York. She made her stage debut at the age of six in Philadelphia in the

LENA HORNE

play *Madame X.* Traveling with her mother, who was a member of the Lafayette Stock Players, Lena decided early in life that she wanted to become an actress. Her mother sent her to Fort Valley, Georgia, to attend a boarding school where her uncle was the dean. At age 14, she returned to New York to complete her education.

Still desiring a career on the stage, she joined the chorus of the show playing at the Cotton Club in Harlem; after two years, she was featured as the show's leading singer and dancer. Next, she was the featured soloist with Noble Sissle's band and was later featured in the *Blackbirds of 1939.* When Charlie Barnet signed her as soloist with his orchestra, Lena became the first Negro singer to be featured by a white band. Radio and recording dates followed, and she was in demand for many night club engagements. Among these clubs were the Mocambo in Hollywood and Café Society Downtown, where a film executive offered her a part in Metro-Goldwyn-Mayer's *Panama Hattie* in 1942.

In both *Cabin in the Sky* and *Stormy Weather,* Miss Horne's name went up in lights at leading motion picture theaters across the country. She was a featured performer in *Broadway Rhythm, As Thousands Cheer, Two Girls and a Sailor* and other pictures, and has been engaged at the most fashionable night clubs from Manhattan to the Champs Elysées in Paris.

Miss Horne gives generously of her time and talent to help worthy causes. She is well known for her stand against discrimination and bigotry in and out of show business: she refuses to appear before segregated audiences and has turned down lucrative engagements for this reason. During World War II, she volunteered to join the U.S.O. tours. In 1970, she starred in a memorable TV special with Harry Belafonte and is currently filming television commercials.

Houston, Charles Hamilton
Lawyer and NAACP Leader

Charles Hamilton Houston (1895–1950), the architect and dominant force of the legal program of the National Association for the Advancement of Colored People, was born in Washington, D.C. It is said that he "set the pattern for fundamental attacks on barriers to equal justice," even though he did not live to see the fruits of his labors: the decision in the famous case of *Brown* v. *Board of Education* was not reached until four years after his death. He merits credit for devising the legal strategy for the case in which the Supreme Court declared segregation to be unconstitutional, in 1954. He guided the NAACP committee on legal defense through the legal maze of a series of cases on discrimination in education and

CHARLES HAMILTON HOUSTON

labor, restrictive covenants and interstate travel.

Houston's own scholastic record qualified him for his brilliant career: he graduated from the M Street High School at the age of 15, and at 19 he was wearing a Phi Beta Kappa key as an honor graduate of Amherst College. After a brief period of teaching English at Howard University, he entered the armed forces in 1917 and was commissioned a first lieutenant in the infantry, serving overseas as an artillery officer. Following his discharge from the army, he entered the Harvard Law School, and became the student editor of the *Harvard Law Review* for two years. He received his first law degree in 1922 and his law doctorate the following year. He continued his study of law at the University of Madrid, earning the degree of Doctor of Civil Law. Returning to America, he joined his father in Washington in a partnership firm and concentrated his efforts on developing his private law practice until he joined the faculty of the law school of Howard University in 1929.

As vice-dean of the Howard University School of Law, Houston served as full-time administrator from 1929 to 1935. In this short span of time, he created a fully accredited, nationally known and respected law school for the university—it was an unaccredited, little-known institution before he undertook its administration.

Hughes, Bernice Gaines

Officer in the U.S. Women's Army Corps

Bernice Gaines Hughes (1904–), first Negro woman to obtain the rank of lieutenant colonel in the United States armed services, was born in Xenia, Ohio. She enlisted in the U.S. Women's Army Corps as a private in 1942 and was sent to Fort Des Moines, Iowa, for basic training. She graduated from officer candidate school in May 1943 and was commissioned a second lieutenant. In August 1944, she was promoted to first lieutenant; in January 1946, to captain; in April 1949, to the rank of major in the regular army; and in August 1951, she obtained the permanent rank of lieutenant colonel while on active duty in the regular army. She retired with this rank in February 1958.

Lt. Colonel Hughes served as WAC Company Commander in the European theater of operations for seven years and served on the Army General Staff as personnel director in the WAC headquarters in the Pentagon for two years. She was administrative officer with the Special Services Division Headquarters of the Communications Zone in Orléans, France, for three years, and prior to her retirement, she was deputy chief of staff for logistics in the review and analysis division of the General Staff in the Pentagon.

Bernice Hughes has received the following campaign awards: the EAME Campaign Medal; the WAAC Service Medal; the World War II Victory Medal; the National Defense Service Medal; and the American Campaign Medal.

When she retired from the army, Mrs. Hughes returned to her career as a teacher. She had previously obtained two degrees in foreign languages from Ohio State University; after additional work toward her Ph.D., and also special study at the Berlitz School of Languages in Orléans, France, she is now serving as assistant professor of French at Central State University, Wilberforce, Ohio.

Hughes, James Langston

Author

Langston Hughes (1902–1967), one of the most productive writers of the 20th century, was born in Joplin, Missouri. Author of poems, novels, plays, biographies, histories, essays and books for children, he received the Witter Bynner prize for excellence in poetry, in 1926; both Rosenwald and Guggenheim fellowships; the Anisfield-Wolfe award, in 1953; and the Spingarn Medal, in 1960.

Hughes rose to prominence in the American literary world in 1926 with the publication of his first book of poetry, *The Weary Blues*. His first short story was written while he was a student at Central High School in Cleveland, Ohio, from which he graduated in 1920. He attended Columbia University, leaving to travel around the world, observing, collecting and writing. Later, he went to Lincoln University, where he received his B.A.

Hughes presented in his colorful and vivid writings his experiences gathered in the 1930's in trips to Africa and to Europe by way of the West Coast, China and Siberia.

JAMES LANGSTON HUGHES

His works have been translated into more than 25 different languages, including German, French, Hindi, Bengalese, Gujarati and Spanish.

Some of his collections of poetry are: *Weary Blues, Fine Clothes to the Jew, Dear Lovely Death, Shakespeare in Harlem, One-Way Ticket,* 1949, and *Ask Your Mama,* 1961. Other books published by Hughes include *Not without Laughter,* 1930; *The Big Sea,* 1940; *The Poetry of the Negro,* 1949; *Simple Speaks His Mind,* 1950; *The First Book of Negroes,* 1952; *Laughing to Keep from Crying,* 1952; *Famous American Negroes,* 1954; *Famous Negro Music-Makers,* 1955; *The First Book of Jazz,* 1955; *The First Book of the West Indies,* 1956; *I Wonder as I Wander,* 1956; *Famous Negro Heroes of America,* 1958; *Tambourines to Glory,* 1958; *An African Treasury,* 1960; *The First Book of Africa,* 1960; *The Best of Simple,* 1961;

Fight for Freedom, 1962; *Five Plays,* 1963; *New Negro Poets,* 1964.

Langston Hughes' works are universal in appeal because they contribute to the understanding of all the peoples of the world. As a lecturer, he invaluably aided the development of young writers and college students. He served as poet-in-residence at Atlanta University and as a visiting professor at the Laboratory School of the University of Chicago.

Hurston, Zora Neale

Anthropologist and Novelist

Zora Neale Hurston (1903–1960), anthropologist and novelist, was born in Eatonville, Florida. A graduate of Barnard College in New York City, where she was a student of Dr. Franz Boas in the field of anthropology, she was recommended by him to the Association for the Study of Negro Life and

ZORA NEALE HURSTON

History to make a special study of a Negro community at Plateau, Alabama. The purpose of the study was to collect materials of anthropological and historical value about the descendants of the last slaves to reach the United States, in 1859. From this study, Miss Hurston wrote an article in 1927 for the *Journal of Negro History* entitled "Cudjo's Own Story of the Last African Slaver."

With her valuable collection of folklore, Miss Hurston turned novelist, using her first-hand materials and her gift for narration to produce a number of fictional works. In her book *Mules and Men,* it is evident that the author is a trained anthropologist; the work is a collection of true stories of humble Negroes presented in their local setting. *Tell My Horse* is another anthropological study dealing with the life of the Haitian Negro; and *Jonah's Gourd Vine* is a work of fiction. *Their Eyes Were Watching God* is a startling story of Southern Negroes, which may be classified as a historical novel, since it covers such delineations of life as poverty, race hate, segregation and the economic struggles of the Negro.

Miss Hurston's works are unusually vivid because she lived among the people, winning their confidence and actively taking part in their lives. As a trained scientist, she observed keenly; then she transformed her findings into an exciting narrative.

Jackson, Luther Porter

Historian

Luther Porter Jackson (1892–1950), noted historian of Virginia, was born in Lexington, Kentucky. As a child, he delighted in asking questions; and when he learned to read, he often sat by an oil lamp, reading to find the answers to his questions. While attending Fisk University, he became interested in the history of the Negro and was astonished to find that very little had been written about his race. Determined to add to the little information that was in the current books about the customs, contributions and activities of the Negro, he prepared himself for a career in the field of history.

Graduating from Fisk in 1914, he taught school for brief periods at Voorhees Institute and at Kansas Industrial College before obtaining his M.A. degree from Columbia University in 1922. He accepted an appointment at Virginia State College in 1922; and in 1937, he received his Ph.D. degree in history from the University of Chicago. He was promoted to professor of history and chairman of the social science department at Virginia State College. Professor Jackson spent considerable time in research on the history of the Negro in Virginia. Some of his scholarly articles are: "Economic Advancement of Negroes in Virginia," "Negro Business Enterprises," "Education and Schools," "Building the Family—Legal Marriage," "The Negro in the Days of Slavery" and "Virginia Negro Soldiers and Seamen in the American Revolution."

Professor Jackson was active in movements for civil rights in Virginia. He worked to facilitate voting by Negroes and for the abolition of the "lily-white primary" and the poll tax. He founded the Virginia Negroes' League as an organ to promote this drive, and, in 1949, he delivered a paper on "Virginia and the Civil Rights Program" before the Virginia Social Science Association at the University of Virginia. Throughout his career, he worked actively with Carter G. Woodson and the Association for the Study of Negro Life and History, serving on the editorial staff of the *Journal of Negro History* and the *Negro History Bulletin.*

Jackson, May Howard

Sculptor

May Howard Jackson (1877–1931), a sculptor who broke with academic tradition, was born in Philadelphia, where she studied at the Pennsylvania Academy of Fine Arts. Graduating in 1899, she established her own studio, where she worked quietly on the subjects that stimulated her interest. After her marriage, she moved her studio to Washington, D.C., and continued to sculpt racial figures. She departed from the tradition of going to Europe to study the old European masters and, instead, became intrigued with the Negro types in her environment and executed many works of art embodying the various distinctive traits of the individuals she modeled.

Racial themes were unpopular in the early quarter of the century, and Mrs. Jackson, therefore, achieved in a field that had not been touched by any other American sculptor of her time. In a series of portrait busts, she found individuality in each of her subjects—Paul Laurence Dunbar, Kelly Miller, Dr. Du Bois and Francis Grimké. "The Mulatto Mother and Her Child" is definitely symbolic and social: the sculptor has expressed in the figure the double heritage of mixed blood—some features are Caucasian, some Negroid. "The Head of a Child" is another execution of her social philosophy, as the artist has portrayed in the figure the prophecy of a new, emerging view of humanity.

Jarboro, Caterina

Opera Star

Caterina Jarboro (1903–), the first Negro woman singer to star in an all-white opera company in the United States, was born Catherine Yarborough in Wilmington, North Carolina. In 1933, the sensational appearance of Miss Jarboro in the title role of Aïda with the Chicago Opera Company at the Hippodrome, New York City, created a demand for a repeat performance two days later. In 1930, she had sung the role of Aïda at the Puccini Theatre in Milan, Italy.

CATERINA JARBORO

Encouraged by the favorable comments on Miss Jarboro's performance in New York, the manager of the Chicago Opera Company engaged her for a 20-week season of grand opera in the fall of 1933. She was presented in the role of Selika in Meyerbeer's *L'Africaine*. In this production, she won the praise of the foremost critics of the country for her very fine interpretation—both as a singer and as an actress.

Miss Jarboro was educated in the Catholic schools of Wilmington and at the Gregory Normal School. At the age of 13, she went to Brooklyn to live with an aunt and study music. To earn funds for study in Europe, she took part in the musical productions of *Shuffle Along* and *Runnin' Wild*. While in Europe, she studied under singing masters in Paris and Milan. Her triumphant appearances after her return to America in 1933 dwindled rapidly when white Americans realized that she was an American Negro and not an

Italian. Although she made concert tours throughout the country and appeared before an audience of six thousand in a performance with the Chicago Opera Company in 1935, the New York Metropolitan Opera Association refused to accept her membership in its newly formed grand opera company. In her efforts to join the company, however, she did pave the way for future talented and trained Negro women aspirants in opera in America.

Johnson, Charles Spurgeon

Sociologist and Educator

Charles Spurgeon Johnson (1893–1956), eminent sociologist and university president, was born in Bristol, Virginia. This outstanding scholar was named president of Fisk University in 1946 and is one of the few Negro college presidents who achieved notice as a scholar before becoming an administrator. As director of the social science department at Fisk, Dr. Johnson had already been recognized as an able authority in his field. In his research and writings, he had covered the sociological aspects of the American Negro from the rural areas to the urban centers. His major works were written before he assumed the role of university president: *The Negro in Chicago,* 1922; *The Negro in American Civilization,* 1930; *Negro Housing,* 1932; *Economic Status of the Negro,* 1933; *Shadow of the Plantation,* 1934; *Collapse of Cotton Tenancy,* 1934; *Race Relations,* 1934; *The Negro College Graduate,* 1938; *Growing Up in the Black Belt,* 1941; *Patterns of Negro Segregation,* 1943; *To Stem This Tide,* 1943; *Culture and the Educational Process,* 1943; and *Into the Main Stream,* 1947.

Dr. Johnson was educated at Virginia Union University and the University of Chicago and received honorary degrees from Howard, Columbia and Harvard Universities. He was director of research and investigations for the Chicago Urban League from 1917 to 1919; the investigator of Negro migration for the Carnegie Foundation in 1918; a member of the Committee of Race Relations in Chicago, 1919–21; and director of many institutes on race relations throughout the United States.

He was one of 20 American educators selected to advise on the educational reorganization of Japan in 1946 and was a consultant for several of the White House conferences on the problems of youth in American society.

CHARLES SPURGEON JOHNSON

Johnson, Hall

Musician

Hall Johnson (1888–1970), choral conductor and composer, was born in Athens, Georgia. He was educated at Knox Institute in Athens and at Atlanta University, Allen

University and Hahn School of Music, graduating from the University of Pennsylvania School of Music in 1910. He studied further in New York in 1923–24 at the Institute of Musical Art and obtained his Doctor of Music degree in 1934 from the Philadelphia Music Academy. During the 1920's, he was the recipient of several prizes for his musical compositions "Way Up in Heaven," "Sonata," "Flyer" and "Banjo Dance." He toured the nation with *Shuffle Along* and other outstanding musical revues.

In 1925, in New York City, he organized the Hall Johnson Choir, which appeared in many theater programs and on radio. In 1935, after a successful run in the stage production of *Green Pastures,* the choir went to Hollywood to participate in the motion picture version of the play; and Johnson and his choir remained in Hollywood to work in other productions, such as *Lost Horizons.* He organized the Festival Chorus of Los Angeles in 1941 for the purpose of raising funds to provide scholarships for young persons with musical talent.

Johnson received the Harmon Award in 1931 for his rendition of the music for *Green Pastures.* His compositions include the book and music for *Run Little Chillun,* produced in New York in 1933 and in Los Angeles and San Francisco in 1938 and 1939; and *Son of Man,* a religious cantata in the black idiom. He arranged and published countless black spirituals and folk songs, including his *Green Pastures Spirituals.*

Johnson, Henry

World War I Hero

Henry Johnson (1897–1929), hero of World War I who was awarded the French Croix de Guerre, was a redcap from Albany, New York. He served with the 15th National Guard of New York, which became the 369th Infantry during World War I and developed into one of the foremost fighting units in the American Army. It was the first group of Negro combat troops to arrive in France in 1917 and was the first American unit to cut through the German lines to reach the Rhine River. The entire regiment, having never retreated and never lost a soldier as a prisoner, was awarded the Croix de Guerre by the French government.

Henry Johnson and Needham Roberts merited individual citations by the French government for their unusual bravery in action. These two privates, while on guard duty one night, fought off a raiding party of about 20 Germans. Roberts was seriously wounded, but he was capable of keeping Johnson supplied with hand grenades to throw at the advancing Germans. When their ammunition ran out and the Germans attempted to drag the wounded Roberts away, Johnson fought them off with his French combat knife until the Germans retreated. When the encounter was over, four Germans were dead and several more were wounded. The report of this occurrence on May 15, 1918, was called the "Battle of Henry Johnson" in the American papers.

Johnson, J. Rosamond

Musician

J. Rosamond Johnson (1873–1954), an exponent of distinctively Negro music, was born in Jacksonville, Florida. He received a thorough musical education at the New England Conservatory of Music in Boston. Over the years, he pursued an interesting and unusual career as he used his formal training in music to develop a distinctive form of Negro music. Reaching the age of maturity when ragtime was becoming popular in America, Johnson became a composer-producer of vaudeville shows. He rose rapidly from a partnership with the comedian Robert Cole to directing successful

J. ROSAMOND JOHNSON

musical comedies. For a short period he was director of music for the Music School Settlement of New York, but the lure of the theater caused him to return to the vaudeville stage.

His musical comedy *The Red Moon* is remembered for one of its hit songs, "Wrap Me in Your Little Red Shawl." Johnson collaborated with his brother James Weldon by setting his poetry to music; one of the most outstanding works of the two is "Lift Every Voice and Sing," long considered the Negro national hymn. Songs written by Cole and Johnson for Klaw and Erlanger, producers of musical extravaganzas in New York City, were "Under the Bamboo Tree," "The Congo Love Song," "Nobody's Looking But the Owl and the Moon" and "My Castle on the Nile."

Johnson went abroad in 1913 to direct a musical comedy at the Hammerstein Opera House in London. He appeared also at the London Palladium in a new musical comedy.

Returning to America, he worked at the Music School Settlement but soon returned to the stage with the "Rosamond Johnson Quintet." In 1925, he arranged the music for his brother's collection *The Book of American Negro Spirituals.*

Johnson, James Weldon

Author and Diplomat

James Weldon Johnson (1871–1938), teacher, writer, diplomat and secretary of the NAACP, made a lasting impression on the cultural and social life of the Negro in America. He was the author of numerous books of both prose and verse. Some of his more notable works are *Fifty Years and Other Poems; God's Trombones: Seven Negro Sermons in Verse; The Book of American Negro Poetry; Black Manhattan; The Autobiography of an Ex-Colored Man,* a fictional

JAMES WELDON JOHNSON

biography published in 1912; and his own autobiography, *Along This Way*, in 1933.

His famous poem "Lift Every Voice and Sing" (1900), which his brother J. Rosamond Johnson set to music, was adopted by many depressed Negroes of the 1930's as their national hymn. His dramatic version of "The Creation" is still performed today, by dramatic readers, over television networks. One of his most notable poems praises the nameless authors of the Negro spirituals: "O Black and Unknown Bards of Long Ago." Johnson was a contributor to the *Nation, Crisis* and several other national magazines, editor of the New York *Age* newspaper and an extremely popular columnist for 10 years.

Johnson was born in Florida and was educated in Atlanta and New York City. He practiced law in Florida and taught school in his native state for a few years before joining his brother J. Rosamond Johnson in New York, to collaborate with him in writing musical comedies. He served as executive secretary of the NAACP and led the campaign for the Dyer Anti-Lynching Bill of 1921. Previously, Johnson had served the United States government as consul in Nicaragua. He was professor of creative literature at Fisk University at the time of his death.

In his book *Negro Americans, What Now*, published in 1934, he helped to explain the Negro's cultural contributions and achievements in literature and music and gave his own philosophy and expectations for the future of the Negro.

Johnson, John Harold

Publisher

John Harold Johnson (1918–   ), editor and publisher of *Ebony, Jet* and *Negro Digest* and president of Johnson Publishing Company, was born in Arkansas City, Arkansas. He was educated at the University

JOHN HAROLD JOHNSON

of Chicago and the Northwestern University School of Commerce. He started his career with the Supreme Liberty Life Insurance Company in 1936, while still attending school. In 1942, he borrowed $500, in order to start publication of the *Negro Digest;* and within six months' time, he gave up his job as publicity director with the insurance company to devote all of his energies to the magazine.

The company now publishes *Ebony, Jet, Black Stars, Black World* and *Ebony Jr!* magazines and has several affiliates, including a book division, a book club, and Ebony-Jetours (a travel service).

Johnson is a member of the board of directors of Twentieth Century Fox, the Marina City Bank of Chicago and the Service Federal Savings and Loan Association of Chicago. In 1972, he opened a new $8 million Johnson Publishing Company building in Chicago and purchased the Chicago radio station WGRT.

In 1966, he received the Spingarn Medal of the NAACP. In 1970, he was presented with the University of Chicago Alumni Association's Professional Achievement Award. In 1972, he became the first black publisher to be named "Publisher of the Year" by the Magazine Publishers Association. Johnson is a member of several business and civic organizations and is a 33rd degree Mason.

Johnson, Malvin Gray

Artist

Malvin Gray Johnson (1896–1934), painter of vivid Southern landscapes in water color, was born in Greensboro, North Carolina. He studied at the National Academy of Art, where he developed skill as a painter of life sketches and water scenes. He was a restless experimentalist, changing styles feverishly and turning from one school of art to another. At one time, he was an impressionist painter; then he turned to cubism; and finally, with a combination of sardonic humor and mystical pathos, he painted Negro folk types based on African idioms.

His original Southern landscapes are his greatest contribution to American art. They include vivid local color and a gallery of peasant types in such paintings as "Convict Labor," "Red Road," "Brothers," "Uncle Joe" and "Dixie Madonna"—acclaimed by critics as being outstanding works in the difficult medium of water color.

In 1928, Johnson won the Otto Kahn Special Prize in the Harmon show for his "Swing Low, Sweet Chariot," in which he depicts the emotions of down-trodden slaves who, after a day of toil, went to the edge of the river to call upon God for freedom. The painter showed, in a cloud phantasy over the heads of the praying slaves, a concept of their consciousness. Technically, the painting was unsatisfactory; but the judges gave him the prize as a means of encouraging the artist to perfect the idea toward which he was groping.

Johnson, Mordecai Wyatt

Educator and Minister

Mordecai Wyatt Johnson (1890–   ), university president and Baptist minister, was born in Paris, Tennessee. His gift as an orator became evident while he was in high school and influenced him to select the ministry as a career. He was educated at Morehouse College in Atlanta, the University of Chicago, and Colgate-Rochester Divinity School. In 1923, he earned his Master of Sacred Theology degree from Harvard University, where he attracted national attention for his delivery of a speech entitled "The Faith of the American Negro."

Dr. Johnson taught economics and history at Morehouse College from 1911 to 1913, leaving there to pastor a church in West Virginia. He was the first Negro to be appointed president of Howard University,

MORDECAI WYATT JOHNSON

taking office in 1926. When he assumed the administration of the university, it consisted of a cluster of unaccredited departments instead of colleges. At the time of Dr. Johnson's retirement in 1956, the institution had grown to ten distinct schools and colleges with an enrollment of more than 6,000 students. By 1965, the School of Medicine had graduated over half the black doctors in the United States. Dr. Johnson was responsible for securing congressional passage, in 1928, of an act for annual funds to the university for its support. He received the Spingarn Medal in 1929. In 1973, he began work on a book about his years as president of Howard.

Johnson, Sargent C.

Sculptor

Sargent C. Johnson (1888–1967), famous contemporary sculptor, was born in Boston and became well known as an artist in California in 1925, when his works were exhibited by the San Francisco Art Association. From 1928 to 1935, he exhibited his works in the Harmon Foundation art shows, where he was repeatedly a prize winner. His black porcelain bust of a Negro boy, "Sammy," shows his strongly simplified style and modern techniques, as well as the primitive African influence seen in many of his works.

Johnson had experimented with metal appliqué, wrought metal and various other composite materials, and he did Mexican gouache drawings. His most representative works, however, are of American Negro types; "Chester" and "Anderson" are portrayals of Negro youths.

Johnson studied at the Boston School of Fine Arts and under Bentiamino Bufano and Ralph Stockpole. His works are represented in the permanent collections of the San Diego Fine Arts Gallery and the San Francisco Museum of Art.

Jones, Eugene Kinckle

National Urban League Leader

Eugene Kinckle Jones (1885–1951), executive secretary of the National Urban League from 1919 to 1941, was born in Richmond, Virginia. He attended Wayland Academy and graduated from Virginia Union University with the B.A. degree in 1906; the university honored him with an LL.D. in 1924. He earned his M.A. degree at Cornell University in 1908.

Convinced in his youth that the salvation of the Negro lay in equal opportunity for employment, Jones became one of the leaders in organizing the National Urban League in 1911. The league undertook to open new opportunities for Negroes in industry and to assist Negroes in their problems of adjustment in the Northern urban centers. Branches were opened in large cities for the purpose of meeting the migrants, directing

EUGENE KINCKLE JONES

them to jobs, housing them and giving them general information on how to live in the city. Jones, as the first executive secretary, established the structure and the program of the organization during its first 30 years.

The power of the league placed Jones in the front ranks of leadership. He was called upon by the United States Department of Commerce to serve as advisor on Negro affairs from 1933 to 1937. He was chairman of the Negro advisory committee for the Texas Centennial Exposition in 1936 and for the New York World's Fair in 1939, and a member of the Fair Employment Board of the United States Civil Service Commission in 1948.

Jones, Lois Mailou

Artist

Lois Mailou Jones (1905–   ), professor of design and watercolor painting at Howard University, Washington, D.C., was born in Boston, Massachusetts, studied at the Museum School of Fine Arts in Boston and received her A.B. degree from Howard University, *magna cum laude.*

Considered a major painter, the artist has had a varied career. She was at one time a costume designer, a free-lance textile designer and a book illustrator. She headed the department of art at the Palmer Memorial Institute, Sedalia, North Carolina, before joining the faculty at Howard in 1930.

During the 1930's, Lois Mailou Jones tended toward an Impressionistic style. After the war, when she returned to Paris to paint and work, her style began to evolve and become more literal, though tempered by her own personal vision. In the 1950's, she married and spent summers, through 1969, studying and painting in Haiti. A grant from Howard made the summer of 1969 possible.

On a second grant from Howard, Miss Jones traveled and worked in Africa on sab-

batical leave, in 1970–71. Again her style evolved. Originally a landscape artist, Miss Jones attributes her use of the black subject and the growing warmth in her work to her colleague, Alain Locke.

She is considered a catalyst for artists, especially black artists. Yet her own work retains creativity. She has exhibited in major galleries in the United States and in Europe. In 1973, *"Retrospective,"* an art show spanning the years 1930–72, opened at the Museum of Fine Arts, Boston. In 1974, Miss Jones organized and participated in a show featuring black artists from Haiti, Africa and the United States. The show was held at the Acts of Art Gallery in New York City.

Jones, Virginia Lacy

Educator

Virginia Lacy Jones (1912–   ), director of the Atlanta University School of Library Service, was born in Cincinnati, Ohio, and was educated in the public schools of that city. She was graduated in 1933 from Hampton Institute with a B.S. in library science. She has an M.S. from the University of Illinois and a Ph.D. from the University of Chicago.

Before assuming her present position in 1945, she was dean of the School of Library Service at Atlanta. She is a member of the President's Advisory Committee on Library Training and Research and a member and former president of the Association of American Library Schools and the American Library Association. In 1971, she was elected to the executive board of the American Library Association.

Dr. Jones has published two books: *U.S. Government Publications on the American Negro, 1916–1937,* and *Problems of Negro Public School Library Service in Selected Southern Cities.* She is the author of many articles, including "Book Parties, a New

Adult Service," *Library Journal,* November 1943; "Administrative Provision for College Library Service," *Negro College Quarterly*, March 1947; "Wanted—18,000 Librarians," *Opportunity,* October–December 1947; and "Negro School Library Service in the South," *Top of the News,* December 1947.

Julian, Percy L.

Chemist

Percy L. Julian (1899–1975), research chemist, millionaire and former teacher, was president of Julian Associates and director of the Julian Research Institute in Franklin Park, Illinois.

Dr. Julian was born in Montgomery, Alabama, the son of a railway mail clerk. His grandfather, a former slave, had lost his right hand as punishment for learning to read.

PERCY L. JULIAN

Julian has 15 honorary degrees. He is a graduate of DePauw University (B.A. 1920); Harvard University (M.A. 1923); and the University of Vienna (Ph.D. 1931). He received an Austin Fellowship for graduate studies at Harvard. In 1928, he became an associate professor and head of the chemistry department at Howard University. In 1929, with a General Education Board fellowship, he studied in Vienna. In 1931, with a full professorship and with his Ph.D., he returned to Howard. He became a research fellow at DePauw in 1932. In 1936, after four years at DePauw, he found himself unable to obtain a faculty appointment at any major white college or university, including DePauw.

Julian left the academic world and became research director of the soya products and vegetable oil division of the Glidden Paint Co. of Chicago. He left Glidden in 1954 to form his Julian Laboratories, where he developed soybean products, hormone preparations and other pharmaceuticals. In 1961, he sold the firm for $2,338,000. He founded his present organizations in 1964.

Just, Ernest E.

Biologist

Ernest E. Just (1883–1941), brilliant investigator of biological phenomena relating to the structure of the cell, was born in Charleston, South Carolina. He is the author of 2 major books and more than 60 scientific papers in his field. After receiving his B.A. degree with high honors from Dartmouth and his Ph.D. degree from the University of Chicago, he began teaching at Howard University and, by 1912, had earned the rank of professor of zoology. He utilized his highly trained mind in formulating new concepts of cell life and metabolism and made pioneer investigations into the mysteries of egg fertilization, artificial parthenogenesis, and cell division.

ERNEST E. JUST

A member of the Phi Beta Kappa honor society, Dr. Just received the Spingarn Medal in 1914 for his outstanding contributions in biology. He has served as associate editor of the journal *Physiological Zoology* (Chicago), the *Biological Bulletin* (Woods Hole, Massachusetts), and the *Journal of Morphology* (Philadelphia); and as vice-president of the American Society of Zoologists.

King, Martin Luther, Jr.
Leader in the Civil Rights Movement

Martin Luther King, Jr. (1929–1968), Nobel Peace Prize winner and civil rights leader, was born in Atlanta. He was educated at Morehouse College and the Crozer Theological Seminary, where he earned the Pearl Plafkner Prize for scholarship. He received his Ph.D. degree from Boston University in 1955 and D.D. degrees from both Boston Theological Seminary and the University of Chicago Theological Seminary.

As pastor of the Dexter Avenue Baptist Church in Montgomery, Alabama, Dr. King assumed leadership of the Montgomery bus boycott, which ended segregation on city buses. The use of non-violence by the Montgomery Improvement Association proved successful as a technique in combating discrimination, and it put the name of its advocate, Martin Luther King, in the headlines. From that date on, he became the symbol of the Negro revolution in America and was named the "Man of the Year" in 1963 by *Time* magazine.

Dr. King, along with a group of Atlanta ministers, organized the Southern Christian Leadership Conference to stage massive demonstrations and carry the struggle for equality into other areas of the nation. Birmingham, with its snarling police dogs and its bombs, became the first main battleground for civil rights, and Martin Luther King led

MARTIN LUTHER KING, JR.

his people to a Christian forbearance that nourished hope in obtaining justice. Jailed as the leader of the demonstration, King wrote his famous "Letter from a Birmingham Jail."

The March on Washington in 1963 by all of the organizations involved in the civil rights movement culminated with Dr. King's moving speech and led to passage of the Civil Rights Act in 1964. To implement the gains expressed in the Civil Rights Act, Dr. King organized the voter registration drives in Alabama. In the dramatic march from Selma to Montgomery in 1965, with local race hatred and the Ku Klux Klan murders highlighting the event, Dr. King exposed to the nation the injustice prevailing in America and became the outstanding spokesman for the Negro people.

In 1966, he aimed his activities at the slums of Chicago. He was planning a poor people's march on Washington, when, on April 4, 1968, in Memphis, he was killed by an assassin's bullet.

Koontz, Elizabeth Duncan

Educator

Elizabeth Duncan Koontz (1919–), now director of the Women's Bureau in the U.S. Department of Labor, served as president of the Department of Classroom Teachers of the National Education Association in 1965. The Department of Classroom Teachers is one of the world's largest educational organizations; its membership of over 825,000 teachers includes the majority of the members of the National Education Association. Having served as secretary for two terms, in 1961 and 1962, and as vice-president from 1963 to 1964, she was elected president at the 102nd Annual Convention.

Mrs. Koontz was educated in the public schools of Salisbury and received her B.S. degree in English and education from Livingstone College. She earned her M.A. degree

at Atlanta University and studied further at Columbia University, the University of Indiana and at North Carolina College in Durham, North Carolina. In connection with her teaching career, she has been active in the local educational associations, serving two terms as president of the Salisbury Chapter of the North Carolina Teachers' Association.

In 1962, Mrs. Koontz was one of two classroom teachers who traveled to West Berlin to observe the effects of the Berlin Wall on education. She represented the National Education Assocation at the invitation of the West Berlin Teachers' Association.

Mrs. Koontz is a member of the North Carolina Chapter of the Council for Exceptional Children and the National Association for Retarded Children. She received two citations, in 1962 and 1963, for outstanding professional service and achievement in the teaching profession, from the Piedmont District of the North Carolina Teachers' Association and from the Future Teachers of America. In 1967, she became the first black to be elected president of the NEA. She is listed in *Who's Who of American Women* for 1974–75.

Lanier, Raphael O'Hara

Educator and Diplomat

Raphael O'Hara Lanier (1900–1962), college administrator and United States minister to Liberia, was born in Winston-Salem, North Carolina. He attended Lincoln University in Pennsylvania and Stanford University in California. Awarded a Rosenwald Fellowship in 1931, he studied at Harvard University for a year; later, he was honored by Liberia College of Monrovia with an LL.D. degree. After two years of teaching history at Tuskegee Institute in Alabama, he became dean and director of the summer school at Florida A. and M. College in Tallahassee for eight years. He then was dean of Houston College in Texas for five years before joining the division of Negro Affairs in the National Youth Administration office in Washington, D.C.

In 1940, he returned to his profession as dean of instruction at Hampton Institute in Virginia, where he later served as acting president. In 1945, he accepted a position as special assistant in the bureau of services of the United Nations Relief and Rehabilitation Administration. Later, Dr. Lanier was appointed by the United States to serve as minister to Liberia for two years. Upon his return to America, he accepted the presidency of Texas Southern University in Houston, Texas.

Dr. Lanier contributed many scholarly articles to the professional journals in his field and served on the editorial boards of the following: *Journal of Negro Education, Negro College Quarterly,* and the *Quarterly Review of Higher Education among Negroes.* He was a member of the advisory board of the Southern Negro Youth Congress, the national committee of the National Urban League and the National Education Association; and he served as a trustee of the American Teachers' Association.

Lawless, Theodore K.

Physician and Philanthropist

Theodore K. Lawless (1894–1971), dermatologist and philanthropist in Chicago's black district, was one of the world's leading skin specialists. Born in Thibodaux, Louisiana, he was educated at Talladega College in Alabama, the University of Kansas, and Northwestern, where he obtained his M.D. Later, he studied at Harvard and Columbia. Afterward, he received additional training in Europe. His reputation as a dedicated and skillful dermatologist brought him a daily av-

THEODORE K. LAWLESS

erage of one hundred patients, both black and white.

This distinguished dermatologist used his considerable earnings generously. Dillard University in New Orleans has a chapel that bears his name; and he also secured for the school an apartment building valued at about $700,000. The Beilinson Hospital Center in Israel has a dermatology clinic bearing the name of Dr. Lawless, who helped to raise $500,000 for the structure.

He was a senior attending physician at Provident Hospital in Chicago, and from 1924 to 1941 he taught at the Northwestern University School of Medicine. Besides his skill in the field of common skin diseases, he contributed to the scientific treatment of leprosy and syphilis.

Dr. Lawless received the Harmon Award in 1929 for achievement in medicine, and the Beatrice Caffrey Merit Award in 1970.

Lawrence, Jacob

Artist

Jacob Lawrence (1917–), one of the nation's foremost contemporary painters, was born in Atlantic City, New Jersey. He has earned an outstanding reputation by developing more than a dozen series of historical stories with as many as 60 pictures on a single subject, spending time in historical research in order to depict a story, an event or an institution. For instance, in "Migration" the artist illustrates the migration of Negroes into the North during World War I and their subsequent life in the slums. This series contains 60 pictures, which were purchased by the Museum of Modern Art in New York and the Phillips Gallery in Washington, D.C.

Lawrence began drawing and painting as a child in Philadelphia. In 1931, his family moved to New York, where he studied under Charles Alston at Utopia House and at the Harlem Art Center.

During World War II, Lawrence joined the United States Coast Guard and executed a series of paintings depicting wartime activities. This series, now in the United States Coast Guard archives, is preserved as a permanent record of the role played by this branch of the armed services in World War II. After the war, he was granted a Guggenheim Fellowship to do another series on the war. This group of 14 paintings, depicting the boredom of the servicemen, the battle fatigue, mail from home and air raids, is thought by many to be his best work.

Physical and emotional exhaustion forced the painter to enter New York Hillside Hospital in 1950. As his health improved, he started on a group of paintings depicting hospital life, such as "Sedation," "Depression," "Psychiatric Therapy" and "Occupational Therapy." After regaining his health, he returned to painting and produced a series of 12 pictures on theatrical life.

Lawrence has painted portraits for two covers of *Time magazine*. The first, a portrait of former Biafra's Lieutenant Odummegwu Ojukwu, appeared on August 23, 1968. The second, of Jesse Jackson, appeared on April 6, 1970. In 1968, Lawrence illustrated a juvenile book on Harriet Tubman, *Harriet and the Promised Land*. He has contracted for another, a new collection of *Aesop's Fables*. Lawrence received the Spingarn Medal of the NAACP in 1970, the first artist so honored.

Locke, Alain Leroy

Literary Critic

Alain Leroy Locke (1886–1954), literary and art critic and interpreter of the Negro's contribution to American culture, was born in Philadelphia. He attended school there and earned the B.A. degree (1907) and Ph.D. degree (1918) at Harvard University. As a Rhodes Scholar from Pennsylvania, he did graduate work at Oxford University from 1907 to 1910. He also studied at the Univer-

ALAIN LEROY LOCKE

sity of Berlin from 1910 to 1911, and was professor of philosophy at Howard University from 1912 until his retirement in 1953.

When he assumed the editorship of the volume *The New Negro* (New York, 1925), Locke became an interpreter of the Negro's increasing contribution to American culture.

Alain Locke, as critic and art historian, was one of the Negro's chief intellectuals. He was the author of *Race Contacts and Interracial Relations,* 1916. His famous *Bronze Booklets* include his studies of Negro music and art. At the time of his death, he was in the process of writing his major work, *The Negro in American Culture,* under a grant from the Rockefeller Foundation. Completed by Margaret Just Butcher, the book was published in 1956.

Logan, Rayford Whittingham

Historian

Rayford Whittingham Logan (1895–), university professor and historian, was born in Washington, D.C., and graduated with honors from Williams College in Massachusetts in 1917. He obtained his M.A. degree in 1932, and the Ph.D. degree from Harvard University in 1936. After serving five years at the Virginia Union University as professor of history, he moved to Atlanta University, where he was chairman of the department of history for five years. He was appointed professor of history at Howard University in 1938 and was promoted to head of the department in 1942.

As a historian, he exhibited excellent scientific research in the production of his monumental work *The Diplomatic Relations of the United States and Haiti, 1876-1891.* He edited *What the Negro Wants,* 1944, and wrote *The Senate and the Versailles Mandate System,* 1945; *The African Mandates in World Politics,* 1948; and a number of scholarly articles for professional journals.

On his retirement as head of Howard's history department in 1965, Dr. Logan was named professor emeritus. He was reappointed professor of history and Centennial History historian, 1965–69. In 1971, he was again reappointed professor of history. An annual series of Rayford W. Logan lectures was instituted at Howard in 1971 and has continued to the present. Dr. Logan has spoken at all of these lectures. Dr. Logan is listed in *Who's Who in America* for 1974–75. He is a member of the Authors' League and the Cosmos Club in Washington, D.C.

Louis, Joe
(Joseph Louis Barrow)

Athlete

Joe Louis (1914–), world's heavyweight boxing champion from 1937 to 1949, was born in Lexington, Alabama. His family moved to Detroit in search of higher wages

JOE LOUIS

but there, also, had a constant struggle to keep the children fed and clothed. Joe attended Duffield Grammar School, where he found little to interest or stimulate him; and, still a young boy, he left school to go to work. In the Ford plant at River Rouge, he did heavy work that developed his muscles, and the wages he earned were a welcome addition to the family income. While doing a man's job at the plant, Joe amused himself with the neighborhood boys' games of street-boxing. An amateur fighter, Thurston McKinney, who was short of sparring partners, asked Joe to spar with him, and the aspiring champion McKinney was knocked out by the boy.

This was the beginning of a career that was to give Louis his boxing championship title. In the Golden Gloves contest of 1934, Joe won the amateur light heavyweight title; he fought his first professional fight in July 1934. "The Brown Bomber," as he was called later, defeated Jack Knacken, a heavyweight from Chicago; and, after 36 professional fights, he was ready to try for the top title in 1937. On June 22, 1937, he defeated James J. Braddock and became the world's champion heavyweight boxer, holding the title continuously from 1937 to 1949.

During World War II, he was drafted into the army as a private but was soon promoted to sergeant. He was used by the government as a morale builder for the troops, putting on exhibition bouts in a tour of army camps around the world. He received a Legion of Merit medal for his record in the army.

"The Brown Bomber" grossed over four million dollars during the peak years of his boxing career, but, due to various unsuccessful business ventures, he suffered heavy losses. Although his financial situation has been a problem, Joe Louis is still optimistic: he says that boxing was good to him and that he "won't be selling apples on a corner."

McDaniel, Hattie

Actress

Hattie McDaniel (1898–1952), "eternal mammy" of Hollywood and radio, was born in Wichita, Kansas, and educated in the public schools of Denver, Colorado. At the age of 17, she first sang on the radio; and the following year, she won a gold medal given by the WCTU for her recital of the dramatic poem "Convict Joe." She went on tour during 1924 and 1925 and was referred to as the "colored Sophie Tucker."

She was featured in a popular radio show in which she played the role of Hi-Hat Hattie, and in 1933, Paramount Studios gave her a part in the film *The Story of Temple Drake*. Hollywood producers then labeled her "Mammy," and she was given only stereotyped roles afterward. Typical of her films are *Gone with the Wind, The Little Colonel, Saratoga, I'm No Angel* and *Nothing Sacred*.

HATTIE MCDANIEL

In 1939, she received an Oscar award from the Academy of Motion Picture Arts and Sciences for her performance in *Gone with the Wind*.

McKissick, Floyd B.

Businessman

FLOYD B. McKISSICK

Floyd B. McKissick (1922–   ), president of the Floyd B. McKissick Enterprises, Inc., in Soul City, North Carolina, is the former director of the Congress of Racial Equality (CORE) and an early advocate of the concept of black power.

McKissick resigned as director of CORE in 1968, to devote full time to work for black economic power. His national company helps organize and finance black businesses. He is also president of Warren Regional Planning Corporation, Inc., whose main project is the development of Soul City, the cost of which is estimated at $90 million.

Born in Asheville, North Carolina, McKissick graduated from a local high school and attended Morehouse College and North Carolina College in Durham. He received his law degree from the University of North Carolina Law School in 1951, the first black to receive a law degree from that institution. He was admitted to the North Carolina bar in 1952, and to practice before the United States Supreme Court in 1955. In 1962, he received the Ike Smalls civil rights award from the NAACP.

In 1963, McKissick was elected national chairman of the Congress of Racial Equality. In 1966, he replaced the retiring James Farmer as national director.

Under the leadership of McKissick, CORE advocated an end to United States involvement in Vietnam, stressing the need for attention to various social and economic problems and inequities in the United States. McKissick termed the "black problem" an American problem and insisted on the necessity for enforcement of civil rights laws. McKissick used his expertise to revamp the financial affairs of CORE. He raised $3 million for the organization.

In 1966, McKissick was asked to give his views about the change in attitude of many civil rights leaders that occurred during the black revolution of the 1960's. Speaking of CORE, he stated: "Our change is to work for solutions, besides just pointing out the wrongs in society. We believe that we have to get far more involved politically. We are directing a program toward political education, not only voter registration. We are also moving toward the development of an economics section of CORE—teaching self-help programs, developing co-operatives, credit unions, farming co-operatives, small businesses, and teaching Negroes how to get the benefits of Federal programs which are available. . . .

"We're also setting up a cultural-affairs and identity department. Here we're concerned with the teaching of Negro history and the Negro heritage. . . . We're also concerned with developing leadership."

McKissick is the author of *Three-Fifths of a Man* (Macmillan Company, 1969), as well as various articles and essays. He is a lecturer and public speaker. He is chairman of the National Conference of Black Lawyers and of the National Committee for a Two-Party System, Inc.

Marshall, Thurgood

United States Supreme Court Justice

Thurgood Marshall (1908–), Associate Justice of the United States Supreme Court, was formerly United States Solicitor General and director of the Legal Defense Fund of the NAACP. He has been popularly named "Mr. Civil Rights," because of the successful case won by his team of lawyers in 1954 against the "separate but equal" policy of segregated schools in America.

Justice Thurgood Marshall was born in Baltimore, Maryland, in 1908, and attended local public schools. He is a graduate of Lincoln University, in Pennsylvania (A.B., *cum laude,* 1930) and of Howard University Law School (L.L.B., *magna cum laude,* 1933).

Marshall went into private practice in Baltimore in 1933. While he was in private practice, one of his most fruitful and satisfying cases was *Murry* v. *Pearson,* which won the right for blacks to study in the University of Maryland Law School.

From 1936 to 1938, he was part-time assistant to Charles H. Houston, NAACP special counsel. He became director of the NAACP's new Legal Defense and Educational Fund in 1939; his team of lawyers won 29 out of 32 Supreme Court cases.

In 1938, Marshall prepared the Supreme Court brief which resulted in the granting of a black student, Lloyd Gaines, the right to enter the University of Missouri Law School. Marshall was NAACP special counsel from 1938 to 1962.

In addition to the 1938 brief, his first victory as NAACP special counsel, Marshall is known for winning key Supreme Court cases: *Smith* v. *Allwright,* 1944, ending segregated primaries; *Morgan* v. *Virginia,* 1946, invalidating state laws segregating interstate passengers; and *Sweatt* v. *Painter,* 1950, resulting in the admission of black law students to the University of Texas. The 1954 school desegregation decision, *Brown* v. *Topeka Board of Education,* is his greatest victory.

The late President John F. Kennedy appointed Marshall judge of the second court of appeals in 1962. As a federal judge, he was appointed for life, with a salary of $30,000 per year; but, when President Johnson offered him the position of Solicitor General, the people's advocate before the Supreme Court, he accepted. This position included a lower salary as well as uncertain tenure, but Judge Marshall felt that it was time for blacks, who had made so many advances in government, to start making some sacrifices.

In 1967, President Lyndon B. Johnson appointed Marshall to the United States Supreme Court. Justice Marshall became the first black to serve on that body.

Marshall has been popularly named "Mr. Civil Rights," because of the success of the *Brown* v. *Topeka Board of Education* case.

THURGOOD MARSHALL

Mays, William Howard

Athlete

William Howard (Willie) Mays (1931–), famous major league baseball star, was born in Westfield, a steel-mill town about 13 miles from Birmingham, Alabama. He grew up in the home of his uncle after his parents were divorced, but his father frequently visited the household and directed the boy's training. As a student at Fairfield High School, Willie played football and basketball; but during the summer he played baseball on the local sandlot teams. His father arranged for the manager of the Birmingham Barons to try Willie on his team for the summer. The scouts of the major league Giants Club saw Willie in action, bought his contract and placed him on the Giants' farm team in Trenton, New Jersey.

In 1951, Mays was promoted to the Minneapolis Millers. At the spring training camp in Florida, Leo Durocher, manager of the Giants, decided to try him in the major league.

Willie reported for his first major league game at Shibe Park in Philadelphia, in May 1951. Not knowing the names of his teammates, he used the expression "Say, hey" when he wanted their attention. Soon the other players warmed up to him and caught the infectious good humor of the "Say, hey kid." He was voted "Rookie of the Year for 1951," having hit 20 home runs in his first season.

His baseball career was interrupted by the draft in 1952. He spent most of his 21 months of service playing ball and working for the army's physical fitness training program. While he was in the army, the Giants went into a slump, but when he returned, in 1954, the team won the World Series. In the same year, his batting average was the highest in either league, earning for him the title of "Most Valuable Player" in the National League and "Major League Player of the

WILLIAM HOWARD MAYS

Year." The Associated Press poll named him the "male athlete of the year."

In 1966, this outstanding athlete continued to excel in major league baseball: he played for the San Francisco Giants under a contract that paid him more than $100,000 for the season. He has written an autobiography, *Born to Play Ball,* in which he attributes his success to the teamwork of the entire Giants Club.

Miller, Doris

Naval Hero

Doris (Dorie) Miller (1919–1943), Messman First Class, United States Navy, was awarded the Navy Cross for his distinguished devotion to duty, extraordinary courage and disregard of his own personal safety during the attack on the fleet at Pearl Harbor, on December 7, 1941. Miller was born on a

DORIS MILLER

small farm near Waco, Texas, of parents who worked as sharecroppers, eking out a bare existence from their cotton crop. When he was 19 years old, a naval recruiting officer was in Waco, and the young Doris signed up to see the world. His enlistment meant hard work at menial jobs, since the policy of discrimination at the time limited Negroes to service as stewards and cooks.

The brave feat of Dorie Miller during the confusion of the surprise attack on Pearl Harbor was executed when his captain was mortally wounded. Miller moved his captain from the bridge to a place of greater protection from enemy strafing and bombing, and the vicious fires aboard ship; then he returned to an unmanned machine gun. Though untrained as a gunner, he manned the weapon, blasting away at the Japanese planes until he was ordered to abandon the bridge.

On that eventful day in December, he was a messman on the *West Virginia,* which was sunk in Pearl Harbor. This young hero was only 22 years old when he received his citation from Admiral Chester W. Nimitz; the following year, he was listed as missing in action in the Pacific.

Miller, Kelly

Educator and Author

Kelly Miller (1863–1939) was born in Winnsboro, South Carolina, during the Civil War. After spending 17 years in the South, Miller came to Washington, D.C., to attend Howard University, where he received his B.A. degree. After earning his M.A. degree from Johns Hopkins University, he began a teaching career at Howard that spanned 44 years. During his tenure, he served successively as professor of mathematics, professor of sociology, dean of the College of Arts and Sciences, and dean of the Junior College.

KELLY MILLER

As a writer, he helped W. E. B. Du Bois edit *Crisis* magazine and became the first Negro academician to write a weekly column for the Negro press.

Miller was called the father of the Sanhedrin, a 1924 movement which attempted to unite all Negro organizations into one front. Although one meeting was attended by influential leaders from various Negro organizations, including the NAACP and the National Urban League, and many proposals were made, the movement failed to gain the momentum necessary to accomplish its aims.

One of the major spokesmen, writers, and teachers of his race in the early 20th century, Kelly Miller has been referred to as a "marginal man," racially separated from the white world, and intellectually distinct from his own group. In addition to his newspaper columns, he also wrote *Race Adjustment* (1908), *Out of the House of Bondage* (1917), *History of the World War and the Important Part Taken by the Negroes* (1919) and *The Everlasting Stain* (1924).

Mitchell, Abbie

Singer

Abbie Mitchell (1884–1960), dramatic soprano, was ambitious to sing in opera, but this elusive dream was never realized. Charles D. Isaacson wrote in the New York *Morning Telegraph* following her first recital, "What an Aïda this woman would make!" Her diction was highly praised, and many white singers studied her skill in producing pure, clear tones.

Miss Mitchell was born in New York City, attended school in Baltimore and studied voice under Harry T. Burleigh and Emilia Serrano. Gaining stage presence by performing in the musical comedies based on Negro folklore that were produced by her husband, Will Marion Cook, she continued to study musical theory and harmony. After complet-

ABBIE MITCHELL

ing two years of study under Jean de Reszke in Paris, she returned to New York for her first concert, which was highly successful. The critics' suggestion that she sing the role of Aïda spurred her to further study in Paris in the summer of 1913. Returning to America, she began making concert tours; and in a recital at Orchestra Hall in Chicago, she was described by one critic as follows: "I have never before heard singing of such sane and beautiful workmanship." She was accorded the high praise of the critics but was refused admittance to the inner circles of the opera.

Abbie Mitchell exhausted her voice by singing for many years in vaudeville and musical comedies. Then, she turned to dramatic acting and joined the Lafayette Players stock company in New York City. She was the leading actress in their productions of *Madame X, In Abraham's Bosom* and *Help*

Wanted. She eventually accepted an appointment as a member of the faculty of the Tuskegee Institute School of Music. Her son, Mercer Cook, became American Ambassador to Senegal.

Morgan, Garrett A.

Inventor

Garrett A. Morgan (*c.* 1875–1963), inventor of the first automatic stop signal, was born in Paris, Kentucky, during the Reconstruction period. In 1895, he moved to Cleveland, Ohio, where he produced his first invention, a best fastener for sewing machines, in 1901. In 1914, at the Second International Exposition of Sanitation and Safety, he won a gold medal for his invention of a truly practical gas mask. In 1916, he proved the usefulness of this device by rescuing workmen trapped in a tunnel under Lake Erie, and was awarded a gold medal by the city of Cleveland. He sold the patent rights to his stop signal to the General Electric Company for $40,000.

Motley, Archibald John

Artist

Archibald John Motley (1891–), who portrays Negro life in his paintings, was born in New Orleans. His parents moved to Chicago when he was in the third grade. He graduated from Englewood High School there, and, with the help of Dr. Gonzales of Armour Institute, he was encouraged to further his training. At the Art Institute of Chicago, he progressed rapidly. He won two prizes in 1925. The two paintings, "A Mulattress" and "Syncopation," were realistic in theme, dealing with life as the artist observed it in Chicago's Southside. He received the Joseph N. Eisenrath Prize for the painting "Mending Socks," and held one-man exhibits at the Newark Museum (1927) and the New Gallery in New York City (1928).

Awarded a Guggenheim Fellowship, Motley was able to study in France for two years. While in Europe, he exhibited his works for the American-Scandinavian Foundation in Stockholm and Copenhagen in 1930. At the World's Fair in Chicago in 1933–34, he exhibited his paintings "Blues" and "A Surprise in Store." He has been responsible for the mural paintings in the Wood River, Illinois, Post Office building, the Nichols School in Evanston and the Doolittle School in Chicago. His first Harmon Award was received in 1928, and, in 1950, he won an award for his unusual composition entitled "Getting Religion." He understood the life of the deprived Negroes of his environment, portraying them in compositions such as "Old Snuff-Dipper," "Black and Tan Cabaret," "Barbecue in a Garden," "Carnival" and "Parade."

Favorably recognized in the best art circles of Chicago, Motley is a member of the Illinois Academy of Fine Arts.

Motley, Constance Baker

Judge

Constance Baker Motley (1921–), U.S. district judge for the Southern District of New York, was appointed September 9, 1966, by President Lyndon B. Johnson. Prior to her appointment, she was a member of the NAACP Legal Defense and Educational Fund, Inc. (1945–65). Judge Motley, born in New Haven, Connecticut, is a graduate of New York University (A.B. 1943) and of Columbia Law School (L.L.B. 1946).

In her position as associate counsel of the fund, Constance Motley has won many difficult cases in the area of civil rights; her most famous victory was the case of James Meredith against the University of Mississippi. The brilliant argument of Mrs. Motley in defense of Meredith's admission to the university won for him this right, and the barriers of segregation in the universities of the South were

CONSTANCE BAKER MOTLEY

broken. Meredith completed his degree at "Ole Miss" and later returned to the state to demonstrate in the cause of voter registration.

In the election of 1964, Mrs. Motley entered New York politics and ran successfully for a seat in the New York senate. In a special election in 1965 held by the New York City Council to fill a vacancy in the office of the borough president of Manhattan, Mrs. Motley won and was reelected in the city-wide elections of November 1965 to a full four-year term. She was the first woman, as well as the first black, to hold the office of borough president.

Moton, Robert Russa

Educator

Robert Russa Moton (1867–1940), successor of Booker T. Washington as president of Tuskegee Institute in Alabama, was born in Amelia County, Virginia, in 1867. Attend-ing the local school in Prince Edward County for a short while, the poorly trained youth entered Hampton at the age of 19, although he was unable to pass the regular entrance exam. He was given a job in the sawmill and the privilege of attending night school, and within a year he had caught up sufficiently to enter day school. He graduated in 1890, remaining at Hampton as assistant comman-dant, and the next year as commandant, of the semi-military student body.

When Booker T. Washington died in 1915, another Hampton-trained individual was sought to succeed him. Moton was selected to solidify the gains that Washington had made and to put the school on a more secure finan-cial basis. In 1925, in a joint effort for both Hampton and Tuskegee, a five million dollar increase in endowment was achieved by Pres-ident Moton.

He spoke throughout the South to both white and Negro audiences on the delicate issue of race relations and, like his predeces-sor, he was chosen by President Woodrow Wilson to represent the White House in an investigation of complaints of Negro troops abroad. Criticism from other Negro leaders became quite vocal, and it was not until the erection of the Veterans Hospital at Tuskegee that Robert Moton was able to convince his own people of the worth of his leadership. The determined stand that he maintained against the white townspeople who wanted to control the hospital was heroic. After threats and intimidations from the Ku Klux Klan, Moton won the decision for the hospital to be staffed completely by Negro doctors, nurses and other workers.

The publication of his autobiography, *Finding a Way Out,* in 1920, was unfavor-ably received by many Negroes. In 1929, he brought forth an entirely different rendition of what he thought and felt about his people in *What the Negro Thinks.*

ROBERT RUSSA MOTON

Moton received many honorary degrees, including a Master of Arts from Harvard and honorary degrees from Virginia Union, Oberlin, Williams and Howard. He received the Harmon Award in 1930 and the Spingarn Medal in 1932.

Muhammad, Elijah

Black Muslim Leader

Elijah Muhammad (1897-1975) was born in Sandersville, Georgia, during the turbulent years of post-Reconstruction Negro suppression in the South. Born Elijah Poole, he assumed the name Muhammad as a result of his religious conversion in 1930. Due to the cloak of secrecy which surrounds Muhammad, little was known of his early life. He first attracted public attention in Detroit, Michigan, in the mid-1930's, when, as a follower of Wali Farad, founder of the "Nation of Islam," he began preaching racial unity as a religious tenet.

From this early teaching had grown the black nationalist activity known today as the Black Muslim Movement. Muhammad had a profound effect on some blacks and had served a dual purpose with his philosophy. By expounding racial ties and unity, he helped bind a people together for common action. By preaching militancy and solidarity against the majority group, he added to the breach in racial relations. The extent of his impact on the civil rights revolution of the 1960's must be determined by future historians.

Muhammad published a weekly newspaper, *Muhammad Speaks,* in which he revealed his doctrine to his followers. Prior to his death, he resided in a palatial home in Chicago.

Mulzac, Hugh Nathaniel

Seaman

Captain Hugh N. Mulzac (1886–), master of ocean-going steamships, was born in Kingston, St. Vincent Island, British West Indies. He went to England in his early twenties to attend the Swansea Nautical College in South Wales in preparation for a career as a seaman. In 1911, he came to the United States to attend the Shipping Board School in New York and gained practical experience by making periodical ocean voyages, applying himself to the study of wireless techniques and navigation.

During World War I, Hugh Mulzac was shipping out of Baltimore, Maryland, as a second mate on ships transporting war materials to Europe. Ambitious for promotion to chief mate, he appeared before the merchant marine inspectors as a candidate for his master's papers. He passed the exam in 1920 with a high rating, but was forced to continue sailing as a mate because Negroes were denied the rating of captain on American ships. It was only after great pressure was put on the government that Hugh Mulzac was assigned as captain to the *Booker T. Washington* in World War II; but his appointment was with the condition that he hire only Negroes for his crew. He refused to accept the ship under those conditions and stuck to his point until he won the right to man his ship with the best available men, regardless of race.

Nix, Robert N. C.

United States Congressman

Robert N. C. Nix (1905–), Democratic congressman from the second district of Pennsylvania, was born in Orangeburg, South Carolina. He received his secondary education at the Townsend Harris Hall High School in New York City, his college degree from Lincoln University in Pennsylvania and earned his law degree at the University of Pennsylvania Law School. He has practiced law since 1925, and served as special assistant deputy attorney general of Pennsylvania from 1934 to 1938.

Building his political career in the 44th ward, Nix was executive committeeman of the 9th division for 26 years. He was unanimously elected Democratic ward leader of the 32nd ward in 1958. He served as a delegate to the Democratic national convention in Chicago in 1956.

In May 1958, he was elected from the fourth district of Philadelphia to fill the unexpired term of Congressman Earl Chudoff and was inducted into the 85th Congress. He has been reelected to serve for seven more terms, through the 93rd Congress. He is a senior member of the congressional Black Caucus. He is a member of the Post Office and Civil Service and Foreign Affairs Committees, as well as the Postal Service, Postal Facilities, Mail and Labor Management and the Asian and Pacific Affairs Subcommittees. He remains a member of the Pennsylvania legal firm Nix and Nix.

Noble, Jeanne L.

Educator

Jeanne L. Noble (1926–), associate professor at New York University, was born in Palm Beach, Florida, and took her undergraduate training at Howard University. She specialized in guidance and developmental psychology at Teachers' College of Columbia University, where she obtained both the Master's degree and Doctorate. She has studied at England's University of Birmingham.

Dr. Noble was guidance counselor and director of freshman orientation at the City College of New York before her appointment to the Center for Human Relations Studies at New York University. She had also served on the Board of Higher Education of New York City as research assistant in the program of guidance and school counseling. Before coming to New York, Dr. Noble was dean of women at Langston University in Oklahoma and assistant professor of social science at Albany State College in Georgia. She also has been a summer visiting professor at the University of Vermont and Tuskegee Institute in Alabama.

Dr. Noble received the Pi Lambda Theta Research Award in 1956 for her book *The Negro Woman's College Education*. She co-authored a textbook with Dr. Margaret Fisher, in 1960, entitled *College Education as Personal Development*.

In 1964, Dr. Noble accepted Sargent Shriver's offer to head a committee in drawing up plans for the Girls' Job Corps, a department within the federal government's anti-poverty program. In 1965, she received the Bethune-Roosevelt Award for service in the field of education. She is active in Girl Scout work and with the National Social Welfare Assembly. She is a member of the President's Commission on the Status of Women.

Owens, Jesse

Athlete

Jesse Owens (1913–), in his day the foremost sprinter and broad jumper in the world, was the outstanding star of the Olympic games held in Berlin, Germany, in 1936. He won the 100-meter dash, the 200-meter dash and the broad jump, and was the anchor man on the United States 400-meter relay team. He began his track career at the Fairmount Junior High School in Cleveland, Ohio, where he was coached by Charles Riley, who continued as his mentor through East Technical High School and at Ohio State University in Columbus.

Coach Riley's fleet-footed pupil won distinction for the high school in 1933 at the National Interscholastic Championships held at the University of Chicago, and furthered his reputation as a track star at Ohio State University, where he received his B.A. degree in 1937. Recipient of the Associated Press citation as the outstanding track athlete of the first 50 years of the 20th century, Owens has worked with boys in Chicago in hope of combating juvenile delinquency through sports and has served on the Youth Commission of Illinois. The United States Department of State sent him as a good-will ambassador to India in 1955.

JESSE OWENS

Parks, Gordon Roger

Photographer and Journalist

Gordon Roger Parks (1912–), master of the camera, was born on a small farm in Fort Scott, Kansas. He was named "Magazine Photographer of the Year" in 1961 by the American Society of Magazine Photographers. Syracuse University has honored him with the Newhouse Award in photography; and he has received honors in the Art Directors Show, as well as the News Pictures of the Year competition.

A high school dropout, Parks spent his youth working as a waiter, lumberjack, piano player, band leader and basketball player. In Chicago, in 1937, David P. Ross, director of the South Side Community Art Center, encouraged him to study photography by providing a darkroom where he could develop his pictures.

The popularity of photography was reaching a peak in the 1930's through the numerous pictorial magazines, such as *Life* and *Look*. Parks gave a one-man show of his work, and, as a result of the show, won a Rosenwald Fellowship for further study and experimentation. After a year spent at the Farm Security Administration unit under the direction of Roy Stryker, Parks joined Elmer Davis in the overseas division of the Office of War Information.

In 1949, he became a free-lance photographer with *Life* magazine, covering such assignments as stories on a gang leader of Harlem; crime in the United States; poverty in Brazil, using a boy named Flavio as his subject; and discrimination and segregation in the United States.

Parks has had several books of his photographs and writings published. In 1969, he directed a film version of his book *The Learning Tree,* which is based on his youth in a small town in Kansas. In 1971, he directed the hit film, *Shaft,* and its sequel, in 1972, *Shaft's Big Score.*

Peçanha, Nilo

Leader of Brazil

Nilo Peçanha (1860–1924), President of the Republic of Brazil in 1909–10, was of undoubted Negro ancestry. Born in Campos, near Rio de Janeiro, he completed his law studies in 1887. As a lawyer and politician, he championed the abolition of slavery early in his career, which automatically designated him as a confirmed and active member of the Republican movement. In 1890, he was chosen deputy to the Constituent Assembly and was elected to the first Congress of the Republic. He was re-elected continuously until 1903, when he was elected to the legislature by the constituents of the state of Rio de Janeiro.

Nilo Peçanha ran as vice-president on the ticket with Alfonso Pena and was successful in winning the election. On the death of President Pena in June 1909, Peçanha took over the presidency of Brazil and completed the term in November 1910. He was returned to the Senate in the election of 1912 and was later elected president of the state of Rio de Janeiro. In 1917, he was appointed minister of foreign affairs under the administration of President Wenceslau Braz.

Petry, Ann Lane

Author

Ann Lane Petry (1911–), practicing pharmacist and novelist, was born in Old Saybrook, Connecticut, of a family whose members traditionally were pharmacists. Her grandfather was a pharmaceutical chemist; and her father, Peter C. Lane, her uncle and her aunt were pharmacists. The young daughter was expected to carry on the tradition, even though she became interested in writing while in high school. She completed high school in 1929 and dutifully enrolled in the College of Pharmacy at the University of Con-

ANN LANE PETRY

necticut in New Haven, then went to work in her family's drugstores, as was expected.

Listening to the stories of the people who visited the stores, Ann began to formulate ideas for short stories. During her spare time, she turned to writing again but received rejection slips for every story she submitted to magazines. In 1938, she married George Petry and moved to New York, where she worked for the *Amsterdam News*, preparing advertising copy. In 1941, she joined the staff of the *People's Voice*, covering general news stories and editing the women's page.

Searching for news stories in the slums of Harlem was an important experience for Ann Petry. Appalled by the destitute plight of the Negro children of the area, she accepted a position with the New York Foundation in 1944, to engage in an experimental study of the effect of segregation upon the minds of children. Working with the public school children of Harlem, she resumed her writing by producing plays for the children. Next, she joined the American Negro Theatre group, but turned again to writing short stories.

One of her short stories appeared in *Crisis* in 1943 and gained the attention of an editor of the Houghton Mifflin publishing company, who contacted her about a novel. This encouraged her to start her first book, *The Street*; and, to her surprise, the company awarded her a $2,400 literary fellowship in 1945. The book, published in 1946, won fame for the young author. Her second, *Country Place,* followed in 1947; *Harriet Tubman: Conductor on the Underground Railroad* appeared in 1955. Her other works are *The Drugstore Cat, In Darkness and Confusion, Cross Section,* and "Like a Winding Sheet," named best American short story for 1946.

Miss Petry lives and writes in Old Saybrook, where she is a practicing pharmacist at James' Pharmacy. In 1963, she wrote a novella, *Miss Muriel,* which she said contained material to appear in a larger work in progress.

Pickens, William

Scholar and Educator

William Pickens (1881–1954), educator and author, was born in South Carolina. His parents were former slaves who moved twenty times during his youth, in an effort to support their children. As the child of sharecroppers, William had to work the land instead of going to school; and it was not until his family settled near Little Rock, Arkansas, that fairly decent schools were available to him. He had to put in a half-day of work in the morning before school and then return to the fields in the afternoon.

Pickens' determination to learn survived the years of hard work and frustration. And in 1902, he earned his B.A. degree from Talladega College in Alabama. In 1904, he was awarded a B.A. degree from Yale University, where he was elected to the Phi Beta Kappa honor fraternity. In 1906, Pickens received a diploma from the British Esperanto Association. He received three honorary degrees—from Fisk University, Selma University and Wiley College in Marshall, Texas. He was instructor of Latin and German at Talladega from 1904 to 1909, then was promoted to professor of languages from 1909 to 1914. He spent one year at Wiley College as professor of languages before assuming the office of dean at Morgan College in Baltimore, Maryland.

In 1920, he accepted the job of field secretary for the National Association for the Advancement of Colored People; and in 1942, he became chief and director of the interracial section of the Savings Bond Division of the U.S. Treasury Department.

Pickens was the author of *Abraham Lincoln, Man and Statesman,* 1909; *The Heir of Slaves,* 1910; *Frederick Douglass and the Spirit of Freedom,* 1912; *Fifty Years of*

WILLIAM PICKENS

Emancipation, 1913; *The Ultimate Effects of Segregation and Discrimination,* 1915; *The New Negro,* 1916; *Bursting Bonds,* an autobiography, 1923; and many articles. He was the leader of the Federal Forum Projects for the United States Department of the Interior in 1937–38.

Poitier, Sidney

Actor

Sidney Poitier (1927–   ), first black Academy Award winner (for his performance in *Lilies of the Field,* 1963), was born in Miami, Florida. He was educated by private tutors and in public high school in Nassau, New Providence, Bahamas. At 15 he had to leave school to work. He was variously a drug store clerk, parking lot attendant and a longshoreman.

After World War II, during which he enlisted in, and served four years in, the U.S. Army, he joined the American Negro Theater

SIDNEY POITIER

as janitor in exchange for acting lessons. He played minor roles with the group and through a producer won a Broadway bit part. Roles in *Lysistrata, Freight* and *Anna Lucasta* followed.

He became nationally known as a film star with his role of Miller in *The Blackboard Jungle* in 1955. In 1959, he created one of his most famous roles in the play *A Raisin in the Sun.*

His film credits include: *A Patch of Blue, In the Heat of the Night, Guess Who's Coming to Dinner* and *The Lost One.*

Films of his own making include *For Love of Ivy* (1968) and *In a Warm December* (1973). He produced (with Harry Belafonte) and starred in *Buck and the Preacher* (1972). He is a member of and helped found First Artists Productions, which includes Paul Newman, Barbra Streisand and Steve McQueen.

Powell, Adam Clayton

Minister

Adam Clayton Powell, Sr. (1865–1953), builder of America's largest Negro congregation, the Abyssinian Baptist Church of New York City, was born in a one-room log cabin in Franklin County, Virginia. He was one of 16 children of a former slave who bore the brand "P" on his back. At the close of the Civil War, this large family could not afford regular schooling for their children; but the precocious young Adam was so eager to learn that he memorized the alphabet forward and backward within his first two days in school.

His desire to learn took him through the meager schools of his county and on to Wayland Academy (now Virginia Union University), where he graduated in 1892. He entered the Yale University Divinity School in 1895. In 1908, Powell became the pastor of the Abyssinian Baptist Church of New York City. The church, located in downtown

ADAM CLAYTON POWELL

New York, had a membership of only 1,600 and an indebtedness of $146,354. By 1921, Reverend Powell had built the present church on West 138th Street at a cost of $350,000. When he retired in 1937, the membership had reached 14,000 and assets of the church totaled $400,000. Today, the church has more than 15,000 members and is a major force in the total life of the Negroes of New York City. It is a community within itself, with departments that include social service, recreation, crime prevention, adult education, a day nursery and an employment agency. During the depression of the 1930's, the church provided soup kitchens to serve thousands of jobless Negroes in Harlem.

In 1928, Reverend Powell received the Harmon Award as leader of the best-organized church among Negroes in America. He also received many honorary degrees from leading universities in America and lec-

tured on race relations at Colgate University and at many other colleges. His books include an autobiography, *Against the Tide,* 1938; *Saints in Caesar's Household,* 1939; *Picketing Hell,* 1942; *Riots and Ruins,* 1945; and *Upon This Rock: The History of the Abyssinian Baptist Church,* 1949.

Powell, Adam Clayton, Jr.
United States Congressman

Adam Clayton Powell, Jr. (1908–1972), former U.S. congressman, was born in New Haven, Connecticut, and educated in New York City, where his illustrious father was the pastor of the largest Negro church in America, the Abyssinian Baptist Church. Powell graduated from Colgate University in 1930 and earned his Master's degree at Columbia University in 1932. While assistant

ADAM CLAYTON POWELL, JR.

pastor to his father in the 1930's, young Powell sent pickets to march in front of the flourishing white establishments in the heart of Harlem that depended on Negro patronage but had no colored employees. He assumed the leadership of his father's church in 1937 and, in 1942, became founder, editor-in-chief and co-publisher of the militant newspaper the *People's Voice*.

Adam Clayton Powell, Jr., was to become one of the "new breed" of religious leaders—a fighting radical identifying himself with the "marching blacks." As chairman of the Harlem Coordinating Committee, he helped to promote Negro job opportunities in Harlem's white business firms. In 1941, with the help of his congregation and his personal popularity, he became the first Negro elected to serve on the New York City Council. While on the council, he pressed for the hiring of Negro motormen and conductors on public transportation facilities. He also worked for the hiring of Negroes on the faculties of the city colleges of New York.

In 1943, he won the endorsement of Democrats, Republicans and the American Labor Party for the congressional nomination. He was elected to the House of Representatives in 1944 and was re-elected until late 1969, even though he was repudiated by the regular Democratic organization in the 1958 election.

Powell was denied his seat in the House in 1967. The Supreme Court later ruled that the House had acted illegally. Powell was re-elected in 1968, but failed to regain his former power. He was defeated in the 1970 Democratic primary and spent most of the time until his death in retirement at his home in Bimini. He died in a Miami, Florida, hospital, April 6, 1972.

Powell's most serious venture into foreign policy was his attendance at the 1955 Bandung Conference in Indonesia, where 29 Asian and African nations met to discuss their problems. He attended the meeting alone, at his own expense and over what he called the "strong opposition of the State Department." The United States government officially boycotted the conference. Powell credited himself with blunting Communist attacks on America by announcing that racial discrimination was on the way out. Later, President Dwight D. Eisenhower congratulated and commended Congressman Powell for his initiative and success regarding the trip to Bandung.

Price, Mary Leontyne

Opera Singer

Leontyne Price (1927–   ), third black to sing with the Metropolitan Opera, and its first black star, began her career singing in a church choir in Laurel, Mississippi. She made her opera debut in 1957 with the San Francisco Opera, and made her debut at the Metropolitan in 1961 in a performance of *Il Trovatore*.

Miss Price has sung at every major opera house in the world, including La Scala, the Paris Opera, the Rome Opera, the Vienna Staats-Opera, the Berlin Opera and the Hamburg Opera.

In 1966, she starred in *Antony and Cleopatra* at the opening of the new Metropolitan Opera House in New York's Lincoln Center.

After an absence of several seasons from the Metropolitan, Miss Price returned for the 1974 season with leading roles in *Madama Butterfly* and *Don Giovanni*.

She received the Presidential Medal of Freedom in 1964 and the Spingarn Medal of the NAACP in 1965. She is a Fellow of the American Academy of Arts and Sciences and a member of the advisory board of the National Cultural Center.

Quarles, Benjamin

Historian

Benjamin Quarles (1904–), scholar in the field of American Negro history, was born in Boston, Massachusetts, where he received his early education in the public schools. His bachelor's degree was earned at Shaw University in Raleigh, North Carolina, in 1931. As the recipient of a junior fellowship and grant-in-aid from the Social Science Research Council—the President Adams Fellowship in Modern History from the University of Wisconsin—he earned his doctoral degree in 1940.

Dr. Quarles served as professor of history and dean of instruction at Dillard University in New Orleans before assuming his present professorship at Morgan State College in Baltimore, Maryland. Among the numerous books written by this outstanding historian are: *Frederick Douglass,* 1948; *The Negro in the Civil War,* 1953; *The Negro in the American Revolution,* 1961; and *Lincoln and the Negro,* 1962. The last work, a well-balanced, meticulously documented and finely written book, is a dramatic story of Lincoln, the Civil War and the role of the Negro, which is not generally included in works on the period. In fact, *Lincoln and the Negro* is Professor Quarles' most outstanding contribution to this neglected area of American history. Dr. Quarles has received two Rosenwald fellowships and a Guggenheim fellowship. He has recently been named chairman of Maryland's commission on black history and culture.

Active in the Association for the Study of Afro-American Life and History, he is an associate editor of the *Journal of Negro History* and a contributing editor to *Phylon.* His book *Black Abolitionists* was published in 1969.

Randolph, Asa Philip

Labor and Civil Rights Leader

Asa Philip Randolph (1889–), former vice-president of the American Federation of Labor-Congress of Industrial Organizations (AFL-CIO), is known as the organizer of the Brotherhood of Sleeping Car Porters in 1925 in New York City. He was president of the Brotherhood until his retirement in 1968. In 1957 he became a vice-president of AFL-CIO and now serves on its executive council.

The militant civil rights leader was born in Crescent City, Florida, and attended City College in New York City. Active in civil rights since the 1920's, he organized and directed the 1941 "March on Washington," which led President Franklin D. Roosevelt to create the Fair Employment Practices Commission, opening thousands of jobs to blacks during World War II.

ASA PHILIP RANDOLPH

Randolph was a leader of the Committee against Discrimination in the Armed Forces, which helped influence President Truman to eliminate segregation in the armed forces of the United States. He organized the youth march on Washington in 1958 to demonstrate in favor of implementing the Supreme Court's school desegregation decision of 1954. Again in 1963, he was one of the leaders of the march on Washington demonstrating for the passage of the Civil Rights Bill. He served as honorary chairman of the White House Conference on Civil Rights in 1966, which was held to discuss means of enforcing the Civil Rights Acts of 1964 and 1965.

Randolph has organized various movements and programs on behalf of blacks, including the League for Non-Violent Civil Disobedience against Military Segregation, the National Negro Congress and the Non-Partisan League of the CIO.

Redding, Jay Saunders

Scholar and Author

Jay Saunders Redding (1906–   ), professor of American Studies and Humane Letters at Cornell University, Ithaca, New York, was born in Wilmington, Delaware. He received both his Bachelor of Philosophy degree and his Master of Arts degree from Brown University and studied Elizabethan drama at Columbia University. His career as a teacher began at Morehouse College in Atlanta, Georgia, and, after several appointments in various colleges of the South, he settled at Hampton Institute in 1943 as professor of creative literature. A member of Phi Beta Kappa honor fraternity, he received a Rockefeller Foundation fellowship in 1940 and a Guggenheim in 1944. In 1969, he became professor of American history at George Washington University. In

1971, he co-edited an anthology, *Cavalcade*, with Arthur P. Davis.

As a writer, Redding has produced the following books: *To Make a Poet Black*, 1939; *No Day of Triumph*, 1942; *Stranger and Alone*, 1950; and *On Being Negro in America*, 1951. He has published articles in the *Atlantic Monthly, Harper's, Saturday Review of Literature, American Mercury, New Republic, Survey Graphic, Antioch Review* and *Transition*. His *No Day of Triumph* won the 1944 Mayflower Award, which is given annually for the best book written by a resident of North Carolina, regardless of race or color. For the Lippincott series on the different peoples who constitute the U.S.A., he wrote *They Came in Chains*.

As a critique of social life among Negroes in America, *Stranger and Alone* deals with the serious issue of Negro leaders in the field of education. It exposes conditions in Negro colleges, with special reference to the administrative activities. The first theme of this novel is that education in Negro colleges is geared to keeping the Negro submissive, thus training him for failure in terms of American values. The novel's second objective is to point out that militant leaders do not exist in the South.

Rivers, Francis E.

Lawyer

Francis E. Rivers (1893–), retired judge, president and chief policy maker of the NAACP Legal Defense and Education Fund, was born in Kansas City, Kansas. A Phi Beta Kappa graduate of Yale University in 1915, he applied to 60 New York banking and insurance firms in search of employment, but found, nothing available for a brilliant young Negro. After several attempts to undertake business ventures in Harlem, he won a scholarship to the Columbia University Law School. Upon graduation

FRANCIS E. RIVERS

in 1922, he was admitted to the bar; but when he applied to a score of downtown law firms for employment, he was again denied work. Finally, after he secured part-time work in the post office, Jonah Goldstein, of the prominent firm of Goldstein and Goldstein, heard of his plight and took him into the firm. Later, he was associated with the firm of Finkelstein and Welling for two years before opening his own office in New York City in 1925.

Taking an interest in the tangled political affairs of Republican-dominated Harlem, Rivers ran for the New York legislature on the Republican ticket from the 19th district in 1929 and was elected. In the legislature, he aroused the vested interest group of Harlem by introducing bills calling for minimum wages, and other bills designed to force Harlem landlords to repair their property in order to collect rents. These were unsuccess-

ful, but he did get a bill passed to create the 10th municipal district court in Harlem, ensuring the election of two Negro justices for the first time. Rivers was nominated for one of the posts in 1930, but Harlem went Democratic and he was defeated. In 1937, he was appointed Manhattan district attorney, serving under Thomas Dewey and Frank Hogan until 1943. When Dewey became governor, he appointed Rivers a justice of the city courts. He was nominated by the Republican Party and the American Labor Party and was easily re-elected in 1943. During this period, Judge Rivers was involved in the fight with the American Bar Association (A.B.A.) over admitting Negro lawyers to membership. He won the right of membership in the A.B.A. and the support of all of the political parties in the election of 1953.

Judge Rivers retired from the bench in 1963; he became president and chief policy-maker of the NAACP Legal Defense and Education Fund on April 1, 1965. This unit is the national legal arm of the entire civil rights movement. He regards this post as another adjunct to the task he assumed in 1963 as chairman of the special committee on civil rights that was formed at a White House conference called by President Kennedy.

Judge Rivers had served as vice-president of the Legal Fund since 1950 and was the first Negro to become its president, as he was the first Negro member of the bar association of New York City and the first Negro city court justice.

Robeson, Paul

Actor

Paul Robeson (1898–1976), dramatic actor and baritone soloist, was born in Princeton, New Jersey, and was educated at Rutgers College, where he was elected to the honor fraternities Cap and Skull and Phi

Beta Kappa. As a member of the varsity football team, he was placed by Walter Camp on the All-American Football Team of 1918. In 1923, he received his law degree from Columbia University, but the talented Robeson was destined for a career on the stage.

His interest in the theater began when he appeared in an amateur production of *Simon the Cyrenian* at the Harlem branch of the YMCA. He played the leading role in Eugene O'Neill's play *Emperor Jones* in London in 1925. After his successful appearance as an actor, he embarked on a concert tour throughout Europe and America as a basso interpreter of black spirituals. In 1928, he sang in Ziegfeld's production of *Show Boat*.

In 1930, he returned to the theater in the role of Othello at the Savoy Theatre in London. His interpretation of the Shakespearean character won spectacular acclaim. He played the same role in two American productions, in 1934 and 1943. His acting in 1943

PAUL ROBESON

captivated American audiences for 296 performances. In 1924, he appeared in O'Neill's *All God's Chillun Got Wings*. He performed the title role in O'Neill's *The Hairy Ape* in London in 1931 and starred in the film production of *Emperor Jones* in 1933.

Possessing a deep sympathy for the social underdog and having experienced the humiliations of second-class citizenship in his native America, Paul Robeson went to Soviet Russia in the late 1940's and resided there periodically until the mid-1960's, when he returned to the United States. He is listed in *Who's Who in America, 1974–75*.

Robinson, Hilyard R.

Architect

Hilyard R. Robinson, architect specializing in slum clearance and housing projects, was responsible for organizing and conducting the slum housing survey in the District of Columbia in 1933. As a professor of architecture and chairman of the department of architecture at Howard University for 13 years, he was given the contract to serve as principal designer of the Howard city slum clearance project in Washington in 1933. In 1934, he was appointed consulting architect to the National Capitol Advisory Committee, for the selection of sites for slum clearance and as senior architect for the United States Suburban Resettlement Administration. The Washington Board of Trade appointed him a member of the design committee to plan renovation of the blighted areas of the capital city.

His most outstanding construction project was the 1.8-million-dollar Langston Public Works Administration Housing Project for Negroes. He collaborated with Paul R. Williams in designing the men's dormitory at Howard University. His second large public project was the Alabama Avenue, S.E., government housing project in 1940.

HILYARD R. ROBINSON

Robinson received his training at the University of Pennsylvania and at the Columbia University School of Architecture. He continued his training at the University of Berlin and made a special tour of Europe and Soviet Russia to study and examine housing structures. In 1926, Robinson's design was chosen for the historic restaurant in the new Henry Hudson Hotel in Troy, New York. In 1927, he was awarded the first, second and fourth prizes offered by the journal *Architecture*.

Robinson, Jackie

Athlete

Jackie Robinson (1919-1972), elected to the Baseball Hall of Fame in 1962, was born on a sharecropper's farm near Cairo, Georgia. His father deserted the family six months after Jackie was born, and the following year, his mother moved to Pasadena, California, where she worked with a determination to do the best she could for her children. As soon as the boys were old enough, they began to work in order to contribute to the family's income. Jackie's first regular job was delivering papers in the neighborhood.

He attended Muir Technical High School, where he enjoyed competing in athletics. He excelled in football, basketball, baseball and track, but no major college offered him a full scholarship. He entered Pasadena Junior College, where he played quarterback on the football team and was noticed by college scouts. He made headlines as a track star, setting a new world record for the junior college broad jump. In baseball, he was named the most valuable junior college player in southern California.

Upon graduating from Pasadena Junior College, Jackie had a wide choice of scholarships to senior colleges. He entered U.C.L.A., and it was predicted by George T. Davis of the *Herald Express* that he would go down in history as the greatest all-round athlete of the Pacific Coast Conference. In the fall of 1941, Jackie began playing professional football, but his career was interrupted when Pearl Harbor was attacked by the Japanese and he was drafted into the army. He attended officer candidate school and was appointed to serve as a morale officer. Upon his discharge from the army, he accepted a coaching job at Sam Houston College in Texas, but resigned in April 1945 to play baseball with the Kansas City Monarchs.

When Branch Rickey, owner of the Brooklyn Dodgers, decided to pioneer in hiring Negro ball players, he settled on Jackie Robinson, who was hired on October 23, 1945. Tension mounted across the nation at the prospect of a Negro playing on a major league baseball team. Robinson made his debut in Jersey City on April 18, 1946, as the second baseman of the Montreal Royals. His season with the Dodgers' farm team culminated in

JACKIE ROBINSON

triumph in the 1946 Little World Series in Louisville, Kentucky, where Jackie emerged as a hero in the final and decisive game. The next season, Rickey moved Jackie up to the National League as first baseman, and with Jackie on the team, the Dodgers won the pennant in 1947 and five more times in the following 10-year period.

In 1949, Jackie Robinson was named the National League's Most Valuable Player. After 10 years of major league baseball, at the age of 38, Jackie retired from his athletic career. He was formerly chairman of the board of the Freedom National Bank and vice-president of Proteus Company.

Robinson, Luther

Dancer

Luther (Bill "Bojangles") Robinson (1878–1949), the nation's first great tap dancer, was born in Richmond, Virginia. His parents died while he was an infant, leaving him, an older brother and a sister to be cared for by their grandmother. The boys' education was very limited, since they had to spend most of their time earning money to help support the poverty-stricken family.

Luther began his dancing career as a shoe-shine boy; when business was slow, he would dance in taverns and barbershops or even on the sidewalks. More nickels and dimes were thrown to him for dancing than he earned from all of his other odd jobs. His performances brought him a degree of popularity that did not fit his name, Luther; so he began to use his brother's name, Bill.

Shortly after changing his name, he gave up dancing to work as a stableboy at Benning's Race Track near Washington, D.C. At a local dance hall, he was observed executing some fancy dance steps by Eddie Leonard, a veteran of vaudeville, who signed Bill up for a job in his show *The South before the War*. When this show closed, Bill teamed up with George Cooper in a vaudeville act, but Cooper soon died of cancer and Robinson abandoned the stage. Taking a job as a waiter, he accidentally spilled a bowl of hot oyster stew down a customer's back. The customer was Morty Farkins, of the Western Vaudeville Manager's Association, who became Robinson's manager for the remainder of his career.

Under Farkins' management, Robinson was destined to dance his way to fame and fortune. During the twenties he appeared on Broadway with the *Blackbirds* and *Brown Buddies*. In the thirties, as a Hollywood star, his fame spread around the world. His most popular movies, made with Shirley Temple, were *In Old Kentucky*, *The Littlest Rebel*, *One Mile from Heaven*, *Rebecca of Sunnybrook Farm* and *The Little Colonel*. He was capable of dancing one hour and 15 minutes without repeating a single step, and he held the world's record for running backwards. He celebrated his 62nd birthday by dancing 62 blocks down Broadway. Robinson was known for his generosity: he earned a fortune, and he gave away a fortune to needy fellow actors and charitable causes.

Robinson, Ray (Sugar Ray)

Athlete

Sugar Ray Robinson (1920–), holder of three world championship boxing titles, was born Walker Smith, Jr., in Detroit, Michigan, where he grew up in the slum district known as Paradise Valley. Walker was only seven years old when his parents were divorced, and the children had to help their mother financially to keep the family together. She encouraged her son's love for sports and managed to eke out 25 cents a month for membership dues in the Brewster Community Center, where he began to imitate the older boys in shadowboxing, skipping rope and taking punches at the bag.

Friends and relatives encouraged Mrs. Smith to move to New York, where she obtained work at the Riverside Laundry and Supply Company for $12 a week.

When Walker was introduced to George Gainford, the boxing coach of the Salem Crescent Athletic Club, his love for boxing blossomed; and in a matter of weeks, he was competing in amateur tournaments. One night, Gainford took some of his boxers to Waterbury, Connecticut, to see some amateur boxing matches. On that occasion, one of the boxers did not show up, and Walker was put into the ring in his place. He did not have an AAU membership card, so a card was borrowed from another fighter, named Raymond Robinson. Walker Smith scored a quick knockout and returned to New York as Ray Robinson. The adjective "Sugar" was added by Gainford, who made the remark that he was "sweet as sugar."

At the age of 20, Robinson entered the professional ring in Madison Square Garden.

After a non-title bout with the lightweight champion, Sammy Angot, Sugar Ray set out to win the welterweight crown. In 1943, he was drafted into the army and was assigned to the same troupe as Joe Louis. They toured the United States entertaining troops with boxing routines and were allowed time off for their professional matches.

Sugar Ray finally got a chance to officially earn the welterweight title by defeating Tommy Bell in a 15-round contest. He won the middleweight championship of Pennsylvania in 1950 and sought a match with the world-title holder, Jake La Motta. The match was held in Chicago in 1951, with Sugar Ray winning the contest in the 13th round. The following year, he fought Joey Maxim for the light heavyweight crown in New York but was overcome by heat prostration between rounds near the end of the fight. He retired for a while, but returned to the ring for almost a decade, fighting men 10 years younger than himself. Sugar Ray Robinson was one of the greatest all-round fighters the sports world has seen in this century.

Rowan, Carl T.

Government Official

Carl T. Rowan (1925–   ), newsman, author and diplomat, is a widely syndicated newspaper columnist who resigned in 1965 as director of the United States Information Agency to return to journalism. He joined the Publishers-Hall Syndicate in 1965 and has since received over a dozen awards for his work.

A native of Ravenscroft, Tennessee, Rowan is a graduate of Oberlin College (B.A. 1947) and the University of Minnesota (M.A., journalism, 1948). He holds 13 honorary degrees.

In 1948, he joined the staff of the *Minneapolis Tribune* and remained there until he was appointed to the Department of State as

CARL T. ROWAN

deputy assistant secretary of state for public affairs in 1961. While on the staff of the *Tribune,* he reported many of the major news events of the 1950's and covered assignments for leading magazines, such as the *Saturday Evening Post, Look* and *Ebony.* Each year he won awards for his news coverage.

In January 1964, President Lyndon B. Johnson appointed Carl Rowan director of the United States Information Agency. Mr. Rowan gave up this post in 1965, to return to journalism. Before receiving this appointment, Mr. Rowan served as ambassador to Finland. In 1954, he lectured in Asia for the State Department on "The Role of the Newspaper in Change." He is the author of several books: *South of Freedom,* 1953; *The Pitiful and the Proud,* 1956; *Go South to Sorrow,* 1957; *Wait till Next Year,* 1960 (a biography of Jackie Robinson); and *No Need for Hunger,* 1962.

Mr. Rowan was selected "Minneapolis' outstanding young man of the year" by the Minneapolis Junior Chamber of Commerce, in 1954; he received the Sidney Hillman Award for the best newspaper reporting in the nation during 1952. He was awarded an honorary Doctor of Letters degree from Oberlin College in 1962.

Rudolph, Wilma Glodean

Athlete

Wilma Glodean Rudolph (1940–), winner of three gold medals in the 1960 Olympics in Rome, grew up in Clarksville, Tennessee. She has set phenomenal records and has capitivated a worldwide audience as a track star. Beginning in high school, for five years Wilma won all of the dashes that she entered, ranging from 50 to 220 yards. She was also an all-star basketball player on the local high school team in Clarksville, and in 25 games in 1956 she scored 803 points. In this same year, she was a member of the United States Olympic team. In 1960, she gained international fame at Rome as a member of the U.S. team.

Also in 1960, she won second place in the competition for the James E. Sullivan Award, given to the top amateur athlete in the U.S. (In 1961, she received this award.) She won the 1960 Helm World Trophy for the outstanding athlete in North America, the *Los Angeles Times* award for women's track and field events and the *Mademoiselle* award for outstanding achievements for the year. Also, she was chosen as one of the 10 outstanding women in the United States by the *New York Times* and was voted the most outstanding athlete of the year by the European Sportswriters' Association. In the year 1960 alone, Miss Rudolph received a total of 18 awards and citations.

While Wilma was a student at Tennessee A. and I. University in Nashville, Coach

Edward S. Temple was the person most responsible for her achievements. In Melbourne, Australia, at the opening of the Olympic games in 1956, Coach Temple electrified the track world when six of his women athletes won positions on the United States Olympic track and field team. Wilma Rudolph was one of these women, and she succeeded in glamorizing a sport that previously had been considered unsuitable for women.

Sampson, Edith Spurlock

Circuit Court Judge

Edith Spurlock Sampson (1901–), distinguished lawyer and alternate delegate to the United Nations General Assembly in 1950, was born in Pittsburgh, Pennsylvania. She began her career as a social worker, having obtained her training at the New York School of Social Work and at the School of Social Service Administration of the University of Chicago. While she was engaged as a social worker in Chicago, she studied law at the John Marshall Law School and Loyola University, where she earned her Master of Laws degree in 1927. In 1952, she received the honorary degree of Doctor of Laws from the John Marshall Law School.

She established her law office in Chicago in 1926, specializing in criminal law and domestic relations, and served as probation officer and referee in the juvenile court of Cook County from 1930 to 1940. She was the first black woman appointed as an assistant state's attorney for Cook County, Illinois. In 1949, as a member of the World Town Hall of the Air, Mrs. Sampson visited more than 20 countries, participating in open debates on current political questions with leading citizens in each country. It was after this extensive tour that President Truman recognized her qualifications and appointed her to serve as alternate delegate to the United Nations General Assembly in 1950. She was

sent abroad as guest lecturer for the United States in 1951 and 1952 and, in 1955, received an award from the Society of American Friends for her Middle East lecture tour. In 1964, she became an associate judge of the Cook County circuit court. She is listed in *Who's Who of American Women, 1974–75.*

Savage, Augusta

Sculptor

Augusta Savage (1900–1962), one of America's foremost sculptors, was born in Green Cove Springs, Florida, and was educated at the Florida A. and M. College and at the Cooper Union Art Institute in New York, where she studied under George Brewster for two years. Abroad, she studied under Felix Beuneteau and at the Grande Chaumière in Paris, with the aid of fellowships awarded by the Rosenwald Fund and the Carnegie Foundation. She had been disap-

AUGUSTA SAVAGE

pointed previously when she was denied, because she was a Negro, a scholarship she had won for study at Fontainebleau, France. The action of the committee allocating the scholarships for the French government brought protests in the American papers. Later, she won a scholarship to study at the Royal Academy in Rome, but she lacked sufficient funds for the trip.

While a student at Cooper Union, Miss Savage became interested in Negro types, and she has produced such striking works as the "African Savage," "The Tom Tom" and "The Negro Urchin." She received citations in Paris for her exhibit at the spring Salon at the Grand Palais in 1929, and was awarded the Colonial Exposition medallion by the French government in 1931. In 1939, she was commissioned to execute a sculptural group symbolic of the Negro's contribution to music for the Community Arts Building at the New York World's Fair.

Miss Savage was former director of the Harlem Community Art Center, where she was an effective teacher. One of her pupils, William Artis, won the Harmon Art Award in 1933. She sculptured a score of prominent Americans and exhibited her works in many American galleries, including the Chicago Art Institute. "The Negro Urchin" is one of her technically most successful works. Some of her other works are "The Gamin," "Envy," "Martyr," "The New Negro," "Green Apples" and "Lift Every Voice and Sing," which was exhibited at the New York World's Fair in 1939.

Schuyler, Philippa Duke

Musician

Philippa Schuyler (1932–1967), child prodigy, concert pianist and composer, was born in New York City, the daughter of George Schuyler, journalist, novelist and editor of the *Pittsburgh Courier*. Her parents planned her education to meet the needs of her I.Q. of 185, recognizing that the slow pace of the regular school system would be frustrating to the gifted Philippa. At the age of three, she had already begun writing poetry, playing the piano and composing music. At 14 years of age, she had composed two hundred musical selections.

The precocious Philippa completed the eighth grade of the Sacred Heart Annunciation Girls' School when she was 10 years old. After completing Father Young's High School, she did not enter college; instead, she was tutored in languages, history, psychology and other subjects while she filled concert engagements as a child prodigy. In the young composers' contest held at Detroit's Grinnell Foundation, Philippa won first and second prizes for her compositions "Manhattan Nocturne" and "Rumpelstiltskin" from the *Fairy Tale Symphony*. The first-prize composition, "Manhattan Nocturne," scored for a hundred-piece symphony orchestra, has been performed by the New York Philharmonic symphony orchestra and the Chicago and San Francisco symphony orchestras.

Fluent in French, Spanish and Italian, she traveled throughout the world on concert tours. She told of her exciting adventures in her book *Adventures in Black and White*. She was in the Congo in 1960, when the revolution occurred, and was kidnapped in Nigeria and poisoned in West Africa. During her travels, she performed for European, African and Asian royalty.

Miss Schuyler was awarded more than two dozen prizes and citations for her artistry. Her published works include *Six Little Pieces* and *Eight Little Pieces* for the piano, and *Sleepy Hollow Sketches*. Prior to her tragic death in a plane crash in 1967, Miss Schuyler had appeared as guest soloist with the major symphony orchestras of the nation.

Spaulding, Asa T.

Businessman

Asa T. Spaulding (1902–   ), retired president of North Carolina Mutual Life Insurance Company in Durham, North Carolina, is now president of Asa T. Spaulding Consulting and Advisory Services. The firm provides advisory services to corporations throughout the United States. When Spaulding retired from North Carolina Mutual, the company was the largest black-owned insurance company in the world. Born in Columbus County, North Carolina, Spaulding is a graduate of New York University (B.S. 1930) and the University of Michigan (M.A. 1932). He has honorary degrees from five universities, including Duke (L.L.D.) and the University of North Carolina (L.L.D.). Spaulding went to work as a youth for North Carolina Mutual, then managed by his uncle. He was elected to the presidency in 1959.

ASA T. SPAULDING

In 1964, he was named the first black director of W. T. Grant Co. He serves on state and federal government commissions. He is a trustee of Howard and Shaw Universities and of the National Urban League. His writings on insurance have appeared in the *Congressional Record.*

Still, William Grant

Musician

William Grant Still (1895–   ), classical composer, called by his peers the "dean of black composers," was born in Woodville, Mississippi. He became the first black to conduct a major symphony orchestra in the United States when he directed the Los Angeles Philharmonic in 1936.

Originally planning a career in medicine, Still studied at Wilberforce University, then at Oberlin Conservatory of Music and the New England Conservatory of Music. He was a dedicated student of composition under the tutorship of George Chadwick and Edgard Varése, and composed more than one hundred musical selections, including five symphonies, six operas, ballet music, spirituals and musical poems. He has received Guggenheim and Rosenwald fellowships, and the National Association of American Composers and Conductors cited him for his *Symphony in G Minor* and *Africa.* In 1928, he won the Harmon Award for Distinguished Achievement among Negroes.

Still first became engrossed in arranging and orchestrating musical comedy melodies in New York, but he deliberately turned from light music to experimenting in serious renditions of Negro music. His *Afro-American Symphony* was presented by the Rochester symphony orchestra in 1931. *Africa,* a symphonic poem, was performed by Barrare's Little Symphony in Rochester and at the Festival of American Music held in Hamburg, Germany. Another symphonic poem,

WILLIAM GRANT STILL

From the Journal of a Wanderer, was performed by the Chicago and Rochester symphony orchestras.

Other notable works of the composer are *Darker America, From the Heart of a Believer, From the Land of Dreams, Levee Land, From the Black Belt* and *Log Cabin Ballads.* His stage works include a ballet, *Sahdji,* and his opera *Troubled Island.*

Terrell, Mary Church

Civic Leader

Mary Church Terrell (1863–1954), a woman who championed human rights, was born in Memphis, Tennessee, and was educated at Oberlin College. Her father was a former slave who had amassed a fortune through his real estate business. Rather than have his daughter attend the poorly equipped segregated schools of Memphis, he sent her

to Ohio to attend school. After graduating from Oberlin College, she made her home in Washington, D.C.

In 1895, Mrs. Terrell was appointed to the District of Columbia School Board; and in 1904, she was a delegate to the International Council of Women in Berlin, where she addressed the Council in French, German and English. She was an active worker for woman's suffrage and the passage of the Nineteenth Amendment, which granted women the right to vote. In 1909, she became a charter member of the NAACP. In 1953, she took an active part in demonstrations protesting segregated public facilities in Washington, D.C.

As a writer, lecturer, organizer and demonstrator, she fought segregation in the restaurants of the nation's capital. With other citizens, she brought a test case to the Supreme Court that demanded the enforcement of an old law banning discrimination of "respectable citizens" in restaurants. The Court ruled that the old law was still valid, and desegregation of hotels, restaurants and theaters soon followed. In 1940, Mrs. Terrell had published her autobiography, *A Colored Woman in a White World.*

Thurman, Howard

Theologian

Howard Thurman (1900–), clergyman and philosopher, was born in Daytona Beach, Florida. He has been rated as an ambassador of goodwill for his visits to hundreds of college campuses in America, Canada and abroad in his crusade against the intellectual apathy of college students. His penetrating insights into life situations and his unique approach to college students have been the keynote of his success as a clergyman-philosopher. Audiences are spellbound by his eloquence. During his career, he was called upon to serve as resident guest

HOWARD THURMAN

lecturer at the Colgate-Rochester Divinity School; and in 1935, he toured Canada, lecturing at many institutions of higher learning. In India, he lectured at 45 Indian colleges. The Indian newspaper *Madras Guardian* reported an Indian student as saying that he would follow Dr. Thurman to America to learn more of Negro life in the United States.

Dr. Thurman received his educational training at the Florida Baptist Academy and later graduated from Morehouse College in Atlanta and earned his B.D. degree at the Colgate-Rochester Divinity School. He was a Kent Fellow at Haverford College, where he studied under the great mystic scholar Rufus Jones, and has been associated with several of the major Negro colleges as professor of philosophy and religion. From 1932 to 1944, he was professor of systematic theology and dean of the Andrew Rankin Chapel

at Howard University. In 1944, he was minister of the Church for the Fellowship of All Peoples in San Francisco; and, in 1946, he was an Ingersoll lecturer on the "Immortality of Man," at Harvard University. His last appointment was at Boston University, where he served as professor and dean of the chapel until his retirement.

Dr. Thurman is the author of *The Greatest of These,* 1945; *Deep River,* 1946; *Negro Spiritual Speaks of Life and Death,* 1947; *Meditations for Apostles of Sensitiveness,* Series I, 1947, and Series II, 1948; and *Jesus and the Disinherited,* 1948

Tobias, Channing H.

Leader in Interracial Cooperation

Channing H. Tobias (1882–1961), outstanding proponent of interracial cooperation, was born in Augusta, Georgia. He played a prominent role in the affairs of race relations during the thirties and forties as an intermediary between Negroes and the White House. His career in YMCA work placed him in a position to carry out his resolve to employ Christian principles as a basis for promoting race relations.

He became student secretary of the National Council of the YMCA in 1911 and secretary of the council's colored department in 1923. He accepted the directorship of the Phelps-Stokes Fund in 1946. While serving with the YMCA, he was a delegate and chairman of the committee on race relations at the 1937 world conference of the YMCA, in Mysore, India. He was again delegate to this conference in Denmark in 1950. During World War II, he was associate administrator of the New York State war finance committee.

Besides directing the Phelps-Stokes Fund, Tobias served on the board of directors of the Marshall Field Foundation, the Jessie Smith Noyes Foundation, the Stettinius Associates of Liberia, the American Bible Society and the Modern Industrial Bank of New York City. As chairman of the board of directors of the NAACP, his position of strength and leadership was recognized in Washington. He was placed on the Advisory Committee on Selective Service and on the Army and Navy Committee on Welfare and Recreation during World War II. President Truman appointed him to serve on his Committee on Civil Rights in 1946.

Tobias traveled around the world in 1935 and through Africa in 1946. He received the Harmon Award for religious service in 1928 and the Spingarn Medal in 1948. His role in interracial cooperation was deeply influenced by his educational background. As an orphan, he was befriended and helped through college by President Walker of Paine College in Augusta, Georgia. To prepare for the ministry, he was sent to Drew University in Madison, New Jersey. During his lifetime, he received a number of honorary degrees, the most notable being that of Doctor of Laws from New York University in 1950. This was the first such award to a Negro in the history of the university.

Even though he was an independent in politics, he was in frequent and close touch with the White House and various government agencies because of his general acceptance as an elder statesman. He commanded a following among Negroes of all social and economic backgrounds in all parts of the country.

Townsend, Willard Saxby
International Labor Leader

Willard Saxby Townsend (1895–1957), organizer of the United Transport Service Employees Union and international labor leader, was born in Cincinnati, Ohio, and was educated in the public schools of that city and at the Illinois College of Chiropody. After completing the course in chiropody, he returned to Cincinnati to establish a practice and enjoyed a relatively stable career for four years. As a result of his experience as a soldier in World War I, Townsend became interested in organizing a Cincinnati company for the Ohio National Guard. The organization of this company proved to be a success, and he earned promotion to the rank of first lieutenant in 1924. He served for several years as commanding officer of the group.

His activities with the National Guard, plus his unsuccessful bid for a seat on the city council in the election of 1924, caused his practice as a chiropodist to fail completely. He decided to go back to school, major in chemistry and become a teacher. While working as a redcap, dining-car waiter and Pullman porter on the various railroad lines in Canada, he was able to complete two

CHANNING H. TOBIAS

WILLARD SAXBY TOWNSEND

years of study at the University of Toronto. Townsend accepted a job as a schoolteacher in Texas until the start of the economic depression of 1929, when he returned to Chicago. It was at this point in his career that he was able to use his skill in organization and leadership, for he began the long and arduous task of organizing the redcap workers of America.

In the 1930's, Townsend traveled throughout the nation organizing the men who worked as redcaps into the national body of United Transport Service Employees (U.T.-S.E.). The organization was affiliated with the Congress of Industrial Organizations (C.I.O.), and as national president of the U.T.S.E., he automatically became a member of the executive board and, incidentally, the first Negro vice-president in organized labor. He was a member of the C.I.O. Committee to Abolish Discrimination and was selected as the international representative of labor to conferences in Cuba, Mexico, Japan and Germany.

In 1947, he served as a member of the Committee of the World Federation of Trade Unions to study conditions in Japan, China, Korea, the Philippines and the Malay States. He attended the International Confederation of Free Trade Unions' Conference at Berlin in 1952 and was selected to go to Japan again on a special mission for organized labor. Upon his return from Japan in 1952, he wrote a handbook entitled *Trade Union Practices and Problems,* which was translated into Japanese for the purpose of instructing laborers of Japan about the purposes and functions of organized labor. While in Japan, he was invited to address the Japanese Diet. He so impressed the politicians, as well as the ranks of labor, that a monument was erected in his honor.

When the American Federation of Labor and the C.I.O. merged in 1955, Townsend was elected to the joint executive council. His death in 1957 ended a career which started in a Negro slum area of Cincinnati and culminated in a position in the highest ranks of international labor.

Trotter, William Monroe
Civil Rights Leader and Journalist

William Monroe Trotter (1872–1934), a reform journalist and militant civil rights leader, was born in Boston, Massachusetts. He graduated from the Hyde Park High School in 1890 as an honor student and entered Harvard University, where he received his Bachelor's degree *magna cum laude.* He had been elected to the Phi Beta Kappa honor fraternity during his junior year.

Trotter's career was launched in Boston as a real estate broker, but his ultimate goal was achieved in 1901, when he established the militant newspaper, the *Guardian*. Every detail was carefully planned in terms of location and symbolism: he selected the building that William Lloyd Garrison had used for the publication of the *Liberator* and where Harriet Beecher Stowe's *Uncle Tom's Cabin* had been printed. The main purpose of the paper was "propaganda against discrimination based on color and denial of citizenship rights because of color."

In explaining why he accepted the hazardous, insecure life of an agitator, he said, "The conviction grew upon me that pursuit of business, money, civic or literary position was like building a house upon sands; if race prejudice and persecution and public discrimination for mere color was to spread up from the South and result in a fixed caste of color . . . every colored American would be really a civil outcast, forever an alien, in the public life."

The *Guardian* became a national institution, and so did its editor, William Monroe Trotter. He opposed all compromises on civil rights, whether they were proposed by Booker T. Washington or President William Howard Taft. On July 30, 1903, at the Columbus Avenue African Zion Church in Boston, Booker T. Washington was the featured speaker. Trotter and his followers hissed and interjected remarks to such an extent during the course of Washington's address that the police had to be called; some sources say that Trotter threw a stench bomb in the audience. Trotter and his cohorts were duly arrested, fined and sentenced to the Charles Street Jail for 30 days. He explained his reasons for creating a furor on the grounds that Washington had a veritable monopoly on the prevalent media of publicity, and there was no other way to reach the public with his views on civil rights for the Negro. He detested Washington's leadership and compromising position, collaborating instead with W. E. B. Du Bois, in 1905, in the organization of the Niagara movement, forerunner

of the National Association for the Advancement of Colored People.

As the "watchdog" of discrimination, Trotter did not hesitate to protest to the President of the United States. In 1906, he challenged Theodore Roosevelt over the discharge of three companies of the 25th United States Infantry Regiment in an incident in Brownsville, Texas. In 1910, he organized a successful demonstration against the showing of the Negro-baiting play *The Clansman* in Boston; and again, in 1915, he picketed the theater where *Birth of a Nation* was being shown. He was arrested, tried and eventually acquitted for this demonstration.

President Wilson, like Booker T. Washington, was disliked by Trotter. Trotter led a delegation to protest the discriminatory policy against Negro employees in government offices. His greatest feat occurred in 1919, when the Paris Peace Conference was convened. Trotter applied for a passport, wishing to attend the meeting in order to place the Negro question in the United States before the Allied statesman who had said the war would "make the world safe for democracy." Trotter was denied the passport; but he learned to cook and, to reach Europe, obtained a job on a transatlantic steamer as a second cook. In Paris, he appeared at the conference as a delegate of the National Equal Rights League and as secretary of the Race Petitioners to the Peace Conference. The chiefs of state, including Woodrow Wilson, refused to include any proviso outlawing discrimination in the Covenant of the League of Nations, as proposed by the Japanese delegation.

Returning home, Trotter continued his militant struggle until his death in 1934. By this time, he was practically penniless, having exerted all of his efforts in the fight for civil rights.

Vann, Robert L.

Publisher

Robert L. Vann (1887–1940), founder of the *Pittsburgh Courier* newspaper in 1910, was born in the backwoods of North Carolina. He was the son of an ex-slave tenant farmer who lived in such a remote rural area that Robert was 10 years old before he saw his first railroad train. From a little two-page news sheet, published by a Negro employee of a Pittsburgh pickle factory, Vann built his giant *Pittsburgh Courier*. At the time, he had just obtained his law degree from the University of Pittsburgh Law School.

The struggling young lawyer noticed the popularity of the little news sheet filled with the crude verse of its publisher, and after contacting the owner, Vann decided to convert it into a newspaper. With a few associates whom he interested in the project—and little capital—he published the first edition on March 10, 1910. The venture was a success, and as a spokesman for the Republican Party, it became the news media for the Negro community in Pittsburgh. By the 1930's, its circulation reached from coast to coast, with branch offices and outlets throughout the United States.

During the economic depression of the thirties, Vann saw fit to change the support of the *Courier* from the Republican Party to that of the New Deal Democrats. For his support of the Roosevelt program, he was appointed assistant United States attorney general in the late thirties.

Waters, Ethel

Actress

Ethel Waters (1900–77), veteran of 30 years in the entertainment world, was born in Chester, Pennsylvania, of a poverty-stricken family. Marriage at the age of 12 and employment as a maid earning $4.75 a week.

ETHEL WATERS

were hardly an escape from her dire circumstances. However, she possessed an unusual voice, and at age 17, she obtained a job singing at Lincoln Theater in Baltimore. In 1923, she substituted for Florence Mills at the Plantation Club in New York, introducing the song "Dinah," which created a sensation and resulted in her rapid rise to fame. For the next 10 years, she played in Negro theaters throughout America.

Her first Broadway appearance was in 1927 in *Africana;* it was followed by *Blackbirds, Rhapsody in Black, As Thousands Cheer, At Home Abroad* and *Mamba's Daughters.* She also won acclaim with her first film appearance in 1929 in *On with the Show.* Her performances in the show and film *Cabin in the Sky,* in the play *The Member of the Wedding,* and in the film *Pinky* were great successes. Not satisfied with many of the roles that producers offered Negroes, she delayed accepting a role in *Cabin in the Sky* until she was assured that the portrayal of Petunia was symbolic of the very best in Negro womanhood.

She is especially known for her singing of "Dinah," "Stormy Weather," and "Am I Blue." Miss Waters established herself as a sensitive dramatic actress in the Broadway production of *A Member of the Wedding,* for which she won the New York Drama Critics' Award in 1941. Her autobiography, *His Eye Is on the Sparrow,* was published in 1951. Now retired, Miss Waters is listed in *Who's Who of Amercian Women, 1974–75*

Weaver, Robert Clifton

Presidential Cabinet Member

Robert Clifton Weaver (1907–   ), professor of urban affairs at Hunter College in New York City since January 1969, became the first black to hold a Cabinet position in the United States Government when President Lyndon B. Johnson appointed him in

ROBERT CLIFTON WEAVER

1966 to the newly created Cabinet post of Secretary of Housing and Urban Affairs.

Born in Washington, D.C., and educated at Harvard University (B.S., 1929; M.A., 1931; Ph.D., 1934), Weaver entered government service in 1933 as a race relations officer in the Department of the Interior. Serving the Roosevelt New Deal program, he was employed as an advisor-specialist in problems of discrimination in housing and employment. He was appointed to the Housing Authority Administration in 1937 as a special assistant. During World War II, he became chief of the minority group service division of the War Production Board (1940–42). In these positions, he worked untiringly to bring about full integration in all departments of the Federal government.

Near the close of World War II, he was assigned to work with the United Nations Relief and Rehabilitation Administration. While he was away from Washington, he taught at two major universities—Columbia University in New York and New York University. Subsequently, the John Hay Whitney Foundation appointed him to administer its fellowship program. Actively participating in the affairs of the Democratic Party while residing in New York, he was appointed by Governor Harriman as state rent commissioner. He was vice-chairman of the New York City Housing and Redevelopment Board; and during the 1960 presidential campaign, he served as adviser on civil rights to the presidential candidate, John F. Kennedy, who later appointed him administrator of the Housing and Home Finance Agency, where he served for five years.

With this record of service and extensive knowledge of the increasing problems in America's urban centers, Robert Weaver was nominated by President Lyndon B. Johnson on January 13, 1966, to the newly created cabinet post of Secretary of Housing and Urban Development. He is the author of 4 books and holds 30 honorary degrees from institutions around the country. He resigned from the Cabinet in 1969 to return to academic life.

Wesley, Charles Harris
Historian and Educator

Charles Harris Wesley (1891–), historian and lecturer, was born in Louisville, Kentucky. He attended Louisville's Central High School and at the age of 15 entered Fisk Preparatory School. After his graduation from Fisk University, he was awarded a scholarship to Yale University to study for his Master's degree in economics. Next, he began teaching languages and history at Howard University; but, feeling the need of further preparation in languages, he went to Paris to study at the Guilde Internationale.

He was ordained a minister in the African Methodist Episcopal (A.M.E.) Church in 1919 and pastored three churches in Washington, D.C., while serving as chairman of the department of history, dean of the college of liberal arts and dean of the graduate school at Howard University. In 1920, he received the Austin Teachers' Scholarship to study at Harvard for his Ph.D. degree, and in 1930, as a Guggenheim Fellow, he went to London, where he did research on slavery and emancipation in the British Empire.

In 1942, Dr. Wesley accepted the presidency of Wilberforce University in Ohio, which was made up of three separate units— Wilberforce, an A.M.E. school administered by a president; Payne Theological Seminary, directed by a dean; and the Normal and Industrial Department, administered by the state of Ohio. In his first five years as administrator, he paid off the long-standing debt, launched a building program and upgraded the academic standards of the university. In 1947, the state board of trustees appointed

CHARLES HARRIS WESLEY

him director of Central State University, formerly the vocational division of Wilberforce University. From 1947 to 1965, Charles H. Wesley built a new college on an old campus, as Central State University became a full-fledged institution for higher education. Immediately after the two schools separated, Dr. Wesley launched a program of integration, encouraging white students to enter the university, since the charter granted by the state of Ohio had not stipulated any form of segregation.

During his 23 years of service in the state of Ohio, he served as president of the Association of Ohio College Presidents and Deans, chairman of the Inter-University Council of the State of Ohio and a member of the Governor's Committee on Community Colleges in Ohio. He is the recipient of many honorary degrees and awards, including the Distinguished Alumni Award from Fisk University and an honorary degree from the University of Cincinnati.

Upon retirement from Central State University, Dr. Wesley became executive director of the Association for the Study of Negro Life and History (now Afro-American Life and History) in Washington, D.C. He retired in 1972 after serving in this position for 15 years.

Wharton, Clifton Reginald

Diplomat

Clifton Reginald Wharton (1899–   ), former United States minister to Romania, was born in Baltimore and was educated at the Boston University Law School. Of the 30 or so blacks in the State Department as of 1959, Wharton was the only one to have attained the rank of minister as a non-political appointee.   After passing

CLIFTON REGINALD WHARTON

the civil service examination, his first assignment was as vice-consul and secretary to the minister to Liberia. Since the notion that European countries would not accept a colored American envoy determined the policy of the foreign service department of the United States, until 1947 Wharton was given the lowest rank and served only in posts designated by the State Department as "Negro posts."

The appointment of Wharton as United States minister to Romania in 1957 created almost no excitement at all. Instead, the new image of America which was emerging in the late fifties went unnoticed even in the Negro press. The dispatching of a Negro diplomat to direct a European legation disproved the State Department's theory that European governments would not accept Negroes. In 1961, Wharton was appointed by President John F. Kennedy as ambassador to Norway.

White, Clarence Cameron

Musician

Clarence Cameron White (1880–1960), noted violinist and composer, was born in Clarksville, Tennessee. His parents, Dr. and Mrs. J. W. White, moved to Washington, D.C., where the young musician was educated in the public schools and at Howard University. To develop his musical talent, he was sent to Oberlin and studied the violin, gaining experience as first violinist in the orchestra there. Upon graduation from the Conservatory at Oberlin, he returned to Washington and taught at the Washington Conservatory of Music and in the public schools.

He was in London, where he was a pupil of the noted Russian violinist Zacharewitsch, and, from 1908 to 1911, of Coleridge-Taylor. He was first violinist in the String Players' Club of Croydon, which was conducted by Coleridge-Taylor. By 1912

CLARENCE CAMERON WHITE

"drank in the crusader's spirit" from the New England men and women who came to Atlanta University to teach. Upon graduation from Atlanta University, he was employed by the Atlanta Life Insurance Company and worked as a layman in the local branch of the National Association for the Advancement of Colored People. Even though he was endowed with a "protective coloration" of white skin, his childhood experiences in the racial powderkeg of Atlanta caused him to join in the crusade of the NAACP. He was brought to the New York office as an assistant to the executive secretary, James Weldon Johnson. Upon Johnson's retirement, Walter White took over the leadership of the association, and for all of his militancy he remained remarkably optimistic.

The NAACP under White's direction fought diligently and forcefully for equality in civil rights, focusing attention on the evils

he had returned to America and opened a private studio in Boston.

In 1924, White accepted the appointment as director of music at West Virginia State College. His summers were spent profitably in travel and study. In collaboration with John F. Mathews, professor of Romance languages at the college, he wrote the opera *Ouanga,* based upon the life of the Haitian liberator, Dessalines. The American Opera Society presented it in concert form in Chicago. As the composer of *Ouanga,* White received the coveted David Bispham Medal, which is awarded for the most important American operatic composition of the year.

White, Walter Francis

Leader in the NAACP

Walter Francis White (1893–1955), former militant executive secretary of the NAACP, was born in Atlanta, Georgia, and

WALTER FRANCIS WHITE

and horrors of lynchings and pushing relentlessly for an end to discrimination and segregation in travel and education. He wrote, lectured, traveled and gathered vital evidence on lynchings and discrimination in the United States.

White became a writer of considerable merit as he collected an abundance of material to develop what became known as the "purpose novel." His first book, *The Fire and the Flint,* reveals the evils suffered by Negroes. *Flight* appeared in 1926, portraying the struggles of a Negro woman in regaining her respectability in the community. In *Rope and Faggot: A Biography of Judge Lynch,* the author gives an account of his firsthand experiences with lynchings during his 10 years of work with the NAACP. His final book, *How Far the Promised Land,* is a summation of the struggles of the Negro for first-class citizenship in America and an optimistic view of fully obtaining this goal in the future.

The famous 1954 decision of the Supreme Court against segregated schools was one of the goals that Walter White set out to achieve. A chief spokesman for the Negro, he was the recipient of many honors, including the Spingarn Medal from the NAACP.

Wilkins, Roy

Leader of the NAACP

Roy Wilkins (1901–), executive director of the National Association for the Advancement of Colored People, was born in St. Louis, Missouri. His mother died when he was only three years old, and her three children were reared by relatives in St. Paul, Minnesota, where the unsegregated environment insulated them from racial insults. Roy was editor of his high school newspaper, and at the University of Minnesota, he became editor of the *University Daily,* which had a circulation of ten thousand copies. Racial discord struck him on the occasion of a

ROY WILKINS

lynching in Duluth, and it prompted him to enter an oratorical contest with a strong anti-lynching speech.

Upon graduation, Wilkins accepted a job with the *Kansas City Call* and rapidly rose to the position of managing editor. In 1930, he waged a vigorous campaign against an anti-Negro senator from Kansas. His experiences in Kansas City, where he was confronted with discrimination and personal indignities, shocked him into the role of a crusader and led eventually to his appointment to the NAACP staff in 1931. He was the editor of *Crisis,* official NAACP magazine, from 1934 to 1949, and represented the organization in the negotiations of the Philadelphia transit strike in 1943.

In 1955, Roy Wilkins became the executive secretary of the NAACP. He assumed this position soon after the Legal Defense Fund had won the famous school desegregation case in 1954, and thus had to face criticism from Negroes over the question of the role of the organization in implementing the Court's decision by open demonstrations. In the Negro revolt of the 1960's, NAACP leadership was openly challenged by the newer, more militant organizations that came to the forefront. There was a widespread doubt that the slow wheels of legal actions in the courts—that took so long and cost so much to bring so little to so few—would ever get to the roots of desegregation, and Wilkins had to bring the NAACP into the more extensive action program. In 1964, Wilkins became executive director of the NAACP.

In 1964, he received the Spingarn Medal of the NAACP. He also received the Freedom House Award (1967); the Theodore Roosevelt Distinguished Service Medal (1968); and the Medal of Freedom (1969).

DANIEL HALE WILLIAMS

Williams, Daniel Hale

Physician

Daniel Hale Williams (1856–1931), pioneer in radical heart surgery and in the establishment of Provident Hospital in Chicago, was born in Pennsylvania. He received his preparatory and college education in Pennsylvania and Wisconsin, and was encouraged to enter the Chicago Medical School, where he earned his medical degree in 1883. He established the country's first interracial hospital in 1891, where he performed, in 1893, an operation on James Cornish, a street fighter who had suffered a knife wound in an artery a fraction of an inch from his heart. The opening of the patient's chest and repair of the wound saved his life. Dr. Williams had accomplished what was formerly thought impossible, and his fame and skill as a surgeon became widely known.

Williams was called to Washington to reorganize the Freedmen's Hospital of Howard University in 1894. He collected a staff of

20 specialists and organized the medical college into departments; the first nursing school was created at Freedmen's under his leadership. He resigned from Freedmen's in 1898 and returned to Chicago, where he became the only Negro on the staff at St. Luke's Hospital. Resuming his association with Provident Hospital, he was affiliated with the Northwestern University School of Medicine. In 1913, he was elected a Fellow of the American College of Surgeons.

Williams, Paul R.

Architect

Paul R. Williams (1896-   ), outstanding black architect and president of Paul R. Williams and Associates, an architectural firm that designs both homes and commercial buildings, was born in Los Angeles, California.

Williams attended the University of Southern California and the Beaux Arts Institute.

PAUL R. WILLIAMS

He holds honorary degrees from Howard University and Tuskegee Institute.

His early working experience with both residential and commercial-type structures taught him how to plan homes in relation to their surroundings.

In California, Williams has designed homes for movie stars Cary Grant, Frank Sinatra, Julie London, Betty Grable and the late Bill Robinson and Tyrone Power. He was associate architect for the planning of the Federal Customs building in Los Angeles and the Los Angeles Airport. He has designed over 3,000 homes in the United States and South America.

Williams served under two Presidents. Calvin Coolidge appointed him to the National Monument Commission, and Dwight Eisenhower appointed him to the National Housing Advisory Committee. Williams has been a fellow of the American Institute of Architects since 1957.

Woodruff, Hale A.

Artist

Hale Woodruff (1900–   ), professor emeritus of art at New York University, New York City, was born in Cairo, Illinois, and studied at the John Herron Art Institute, Harvard University, the Academie Moderne in Paris and the Academie Scandinave.

Woodruff, who was called a "modern master" by the art critic of the *Atlanta Constitution,* was painting local Georgia subject matter when he began his career as art instructor at Atlanta University. To point out the need for slum clearance and better housing, he painted two panels as part of a WPA project, *Shantytown* and *Mudhill Row.* Woodson's more recent major paintings include *The Amistad Mutiny* and *The Founding of Talladega.*

The author of seven publications on art, Woodruff has exhibited in major galleries throughout the United States. In 1971, he exhibited at the Museum of Modern Art in New York City. Also in 1971, he received a special award from the Barristers' Wives of New York City. He is the subject of an essay, "Hale Woodruff," written by fellow artist Lois Mailou Jones and published in 1974. He is a member of the Committee on Art Education of the Museum of Modern Art, New York, the Society of Mural Painters and the New Jersey Society of Artists.

Woodson, Carter G.

Historian

Carter G. Woodson (1875–1950), the founder of the Association for the Study of Negro Life and History, was born in New Canton, Virginia, and was educated at Berea College in Kentucky and at the University of Chicago, where he earned his B.A. degree in 1907 and his M.A. degree in 1908. He earned the Ph.D. degree at Harvard Univer-

CARTER G. WOODSON

sity in 1912, then studied at the Sorbonne in Paris. After serving as an elementary school teacher, high school principal, teacher, college professor and dean of the college of liberal arts at Howard University and at West Virginia State College, he retired from teaching in 1922 to devote all of his time to research and writing.

He had organized the Association for the Study of Negro Life and History in Chicago in 1915, contending, against the prevailing white authorities, that the Negro had an important past and had contributed to the mainstream of civilization. In 1916, the association was incorporated and the first issue of the *Journal of Negro History* was published. Because of his determination and staunch belief in the ultimate acceptance of the Negro through established historical truths, Dr. Woodson is now venerated by scholars of both races and has rightly earned the title

of "the father of modern Negro historiography."

In 1921, Dr. Woodson organized the Associated Publishers to make available books about Negroes, which were rarely accepted by the commercial publishers of America. The observance of National Negro History Week was first begun by the association, and its results penetrated deeply into the segregated schools of the South, giving inspiration and a sense of self-esteem to many students during the Negro revolt of the 1960's. The *Negro History Bulletin* was founded in 1937 as a medium of information for the general public and school children.

While diligently organizing and promoting the *Journal,* the Associated Publishers, Negro History Week and the *Bulletin,* Dr. Woodson searched for documents, collected information and compiled, edited and wrote many books. He published the following works: *The Disruption of Virginia,* 1912; *The Education of the Negro prior to 1861,* 1915; *A Century of Negro Migration,* 1918; *History of the Negro Church,* 1921; *The Negro in Our History,* 1922; *Negro Orators and Their Orations,* 1925; *Free Negro Heads of Families in the United States in 1830,* 1925; *The Mind of the Negro as Reflected in Letters Written during the Crisis, 1800-1860,* 1926; *Negro Makers of History,* 1928; *The Rural Negro,* 1930; *The Story of the Negro Retold,* 1935; *The African Background Outlined,* 1936; and *African Heroes and Heroines,* 1939.

Dr. Woodson was the recipient of the Spingarn Medal, in 1926, for his contributions to the advancement of the Negro. When he died, Dr. Woodson left his estate to the association to carry on the program that he had initiated. By 1965, his contention that the Negro had a past worthy of study had been adopted by the leading institutions and scholars of America, and they were developing programs to fill the long-neglected gap in their versions of the history of mankind. Woodson had set the pace for research in this area over half a century earlier.

Work, Monroe Nathan

Scholar and Publisher

Monroe Nathan Work (1866–1945), publisher and compiler of the *Negro Yearbook,* was born in Iredell County, North Carolina. He was educated at the Chicago Theological Seminary and at the University of Chicago, from which he was awarded the degrees of Bachelor of Arts in philosophy and Master of Arts. He began his career as professor of pedagogy and history at the Georgia State Industrial College in 1903 and accepted the position of director of the department of records and research at Tuskegee Institute in 1908, serving in this capacity until his retirement in 1938.

As director of the department of research, he was in a position to collect pertinent data and statistics on the Negro, which led to the biennial publication of the *Negro Yearbook.* This type of book supplied factual material that was needed by schools and libraries throughout the nation. Through his research in Europe and America, Dr. Work obtained important data for his compilation of the *Bibliography of the Negro.* This publication was a significant achievement because it was the first effort of its kind. In one volume, he presented the works or publications about Negroes in all parts of the world from ancient times to 1928.

In 1928, he received the Harmon Award in Education for "scholarly research and educational publicity through periodic publication of the *Negro Yearbook* and the compilation of a *Bibliography of the Negro.*" The University of Chicago Alumni Association presented him with the Alumni Citation, in 1942, in recognition of his 40 years of public service.

Wright, Richard

Author

Richard Wright (1908–1960), a product of violence and oppression, wrote of this type of brutal existence in his novels. He was born in poverty in Natchez, Mississippi, and his childhood was a twisted strand of hunger, ignorance, prejudice and religious fanaticism. His family moved from a plantation in Mississippi to the city of Memphis, where the father soon deserted the mother and their two children. In his autobiography, *Black Boy,* Wright tells of the bitter pangs of hunger that he experienced during this period of his childhood. The boys had to be placed in an orphans' home until the mother could save enough money to return them to their grandmother in Jackson.

Before Wright completed high school, his

RICHARD WRIGHT

mother had suffered a paralytic stroke; she remained bedridden for 10 years. In spite of the adverse circumstances of his youth, he had decided that he wanted to become a writer. Leaving Jackson for Memphis after completing high school, he took menial jobs to survive while he borrowed books from the library to read at night. One of the first books he read, H. L. Mencken's *A Book of Prefaces,* impressed him with its ironic style, and he realized that words could be used as weapons. Thus, Wright set his course and saved his money for the fare to Chicago.

After two years of saving, he and his brother took their invalid mother to Chicago. The ignorance and prejudice which they hoped to escape when they left the South were to appear in another form in Chicago. Negroes in Chicago in the economic depression of the thirties were reduced to bitter struggle against hunger and starvation. Wright became a member of the Federal Writers' Project in 1935 and moved to the New York project in 1937. His *Uncle Tom's Children* won him a $500 prize in 1938, and the following year he won a Guggenheim fellowship in creative writing and the Spingarn Medal from the NAACP.

His novel *Native Son,* with its vivid portrait of Bigger Thomas, reveals the ugly roots of the experiences the author had known. During the depression he joined the Communist Party, but he withdrew from it in 1944 and told the story of his disillusionment with communism in *The God That Failed.* After 1946, Wright lived in Paris, where he continued to write. Some of his other works are *The Outsider,* a novel; and *Black Power* and *The Color Curtain,* non-fiction books, the former about life in Ghana on the eve of its independence, the latter covering the Asian-African Bandung Conference of 1955.

Yerby, Alonzo Smythe

Physician and Educator

Alonzo Smythe Yerby (1921–), head of the department and professor of health services administration at the Harvard University School of Public Health, was born in Augusta, Georgia. A graduate of the University of Chicago in 1941, and of the Meharry Medical College in 1946, he earned the M.P.H. in public health practice and medical care administration at Harvard in 1948. He was assigned by the United Nations as field medical officer for the International Refugee Organization in the United States Zone of Germany in 1948 and 1949. In this position, he was responsible for the supervision of the preventive and curative medical services for approximately 25,000 displaced persons in refugee camps in Bavaria.

In November 1949, he was appointed

ALONZO SMYTHE YERBY

deputy chief of medical affairs in the Office of the U.S. High Commissioner for Germany. Dr. Yerby was responsible for the exchange program of German, other European and American medical personnel in the rehabilitation and reorientation program of the German Health Services. Upon his return to America in 1950, he became the associate medical director of the Health Insurance Plan of Greater New York and a staff physician at the Sidney Hillman Health Center in New York City. From 1957 to 1960, he was deputy commissioner for medical affairs for the New York State Department of Social Welfare.

Dr. Yerby became the executive director of medical services for the New York City Department of Health and medical welfare administrator of the Department of Welfare in 1960. In 1965, he served as commissioner of the New York City Department of Hospitals. He also served as assistant professor of administrative medicine at the Columbia University School of Public Health and Administrative Medicine from 1960 to 1966. He assumed his position at Harvard in September of 1966.

He is the recipient of the New York City Public Service Award for Professional Achievement; the 1965 Award for Exceptional Achievement in Preventive Medicine from the New York State Academy of Preventive Medicine; and the Haven Emerson Award, in 1966, from the Public Health Association of New York City.

Yerby, Frank

Author

Frank Yerby (1916–), successful commercial writer of historical fiction, was born in Augusta, Georgia. He graduated from the local Paine College in 1937 and received his M.A. from Fisk University in 1937. He studied further at the University of Chicago before launching his career as a teacher at Florida A. and M. College and Southern University in Baton Rouge, Louisiana. During World War II, he was employed by the Ford Motor Company and at Ranger Aircraft in Jamaica, New York. He was greatly encouraged when his first short story to be published received the O. Henry Memorial Award for the best short story of the year.

In 1946, with the publication of his first novel, *The Foxes of Harrow,* Yerby won recognition and acclaim and created a controversy as well. In writing the historical novel, he drew characters from all ethnic groups in the American scene and avoided the pitfalls of argumentative interpretations. Instead, he concentrated upon the pleasure principle of literature: his main objective was to entertain by re-creating a particular era in history. Critics looked for errors in historical fact and in characterization, but the only evidence they could find to prolong their criticism was a comparison of Yerby's *The Foxes of Harrow* with Margaret Mitchell's *Gone with the Wind.* Both authors used the Civil War as their setting, but Yerby was far more economical in the unfolding of his historical chronicle than Miss Mitchell, and he made his main Negro characters superior: Inch was a man of letters, and the slave girl was a princess. The characterizations are far different in *Gone with the Wind.*

When *The Foxes of Harrow* became a successful motion picture, the author left his teaching career and settled down to the production of popular fiction. His second book in the series, *The Vixens,* 1947, deals with the period of Reconstruction. The last in the trilogy, *Pride's Castle,* covers the period from the 1870's to the 20th century. *Floodtide* discusses the Cuban revolution and the American scene around 1850; *The Gold-*

en Hawk is a picaresque novel based on a sea adventure. A prolific author, Yerby has averaged almost a book a year since 1946. *The Voyage Unplanned*, his most recent work, was published in April 1974. He is a frequent contributor to *Harper's Magazine*.

Young, Charles

Officer in the United States Army

Charles Young (1864–1922), graduate of the United States Military Academy, was born in Kentucky and moved with his family to Ohio when he was nine years old. He attended high school there, and taught in the public schools, and was admitted to the United States Military Academy in 1884. He graduated in 1889 and was commissioned as a second lieutenant in the U.S. Cavalry. In 1894, he became professor of military science and tactics at Wilberforce University in Ohio.

During the Spanish-American War, Young served as a major in charge of the 9th Ohio Regiment, which was composed of Negro

CHARLES YOUNG

volunteers. After the war, he remained in the army, serving in the United States, the Philippines, Mexico and Haiti; and by 1916, he had attained the rank of lieutenant colonel. The Negro people of America followed the career of Charles Young with interest and pride. The bravery he displayed, the prejudice he suffered and his determination in spite of discrimination and disappointment were all a part of their own daily lives.

In 1917, when the United States entered World War I, the friends and followers of Colonel Young assumed that he would be given a post equal to his rank and ability. Instead, he was suddenly retired; the reason given was that he was physically unfit for duty. Stung by the injustice of this finding, Young mounted his favorite horse at Wilberforce, Ohio, and rode the 500 miles to Washington, D.C., to prove to high-ranking army officials, as well as his fellow colored citizens, that he was indeed fit for service. Finally, after continued demands by the public, the army reinstated him, and he was assigned to train Negro troops at Fort Grant, Illinois.

Later, Colonel Young was sent as military attaché to Liberia. He died in Lagos, Nigeria, in the service of his country, and was buried in Arlington National Cemetery.

Young, Whitney Moore

Leader of the National Urban League

Whitney Moore Young (1921–1971), former executive secretary of the Urban League, was born at Lincoln Ridge, Kentucky. He attended Kentucky State College in Frankfort and received his M.A. degree at the University of Minnesota in 1947. He also obtained training at the Massachusetts Institute of Technology, and at Rhode Island State College during World War II, and taught school for a brief period before joining the Urban League in St. Paul, Minne-

WHITNEY MOORE YOUNG

sota. In 1950, he was executive secretary of the Omaha, Nebraska, office.

In the Negro revolt of the 1960's, Whitney Young, as executive director of the National Urban League, accepted the challenge of directing the organization into a more dynamic role in the struggle for civil rights. The league does research concerned with community attitudes toward the prevalent social ills of discrimination.

When Young was studying at Minnesota, he took time to join the Congress of Racial Equality and participated in student demonstrations that resulted in the integration of eating facilities near the university. He was dean of the Atlanta School of Social Work when he was appointed to direct the national office of the league. Young was in Atlanta when the students began sit-ins in that city and, from his experience and wisdom, he was able to give them invaluable assistance. He attempted to restore the league to the front rank of leadership in the revolution of the 1960's.

Bibliography

This bibliography is intended to guide the reader to additional works about individual Negroes and their contributions to society. The author also would like to inform the reader of the availability of several excellent general studies about the history of the Negro people. Among these more comprehensive works are: *From Slavery to Freedom*, by John Hope Franklin; *The Negro in American History*, by Benjamin Quarles; and *The Negro in Our History*, by Carter G. Woodson, which has been revised and brought up to date by Charles H. Wesley. *The Story of the Negro Retold*, by Carter G. Woodson and Charles H. Wesley, is an outstanding general reference book for younger readers.

AUTOBIOGRAPHY

ADAMS, JOHN QUINCY. *Narrative of the Life of John Quincy Adams: When in Slavery and Now as a Freeman.* Harrisburg, Pa., 1872.

ALLEN, RICHARD. *First Bishop of the A.M.E. Church: The Life, Experience and Gospel Labors of the Rt. Rev. Richard Allen.* Philadelphia, 1793.

ANDERSON, JOHN. *The Story of the Life of John Anderson, the Fugitive Slave.* London, 1863.

ANDERSON, MARIAN. *My Lord, What a Morning.* New York, 1956.

ASHER, JEREMIAH. *An Autobiography.* Philadelphia, 1862.

BALL, CHARLES. *Fifty Years in Chains: Or, the Life of an American Slave.* New York, 1859.

BIBB, HENRY. *Narrative of the Life and Adventures of Henry Bibb, an American Slave: Written by Himself.* New York, 1849.

BILLINGTON, RAY ALLEN (ed.). *The Journal of Charlotte L. Forten: A Free Negro in the Slave Era.* New York, 1961.

BROWN, HENRY BOX. *Narrative of the Life of Henry Box Brown: Written by Himself.* Manchester, England, 1851.

BROWN, WILLIAM WELLS. *Narrative of William W. Brown, a Fugitive Slave: Written by Himself.* Boston, 1847.

BRUCE, HENRY CLAY. *The New Man: Twenty-Nine Years a Slave; Twenty-Nine Years a Free Man.* York, Pa., 1895.

CORROTHERS, JAMES D. *In Spite of the Handicap.* New York, 1916.

DEANE, CHARLES (ed.). *Letters of Phillis Wheatley.* Boston, 1864.

DOUGLASS, FREDERICK. *The Life and Times of Frederick Douglass.* Hartford, Conn., 1881.

———. *My Bondage and My Freedom.* New York, 1855.

DU BOIS, W. E. BURGHARDT. *Dusk of Dawn: An Essay toward an Autobiography of a Race Concept.* New York, 1940.

DUNHAM, KATHERINE. *A Touch of Innocence.* New York, 1959.

EDWARDS, WILLIAM JAMES. *Twenty-Five Years in the Black Belt.* Boston, 1918.

FLEETWOOD, CHRISTIAN A. *The Negro as a Soldier.* Washington, 1895.

FLIPPER, HENRY O. *The Colored Cadet at West Point.* New York, 1878.

FULLER, T. O. *Twenty Years in Public Life.* Memphis, Tenn., 1913.

GIBBS, MIFFLIN W. *Shadow and Light.* Washington, 1902.

GOODWIN, RUBY BERKLEY. *It's Good to Be Black.* Garden City, N.Y., 1953.

GREEN, JOHN P. *Fact Stranger than Fiction: Seventy-Five Years of a Busy Life.* Cleveland, 1920.

HANDY, WILLIAM CHRISTOPHER. *Father of the Blues.* New York, 1941.

HARRIS, THEODORE D. (ed.). *Negro Frontiersman: The Western Memoirs of Henry O. Flipper.* El Paso, 1963.

HEARD, W. H. *From Slavery to the Bishopric of the A.M.E. Church.* Philadelphia, 1924.

HENSON, JOSIAH. *The Life of Josiah Henson.* Boston, 1849.

HENSON, MATTHEW A. *A Negro Explorer at the North Pole.* New York, 1912.

HUGHES, LANGSTON. *The Big Sea.* New York, 1940.
———. *I Wonder as I Wander.* New York, 1956.

HUNTON, ADDIE D. W., and JOHNSON, KATHRYN D. *Two Colored Women with the American Expeditionary Forces.* Brooklyn, N.Y., 1920.

HURSTON, ZORA NEALE. *Dust Tracks on a Road.* Philadelphia, 1942.

JOHNSON, JAMES WELDON. *Along This Way.* New York, 1933.

KECKLEY, ELIZABETH. *Behind the Scenes.* New York, 1868.

KING, MARTIN LUTHER, JR. *Stride toward Freedom: The Montgomery Story.* New York, 1958.

LANE, ISAAC. *Autobiography of Bishop Lane, LL.D., with a Short History of the C.M.E. Church.* Nashville, Tenn., 1916.

LANE, LUNSFORD. *The Narrative of Lunsford Lane, Formerly of Raleigh, N.C.* Boston, 1842.

LANGSTON, JOHN MERCER. *From the Virginia Plantation to the National Capitol.* Hartford, Conn., 1894.

MCKAY, CLAUDE. *A Long Way from Home.* New York, 1937.

MALCOLM X. *The Autobiography of Malcolm X.* New York, 1965.

MAYS, WILLIAM H. *Born to Play Ball.* New York, 1955.

MOTON, ROBERT R. *Finding a Way Out: An Autobiography.* Garden City, N.Y., 1920.

NORTHUP, SOLOMON. *Twelve Years a Slave.* Buffalo, 1853.

PATTERSON, HAYWOOD, and CONRAD, EARL. *Scottsboro Boy.* Garden City, N.Y., 1950.

PAYNE, DANIEL ALEXANDER. *Recollections of Seventy Years.* Nashville, Tenn., 1888.

PENNINGTON, JAMES W. C. *The Fugitive Blacksmith: Or Events in the History of James W. C. Pennington.* London, 1850.

PEYTON, THOMAS R. *Quest for Dignity: An Autobiography of a Negro Doctor.* Los Angeles, 1950.

PROUDFOOT, MERRILL. *Diary of a Sit-In.* Chapel Hill, N.C., 1962.

ROBINSON, JOHN ROOSEVELT (JACKIE). *Baseball Has Done It.* Philadelphia, 1964.

SANCHO, IGNATIUS. *The Life of Ignatius Sancho, an African.* London, 1784.

STILL, JAMES. *Early Recollections and Life of Dr. James Still.* Philadelphia, 1877.

STILL, WILLIAM. *The Underground Railroad: Records, with a Life of the Author.* Philadelphia, 1872.

TAYLOR, SUSIE KING. *Reminiscences of My Life in Camp.* Boston, 1902.

TERRELL, MARY CHURCH. *A Colored Woman in a White World.* Washington, 1940.

TRUTH, SOJOURNER. *Narrative of Sojourner Truth.* Boston, 1875.

VASSA, GUSTAVUS. *The Interesting Narrative of the Life of Olaudah Equiano, or Gustavus Vassa.* 2 vols. London, 1789.

WASHINGTON, BOOKER T. *Up from Slavery.* New York, 1901.

WATERS, ETHEL. *His Eye Is on the Sparrow.* Garden City, N.Y., 1951.

WESTFIELD, CHESTER J. *The Experiences of Company "L," 368th Infantry, a Unit of the Black Buffalo Division: Told in Verse. . . .* Nashville, Tenn., 1919.

WHITE, WALTER F. *A Man Called White.* New York, 1948.

BIOGRAPHY AND HISTORY

ADAMS, RUSSELL L. *Great Negroes, Past and Present.* Chicago, 1964.

ALBANY INSTITUTE OF HISTORY AND ART. *The Negro Artist Comes of Age: A National Survey of Contemporary Artists.* Albany, N.Y., 1945.

ALBERT, OCTAVIA VICTORIA ROGERS. *The House of Bondage: Or, Charlotte Brooks and Other Slaves.* Cincinnati, 1890.

ALEXANDER, CHARLES. *One Hundred Distinguished Leaders.* Atlanta, Ga., 1899.

ALLEN, WILL W., and MURRAY, DANIEL. *Banneker, the Afro-American Astronomer.* Washington, 1921.

ALLEN, WILLIAM G. *Wheatley, Banneker and Horton.* Boston, 1849.

AMERICAN REFORM TRACT AND BOOK SOCIETY. *Aunt Sally: Or the Cross the Way to Freedom. A Narrative of the Slave-Life and Purchase of the Mother of Rev. Isaac Williams, of Detroit, Michigan.* Cincinnati, 1862.

AMORY, CLEVELAND (ed.). *Celebrity Register*. New York, 1963.

APTHEKER, HERBERT. *American Negro Slave Revolts*. New York, 1943.

———. *The Negro in the Abolitionist Movement*. New York, 1941.

———. *One Continual Cry: David Walker's "Appeal to the Colored Citizens of the World, 1829."* New York, 1965.

BAKER, HENRY E. *The Colored Inventor*. New York, 1913.

BARDOLPH, RICHARD. *The Negro Vanguard*. New York, 1959.

BEASLEY, D. *The Negro Trail Blazers of California*. Los Angeles, 1919.

BENNETT, LERONE, JR. *Before the Mayflower: A History of the Negro in America, 1619–1964*. Baltimore, 1966.

———. *What Manner of Man: A Biography of Martin Luther King, Jr.* Chicago, 1964.

Black Heroes of the American Revolution 1775-1783. New York: NAACP, 1965.

BONTEMPS, ARNA W. *Famous Negro Athletes*. New York, 1964.

BRADFORD, SARAH. *Harriet, the Moses of Her People*. New York, 1886.

BRAGG, GEORGE F. *The First Negro Priest on Southern Soil*. Baltimore, 1909.

BRAWLEY, BENJAMIN. *Negro Builders and Heroes*. Chapel Hill, N.C., 1937.

———. *Paul Laurence Dunbar: Poet of His People*. Chapel Hill, N.C., 1936.

———. *Women of Achievement*. Chicago, 1919.

BRODERICK, FRANCIS L. *W. E. B. Du Bois: Negro Leader in a Time of Crisis*. Stanford, Calif., 1959.

BROWN, HALLIE O. (comp.). *Homespun Heroines*. Xenia, Ohio, 1926.

BROWN, WILLIAM WELLS. *The Black Man: His Antecedents, His Genius and His Achievements*. New York, 1863.

——— *The Rising Son: Or the Antecedents and Advancements of the Colored Race*. Boston, 1874.

BRUCE, JOHN EDWARD (ed.). *Short Biographical Sketches of Eminent Negro Men and Women in Europe and the United States*. Yonkers, N.Y., 1910.

BRUNN, HARRY O. *The Story of the Original Dixieland Jazz Band*. Baton Rouge, 1960.

BUCKLER, HELEN. *Dr. Dan: Pioneer in American Surgery*. Boston, 1954.

BUNDY, WILLIAM O. *Life of William Madison McDonald*. Fort Worth, 1925.

CHERRY, GWENDOLYN, THOMAS, RUBY, and WILLIS, PAULINE. *Portraits in Color: The Lives of Colorful Negro Women*. New York, 1962.

CHESNUTT, HELEN M. *Charles Waddell Chesnutt: Pioneer of the Color Line*. Chapel Hill, N.C., 1952.

COOK, H. T. *Life and Legacy of David R. Williams*. New York, 1919.

COOK, MERCER. *Five French Negro Authors*. Washington, 1943.

COOLEY, TIMOTHY MATHER. *Sketches of the Life and Character of the Rev. Lemuel Haynes, A.M., for Many Years Pastor of a Church in Rutland, Vermont, and Late in Granville, New York*. New York, 1837.

COURLANDER, HAROLD. *Negro Folk Music, U.S.A.* New York, 1963.

CRAWFORD, GEORGE W. *Prince Hall and His Followers*. New York, 1914.

CROSS, SAMUEL H., and SIMMONS, ERNEST J. *Alexander Pushkin, 1799–1837: His Life and Literary Heritage*. Washington, 1937.

CROWN, EDMOND D. *The Story of Marcus Garvey and the Universal Negro Improvement Association*. Madison, Wis., 1955.

DALY, JOHN JAY. *A Song in His Heart*. Philadelphia, 1951.

DANIEL, SADIE I. *Women Builders*. Washington, 1931.

DANNETT, SYLVIA G. *Profiles of Negro Womanhood*. Yonkers, N.Y., 1964.

DELGADO, MARTÍN M. *Biografia del Libertador Toussaint L'Ouverture*. Havana, 1957.

DOBLER, LAVINIA, and BROWN, WILLIAM A. *Great Rulers of the African Past*. New York, 1965.

DOVER, CEDRIC. *American Negro Art*. Greenwich, Conn., 1960.

DU BOIS, W. E. BURGHARDT, and JOHNSON, GUY B. *Encyclopedia of the Negro: Preparatory Volume*. New York, 1945.

DURHAM, PHILIP, and JONES, EVERETT L. *The Negro Cowboys*. New York, 1964.

EMBREE, EDWIN R. *13 against the Odds*. New York, 1944.

FAUSET, ARTHUR H. *For Freedom: A Biographical Story of the American Negro*. Philadelphia, 1927.

FLEISCHER, NATHANIEL S. *Black Dynamite: The Story of the Negro in the Prize Ring from 1782 to 1938.* New York, 1938.

FLEMING, BEATRICE J., and PRYDE, MARION J. *Distinguished Negroes Abroad.* Washington, 1946.

FLEMING, G. JAMES, and BURCKEL, CHRISTIAN E. (eds.). *Who's Who in Colored America.* Yonkers, N.Y., 1950.

FOLEY, ALBERT S. *God's Men of Color: The Colored Catholic Priests of the United States, 1854–1954.* New York, 1954.

FONER, PHILIP S. *Frederick Douglass: A Biography.* New York, 1964.

GILBERT, OLIVE. *Narrative of Sojourner Truth, a Bondswoman of Olden Time, Emancipated by the New York Legislature in the Early Part of the Present Century.* Boston, 1875.

GOLDBERG, JOE. *Jazz Masters of the Fifties.* New York, 1965.

GRAHAM, SHIRLEY. *Jean Baptiste Pointe du Sable.* New York, 1953.

———. *Paul Robeson: Citizen of the World.* New York, 1946.

———. *Your Most Humble Servant.* New York, 1949.

———, and LIPSCOMB, GEORGE D. *Dr. George Washington Carver, Scientist.* New York, 1944.

GREENE, LORENZO J. *The Negro in Colonial New England, 1620–1776.* New York, 1942.

HADLOCK, RICHARD. *Jazz Masters of the Twenties.* New York, 1965.

HARE, MAUD CUNEY. *Negro Musicians and Their Music.* Washington, 1936.

———. *Norris Wright Cuney.* New York, 1913.

HARR, WILBER C. *The Negro as an American Protestant Missionary in Africa.* Chicago, 1946.

HARRIS, ABRAM L. *The Negro as Capitalist: A Study of Banking and Business among American Negroes.* Philadelphia, 1936.

HATCHER, WILLIAM E. *John Jasper, the Unmatched Negro Philosopher and Preacher.* New York, 1908.

HEDGEMAN, ANNA. *The Trumpet Sounds: A Memoir of Negro Leadership.* New York, 1964.

HELM, MACKINLEY. *Angel Mo' and Her Son, Roland Hayes.* Boston, 1942.

HILDRETH, RICHARD. *Archy Moore, the White Slave: Or, Memoirs of a Fugitive.* New York, 1857.

HILL, HERBERT. *Anger, and Beyond: The Negro Writer in the United States.* New York, 1966.

HILL, ROY L. *Who's Who in the American Negro Press.* Dallas, 1960.

HOLT, RACKHAM. *George Washington Carver.* Garden City, N.Y., 1943.

HORRICKS, RAYMOND. *Count Basie and His Orchestra: Its Music and Its Musicians.* New York, 1957.

HOSHOR, JOHN. *God in a Rolls Royce: The Rise of Father Divine, Madman, Menace or Messiah?* New York, 1936.

HUGHES, LANGSTON. *Famous Negro Heroes of America.* New York, 1958.

———. *Famous Negro Music Makers.* New York, 1955.

ISAACS, EDITH J. *The Negro in the American Theatre.* New York, 1947.

JACKSON, L. P. *Negro Office-Holders in Virginia, 1865–1895.* Norfolk, 1946.

JAMES, MICHAEL. *Dizzy Gillespie.* London, 1959.

———. *Miles Davis.* London, 1961.

KEEPNEWS, ORRIN, and GRAUER, BILL. *A Pictorial History of Jazz.* New York, 1955.

KERLIN, ROBERT T. *Negro Poets and Their Poems.* Washington, 1935.

KUGELMASS, J. A. *Ralph J. Bunche: Fighter for Peace.* New York, 1952.

LADD, EVERETT C. *Negro Political Leadership in the South.* Ithaca, N.Y., 1966.

LINCOLN, C. ERIC. *The Black Muslims in America.* Boston, 1961.

LOCKE, ALAIN. *Negro Art: Past and Present.* Washington, 1936.

———. *The Negro in Art: A Pictorial Record of the Negro Artist and the Negro Theme in Art.* Washington, 1940.

LOFTON, JOHN M. *Insurrection in South Carolina: The Turbulent World of Denmark Vesey.* Yellow Springs, Ohio, 1964.

LOMAX, ALAN. *Mister Jelly Roll.* New York, 1950.

McCARTHY, ALBERT J. *Louis Armstrong.* New York, 1961.

MILAI, A. *Profile of the Negro, Past and Present.* Pittsburgh, 1965.

MILLER, BASIL W. *Ten Slaves Who Became Famous.* Grand Rapids, Mich., 1951.

MORRIS, SAURIAN. *A Sketch of the Life of Benjamin Banneker: Own Notes Taken in 1836.* Proceedings of the Maryland Historical Society. Baltimore, 1854.

MOTT, ALEXANDER (comp.). *Biographical Sketches and Interesting Anecdotes of Persons of Color.* New York, 1837.

NATHAN, HANS. *Dan Emmett and the Rise of Early Negro Minstrelsy.* Norman, Okla., 1962.

NELL, WILLIAM C. *The Colored Patriots of the American Revolution.* Boston, 1855.

NOBLE, PETER. *The Negro in Films.* London, 1948.

OAK, VISHNU V. *The Negro Entrepreneur.* Yellow Springs, Ohio, 1948.

OLIVER, PAUL. *Bessie Smith.* New York, 1961.

OTTLEY, ROI. *The Lonely Warrior: The Life and Times of Robert S. Abbott.* Chicago, 1955.

OWENS, WILLIAM A. *Slave Mutiny.* New York, 1953.

PEARE, CATHERINE O. *Mary McLeod Bethune.* New York, 1951.

PETRY, ANN L. *Harriet Tubman, Conductor on the Underground Railroad.* New York, 1955.

PIERSON, DONALD. *Negroes in Brazil.* Chicago, 1942.

PONTON, MUNGO M. *Life and Times of Henry M. Turner.* Atlanta, Ga., 1917.

PRICE, HUGH D. *The Negro and Southern Politics: A Chapter of Florida History.* New York, 1957.

PUTTKAMMER, CHARLES W. "William Monroe Trotter: An Evaluation of the Life of a Radical Negro Newspaper Editor, 1901–1934." Unpublished Master's thesis, Princeton University, 1958.

QUARLES, BENJAMIN. *The Negro in the American Revolution.* Chapel Hill, N.C., 1961.

———. *The Negro in the Civil War.* Boston, 1953.

QUICK, W. H. *Negro Stars in All Ages of the World.* Richmond, Va., 1898.

RICHARDSON, BEN A. *Great American Negroes.* New York, 1956.

RICHARDSON, C. (ed.). *The National Cyclopedia of the Colored Race.* Montgomery, Ala., 1919.

ROGERS, J. A. *Africa's Gift to America.* New York, 1961.

ROLLIN, FRANK A. *Life and Public Services of Martin R. Delany.* Boston, 1868.

ROLLINS, CHARLEMAE H. *They Showed the Way: Forty American Negro Leaders.* New York, 1964.

RUDWICK, ELLIOTT M. *W. E. B. Du Bois: A Study in Minority Group Leadership.* Philadelphia, 1960.

SANDLE, FLOYD L. *The Negro in the American Educational Theatre: 1911–1964.* Grambling, La., 1964.

SAYERS, RAYMOND. *The Negro in Brazilian Literature.* New York, 1956.

SAYERS, W. C. BERWICK. *Samuel Coleridge-Taylor: Musician.* New York, 1915.

SCHOMFELD, S. J. *The Negro in the Armed Forces.* Washington, 1954.

SCHWARTZ, PAUL (ed.). *Negro Heroes of Emancipation.* New York, 1959.

SCOTT, EMMETT J. *Scott's Official History of the American Negro in the World War.* Chicago, 1919.

SEGAL, RONALD. *African Profiles.* Baltimore, 1962.

SHERWOOD, HENRY N. *Paul Cuffe.* Washington, 1923.

SILVERA, JOHN D. *The Negro in World War II.* Baton Rouge, 1946.

SIMMONS, WILLIAM J. *Men of Mark: Eminent, Progressive and Rising.* Cleveland, 1891.

SMITH, SAMUEL D. *The Negro in Congress, 1870–1901.* Chapel Hill, N.C., 1940.

SOMERVILLE, JOHN A. *Man of Color: An Autobiography.* Los Angeles, 1949.

STERLING, DOROTHY. *Captain of the Planter: The Story of Robert Smalls.* Garden City, N.Y., 1958.

———. *Freedom Train: The Story of Harriet Tubman.* Garden City, N.Y., 1954.

TAYLOR, JULIUS H. (ed.). *The Negro in Science.* Baltimore, 1955.

THOMPSON, DANIEL C. *The Negro Leadership Class.* Englewood Cliffs, N.J., 1963.

THORPE, EARL E. *Negro Historians in the United States.* Baton Rouge, 1958.

TORRENCE, RIDGELY. *The Story of John Hope.* New York, 1948.

TROYAT, HENRI. *Pushkin.* New York, 1950.

VANDERCOOK, JOHN W. *Black Majesty.* New York, 1928.

VEHANEN, KOSTI. *Marian Anderson: A Portrait.* New York, 1941.

WASHINGTON, BOOKER T. *Frederick Douglass.* Philadelphia, 1907.

WAYMAN, A. W. *Life of Bishop James A. Shorter.* Baltimore, 1890.

WESLEY, CHARLES H. *Richard Allen, Apostle of Freedom.* Washington, 1935.

Who's Who of American Women: A Biographical Dictionary of Notable Living American Women. 4th ed. Chicago, 1966.

WIGGINS, LIDA K. *The Life and Works of Paul Laurence Dunbar.* Boston, 1907.

WILLIAMS, ETHEL L. *Biographical Directory of Negro Ministers.* New York, 1965.

WOODSON, CARTER G. *African Heroes and Heroines.* Washington, 1944.

———— (ed.). *Negro Orators and Their Orations.* Washington, 1925.

————. *The Negro Professional Man and the Community.* Washington, 1934.

———— (ed.). *The Works of Francis James Grimké.* Washington, 1942.

————, and WESLEY, CHARLES H. *Negro Makers of History.* Washington, 1958.

WORK, MONROE N. *A Bibliography of the Negro in Africa and America.* New York, 1928.

YOUNG, ANDREW S. *Great Negro Baseball Stars, and How They Made the Major Leagues.* New York, 1953.

———— *Negro Firsts in Sports.* Chicago, 1963.

ARTICLES IN JOURNALS

ABRAMOWITZ, JACK. "John B. Rayner—A Grass-Roots Leader," *Journal of Negro History,* XXXVI (April 1951), 160–93.

AIDLINE-TROMMER, ELBERT. " 'Alexander Pushkin' and Alexander Pushkin," *Opportunity,* VI (August 1928), 241.

"Alain Leroy Locke," *Negro History Bulletin,* XVIII (November 1954), 26, 32.

ALEXANDER, WILL W. "John Hope," *Phylon,* VIII (Spring 1947), 4–13.

"American Ambassador to Finland," *New Yorker,* XXXIX (December 7, 1963), 45–46.

"The American Negro as an Inventor," *Negro History Bulletin,* III (March 1940), 83–84, 94–95.

ANDREWS, CYRIL B. "Ira Aldridge," *Crisis,* XLII (October 1935), 308, 318.

"Angel of Mercy to the Astronauts," *Ebony,* XXI (June 1966), 49–50.

ARNOLD, EDWARD F. "Some Personal Reminiscences of Paul Laurence Dunbar," *Journal of Negro History,* XVII (October 1932), 400–408.

ASENDIO, JAMES. "History of Negro Motion Pictures," *International Photographer,* II (January 1940), 16.

"B. K. Bruce," *Negro History Bulletin,* I (March 1938), 5.

BACOTE, CLARENCE A. "Negro Office-Holders in Georgia under President McKinley," *Journal of Negro History,* XLIV (July 1959), 217–39.

BAKER, HENRY E. "The Negro in the Field of Invention," *Journal of Negro History,* II (January 1917), 21–36.

"Banker with a Mission: J. H. Wheeler," *Business Week* (May 16, 1964), 56 ff.

BAUR, JOHN EDWARD. "Mulatto Machiavelli: Jean Pierre Boyer and the Haiti of His Day," *Journal of Negro History,* XXXII (October 1947), 307–53.

BEATTY-BROWN, FLORENCE. "Leaders in North Carolina: George Moses Horton," *Negro History Bulletin,* V (February 1942), 103.

"Biographical Sketch of Joseph R. Ray," *Negro History Bulletin,* XXIII (April 1960), 163.

BLAYTON, JESSE. "The Negro in Banking," *Bankers Magazine,* CXXXIII (December 1936), 511–14.

BOAZ, RUTH. "My Thirty Years with Father Divine," *Ebony,* XX (May 1965), 88 ff.

BONTEMPS, ARNA W. "Negro Poets, Then and Now," *Phylon,* XI (Winter 1950), 335–61.

BOOKER, S. "Can Negroes Become Big City Mayors?" *Ebony,* XXI (March 1966), 27 ff.

————. "New Face in Congress: J. Conyers, Jr.," *Ebony,* XX (January 1965), 73 ff.

————. "Robert C. Weaver: Quiet Man Wins Spot in Cabinet," *Ebony,* XXI (April 1966), 82 ff.

BREWER, JAMES H. "Robert Lee Vann: Exponent of Loose-Leaf Politics," *Negro History Bulletin,* XXI (February 1958), 100–103.

BREWER, WILLIAM M. "Henry Highland Garnet," *Journal of Negro History,* XIII (January 1928), 36–52.

————. "John B. Russwurm," *Journal of Negro History,* XIII (October 1928), 413–22.

BROOKS, ALBERT N. D. "Profile of a Fighter, Adam Clayton Powell," *Negro History Bulletin,* XX (May 1957), 170, 191.

BROWN, CHARLES A. "A. H. Curtis: An Alabama Legislator, 1870–1876," *Negro History Bulletin,* XXV (February 1962), 99–101.

————. "John Dozier: Member of the General Assembly of Alabama," *Negro History Bulletin,* XXXVI (December 1962), 113, 128.

————. "Lloyd Leftwich: Alabama State Senator," *Negro History Bulletin,* XXXVI (February 1963), 161–62.

————. "William Hooper Council: Alabama Legislator, Editor and Lawyer," *Negro History Bulletin,* XXVI (February 1963), 171–72.

BROWN, HOLLOWAY. "Silas Mosley: Ambassador of Good Will in Japan," *Negro History Bulletin,* XXIII (May 1960), 171, 191.

Brown, Wesley A. "Eleven Men of West Point," *Negro History Bulletin*, XIX (April 1956), 147–57.

"Brown Skin and Bright Leaf: The Story of the Negro's Role in the Tobacco Industry," *Negro History Bulletin*, XIX (October 1955), 3–10; XIX (November 1955), 27–33.

Browning, James B. "James D. Sampson," *Negro History Bulletin*, III (January 1940), 56.

Bryant, Girard T. "J. B. Rayner, a Negro Populist," *Negro History Bulletin*, III (May 1940), 125–26.

Bush, Joseph B. "The Grandest Olympian: James Cleveland 'Jesse' Owens," *Negro History Bulletin*, XXV (May 1962), 191–93.

Callcott, George M. "Omar Ibn Seid: A Slave Who Wrote an Autobiography in Arabic," *Journal of Negro History*, XXXIX (January 1954), 58–62.

Carneiro, Edison De Souza. "Arthur Ramos (1903–1949)," *Phylon*, XII (Spring 1951), 73–81.

Cartwright, Marguerite. "Etta Moten: Glamorous Grandmother," *Negro History Bulletin*, XVIII (March 1955), 137–38.

———. "A New Star Is Born: Charlotte Wesley Holloman," *Negro History Bulletin*, XVII (April 1954), 153–54.

Clarana, José. "Plácido: Poet and Martyr," *Crisis*, VI (June 1913), 82–83.

Clark, Dovie King. "Peter Humphries Clark," *Negro History Bulletin*, V (May 1942), 176.

Clement, Rufus E. "Richard Robert Wright," *Phylon*, IX (Spring 1948), 62–65.

Cobb, W. Montague. "Daniel Hale Williams, M.D., 1858–1931," *Journal of the National Medical Association*, XLV (September 1953), 379–85.

———. "Daniel Hale Williams: Pioneer and Innovator," *Journal of the National Medical Association*, XXXVI (September 1944), 158–59.

———. "'Dr.' James Still, New Jersey Pioneer," *Journal of the National Medical Association*, LX (March 1963), 196–99.

———. "Martin Robison Delany, 1812–1885," *Journal of the National Medical Association*, XLIV (May 1952), 232–38.

Coleman, Edward M. "William Wells Brown as an Historian," *Journal of Negro History*, XXXI (January 1946), 47–59.

Collier, Eugenia W. "James Weldon Johnson: Mirror of Changes," *Phylon*, XXI (Winter 1960), 351–59.

Collyer, C. "Edward Wilmot Blyden: A Correspondent of William Ewart Gladstone," *Journal of Negro History*, XXXV (January 1950), 75–78.

Congdon, T. B., Jr. "Ann Lowe, Society's Best-Kept Secret: Only Negro American Dress Designer," *Saturday Evening Post*, CCXXXVII (December 12, 1964), 74–76.

Cook, Mercer. "Julian Raimond," *Journal of Negro History*, XXVI (April 1941), 139–70.

———. "Ralph Johnson Bunche—Statesman," *Phylon*, IX (Winter 1948), 303–9.

Cooper, Wayne. "Claude McKay and the New Negro of the 1920's," *Phylon*, XXV (Fall 1964), 297–306.

Cornely, Paul B. "Charles R. Drew (1904–50): An Appreciation," *Phylon*, XI (Summer 1950), 176.

Crowe, Mary Davis. "Richard Theodore Greener," *Negro History Bulletin*, VI (December 1942), 58.

Davis, Harry E. "Prince Saunders, a Distinguished Statesman," *Negro History Bulletin*, III (May 1940), 127.

Diggs, Charles C., Jr. "Negro Congressman," *Negro History Bulletin*, XXVII (February 1964), 114 ff.

Dillard, Irving. "James Milton Turner: A Little Known Benefactor of His People," *Journal of Negro History*, XIX (October 1934), 372–411.

"Doctor Gets Call, to Mayor's Chair: Dr. S. F. Monstime," *Ebony*, XX (October 1965), 171–72.

"Doctor on Wheels: J. A. Bailey," *Ebony*, XIX (October 1964), 83–84.

Dodson, Owen. "Countee Cullen (1903–1946)," *Phylon*, VII (Spring 1947), 19–20.

Drew, Charles R. "Negro Scholars in Scientific Research," *Journal of Negro History*, XXXV (January 1950), 135–49.

Duncan, J. "Negro Composers of Opera," *Negro History Bulletin*, XXIX (January 1966), 79 ff.

Dwight, Edward H. "Robert S. Duncanson," *Negro History Bulletin*, XVIII (December 1954), 53–54.

EISENBERG, BERNARD. "Kelly Miller: The Negro Leader as a Marginal Man," *Journal of Negro History,* XLV (July 1960), 182–97.

"El-Hadj Omar," *Negro History Bulletin,* I (March 1938), 6.

ELMES, A. F. "Garvey and Garveyism," *Opportunity,* III (May 1925), 139–41.

FARIS, KENNETH. "Small Portrait of Richard Wright," *Negro History Bulletin,* XXV (April 1962), 155–56.

FARRISON, W. EDWARD. "William Wells Brown, America's First Negro Man of Letters," *Phylon,* IX (Spring 1948), 13–24.

FELDMAN, EUGENE. "James T. Rapier, Negro Congressman from Alabama," *Phylon,* XIX (Winter 1958), 417–23.

"First Negro Elected Judge," *Literary Digest,* LXXXIII (November 29, 1924), 12.

FISHER, MILES M. "Lott Cary, the Colonizing Missionary," *Journal of Negro History,* VII (October 1922), 380–418.

FORD, C. E. "Negro Singers I Have Heard," *Negro History Bulletin,* XVIII (February 1955), 119–20.

FRANKLIN, JOHN HOPE. "George Washington Williams, Historian," *Journal of Negro History,* XXXI (January 1946), 60–90.

FULLER, HOYT W. "Negro Writer in the United States," *Ebony,* XX (November 1964), 126 ff.

GARVIN, ROY. "Benjamin 'Pap' Singleton and His Followers," *Journal of Negro History,* XXXIII (January 1948), 7–23.

GRAY, GLADYS J. "George Lewis Ruffin," *Negro History Bulletin,* V (October 1941), 18–19.

GREENEBAUM, E. "She Believes in Her People: Kathryn Johnson, Dealer in Racial Self-Respect," *Woman's Journal,* XIII (July 1928), 11.

GRIMKÉ, ANGELINA. "Biographical Sketch of Archibald H. Grimké," *Opportunity,* III (February 1925), 44–48.

GROSS, BELLA. "Life and Times of Theodore S. Wright, 1797–1847," *Negro History Bulletin,* III (June 1940), 133–38, 144.

GUZMAN, JESSIE P. "Monroe Nathan Work and His Contributions," *Journal of Negro History,* XXXIV (October 1949), 428–61.

"H. Council Trenholm," *Negro History Bulletin,* XXVI (May 1963), 231–32.

HAMLIN, WILHELMINA A. "Luther Porter Jackson: Historian," *Negro History Bulletin,* VI (November 1942), 34–35, 46–47.

HARRISON, WILLIAM. "William Monroe Trotter," *Phylon,* VII (Fall 1947), 237–45.

HARTGROVE, W. B. "The Story of Josiah Henson," *Journal of Negro History,* III (January 1918), 1–21.

HASTIE, WILLIAM H. "Charles Hamilton Houston, 1895–1950," *Negro History Bulletin,* XIII (June 1950), 207–9.

HAWKINS, H. "Edward Jones: First American Negro College Graduate?" *School and Society,* LXXXIX (November 4, 1961), 375–76.

HOGGAN, FRANCES. "A Black Statesman of the Last Century," *Crisis,* I (February 1911), 26–27.

HOLMES, D. O. W. "Kelly Miller," *Phylon,* VI (Summer· 1945), 121–25.

HOLMES, EUGENE C. "Alain Leroy Locke: A Sketch," *Phylon,* XX (Spring 1959), 82–89.

"Honoring Cudjo Lewis: America's Last Piece of African Black Ivory," *Literary Digest,* CXI (November 21, 1931), 36–37.

"Hope for the Heart: Robert Clifton Weaver," *Time,* LXXXVII (March 4, 1966), 31–33.

HOUSTON, G. DAVID. "A Negro Senator: B. K. Bruce," *Journal of Negro History,* VII (July 1922), 243–56.

HUGLEY, GWENDOLYN. "Charles Waddell Chesnutt, Pioneer in the Fiction of Negro Life," *Negro History Bulletin,* XIX (December 1955), 54–55.

"Ira Aldridge," *Opportunity,* III (March 1925), 88–90.

JAMES, MILTON M. "Laura Wheeler Waring," *Negro History Bulletin,* XIX (March 1956), 126–28.

————. "William Edmundson, Sculptor," *Negro History Bulletin,* XXII (November 1958), 41.

"James Derham," *Journal of the National Medical Association,* IV (October–December 1912), 50.

"James McCune Smith, 1811–1865," *Journal of the National Medical Association,* XLIV (March 1952), 160.

"James Weldon Johnson: Brief Biography," *Crisis,* XLV (September 1938), 291.

JANIFER, E. "H. T. Burleigh Ten Years Later," *Phylon,* XXI (Summer 1960), 144–54.

"John Hope Franklin at Cambridge," *Ebony,* XVIII (September 1963), 160 ff.

JOHNSON, CHARLES S. "Edwin Rogers Embree," *Phylon,* VII (Winter 1947), 317–34.

JONES, PAUL W. L. "The Greatest Negro Harness Horse Owner, Peter Lee Hinsley," *Crisis,* XLIV (September 1937), 266, 284.

KAPLAN, SIDNEY. "Jan Ernst Matzeliger, and the Making of the Shoe," *Journal of Negro History,* XL (January 1955), 8–33.

KATZ, W. "George Henry White: A Militant Negro Congressman in the Age of Booker T. Washington," *Negro History Bulletin,* XXIX (March 1966), 125 ff.

LANDON, FRED. "Canadian Negroes and the John Brown Raid," *Journal of Negro History,* VI (April 1921), 174–82.

LAPP, RUDOLPH M. "The Negro in Gold Rush California," *Journal of Negro History,* XLIX (April 1964), 81–98.

LATIMER, CATHERINE A. "Catherine Ferguson," *Negro History Bulletin,* V (November 1941), 38–39.

LAWLAH, JOHN W. "George Cleveland Hall, M.D., 1864–1930," *Journal of the National Medical Association,* XLVI (May 1954), 207–10.

"Lemuel Haynes, the Servant of All the People of New England," *Negro History Bulletin,* I (December 1937), 1, 3.

LEWIS, JULIAN H. "Contribution of an Unknown Negro to Anesthesia," *Journal of the National Medical Association,* XXIII (January–March 1931), 23–24.

LEWIS, STEPHEN J. "The Negro in the Field of Dentistry," *Opportunity,* II (July 1924), 207–11.

LINDSAY, ARNETT G. "The Negro in Banking," *Journal of Negro History,* XIV (April 1929), 156–201.

LOCHARD, METZ T. P. "Robert S. Abbott: Race Leader," *Phylon,* VIII (Summer 1947), 124–32.

LOFTON, JOHN M. "Denmark Vesey's Call to Arms," *Journal of Negro History,* XXXIII (October 1948), 395–417.

LOGAN, RAYFORD W. "Carter G. Woodson," *Phylon,* VI (Winter 1945), 315–21.

"Lorenzo Dow Turner: Profile of a Scholar," *Negro History Bulletin,* XXI (November 1957), 26, 47.

LOVE, ROSE LEARY. "A Few Facts about Lewis Sheridan Leary, Who Was at Harpers Ferry in John Brown's Raid," *Negro History Bulletin,* VI (June 1943), 198, 215.

McCONNELL, ROLAND C. "Isaiah Dorman and the Custer Expedition," *Journal of Negro History,* XXXII (July 1948), 344–52.

"Mary Church Terrell," *Negro History Bulletin,* XVIII (October 1954), 2, 6.

MASSAQUOI, H. J. "Gus Hawkins, Fifth Negro Congressman," *Ebony,* XVIII (February 1963), 38 ff.

MATTHEWS, MIRIAM. "William Grant Still: Composer," *Phylon,* XII (Summer 1951), 106–12.

MEADE, GEORGE P. "A Negro Scientist of Slavery Days: Norbert Rillieux," *Negro History Bulletin,* XX (April 1957), 159–63.

MENARD, E. "John Willis Menard: First Negro Elected to the U.S. Congress," *Negro History Bulletin,* XXVIII (December 1964), 53–54.

"Menelik," *Negro History Bulletin,* I (March 1938), 7.

MILES, ETHEL W. "George Cleveland Hall," *Negro History Bulletin,* V (May 1942), 183–84.

MILTON, NERISSA L. "James A. Porter," *Negro History Bulletin,* XVIII (October 1954), 5–6.

———. "Know Your Congressman: Hiram Rhoades Revels," *Negro History Bulletin,* XVIII (February 1955), 112–13.

"Mrs. Bethune: Spingarn Medalist," *Crisis,* XLII (July 1935), 202, 212.

MOORE, WILLIAM H. A. "Richmond Barthé: Sculptor," *Opportunity,* VI (October 1928), 334.

MORE, W. H. "Lemuel Haynes," *Journal of Negro History,* IV (January 1919), 22–32.

MORRISON, A. "Top Judge: William Henry Hastie," *Ebony,* XIX (March 1964), 111 ff.

NABRIT, S. MILTON. "Ernest E. Just," *Phylon,* VII (Summer 1947), 121–25.

"Negro Abraham," *Negro History Bulletin,* V (April 1942), 149–50.

"Negro Architects of Today in Action," *Negro History Bulletin,* III (April 1940), 103–4.

"Negroes Distinguished in Science," *Negro History Bulletin,* II (May 1939), 67–70.

"Negroes in the Field of Philosophy," *Negro History Bulletin,* II (June 1939), 76, 80.

"Norris Wright Cuney: A Son of Texas," *Negro History Bulletin,* V (March 1942), 139–40.

"O. Richard Reid, Portraitist," *Opportunity,* VI (February 1928), 51.

O'CONNOR, J. "A Negro President at Georgetown University Some Eighty Years Ago: Patrick Francis Healy," *Negro History Bulletin,* XVIII (May 1955), 175–76.

"Opening the Cockpit Doors: First Negro Commercial Airline Pilot," *Time,* LXXXI (May 3, 1963), 24.

OSBORN, GEORGE C. "Woodrow Wilson Appoints Robert H. Terrell Judge of the Municipal Court, District of Columbia," *Negro History Bulletin,* XXII (February 1959), 111–15.

PADGETT, JAMES A. "Diplomats to Haiti and Their Diplomacy," *Journal of Negro History,* XXV (July 1940), 265–330.

———. "Ministers to Liberia and Their Diplomacy," *Journal of Negro History,* XXII (January 1937), 50–92.

PARRIS, GUICHARD. "George T. Downing," *Negro History Bulletin,* V (November 1941), 42.

PARRY, ALBERT. "Abram Hannibal, the Favorite of Peter the Great," *Journal of Negro History,* VIII (October 1923), 359–66.

PERKINS, A. E. "James Henri Burch and Oscar James Dunn in Louisiana," *Journal of Negro History,* XXII (July 1937), 321–34.

PHILLIPS, F. L. "Benjamin Banneker, Negro Astronomer and Mathematician," *Colonial Historical Series,* XX (1917), 114–20.

PHILLIPS, WALDO B. "Jim Noble: Oklahoma's Negro Governor," *Phylon,* XX (Spring 1959), 90–92.

POIRIER, N. "Sidney Poitier's Long Journey," *Saturday Evening Post,* CCXXXVII (June 20, 1964), 26 ff.

PORTER, DOROTHY B. "David Ruggles, 1810–1849: Hydropathic Practitioner," *Journal of the National Medical Association,* XLIX (January 1957), 67–72; XLIX (March 1957), 130–34.

——— "Sarah Parker Remond, Abolitionist and Physician," *Journal of Negro History,* XX (April 1935), 287–93.

PORTER, KENNETH W. "John Caesar: Seminole Negro Partisan," *Journal of Negro History,* XXXI (April 1946), 190–207.

"Portrait of a Leader: Thurgood Marshall, a Biographical Sketch," *Negro History Bulletin,* XIX (November 1955), 26, 39.

"Proud New Victory for Navy Destroyer, USS Taussig, under Command of Negro Skipper," *Ebony,* XXI (July 1966), 25 ff.

PUSHKIN, ALEXIS. "The Negro of Peter the Great," *Opportunity,* II (February 1924), 54–58; II (March 1924), 84–88; II (April 1924), 118–21.

QUARLES, BENJAMIN. "Peter Jackson Speaks of Boxers," *Negro History Bulletin,* XVIII (November 1954), 39–40.

"Raceless Bill Cosby," *Ebony,* XIX (May 1964), 131 ff.

REDDICK, L. D. "Carter G. Woodson (1875–1950): An Appreciation," *Phylon,* XI (Summer 1950), 177.

———. "Dizzy Gillespie in Atlanta," *Phylon,* X (Spring 1949), 44–49.

REDDICK, RUTH. "T. Thomas Fortune," *Negro History Bulletin,* V (November 1941), 42–43.

RICHARDSON, JOE M. "A Negro Success Story: James Dallas Burrus," *Journal of Negro History,* L (October 1965), 274–82.

"Robert Smalls," *Negro History Bulletin,* I (May 1938), 5.

ROBINSON, L. "Dorothy Dandridge: Hollywood's Tragic Enigma," *Ebony,* XXI (March 1966), 70 ff.

———. "First Negro Astronaut Candidate," *Ebony,* XVIII (July 1963), 71 ff.

ROMERO, PATRICIA. "Early Organization of Red Caps," *Negro History Bulletin,* XXIX (February 1966), 101 ff.

ROSENBERG, CHESTER. "Duke Ellington," *Crisis,* XLIII (February 1936), 40 ff.

ROY, JESSIE H. "Colored Judges," *Negro History Bulletin,* XXIX (November 1965), 37–38.

———. "Gabriel Prosser; William and Ellen Craft," *Negro History Bulletin,* XXII (October 1958), 17 ff.

———. "Pinpoint Portrait of Judge Marjorie Lawson," *Negro History Bulletin,* XXVI (May 1963), 252.

———. "Pinpoint Portrait of Mrs. Constance B. Motley," *Negro History Bulletin,* XXVI (April 1963), 221.

SAVAGE, W. S. "James Beckwourth—Negro Fur Trader," *Negro History Bulletin,* XVII (March 1954), 123–24.

———. "The Negro Cowboy of the Texas Plains," *Negro History Bulletin,* XXIV (April 1961), 157 ff.

———. "The Negro in the History of the Pacific Northwest," *Journal of Negro History,* XIII (July 1928), 255–64.

———. "The Negro on the Mining Frontier," *Journal of Negro History,* XXX (January 1945), 30–46.

———— "The Negro in the Westward Movement," *Journal of Negro History,* XXV (October 1940), 531–49.

SCHOMBURG, ARTHUR A. "Two Negro Missionaries to the American Indians: John Marrant and John Stewart," *Journal of Negro History,* XXI (October 1936), 394–405.

SEEBER, EDWARD D. "Phillis Wheatley," *Journal of Negro History,* XXIV (July 1939), 259–62.

SHEELER, J. REUBEN. "James Madison Nabrit," *Negro History Bulletin,* XXIV (January 1961), 75–76.

SHERWOOD, H. N. "Paul Cuffe," *Journal of Negro History,* VIII (April 1923), 153–229.

SHUSTER, RHODA. "Ralph Bunche: United Nations Mediator," *Negro History Bulletin,* XIX (May 1956), 174–76.

SINGLETON, VELMA. "John Wesley Work, Sr.," *Negro History Bulletin,* V (February 1942), 115–16.

SMITH, H. L. "Negro Artist in America Today," *Negro History Bulletin,* XXVII (February 1964), 111–12.

SMITH, LUCY H. "Negro Musicians and Their Music," *Journal of Negro History,* XX (October 1935), 428–32.

SMITH, ROBERT A. "Claude McKay: An Essay in Criticism," *Phylon,* IX (Fall 1948), 270–73.

SMITH, WILLIAM G. "Ethel Waters," *Phylon,* XI (Summer 1950), 114–20.

SPELLMAN, FONZELL. "The Twentieth Century's Greatest Negro Anthologist," *Negro History Bulletin,* XXXVI (January 1963), 137.

STAFFORD, A. O. "Antar, the Arabian Negro Warrior, Poet and Hero," *Journal of Negro History,* I (April 1916), 151–62.

STANGE, D. C. "Note on Daniel Payne," *Negro History Bulletin,* XXVIII (October 1964), 9–10.

SWEAT, EDWARD F. "Francis L. Cardozo: Profile of Integrity in Reconstruction Politics," *Journal of Negro History,* LXVI (October 1961), 217–32.

TALLEY, TOMASINA. "Another Negro Historian: Lorenzo Johnson Greene," *Negro History Bulletin,* V (November 1942), 38 ff.

TANNER, HENRY O. "The Story of an Artist's Life [Meta Warrick]," *World's Work,* XVIII (June 1909), 11661; XVIII (July 1909), 11769.

"Three Negro Senators: Revels, Bruce, Brooke," *Negro History Bulletin,* XXX (January 1967), 4 ff.

"The Thrilling Escape of William and Ellen Craft," *Negro History Bulletin,* I (October 1937), 1, 5.

THRUELSEN, R. "Pullman Porter," *Saturday Evening Post,* CCXXI (May 21, 1949), 38 ff.

"Top Nurse in Uniform: Highest-Ranking Negro Woman in the U.S. Army Nurse Corps," *Ebony,* XXI (September 1966), 50.

ULANSKY, ENUGU. "The Integrated Careers of Alain Locke, Philosopher of the New Negro," *Negro History Bulletin,* XXVI (May 1963), 240–43.

VILLARD, OSWALD G. "A. Philip Randolph," *Phylon,* VIII (Fall 1947), 225–29.

"Walter Gilbert Alexander, M.D., 1880–1953," *Journal of the National Medical Association,* XLV (July 1953), 281–83.

WEEKS, STEPHEN B. "George Moses Horton: Slave Poet," *Southern Workman,* XLIII (October 1914), 571.

WESLEY, CHARLES H. "Carter G. Woodson, as a Scholar," *Journal of Negro History,* XXXVI (January 1951), 12–24.

WILLIAMS, FRED H. "Richard DeBaptiste," *Negro History Bulletin,* XXII (May 1959), 178.

WOODSON, CARTER G. "James Edwin Campbell, a Forgotten Man of Letters," *Negro History Bulletin,* II (November 1938), 11.

WOODWARD, I. A. "Joshua Johnston: Baltimore's First Slave Artist of Distinction," *Negro History Bulletin,* XXI (April 1958), 166.

WOODY, R. H. "Jonathan J. Wright, Justice of the Supreme Court of South Carolina, 1870–1877," *Journal of Negro History,* XVIII (April 1933), 114–31.

WORK, M. N. "The Life of Charles B. Ray," *Journal of Negro History,* IV (October 1919), 361–71.

WRIGHT, RICHARD. "Negro Companions of Spanish Explorers," *American Anthropology,* IV (July 1902), 217.

Picture Credits

The author is grateful to the following for their aid in the search for unusual and interesting photographs with which to illustrate the text. Those pictures which have not been listed are in the private collection of United Publishing Corporation, Washington, D.C.

Key: T: Top;   B: Bottom;   L: Left;   R: Right;   C: Center

American Oil Company, Chicago: 74, 163
Cincinnati Historical Society, Cincinnati: 64
Fabian Bachrach: 251, 261, 266
Langston Hughes, New York: 208
Library of Congress, Washington: 2CR, 8R, 12L, 40TL, 65, 76L, R, 79L, 98, 109, 125R, 199, 203, 260L, 265
National Association for the Advancement of Colored People, New York: 242
New York Public Library-Schomburg Collection, New York: 2TL, TR, CL, BL, BC, BR, 10, 16, 24, 27, 34, 36, 40C, 44, 60R, 100R, 107R, 111, 114, 116, 120, 130, 131, 134, 165, 167, 175, 213R, 222, 229, 243
Scurlock Studios, Washington: 80

Index

Biographical Entries Listed by Last Names

Biographical Entries Listed by Major Activities